FUNDAMENTALS OF
GAME
DEVELOPMENT

Heather Maxwell Chandler
Rafael Chandler

JONES & BARTLETT
LEARNING

World Headquarters
Jones & Bartlett Learning
40 Tall Pine Drive
Sudbury, MA 01776
978-443-5000
info@jblearning.com
www.jblearning.com

Jones & Bartlett Learning
Canada
6339 Ormindale Way
Mississauga, Ontario L5V 1J2
Canada

Jones & Bartlett Learning
International
Barb House, Barb Mews
London W6 7PA
United Kingdom

Jones & Bartlett Learning books and products are available through most bookstores and online booksellers. To contact Jones & Bartlett Learning directly, call 800-832-0034, fax 978-443-8000, or visit our website, www.jblearning.com.

Substantial discounts on bulk quantities of Jones & Bartlett Learning publications are available to corporations, professional associations, and other qualified organizations. For details and specific discount information, contact the special sales department at Jones & Bartlett Learning via the above contact information or send an email to specialsales@jblearning.com.

 Artists courtesy of Interabang Entertainment. All artwork © 2010 Interabang Entertainment, LLC, all rights reserved.

Production Credits
Publisher: David Pallai
Editorial Assistant: Molly Whitman
Production Director: Amy Rose
Associate Production Editor: Tiffany Sliter
Production Assistant: Lindsey Jones
Associate Marketing Manager: Lindsay Ruggiero
V.P., Manufacturing and Inventory Control: Therese Connell
Cover and Title Page Design: Kristin E. Parker
Cover Image: Courtesy of Cryptic Studios, Inc. Trademark & © 2009 CBS Studios Inc. All rights reserved. STAR TREK and related marks are trademarks of CBS Studios Inc.
Composition: Glyph International
Printing and Binding: Malloy, Inc.
Cover Printing: Malloy, Inc.

Library of Congress Cataloging-in-Publication Data
Chandler, Heather Maxwell.
  Fundamentals of game development / Heather Maxwell Chandler and Rafael Chandler.
    p. cm.
  Includes index.
  ISBN-13: 978-0-7637-7895-8 (pbk.)
  ISBN-10: 0-7637-7895-8 (ibid.)
  1. Computer games—Programming. I. Chandler, Rafael. II. Title.
  QA76.76.C672C437 2010
  794.8'1526—dc22
                        2010004325

6048
Printed in the United States of America
14 13 12 11 10   10 9 8 7 6 5 4 3 2 1

Credits

■ Contributors

Our sincere appreciation to the following contributors who made this book possible.

Interviews with Industry Experts

Thomas Buscaglia, Esq.

Carey Chico

Don Daglow

Stephanie Deming

Jaime Fristrom

Tracy Fullerton

Raymond Herrara

Daniel Higgins

Clint Hocking

Lee Jacobson

Jeff Matsushita

Jay Powell

Stuart Roch

Amanda Rubright

Tobi Saulnier

Coray Seifert

Wade Tinney

Art Contributions from Interabang Entertainment

Jerry Dunham: Monstars

Fred Gago: Cargo Drop

Shawna Mills: Design Monster; Taxi; Pretty Bee

Chris Sauquillo: Dragon Slayer; Tumble Caps Hillbilly; Tumble Caps Russian

Shan Shankaran: Lyra

Adam Paul Thomas: Mac and rizo; Marlo2b

Evan Washington: Punk Girl; Super Nerd

Game Development Studios Featured on Accompanying CD

Actual Entertainment

Batovi Games Studio

Cryptic Studios

DigitalFlux

Illfonic

Lunchtime Studios

Sundog Software

■ Brand Names and Products

Without these companies and their products, we wouldn't have such a strong and well-rounded game development industry.

Two Worlds is a trademark of Zuxxez Entertainment AG in the USA and EU, and is or may be a trademark of Zuxxez Entertainment AG in other countries.

Monster Madness: Grave Danger is a trademark of SouthPeak Interactive LLC in the USA, and is or may be a trademark of SouthPeak Interactive LLC in other countries.

Dark Messiah Might and Magic, Ghost Recon, Ghost Recon Advanced Warfighter, Splinter Cell, Splinter Cell: Chaos Theory, and Ubisoft are trademarks of Ubisoft Entertainment in the U.S. and/or other countries.

Heavy Gear is a trademark of Dream Pod 9, Inc.

Modern Warfare and Vigilante 8 are trademarks and Activision, Call of Duty, Call to Power, and Guitar Hero are registered trademarks of Activision Publishing, Inc.

Rainbow Six, Rainbow Six Lockdown, Rainbow Six Raven Shield, and Red Storm are trademarks of Red Storm Entertainment in the U.S. and/or other countries. Red Storm Entertainment, Inc. is a Ubisoft Entertainment company.

Dark Reign is a trademark of Auran.

MAG is a trademark of Zipper Interactive.

Excel, Halo, Microsoft, Visual C++, Visual SourceSafe, Windows, Windows Live, Xbox, Xbox 360, and Xbox Live are either registered trademarks or trademarks of Microsoft Corporation in the United States and/or other countries.

App Store, iPhone, iPod, iPod touch, iTunes, Mac, and Macintosh are trademarks of Apple Inc., registered in the U.S. and other countries.

Linux is the registered trademark of Linus Torvalds in the U.S. and other countries.

Donkey Kong, F-Zero, GameCube, Game Boy Game Boy Advance, Metroid Prime NES, Nintendo, Nintendo DS, Nintendo DSi, Nintendo Entertainment System, Pilotwings, Super Mario Bros., Super Mario Bros. 3, Super Mario World, Super NES, Super Nintendo Entertainment System, The Legend of Zelda, Wii, Wii Fit, and Wii Play are trademarks or registered trademarks of Nintendo.

PlayStation, PS2, PS3, and PSP are registered trademarks or trademarks of Sony Computer Entertainment Inc.

Marvel is a trademark of Marvel Characters, Inc.

Mortal Kombat is a registered trademark of Midway Amusement Games.

Quake is a registered trademark of id Software, Inc.

Asteroids and Centipede are trademarks of Atari Interactive, Inc.

Pac-Man is a registered trademark of Namco Bandai.

Intellivision is a registered trademark of Intellivision Productions, Inc.

SEGA, SEGA Master System, and Sonic the Hedgehog are registered trademarks or trademarks of the SEGA Corporation.

Myst is a registered trademark of Cyan Worlds.

DOOM is a registered trademark of Id Software, Inc. in the United States and/or other countries.

Counter-Strike is a trademark and Half-Life is a registered trademark of Valve Corporation.

Final Fantasy and Supreme Commander are registered trademarks of Square Enix Co., Ltd.

World of Warcraft is a registered trademark of Blizzard Entertainment.

Gears of War is a registered trademark of Epic Games, Inc. in the United States of America and elsewhere.

Blu-ray Disc is a trademark of the Blu-ray Disc Association.

Gran Turismo is a registered trademark and MotorStorm is a trademark of Sony Computer Entertainment America.

The Elder Scrolls, Oblivion, Bethesda Game Studios, Bethesda Softworks, Morrowind, ZeniMax, and related logos are registered trademarks or trademarks of ZeniMax Media Inc. in the U.S. and/or other countries.

Spider-Man is a trademark of Marvel Characters, Inc.

James Bond is a trademark of Danjaq, LLC.

NFL is a registered trademark of the National Football League.

Harry Potter characters, names, and related indicia are trademarks of Warner Bros. Entertainment.

Unreal, Unreal Engine, and UnrealScript are trademarks or registered trademarks of Epic Games, Inc. in the United States of America and elsewhere.

Resident Evil is a registered trademark of Capcom Co., Ltd., in the U.S. or other countries.

The Lord of the Rings, The Sims, Ultima, Electronic Arts, EA, and the EA logo are trademarks or registered trademarks of Electronic Arts Inc. in the U.S. and/or other countries.

Brütal Legend is a trademark of Double Fine Productions, Inc.

The Dystopia is a registered trademark of Webzen, Inc.

Rock Band is a trademark of Harmonix Music Systems, Inc., an MTV Networks company.

SingStar is a registered trademark of Sony Computer Entertainment Europe.

DanceDanceRevolution and Silent Hill are registered trademarks of Konami Corporation.

Tetris is a registered trademark of Tetris Holding.

Dungeons & Dragons and Neverwinter Nights are trademarks of Wizards of the Coast LLC in the U.S.A. and other countries.

Mass Effect is a trademark and BioWare is a registered trademark of EA International (Studio and Publishing) Ltd. in the United States and other countries.

Adobe, After Effects, Flash, Photoshop, and Premiere are registered trademarks of Adobe Systems Incorporated in the United States and/or other countries.

Tomb Raider is a trademark of Eidos Interactive Limited.

BioShock is a trademark and/or registered trademarks of Take-Two Interactive Software, Inc.

Autodesk, Maya, and 3ds Max are registered trademarks of Autodesk, Inc., and/or its subsidiaries and/or affiliates in the USA and/or other countries.

Perforce is a registered trademark of Perforce Software, Inc.

Havok Physics is a trademark of Havok.Com Inc.

Alienbrain and Pro Tools are registered trademarks of Avid Technology, Inc. or its subsidiaries in the United States and/or other countries.

Tony Hawk is a registered trademark of Tony Hawk, Inc.

Bugzilla is a trademark of the Mozilla Foundation.

Dolby is a registered trademark of Dolby Laboratories, Inc.

Coca-Cola is a registered trademark of The Coca-Cola Company.

Planetfall is a trademark of Infocom, Inc.

Full Spectrum Warrior and Mercenaries are trademarks and Destroy All Humans is a registered trademark of Pandemic Studios, LLC.

The Emmy name is a trademarked property of The Academy of Television Arts & Sciences and the National Academy of Television Arts & Sciences.

Schizoid is a registered trademark of Torpex Games, LLC.

Jeopardy! is a registered trademark of Jeopardy Productions, Inc.

Wheel of Fortune is a registered trademark of Califon Productions,

Turok is a registered trademark of Classic Media, Inc., an Entertainment Rights group company.

The Aerosmith name and wings logo are trademarks of Rag Doll Merchandising, Inc.

Frontlines: Fuel of War is a trademark of THQ, Inc.

Contents

About the Authors

Heather Maxwell Chandler has been working in the game industry since 1996. Her company, Media Sunshine, Inc., provides consulting services for game developers, publishers, and vendors. Prior to the creation of MSI, she held various production roles at Ubisoft, Activision, Electronic Arts, and New Line Cinema. Heather has worked on more than 30 games, including Two Worlds™, Monster Madness: Grave Danger™, Ghost Recon Advanced Warfighter™, Ghost Recon™ 2, Heavy Gear™, Apocalypse™, Vigilante 8™, Rainbow Six® 3: Raven Shield, Dark Reign™, and Shanghai®: Second Dynasty™.

Heather is also the author of *The Game Localization Handbook* and three chapters in *Secrets of the Game Business, Second Edition*, published by Charles River Media. She has published numerous articles on game development and has lectured at game development conferences all over the world. She graduated with honors from Vanderbilt University (Nashville, Tennessee) and earned an M.A. from the University of Southern California School of Cinematic Arts (Los Angeles, California). For more information, visit www.mediasunshine.com.

Rafael Chandler is a game writer with experience at Zipper Interactive, Slant Six Games, and Ubisoft. He has written or cowritten several games, including MAG™, SOCOM: U.S. Navy SEALs Fireteam Bravo 3™, Ghost Recon 2, and Rainbow Six: Lockdown™. He is the author of *The Game Writing Handbook*, which was a finalist for the 2007 Game Developer Front Line Awards, and he also wrote the script for *Monster Madness: Battle for Suburbia*, a comic book published by Dark Horse that was based on the video game of the same name. Rafael was a speaker at the 2006 Game Writers Conference, the 2007 Russian Game Developers Conference in Moscow (where he taught the six-hour master class), and the 2008 Montreal International Game Summit.

Preface

Presented from the perspective of a video game producer, *Fundamentals of Game Development* introduces the core principles of game production, including the basics of game design, the nuts and bolts of managing game development, and developing a plan to create a game. After reading this book, both students and novice game developers will have a better understanding of the game production process and the necessary steps for creating a game from start to finish.

The book covers the history and business of games and touches on all aspects of the game development process, including preproduction, production, and testing. The book concludes with a case study of a fictional game that demonstrates how to implement the principles and techniques described throughout.

In addition, several industry insiders were interviewed about their game production experiences, and they have generously offered advice and information that anyone involved in game production will find valuable. Enjoy reading the book!

For Instructors

Solutions to the exercise sets, a sample syllabus, class assignments, Microsoft® PowerPoint® slides for lectures, color figures, and more are available for qualified instructors at http://www.jblearning.com/catalog/9780763778958/. Designated instructors' materials are for qualified instructors only. Jones & Bartlett Learning reserves the right to evaluate all requests.

Acknowledgments

We would like to extend a special thanks to David Pallai and Molly Whitman at Jones & Bartlett Learning for shepherding this book through the process. They both provided much-needed support along the way, and they were instrumental in making this book happen. Justin Woodward and his group of artists at Interabang Entertainment—Shawna Mills, Fred Gago, Shan Shankaran, Adam Paul Thomas, Jerry Dunham,

Chris Sauquillo, and Evan Washington—also deserve a special thanks for the amazing color artwork they contributed. Finally, a big thank you to everyone who agreed to be interviewed for the book—your advice will be invaluable to the readers.

Heather Maxwell Chandler
Executive Producer, Media Sunshine, Inc.
heather@mediasunshine.com

Rafael Chandler
Creative Director, Media Sunshine, Inc.
rafael@mediasunshine.com
www.mediasunshine.com

■ About the CD-ROM

The CD to accompany *Fundamentals of Game Development* features the following elements:

- All figures from the book (including those originally in full color) and interactive Microsoft® Excel® spreadsheets
- Contributions from the following game development studios, including screenshots, demos, and descriptions:
  - Actual Entertainment
  - Batovi Games Studio
  - DigitalFlux
  - Illfonic
  - Lunchtime Studios
  - Sundog Software
- A feature of Star Trek® Online, the massively multiplayer online game from Cryptic Studios, Inc.
- All chapter opener art in full color from Interabang Entertainment

1 What Is a Game?

In this chapter:

■ 1.1 Introduction

For well over 4,000 years, games have been a part of the human experience. But given the myriad games and variants that have been designed, how does one define a game? One might describe a game as a play activity defined by interactive challenges, discernible rules, and attainable goals. There will be exceptions to this, of course, but it's a good place to start. Let's look at a classic example: chess.

Chess is a play activity; there is no work involved. It's nothing more than a form of entertainment. The challenges are interactive: In order to participate, the player must move pieces across the board. Chess has clearly defined rules that govern the movement of pieces and the actions of the player, and the game also features an attainable goal: the capture of the opponent's king. So here we have an interactive challenge, well-established rules, and a goal that the player works toward. Video games are also defined by these three principles, but due to their virtual nature, they're far more complex than board games like chess.

■ 1.2 What Is a Game?

The term "video game" originally referred to a specific type of device—a computer system that creates a video display signal for televisions—but it has now become an all-encompassing term. In this chapter, we'll use it as such, except when specifically referring to computer games, which are played only on the personal computer (not consoles, mobile phones, or arcade devices).

Video games are controlled by computer programs. Through user interaction and audiovisual immersion, video games allow players to respond to challenging situations in fantasy worlds. It's important to note that the term "fantasy" refers to the fact that the world in question is virtual, and not real—for example, the player may be exploring the fantasy of playing major league baseball.

1.2.1 Platform

The three main platform categories for games are personal computer (PC), console, and mobile. The PC platform encompasses games made for computers running the Windows®, Mac®, or Linux® OS. These games can be single-player or multiplayer, and web based or run directly from the computer's hard drive. A console is a piece of proprietary game hardware that hooks up to a television such as a Microsoft® Xbox 360® and a Sony PlayStation 3®. A mobile platform consists of anything portable and handheld, including cell phones, PDAs, iPods®, and handheld game systems such as the Nintendo® DSi™ or the Sony/PSP®. As with consoles, handheld game systems are multiuse and can be used to browse the web, listen to MP3 files, or text. New game platforms emerge about every three to five years in order to keep up with the advances in hardware. Each platform has its strengths and weaknesses in regard to games, so developers need to keep these in mind when creating a game.

Porting is when a game is converted from one platform to another. For games released on multiple platforms, the developers need to change the gameplay slightly so it works with the controller, technology, and other elements of the chosen platform.

For example, a game created for a PC would need changes made to the control scheme and user interface (UI) if it were to be ported to a console. An understanding of the key differences between the platforms is useful for better understanding of how the hardware configurations of each platform can influence the type of game being created.

Personal Computer (PC)

As discussed in a later section in this chapter, the personal computer was the dominant game platform for many years. The PC provides powerful graphics and processing power that allow developers to create games that are on the cutting edge of technology. The keyboard and mouse control configuration also allows designers to create games with more complex user inputs and allows players to micromanage large areas of the game. For example, strategy games and simulations are popular on the PC because the player is given a large degree of control over the game UI with the keyboard and mouse.

The main drawback to the PC is that it can be expensive when compared to game consoles. A good gaming PC needs to have the latest hardware upgrades in order to provide the best gameplay experience to the player. PC gamers find themselves frequently upgrading their computers in order to keep up with the latest and greatest gaming technology. In addition, the wide variety of PC configurations makes it difficult for developers to test the game to ensure that it works correctly on all computer configurations because there is no standard PC setup that all gamers are guaranteed to have.

Console

Consoles are proprietary hardware manufactured by third parties such as Sony, Microsoft, and Nintendo. A console is hooked up to a television and its primary purpose is for playing games. In recent years, consoles have become multiuse and can be used to view DVDs or listen to music. Examples of multiuse consoles are the Xbox 360 and the PlayStation 3.

Video game consoles are appealing to game developers because they only need to consider one hardware configuration when creating software for a console. By contrast, PCs offer limitless options because of all the various hardware and software options that the user may add to his or her configuration. Consoles feature simplified control schemes, hook up directly to the TV, and offer less power and more limited memory than PCs. However, because of their relative ease of use their multifunction capabilities (CD/MP3/DVD players, for instance), and their lower price point, they have mass-market appeal. Popular console game genres include shooters, driving games, and sports games.

Handheld

Handheld games are portable, and they feature very simple control schemes (particularly when compared to the PC). Many modern handhelds are online capable, even though they're the least powerful platform. It's common to see multiuse handhelds, such as the PlayStation Portable (PSP®), which can also play music and movies.

1.2.2 Player Mode

Developers also need to consider which player mode the game will feature. There are three main player modes, which can be further subcategorized by the advent of online capability:

Single-player mode is for a single participant. The player competes against the program.

Cooperative multiplayer, also known as co-op, allows two or more players to work in tandem against the program. When played online, each gamer sees the other participants on his or her screen. If two people are playing without an online connection, co-op can take the form of split-screen (in which a line divides the screen and each player looks at his or her half of the screen, as in Halo® 3) or full-screen (in which all of the characters are on the screen at once, as in Marvel™: Ultimate Alliance).

Adversarial multiplayer allows two or more players to compete against one another. In many games, this can take the form of teams battling against one another. In a fighting game like the Mortal Kombat® series, two offline players can face each other on a single screen while sitting side by side on the couch, yelling as they frantically mash buttons. It's possible to play a first-person shooter offline with split-screen (Call of Duty® 4: Modern Warfare™ allows up to four people to play in this manner), but most games with adversarial multiplayer are online, allowing each player to enjoy a full-screen experience. Some games, like Quake® 3, allow free-for-all mayhem, but more and more adversarial multiplayer games organize players into teams (Sony's MAG™ features two teams of up to 128 players).

■ 1.3   1960s: The Birth of Games

Until the 1960s, video games consisted of various programs built on computers by hobbyists and enthusiasts, such as William Higinbotham's Tennis for Two™ (1958). Game hardware was not widely available, and attempts to create commercial games were usually not profitable. Spacewar™, which allowed users to control dueling spaceships, is considered the first game to be made available to consumers. Developed by Steve Russell and various MIT students, Spacewar! was developed in 1961 and distributed in 1962. Though it wasn't a commercial success, it was the first foray into a new industry.

■ 1.4   1970s: The Rise of Arcade Games

During the early 1970s, video games were played primarily on arcade systems and home computers. However, a number of ventures into console gaming were rewarded with mainstream success.

Magnavox released the Odyssey in 1972. The first video game console, the Odyssey featured no audio and was sold with plastic overlays that the player attached to the television screen in order to clearly define the gameplay experience. Overpriced and undermarketed, the system didn't sell very well.

The same year, Atari released Pong™, a wildly popular arcade game that replicated the experience of tennis with a ball (represented by a square) bouncing back and forth between two paddles (represented by short lines). The game was so successful that Atari soon began work on a home version.

In 1977, the company released the Atari 2600™, a cartridge-based system. The 2600 soon became a must-buy holiday gift, and over the next few years, the word "Atari" would become synonymous with "video games," in the same way that "Hoover" is used as a generic term for "vacuum cleaner."

In arcades, where players could enjoy a few minutes of gameplay for a quarter, titles like Space Invaders (1978) and Asteroids™ (1979) proved wildly popular. Atari eventually released many of these arcade games, which further broadened the appeal of the 2600.

However, all was not well at the company. Atari's employees were not credited for their work, and many were unhappy with their working conditions. In 1979, Activision was formed by disgruntled employees who had left Atari. The company immediately began work on production of third-party titles (games developed by companies other than the console manufacturer) for the 2600. Atari sued Activision to prevent the games from being released but lost, which paved the way for other companies to begin third-party game development. Soon, the library of available games for the 2600 was massive. The stage was set for the coming crash.

■ 1.5 1980s: The Crash and Recovery

During the early 1980s, arcade games continued to grow in popularity. The decade kicked off with Pac-Man® and Centipede™, two well-received games released in 1980. Pac-Man's eponymous hero, in particular, became an easily identifiable symbol for the burgeoning video game craze.

In 1981, Nintendo released Donkey Kong®, one of the first games in the platformer genre, which featured a mustachioed protagonist (Jumpman) and his nemesis, a violent ape named Donkey Kong. The game was ported to the Atari 2600, the ColecoVision™, the Intellivision®, and several other platforms.

With the public eagerly awaiting both the highly anticipated Atari 2600 port of Pac-Man and a major movie tie-in, E.T. the Extra-Terrestrial™, the future of games looked bright indeed. But 1982 proved to be a very dark year for the business.

The Pac-Man port was a failure. Expecting a runaway hit, Atari manufactured millions more cartridges than there were 2600 systems, expecting that Pac-Man's popularity would prompt customers to buy systems just so they could play the game. However, the game itself was programmed on an extremely tight schedule, and the 2600's hardware was unable to replicate the game experience properly. As a result, Pac-Man received terrible reviews, and millions of copies went unsold. Atari's reputation was damaged, which would go on to have serious repercussions.

E.T. the Extra-Terrestrial, based on the hit movie of the same name, was released later that year. Again, the game met with harsh criticism, and again, millions of copies went unsold. Worse, the game was based on an intellectual property, so Atari had to pay licensing fees for the rights to the movie. Consumers, frustrated by what many considered to be an unplayable game, returned it in droves. Retailers, upset with the volume of returns, began to wonder if video games were merely a passing fad.

In 1983, the game industry crashed. The glut of systems and games, coupled with the aforementioned high-profile failures, led retailers to devote less and less shelf space to video games. Customers were also purchasing inexpensive home computers, which featured games in addition to other, more practical programs. Since more games were being released but fewer customers were purchasing them, stores tried to return the product to the publishers; if this failed, they simply marked down the games until they sold, then refused to buy more.

Publishers and developers went out of business, though a few (like Activision) survived by switching their focus from video games to computer games. Retailers stopped carrying games. It seemed that the era of console games had come to an end.

By contrast, computer games were doing quite well. The Commodore 64™, released in 1982, became quite popular as a gaming platform thanks to a low price and good marketing. The IBM PC and the monochrome Apple Macintosh® arrived in 1984. In 1985, Commodore released the Amiga™, which was originally intended as a game platform but was ultimately released as a multipurpose computer (though it boasted a huge library of games and was quite popular with game developers and enthusiasts alike). It appeared that computer gaming would fill the void left by consoles.

However, Nintendo was about to unveil a new system. In 1985, the Nintendo Entertainment System® (NES®) was released. Super Mario Bros.® was the system's flagship title, and also one of the best-selling games of all time. It popularized the platformer genre, and it established Mario (formerly known as Jumpman from Donkey Kong) as Nintendo's mascot. The NES was so popular that over the next few years, "Nintendo" became synonymous with "video game," the way that Atari had previously.

Unlike Atari, Nintendo encouraged third-party development but ensured that only Nintendo-approved developers could create cartridges. As a consequence, Nintendo was able to control the number of games that were released.

In 1986, Sega countered with the Sega® Master System™, an 8-bit system intended to rival the NES. However, Sega was unable to dethrone Nintendo, due in part to Nintendo's established foothold in the market.

More success came Nintendo's way in 1987 with the release of The Legend of Zelda®, the first game in a series that would go on to sell over 50 million units combined. Commonly known as Zelda, the game combined role-playing, action, and adventure elements.

In 1989, Nintendo released the Game Boy®, the first handheld console to attain mainstream success. Rival handhelds followed, and though some were technologically superior, they were never able to surpass Game Boy sales.

Sega tried to dethrone Nintendo once more in 1989 with the release of the Sega Genesis™. This 16-bit system was more powerful than the NES and featured better graphics. It beat the Super Nintendo Entertainment System® to market by two years, and allowed Sega to establish itself as Nintendo's primary rival in the early 1990s.

■ 1.6   1990s: The Console Wars

In the 1990s, video games were changed by the advent of 3D graphics and new genres. Arcades declined, but computer games experienced considerable growth. Nintendo released Super Mario Bros. 3® for the NES in 1990 to great critical and commercial success. The most successful nonbundled game ever (meaning that it was not packaged with a console but had to be purchased separately), it sold over 18 million units worldwide.

The company followed this success with the 1991 launch of the Super NES®, which featured launch titles like Super Mario World™, F-Zero™ (a racing game), and Pilotwings™ (a flight simulator). The console was a hit, despite the release of the Sega Genesis two years before.

In response, Sega debuted Sonic The Hedgehog™ in 1991. Sonic was intended as a rival to Mario, and was presented as faster, cooler, and edgier than his counterpart. This competition between the two companies escalated into what some called "the console wars." The battle between the two companies raged for years, but despite their head start and their lower price point, Sega couldn't seem to pull ahead. Eventually, Nintendo won the war, selling nearly twice as many Super NES consoles as the Sega Genesis.

Other companies attempted to enter the battle. NEC released the TurboGrafx-16 in 1989, and both the Atari Jaguar and the 3DO Interactive Multiplayer (published by 3DO) were released in 1993. Despite Atari's return to the fray, all three consoles were casualties of the war, unable to establish a direct rivalry with the two industry titans.

Home computers continued to flourish as a gaming platform. Myst® and Doom were released in 1993. The former, a puzzle game, enjoyed mainstream success. The latter, a first-person shooter, proved wildly popular, due in part to the shareware method of distribution—users could purchase part of the game for a small amount, then pay to play the rest of the game. Furthermore, the burgeoning mod (modification) community helped to keep the game popular, as players created their own levels for Doom and shared them online. This process would be repeated later in the decade with games like Half-Life®, which spawned an extremely popular fan-created mod called Counter-Strike™.

In 1995, the fifth generation of game consoles began with the release of the Sega Saturn and the Sony PlayStation. Originally designed as a CD drive for the Super NES, the PlayStation was reworked into a stand-alone console by Sony when Nintendo canceled the deal.

The following year, the Nintendo 64™ was released. Though the other two consoles played discs, the N64 used cartridges. When the Sega Saturn eventually bowed out of the console war due to mediocre sales, the battle came down to the PlayStation and the N64.

The N64 boasted some well-received titles, such as the first-person shooter GoldenEye 007. However, Nintendo's choice to keep using cartridges instead of pursuing disc media was a costly one; consumers saw cartridges as archaic, and Sony's game lineup was extremely robust. Nintendo's console was easily defeated, and "PlayStation" became the new generic term for "video game." Ironically, Nintendo's decision to sever ties with Sony created a rival that would eventually win the fifth-generation war, with console sales of over 100 million (nearly three times that of the N64).

In 1996, a new first-person shooter called Quake was released for PCs. Though it was hardly the first game to feature online gameplay, it was so successful that many gamers considered online multiplayer to be a feature requirement in subsequent shooters.

Final Fantasy® VII, the critically acclaimed seventh installment in a series that had historically been exclusive to Nintendo, was released in 1997. The game's release on the PlayStation cemented the console's reputation and introduced western audiences to Japanese role-playing games.

Sega tried once again with the Sega Dreamcast™ in 1999. Despite some innovations, such as a built-in modem, the system was a failure, and Sega withdrew from console development thereafter, choosing instead to focus on third-party software development. The time had come for the fastest-selling console in history to take the stage.

■ 1.7   2000s: Online Games and Beyond

Despite numerous successes, PC game sales began to decline. Genres such as adventure games had all but vanished. Massively multiplayer online games (MMOGs) and certain flagship titles continued to sell, but ultimately, console gaming became the standard. During this decade, Sony solidified its lead, Microsoft threw its hat into the ring, and Nintendo started weak and finished strong. The decade opened with a new console-war landscape, as the "big three" were established.

The PlayStation 2 (PS2™) was released in 2000. It featured backward compatibility with the PlayStation, which meant that people could still play their old games on the PS2. Sporting an impressive library of new games, the PS2 was extremely well received and became the fastest-selling console in history.

Microsoft made its entry into console gaming in 2001. The Xbox® featured Xbox Live™, a subscription-based service that streamlined the process of online gaming. Xbox Live was a significant step forward for console users, who finally had access to a growing library of online-enabled games, and it provided a base for Microsoft to dominate online console play in the next generation. Halo®: Combat Evolved, regarded as a "killer app" for the Xbox, drove sales, but Microsoft was unable to close the gap with the PS2.

Nintendo countered with the GameCube™ that same year. The system featured mini-discs, which meant that it couldn't play DVDs, CDs, or previous Nintendo games.

Since both of its rivals played CDs and DVDs, and the PS2 featured backward compatibility, this hurt the GameCube's image. Worse, the system only provided a handful of online-capable games, and it was perceived as more family-friendly and less "edgy" than the other two. This perception helped establish the Xbox, by contrast, as an online-focused console for the mature, tech-savvy gamer. However, that didn't help Microsoft's sales.

The PS2 emerged as the clear victor in this console war, with over 120 million consoles sold, as opposed to the roughly 20 million sold by each of its two competitors.

On the PC gaming front, massively multiplayer online role-playing games (MMORPGs) continued to thrive. Continuing a trend from the 1990s, these sprawling virtual worlds enticed players to participate, often requiring a monthly subscription fee. The most successful of these was World of Warcraft® (2004), which boasted over 11 million subscribers by the end of 2009.

Handheld games made significant process, as Sony released the PlayStation Portable (PSP®) in 2004, featuring a movie player, an MP3 player, and online connectivity; it sold over 50 million units. The Nintendo Double Screen (DS™) was released that same year, and boasted an innovative touch-sensitive screen that the user interacted with via a plastic stylus. The DS was the clear winner in the competition, selling over 110 million units. The Nintendo DSi, which features two built-in cameras and connection to an online store, was released in 2008.

The seventh generation of consoles began with the Xbox 360, which was released in 2005. With an upgraded version of the Xbox Live service, media-streaming technology, and well-received games like Halo 3 (8 million sold) and Gears of War® (5 million sold), the Xbox 360 took the initial lead in the console wars, selling over 30 million units by the end of 2009.

Sony responded with the release of the PlayStation 3 in 2006. The system offered the PlayStation Network, an online gaming service with free access (in contrast to Microsoft's Xbox Live, which players had to pay for in order to enjoy all of the benefits). In addition, the PS3™ featured connectivity with the PlayStation Portable, a built-in Blu-ray DISC™ player, and games like Gran Turismo® 5 Prologue (4 million sold) and MotorStorm™ (3 million sold). It was unable to match the success of the Xbox 360, however, and ended 2009 with over 25 million units sold.

The Nintendo Wii™ was the least powerful system of the "big three" during the seventh generation. It focused on family-friendly games and casual games, leading to a perception that Nintendo had abandoned the hard-core audience that made it a success during the 1980s. Furthermore, instead of the traditional handheld controllers, the Wii sported motion-sensitive controllers that resembled TV remote controls. For these reasons, there was much speculation that the system would be trounced by its competitors. Instead, the Wii dominated the market, selling over 50 million consoles. Its top-selling game, Wii Sports™, sold as many copies, because it was bundled with the system.

Other successful releases included Wii Play™ (20 million sold) and Wii Fit™ (20 million sold). The Wii emerged as the clear victor, prompting Microsoft and Sony to begin development of motion-sensitive peripherals that could compete with the Wii. Microsoft's first venture into motion-sensitive controls is called Project Natal™; using an add-on peripheral for the Xbox 360, it allows users to interact with voice or hand gestures. Sony has announced that it will unveil its motion controller in 2010.

The decade closed with the introduction of a new handheld system: Apple's iPod touch®, a device featuring a touch-sensitive screen and a digital store offering over 100,000 applications. With over 20 million units sold, the system isn't going to topple the PSP or DS as a dedicated handheld gaming system, but the figures are impressive nonetheless. The sales are even more impressive when one considers that Apple also released the iPhone®, a smartphone with similar functionality and access to the App Store℠. Since the iPhone sold over 20 million units, that means developers of applications have a target audience of over 40 million users to cater to. Given the ease of distribution through Apple's digital store, developers have rushed to take advantage of the opportunity, creating over 20,000 games available for purchase. The challenge for those developers is to find a way to get their games into the hands of consumers, which is difficult when one considers the sheer volume of the competition.

■ 1.8 Chapter Summary

Video games are available in a wide variety of formats, and developers must consider these differences carefully when creating games. Also, being knowledgeable about the history of games allows developers to learn from the past and avoid the same mistakes. It also helps them think about new and innovative ways to utilize technology in games.

The next chapter provides an overview of the game industry and discusses how a game evolves from a concept to a retail product. Information is provided about developers and publishers and how they rely on each other to create compelling games.

■ 1.9 Questions and Exercises

1. What are the basic components of a game?
2. What are the differences between the PC, console, and handheld platforms?
3. What are some factors that led to the game crash in the 1980s?
4. How has the Internet impacted the way we play games?
5. If you were to port a game from one platform to another, what are some things that would need to be changed?

2 The Game Industry

In this chapter:

- Game Industry Overview
- Game Concept Basics
- Pitch Documentation
- Pitching a Game to a Publisher
- Managing the Developer–Publisher Relationship
- Legal Agreements
- Licenses
- Console Manufacturers Approval

■ 2.1 Introduction

The process of creating and releasing a game involves numerous steps and can take anywhere from three months to three years. The key people involved in this process are developers and publishers. Developers are responsible for actually making the game, and publishers are responsible for marketing and distributing the game.

Developers must have open communication with their publisher, as the publisher is ultimately responsible for creating the final packaged product and marketing it to potential buyers. Publishers must work well with developers, because without the developers, there are no products to sell. These relationships can get very complex, especially if an independent developer and publisher are working together. More complexity is added if they are working on a console or cell phone title that is submitted to a third party for approval. This chapter discusses the major aspects of the developer–publisher relationship, from pitching a game to a publisher to managing the developer–publisher relationship.

■ 2.2 Game Industry Overview

Most people can come up with an idea for what they think would be a compelling game, but a game is more than just an idea. The idea is the easy part; it's turning the idea into an actual playable game that's the hard part. And once the game is created, potential players need to know that the game is out there so they can play it. As this book will explain, making games requires time, effort, and people. Games also require the support of two main entities—developers and publishers. A game idea can come from either of these groups. For example, a publisher may have access to a licensed book or movie they want to turn into a game, or a developer might have a unique and innovative idea for utilizing technology in a fun and challenging way. Regardless of where the idea comes from, both groups need to work together to make a successful game.

2.2.1   Role of the Publisher

The publisher's responsibilities run the gamut from providing money and resources to manufacturing the actual boxed games that appear on store shelves. The publisher's ultimate goal is to make money by investing in profitable games, both big and small. As discussed later in this chapter, publishers may provide money and resources so that a developer is able to start (or even finish) a game.

When a publisher makes a substantial investment in a game, they are also likely to provide specific feedback on what the game should contain. This could include providing a specific movie license and genre as a starting point for a game or requesting changes to an original game that is already in development. In any case, it is important for developers to consider publisher feedback carefully so they maintain a good working relationship with their publisher.

The publisher is also responsible for distributing the game to retail stores. This includes arranging to have the packaging (box and manual) printed and assembled, creating game discs from the gold master, and then shipping the product directly to stores. If the game is being distributed online, the publisher may provide the actual network resources needed for this type of distribution.

2.2.2   Role of the Developer

The developer's role is to focus on creating a great game. While a developer may be working with a concept handed down from the publisher, it is still the developer's responsibility to refine the concept and create something fun to play. The developer's time is best spent working on the creative and technical aspects of the game, incorporating the publisher's feedback when necessary.

The developer is also responsible for testing the game and addressing any issues that arise. In addition, the developer must provide any necessary support to sales, marketing, and Public relations (PR). More information about what this support entails is discussed in Chapter 15, "Marketing."

■   2.3   Game Concept Basics

When preparing to pitch a game concept to a potential publisher, there are a few elements that need to be defined in regard to the game. The first thing to consider is the fun factor. Though the creation of a game is a fairly straightforward process, it's considerably harder to ensure that the game experience is a fun one. The fun factor is difficult to define, but players know it when they see it. A combination of thrill, challenge, suspense, tension, and emotion, the fun factor is the result of moments of gameplay that are strung together in a sequence that elicits a sense of wonder in the gamer. A fun game can transport one to another world, engrossing the player thoroughly and driving away all thoughts of the real world. When defining a concept for your game pitch, you must focus on elements that define this sense of fun to potential publishers.

This elusive feeling is the result of a focus on core gameplay, and is best created when the game concept is well-defined. In order for the actual game to live up to the fun promised in the game concept, the designers must tune and polish gameplay, make sure that all production values (such as music and voice acting) are high caliber, and vary the game's experience properly. This typically means creating a solid feedback loop: The player takes action, understands the challenge and the nature of failure, overcomes challenges to achieve victory, and receives a satisfying victory of some kind. If well crafted, the pace of gameplay can keep a player occupied for hours.

2.3.1 Rules

A good game has a defined set of rules that govern the player. These rules are instructions and limitations that the player encounters in each game. Rules are an indication of how the player's actions will affect the game world and what the result of those actions will be. Though they may not all be known initially, they should eventually be understood by the player, whether they're learned through experience or explained in a pop-up menu.

When the player understands the rules of a game, it's easier to comprehend the game's objective and thus provide context for the player's actions. This makes it possible for the player to figure out what to do next, as he or she is able to speculate more effectively about what will happen in response to his or her actions.

Victory conditions are different for each game, but effectively they are the necessary actions that will end the game, "beating" it. Not every game features victory conditions; for example, in Oblivion®, the player can complete the main quest and defeat the main enemies, resulting in a cinematic sequence, but gameplay continues and the player is free to explore other parts of the game. However, many games feature a victory condition that the player works toward.

Victory may depend on solving puzzles, reaching a certain area, performing a series of actions in a specific amount of time, or killing a certain number of opponents. Whatever the case, the victory conditions, like the rules, should be presented to the player early on in order to prevent the player from becoming frustrated by repeated failure.

2.3.2 Challenges

During gameplay, the player will encounter opposition and (presumably) emerge victorious. By overcoming obstacles, the gamer can move on to the next sequence. A challenge is a clearly defined event, character, or situation that prevents the player from reaching a goal or target. The player should be aware of the challenge and should have the necessary resources to deal with it effectively, or else the game experience will be a negative one, as the player will perceive the game to be unfair. By overcoming challenges, the player feels a sense of accomplishment, which drives the player to take on the next obstacle.

Challenges should escalate over time, becoming more complex or lethal as the player becomes more comfortable with the game's controls. This will require greater skill on the player's part and will result in greater satisfaction as more serious challenges are overcome. These can take the form of new puzzles, new and more powerful opponents, or new abilities that must be mastered.

In some games, a game level ends with a more powerful enemy (a "boss") or a proportionally more difficult challenge. This challenge is typically followed by a reward of some kind, such as a victory screen or a cinematic sequence that indicates the player has progressed in some way. These end-level challenges are more significant and threatening than the others, and result in a higher level of tension, thrill, and exhilaration when overcome.

■ 2.4 Pitch Documentation

Typically, the pitch process begins with a concept document, which is a short treatment that contains brief descriptions of all of the main areas of a game's design: story, gameplay, market, audio, and so on. This document communicates the main concept to the studio management and/or publisher. The concept document should contain the following elements:

- **Title:** This should be something that stands out and gives the publisher an idea of what the game is about.
- **Genre:** This describes the type of game being made. See the "Genre" section in Chapter 7, "Game Concept," for more information about genres.
- **Platform:** What platform will the game be released on? Why?
- **Target audience:** Who is going to enjoy this game? What are the demographics of your target audience and how does the game fulfill their needs?
- **Premise:** This is a one- to two-sentence description of the game that explains the game's hook and what the player will experience in the game.
- **Game summary:** This is two to three paragraphs that sum up the player's overall game experience. It describes the player's role and what the player can do in the game.
- **Backstory and game world:** This describes the setting of the game and provides a high-level overview of the story. This is also about two to three paragraphs.

- **Gameplay mechanics:** This describes the main gameplay mechanics. What can the player do in the game? What types of challenges will be encountered? How will the player overcome these challenges?

- **Character descriptions:** Who will the player be in the game? Who are the other characters in the game? What types of enemies and nonplayer characters (NPCs) will the player encounter?

- **Mission and story progression:** How does the story unfold during the game? What are the main plot points and how will the player interact with the story?

- **Features and gameplay highlights:** This details the unique selling points of the game and shows how the game stands out from the competition. Think of this as the bulleted list of features that the marketing department might put on the back of the game box to get people interested in buying the game.

- **Technology highlights:** How will technology be used to enhance the gameplay experience? Will it feature cutting-edge graphics, an innovative camera and control scheme, or some type of new multiplayer experience?

- **Art and audio highlights:** This discusses how the art and audio will make the game stand out. Does the game feature music from a well-known composer or celebrity voice actors?

- **Competitive analysis:** How does this game stand out from the competition? What does the game do better than the competition?

- **Team, budget, and schedule:** How much will it cost and how long will it take to make the game? Who will make the game?

Chapters 7, 8, and 9 contain more information about the elements of the pitch document. If a publisher is intrigued by the pitch, a more detailed game design document may be requested for further review.

The game design document is much longer than the concept document; it consists of dozens or hundreds of pages of material, including the nature of the game, the game world, the story, the characters, the gameplay mechanics, and the design of the UI. It transmits critical data to other members of the design team, including programmers, artists, producers, and testers. Through text and illustrations, the designers answer important questions about the game, streamlining the development process and making it possible for other developers to create the necessary code and art assets.

■ 2.5 Pitching a Game to a Publisher

As games get more expensive to make and require larger teams, publishers become more selective about which developers they work with. Wholly owned developers usually have direct access to the people making decisions about which games to develop and thus are not under as much pressure to create and pitch a game idea. If a wholly owned developer does not have an idea for a game, it is likely that the publisher will have a game in mind for the developer.

Independent developers, on the other hand, must find a publishing partner to help them get the game finished and on the store shelves. The developer might have a great game idea and already be in preproduction on it, but unless they can find a publisher, it is unlikely the game will be released or turn a profit. In order to find a partner, developers must pitch their games to potential publishers.

Pitching games is not an easy task, as the developer must be able to successfully communicate the full game experience for the player, even though the game is not completed. In fact, the game might only be in the concept phase and have no tangible assets. The publisher must get a clear understanding from the pitch on whether the game will deliver on this proposed experience and be profitable.

PITCHING TO A PUBLISHER

Don Daglow, President and CEO
Stormfront Studios

Almost every developer pitches to publishers. Earlier in industry history the process was much less formal. Long-term developer–publisher relationships played a big part in developing new games, and ideas would be brainstormed jointly and then green-lighted. Over the last decade the game industry has changed its focus to internal creative teams. Like other entertainment media, game publishers now aggressively seek outside developer pitches as a check and balance in addition to their internal creative efforts.

The good thing about this highly evolved pitch process is that an established developer can readily get a meeting with key decision makers. However, if you waste people's time, you can lose that "open door, call us any time" status. So be sure to make good use of publishers' time when you pitch. You may not get a deal, but make sure you leave the room with your reputation enhanced by what went on during the meeting. The publishers will take your call again the next time you're ready to pitch an opportunity.

Because publishers are pitched several hundred games a year, most of them have some type of pitch process in place that allows them to quickly understand the game's potential. It helps them to decide which games are not suitable for their needs and which games warrant more attention and possibly some initial financial support. The pitch process itself will vary based on such things as the type of game being pitched, to whom it is being pitched, how far along the game is in development, and what type of partnership is needed.

REQUEST FOR PROPOSALS

Don Daglow, President and CEO
Stormfront Studios

Publishers commonly send out a formalized Request for Proposal (RFP), especially for licensed properties or smaller projects. (Larger projects are usually handled by internal teams of publisher employees.) The RFP will include information on the property, target platform, estimated budget, and desired ship date. Publishers do their research before tapping developers, and will send an RFP to the top three to five teams that they believe are the best choices for a particular project. Some publishers may send out an RFP that is a full game design (including gameplay, characters, level designs, etc.). In these cases, publishers are looking for a developer to handle the project as a work for hire, where the design is complete but the developer provides the "hands" to implement it.

Some publishers are looking for the highest quality work, some for the lowest price, but most seek to balance the trade-offs between cost and quality. When developers respond to an RFP, they will do a write-up that responds to the specific requests for content in the RFP, describes key gameplay elements, and provides a ballpark schedule and budget. Prototypes are not usually done on spec in response to RFPs because they are too expensive. However, developers may refer to examples from other games that illustrate key points discussed in their response. Publishers at the RFP stage are most interested in budget, schedule, and whether the game will be fun—if they had big doubts about talent, the developer wouldn't get an RFP in the first place.

Some developers who pitch games do not convey the appropriate information the publisher needs in order to make an initial decision about the game's value. Since publishers are reviewing several hundred games a year, it is imperative that the developer has an understanding of what information and materials are needed for the pitch. The best way to learn how to successfully pitch a game is to talk to other developers and to someone in the publisher's acquisitions department. Lee Jacobson, the vice president of business development and acquisitions for Midway Entertainment, has some concrete advice on what is needed to prepare a game pitch that will get noticed.

HOW TO PITCH A GAME

Lee Jacobson, Vice President of Business Development and Acquisitions
Midway Entertainment

Ten to 15 years ago, games used to be all about the novelty of the gameplay mechanics. Now that games have evolved into more mainstream entertainment, it's really about telling stories and how the stories are executed. Also, as games are getting more expensive, publishers have more departments—such as publishing, marketing, sales, and product development—that are weighing in on game decisions. Because so many people are involved, an independent developer who is pitching an original game must be able to communicate the idea in a very limited amount of time. There are four assets that are invaluable for judging a game's publishing potential.

The first is a very brief treatment of the game. This is a one- to two-page executive summary of the game that explains the essence of the game, how it can be positioned in the marketplace, and how it can be communicated to the customer or retailer. If you have to go through a long dissertation to explain the merits of your game, it is likely the mass-market consumer will not immediately understand the game's appeal.

Don't spend time creating a detailed design document. At the pitch stage, this is not important. For one thing, publishers don't have time to read them. Also, after a publisher starts working with a developer, the publisher's feedback will affect the game's design. Unfortunately, most developers spend lots of time writing a document that details all the gameplay mechanics and all the wonderful features of their game, but are unable to describe their game in one or two sentences that explain why people will want to buy it.

Second, and it really is becoming the norm, is a playable prototype or vertical slice of the game. It doesn't need to be long, but it must show how the final game will look and play—no apologies for visual quality, animation quality, production values, camera cuts, lighting, and so on. Publishers would much rather see a two-minute slice of gameplay where the environment looks amazing than a huge world where you can wander for two hours but looks horrible.

A highly polished demo is more likely to get the developer to the next step in the pitch process. It lets the publisher know that the developer not only understands what the game is about but also knows what the consumer needs to see. This is important; many developers lose sight of this and don't realize it's not about what they think is cool, but what the consumers think is cool.

The third thing is a game trailer. It only needs to be 30 seconds to one minute long, but from the moment it starts, everything—including the mood music, the animation, the setup, and the camera angles—must work together to convey the emotional experience of the game. It has to be edited right, narrated correctly, and interlaced with game footage in order to give the publisher an understanding of how cool the game is.

The high production values of the trailer will reinforce the idea that not only does the developer understand both how to make a game, but also understands how to turn it into an entertainment vehicle. These game trailers can easily be disseminated around the publisher's organization and allow anyone to immediately get a feel for whether the game works or doesn't. Game trailers also are handy since everyone can pop in the video and easily view the highlights of the game.

Fourth, developers can prepare other supporting material to demonstrate that they understand the game's market and what they want the game to do; for example, a very brief overview of the game's competitive title and how the game's features make it different from what is already out there. Don't make the mistake of listing technical features as game features, such as better real-time normal mapping. Instead, focus on what distinguishes the game and how the publisher can sell it to a mass audience. Other information to include is a summary of other games created by the developer and the review scores. Information of this nature helps the publisher determine how risky a particular developer may be. Finally, include a top-line assessment of the schedule and approximate budget; this information will get more detailed as the game makes it further in the process.

The typical deal is the standard developer–publisher model in which the publisher funds 100 percent of the game's development as an advance against future royalties and sales of the game. In this deal, the publisher typically provides the third-party commercial software, the tools, and the development kits. The developer is required to fulfill monthly milestones that are evaluated on a regular basis by the publisher. Various royalty structures can be brought to bear on this. As the risk profile changes from the publisher to the developer, the deal can change.

There are also copublishing deals. In this instance, the game is usually fully funded by the development studio, and they are looking for a publisher who can package the game and distribute it to retailers. The publisher will get a distribution fee, which is usually a percentage of the game's sales. The fee depends on what the publisher brings to the table, which can range from packaging and distributing the game to funding the marketing campaign.

■ 2.6   Managing the Developer–Publisher Relationship

After a developer and publisher have committed to a relationship, the relationship must be maintained, regardless of whether the developer is independent or owned by the publisher. The basics of maintaining the relationships are similar in each case—the publisher needs to be informed of the game's progress, and the developer needs resources and support from the publisher.

Ignoring this relationship can be detrimental to the development process. If the developer does not communicate with the publisher on a regular basis about the progress of the game, the publisher might become frustrated at the perceived lack of progress. This frustration may cause the publisher to allocate needed resources to another project, assign the project to another developer, or cancel the project. If the publisher does not give feedback to the developer throughout the production process, the developer might fulfill all the milestone requirements, but the finished product may not be what the publisher thought it was getting. In cases like this, the publisher might ask for changes after the fact, which means additional costs and resources for both the developer and the publisher.

This relationship is made more complex because both the developer and the publisher have a high stake in the game's success and will do whatever they can to ensure this success. Having people on both sides with a say in how certain things will be in the game brings additional complexity. For example, publishers often assign their own producer to work with the developer, in concert with the developer's producer. This situation of having two producers on the project might create some confusion if the two producers' responsibilities aren't clearly defined.

The publisher producer (PP) is the publishing company's representative and will make sure that all sales, marketing, operations, and testing efforts are in sync with the game's production schedule. He or she is usually responsible for reviewing the developer's milestone deliveries and authorizing payment. Additional responsibilities might include coordinating the marketing and localization tasks on the game, dealing with license approvals, and acting as the developer's advocate at the publisher.

A developer that is owned by the publisher still submits builds for approval but has the advantage of already being on the publisher's payroll. The developer's payment is not tied to completing the milestone deliveries. This does not absolve the developer from delivering completed milestones on time, but it does provide more flexibility regarding when these milestones are reviewed.

The PP is not responsible for the day-to-day management of the development team. This responsibility belongs to the developer producer (DP). The DP is responsible for creating the game development plan and making sure that this plan is completed during the production cycle. The DP deals with any human resource (HR) issues within the team, equipment requests, and anything else that directly affects people on the development team.

DEVELOPER–PUBLISHER RELATIONSHIP

Tobi Saulnier, President
1st Playable Productions

The roles of a producer in an independent studio and a producer in a publisher-owned studio are very different. In some respects they are the same; however, in other aspects the whole relationship with the customer is fundamentally changed.

For example, when working as an independent studio, each contract offers a substantial business risk if any delays or other issues are encountered. You might lose a lot of money and endanger your business, you might lose that customer and endanger your business, and so on. Additionally, since your customers probably each have their own unique processes and systems, for each project you will need to translate between whatever set of processes and systems your customers are using and the internal systems being used by your development team—bug databases, forms, approval processes, and so on.

As a publisher-owned studio, you might incur the wrath of your boss if you go late or over budget, but the consequences are much lower in that your studio is unlikely to be closed (unless that is the only project you are doing and you have repeated performance failures). Also, there's a lot more conformity within an internal studio with respect to processes and systems. Because you only have the one customer, all your processes with the publisher are consistent and can be streamlined. However, your customer now has greatly increased visibility into the project and has a lot more direct control of everything from features to the development approach. For instance, instead of debating the price for a project and providing a service that will cause them to choose you over other developers, you need to be able to justify your budget and negotiate a feasible scope and schedule with your marketing department. So, as an internal studio, the customer management aspect of the producer role is fundamentally different; it becomes more management of organization hierarchy versus management of customers.

In the following interview, Jeff Matsushita discusses how he keeps the development cycle on track. He also discusses the developer–publisher relationship.

DEVELOPER AND PUBLISHER RESPONSIBILITIES

Jeff Matsushita, Executive Producer
Microsoft

Most companies have a formal method of overseeing the progress of titles in production. These processes ensure that the development cycle is on track, that the product is meeting expectations, and that everyone involved with the title is on the same page. Through my game development experiences, I have had the privilege of working with many developers, both internal and external, and gaining some interesting insights into the way developers and publishers work together.

Many factors affect the relationship between the developer and the publisher, such as the terms of the deal, whether the developer is internal or external, and the developer's track record for shipping high-quality titles on time and on budget.

Another factor that influences this relationship is who brings the intellectual property (IP) to the table. For instance, the publisher will feel more strongly about a project when they provide the IP. In this case, the publisher will likely have more feedback in the development process, since they want their license to be represented appropriately. In essence, the publisher becomes the developer's customer. On the other hand, if a developer brings an IP to the table, the publisher will focus on working with the developer to ensure that there is a strong marketing effort to support the developer's vision of the game. These instances are rare, as the developer must bring a strong, established franchise and have a history of executing on it or they must have a high-quality game that is very close to completion.

Because of the increasingly larger budgets necessary to develop and market AAA games, publishers are more cautious with unproven properties and unproven developers. In most cases, publishers will go only to proven developers with established IPs. Additionally, publishers will prefer to work with an internal developer on a new IP so they can have better visibility into the project and can better assess risk.

The *project* is the result of the developer's hard work—the program, the art, the sound, and so on. The *product* is the final package that is advertised to the media, shipped to the distributors, and purchased by consumers. In short, the publisher is responsible for taking the developer's *project* and making it into a *product*. The publisher takes the project, tests it, submits it for approval, creates a marketing campaign, designs the packaging, puts it into the box, and handles sales and distribution of the product. When the IP starts with the publisher, they may also fund the development and provide the initial key creative elements. The key thing is that the publisher takes the efforts of the developer and converts it into something that produces revenue for everyone. In the most basic terms, it can be said that the publisher is in the business of selling games and the developer has the job of making games.

To facilitate this process, a publisher will assign a producer to work on the title. This publisher-side producer is responsible for tracking the overall risk associated with the development of the project, which includes making sure that the developer is providing everything promised in a timely manner and is managing the development team effectively. In addition, the producer works with the developer to help them make the best game possible. The producer will deploy publisher resources for focus testing features and provide feedback to the developer. Finally, the producer also continually herds all of the processes of production to make sure that the development, marketing, testing, and localization efforts remain in sync.

The developer, on the other hand, is responsible for completing the project. Unless there are specific IP-related assets brought to the table by the publisher, this includes everything required to develop the software and is usually provided to the publisher in the form of deliverables predetermined in the early stages of the engagement. The decision on how to manage the project team is the developer's choice. The publisher does not necessarily have a say in how the deliverables are completed so long as they are delivered on time. If, however, the deliverables slip, are of marginal quality, or the developer is showing clear signs that they are suffering from other problems, the publisher will likely show greater interest in how the project is being completed. This does not mean the publisher wants to step in and take over, but they might demand greater visibility into the project to make sure that the game is going well and that their investment is not at risk.

In order to minimize these kinds of things from happening, the developer must provide as much information as possible when delivering milestones to publishers so as to shape expectations properly. For instance, a game rarely shows well early in development. A prototype that has only basic scenes, basic controls, basic visual effects, and so on will not likely impress too many people who have no context in which to place it. When a developer provides these kinds of builds, it is essential they spend the time to carefully set up the deliverables so that everyone understands why the materials are successful and how they show that the development is proceeding with a minimum level of risk to quality, schedule, and even budget. The publisher wants to understand how such a limited portion of the overall game fits into the development plan and how it will evolve into a AAA title.

Another aspect of establishing context is for the developer to be clear about what "done" means. If not explicitly defined, "done" can mean anything from being viewable on a development kit with placeholder art, basic features playable in-game, or bug-free and ready to ship. Naturally, if the publisher is expecting final quality and the developer only meant to provide a first pass, people will end up arguing about the value of the build and inevitably begin questioning the progress of development as a whole. But if there are details on what is included in the deliverable, for example, 10 percent of all animations are finished, polished, and viewable in-game along with the list of animations completed, the publisher can much better assess the state of the game. If the publisher is looking at a deliverable that the developer says is done, and it is obvious that it is not done, the publisher will lose trust in the developer, and the developer is not likely to understand why.

In order to help mitigate this, most publishers prefer that the developer spell out the specifics of the milestones. In these cases, the publisher will not dictate what the content for each deliverable is, but they may have milestone definitions of what is expected at alpha, beta, first playable, and so on that map appropriately with the state of development. The developer is responsible for telling the publisher when the game engine, animations, art, AI (artificial intelligence), and so on will be completed and then managing the project to deliver on these milestones. The only time the publisher gets involved in the development process is if they don't think things are getting finished and their development is at risk.

In every situation, having a strong developer–publisher relationship with open communication is important. The publisher and developer each have obligations to fulfill in this relationship in order for the title to be successful. The most important thing is to spend as much time as possible spelling out the specifics of deliverables. As the only ultimate criterion for a successful development is whether a game is fun—an abstract concept at best—it is important that communication is in the most concrete terms possible.

2.6.1 Independent Developer

Independent developers rely heavily on the publisher to provide the finances for completing a game. In order for the publisher to select the best developer for the job, they will conduct due diligence on the short list of candidates for a given job. Conducting due diligence, or vetting, means that the publisher finds out what they can about the developer's ability to deliver a quality game on time and within budget. Publishers will want to meet with the development team to understand how the developer's production process works and are likely to get references from others who have worked with the developer. It is important for the development team to conduct due diligence on the publisher as well.

After a publisher has signed a developer, they negotiate a delivery and payment schedule for the project milestones. This schedule is affected by factors such as the hardware platform, the scope of the game, terms of the contract, any licensed intellectual properties, and other project variables. No delivery and payment schedule will be exactly the same, although the same types of deliverables will be expected throughout the process.

During the initial preproduction phase, the publisher will expect to get detailed design and technical documentation; a full budget, schedule, and staffing plan; and a gameplay proof of the concept. In some instances, these materials have already been created and presented to the publisher in the initial pitch.

At this stage, the publisher may want further information on what production processes will be used to track the progress of the game. This is a valid concern since the publisher is making an investment in the game and wants to realize a profit on this venture. If the PP is not confident in the DP's ability to manage the production process, the PP may become very involved in the day-to-day production tasks being performed by the team. This is not an ideal situation, as the publisher is not interested in running a development team—that's why the project was assigned to an external vendor in the first place. However, the publisher will do whatever is necessary to protect the investment.

After full production has started on the title, the publisher expects to see regular builds of the game. While reviewing the build, the PP will provide feedback and will request changes to the game. This is expected to happen within a reasonable scope, and the additional feedback will likely improve the overall quality of the game. For example, the PP might ask for a level to be rescripted or for the game controls to be adjusted.

In some cases, the publisher will request a major feature change or a new feature. The DP needs to evaluate these requests to see whether they fit within the agreed-upon scope of the game, as outlined in the documentation and milestone schedule. In some instances, the request replaces a planned feature and thus might not impact the scope or schedule negatively.

In other instances, the feature request will impact the schedule and resources, meaning additional production costs are incurred by both parties. When this happens, the DP must immediately make the publisher aware of the impact: The schedule may need an extension, the developer may need to hire more people, or other features must be cut in order to accommodate the request. If any of these changes happen, the DP and PP must renegotiate the milestones and payments.

A developer dealing with additional feature requests and feedback from the publisher may get frustrated, but if a solid working relationship is established with the PP, this frustration can be minimized. The PP is there to help the developer, and a good PP will work with the developer to deal with any unexpected issues on the project.

WORKING WITH PUBLISHERS

Don Daglow, President and CEO
Stormfront Studios

Choose your publisher wisely and do your research thoroughly. Think of working with a publisher like going on a cruise—you pay for everything in advance, and you can't just turn around and leave if there's a problem. Sometimes publishers may ask developers to add more features to a game without being paid more money, and a developer simply has to say, "I'm sorry. That wasn't in the spec and it's not in the budget or schedule. What should we cut to make room for this new feature?" Other times there will be good-faith misunderstandings that both companies have to work together to resolve (e.g., "Wow, no one ever specified when collision detection would be functional, and we thought it was March and you guys assumed September!").

If you find yourself in conflict with a publisher over game content or a milestone approval, be firm and reasonable in your position but don't get too cynical. Often, your publisher's producer is fighting with his or her boss on your behalf in order to come up with a fair and reasonable way to deal with a problem. In a perfect world, the producer you work with is a foil who brings out the best in your group, just as good editors make good writers better. The best producers challenge their developers and push back to get them to do their best work. This makes for better games—and better royalties.

The following interview details the production model used at Large Animal Games as well as how they manage the developer–publisher relationship.

MANAGING THE DEVELOPER–PUBLISHER RELATIONSHIP

Wade Tinney and Coray Seifert
Large Animal Games

We are a small independent developer that makes games for the casual, downloadable games market. In the past, we would usually have six or so projects in development concurrently, varying in production time from six weeks to six months. This model was successful for us, but now that our catalog of original titles is earning royalties, we are in the position of not having to do as many small projects. Our focus now is on larger projects, with a six- to eight-month development cycle. We have both internally funded projects, like RocketBowl™, as well as third-party publisher-funded projects, such as Saints & Sinners Bingo™, from which we also receive a share of the back end.

Publishers are a relatively new phenomenon in the downloadable game space. There are only a few companies that are actively funding third-party development at the moment.

Although we are not a traditional PC or console game developer, the relationship we have with our publisher is similar. We work with them to create a development plan at the beginning of the project, which defines the core features, the milestones, and the payment schedule. However, the publisher we work with is smaller, which means we have to deal with less corporate overhead and there is greater flexibility in general.

Over the course of a six- to eight-month project, we usually have about eight key milestones, which include such deliverables as design complete, core feature complete, and content complete. The publisher works with us during the development process to ensure these milestones are delivered complete and on time. The publisher provides some QA (quality assurance) resources produces marketing materials, and secures deals with distribution partners.

We have a good relationship with our publisher. We speak with the publisher about once a week, depending on where we are in a project. When issues arise, we may speak with them several times a day. Overall, if things are going well during the development cycle, the publisher is not actively involved. But if the publisher has some concerns, they are brought to our attention and we will address them. The publisher gives good feedback, and it never feels like it is mandated; they trust us to deliver a quality game experience.

For a small developer working in the downloadable games market, having a publisher-backed product can have significant advantages. A publisher can really help push your game to the top and secure a better deal and better promotions with an online game distributor.

In the following interview, Jay Powell discusses development milestones and contract specifics.

DEVELOPMENT MILESTONES

Jay Powell, Chief Customer Officer
Digi Ronin Games

Publishers will include a termination clause in the contract. For example, if a milestone is x number of days late, or fails, the publisher may decide to terminate the contract. In order to enforce this, the contract has to be very specific on what constitutes a milestone. So instead of saying that a set of tasks will be 50 percent complete, the publisher will want a list of actual assets and tasks that are supposed to be completed for a specific milestone.

While a game design document (GDD) and a technical design document (TDD) are usually included as part of a contract, these may not be fully fleshed out before the contract is signed. In this case, the publisher will not require a specific schedule up front but will want to get a list of the milestone breakdowns. A provision is included in the contract to add addendums with the specifically defined mile-stone by a certain deadline. This allows the publisher and developer to have some flexibility as to what should be included in a specific milestone, but also gives the publisher something to check the milestone against when it is delivered for approval. The contract will usually include a well-defined approval process; for example, the publisher will have x number of days to review and send feedback.

Once the publisher reviews the milestone, they will usually have feedback for the developer on things they want changed. The developer needs to be diligent about letting the publisher know when changes are beyond the scope of what is asked for and will require a formal change request. The developer has to walk a fine line, because sometimes a bunch of little things can really add up and impact the scope of the project. On the other hand, the publisher will sometimes ask for small changes that are within reason and don't require change requests.

The process for change orders is defined in the contract. A change order is completed when a publisher requests changes to a milestone that will impact the scope of the project. This change order defines what needs to be done and is presented to the developer. The developer reviews the request and comes back with a plan that details how much money and time will be needed in order to make the change. The publisher can then decide whether these changes are necessary.

2.6.2 Publisher-Owned Developer

As stated earlier, the main benefit of being a wholly owned developer is that the finances are guaranteed, which means the team can concentrate on making the game instead of worrying about getting their milestone payments in a timely fashion.

In this type of relationship, the publisher is also more intimately involved with the team during the development process, which means they can offer more resources to the team. For example, the publisher can temporarily lend the team experts from other internal projects, making it possible for the team to complete a critical task on time. It is also easier for the publisher to make feature requests and grant schedule extensions to ensure that a requested feature gets into the game.

Some publishers will still assign a PP to work with a wholly owned developer. The PP will work with the DP to coordinate testing, marketing, and other tasks for the game. The PP is not likely to run the day-to-day activities of the development team but may be more involved in what production processes are used, especially if there are companywide processes that must be adhered to.

Jamie Fristrom of Torpex Games has this to say about the developer–publisher relationship: "Being owned by another company changes your outlook on staffing. When you are an independent publisher, you try not to hire people until you are sure they are needed. When you are working in-house for another company, you try to get people as soon as possible—even if you are not sure you need them. Because your publisher or owner is trying to place people at several different studios, i.e., they are not focused just on work at your own studio, more time is usually needed to find the right personnel. When they do come along, we usually try to hire them before they are assigned to another developer."

THE ROLE OF THE PROJECT MANAGER

Tobi Saulnier, President

1st Playable Productions

Before Vicarious Visions was owned by Activision, it was an independent developer that worked with many publishers. Having this variety of customers and unique contracts has a major impact on the management of product development.

Vicarious Visions' approach was to assign an internal producer to each title who was called a project manager (PM) to distinguish that role from the publisher producer (PP). The PM is involved very early in the initial project assessment of feasibility. The PM is multidisciplinary and must be able to communicate with art, design, engineering, and the publisher. In addition, the PM must be able to understand the marketing and sales limitations of the project. The PM works directly with the PP, who provides the channel for all marketing plans, financial backing, license requirements, ship dates, and so on.

Although the management at Vicarious Visions provided a lot of support, especially early in the development process, during most of the development the PM was the main point of contact for the PP. This helps streamline the communication between the developer and the publisher. After a project is ready to begin, the PM is provided a project charter that documents the internal goals and assumptions of the game that were developed during the sales process, and this is used to prevent loss of information during the hand-off to the development team.

As the project begins, the PM works closely with the PP on what the constraints are for the IP. For example, specific guidelines are defined on what characters and story elements can be used, what new content can be created, and what themes can be used. As preproduction progresses, the PM works with the development team to make sure that they understand the constraints and that open questions are resolved.

During preproduction, the PM works with the designer and project leads to create the game design and technical design documents, style guide, and development schedule, which defines the details of the remaining milestones.

After the game design document is completed and the title goes into production, the project requires much less marketing interaction and is entirely in the hands of the PM as the team proceeds toward the agreed-upon features and schedule. The PM is responsible for making sure that everyone has what is needed to be productive, presenting the in-progress assets to the PP for review, filling out licensor approval forms, and other things.

The PM role can change depending on how overworked or experienced the PP is. Sometimes, the assigned PP has only one project and thus can provide more support to the PM. In other cases, the PP will have 10 projects and cannot provide a lot of support to the PM. This means the PM must be prepared to step up to handle such diverse tasks as licensor approval paperwork, localization, early testing coordination, and preparation of materials for marketing and PR, even if the PP is ultimately responsible for them.

Ultimately, the PM must do whatever is necessary to keep the project organized and running smoothly. This includes attention to the game, reviewing features, play-testing, monitoring progress through resource allocation, and tracking schedules.

The PM must also write build notes and obtain milestone approvals from the PP. Finally, as soon as the project runs into issues, the PM works with the project leads to find solutions. It helps if the PM has some area of expertise in art, design, or engineering so he or she can understand the hands-on details of how the game is put together. Between all of these roles, the PM is also the team's lead cheerleader, attends to the care and feeding of the team, ensures that milestones are celebrated, and makes sure everyone manages to have some fun between the deadlines.

■ 2.7 Legal Agreements

As a developer, you might be communicating with an attorney or the publisher's legal department on certain matters. For instance, a developer producer participates in negotiating development milestones in the publishing agreement. A publisher producer might work with potential licensees to define the details of a licensing agreement. In each instance, the producer works with qualified attorneys to ensure that all the legalities are properly handled, so it is not necessary for a producer to have a law degree. However, it is helpful for a producer to be knowledgeable about some general legal issues that will be encountered during game development.

Tom Buscaglia, a well-known attorney specializing in games, was interviewed by the author for some general information about legal issues a producer should be aware of. He has also written a series of articles on basic legal information that developers, especially independent ones, should know. For more information, see Appendix D, "Interview Biographies." Information gleaned from the interview is paraphrased throughout this chapter.

2.7.1 Types of Legal Agreements

Legal agreements are contracts between two or more parties that outline the responsibilities and duties of each party to the other. As a producer, you might be involved in negotiating the terms of legal agreements for external vendors, publishers, and licensees. For example, you might determine the milestone schedule and deliverable lists for an external development contract.

2.7.2 Work for Hire

When an external vendor creates something for use in the game, such as music, art assets, or code, he or she owns the created assets and is protected by intellectual property rights. This means you do not have any legal rights to use them in a game, unless you expressly obtain permission from the vendor to do so. However, this does not mean the vendor is obligated to grant you exclusive rights; he or she may want to license these assets to other game companies as well.

This problem can be avoided if a work-for-hire agreement is put into place before any assets are created. This agreement transfers all the rights to the person hiring the vendor, and for all intents and legal purposes, the hiring party is considered the creator of the work. For example, if you hire a composer under a work-for-hire agreement to create music, after the work is completed you own all the music rights free and clear. This means you can use the music in other products you create, or you can license it for use to other parties.

It is important to note that there are only two situations in which a work for hire can exist. The first situation is where an external vendor is commissioned to create a completely new work and signs a work-for-hire agreement before starting anything. In addition, the work must fall within one of nine categories of commissioned work detailed in the Copyright Act: a translation, an instructional text, a test, answers for a test, an atlas, a contribution to a collective work, a compilation, supplementary material, or a contribution to a movie or other audiovisual work. For example, a magazine article could be a work for hire as it is a contribution to a collective work, but a novel could not be a work for hire because it does not fall into any of the previously mentioned categories.

The second work-for-hire situation involves any work created by employees that is within their scope of employment. For example, all the code written by a programmer who is an employee on your development team is work for hire. He or she does not own the rights to the work, as the rights are held by the employer. Of course, this situation can get complicated if working with part-time employees, and in that case a lawyer might need to be consulted. For more information on work-for-hire agreements, please consult the U.S. Copyright's Office circular titled, "Works Made for Hire under the 1976 Copyright Act," which is listed in Appendix C, "Resources."

2.7.3   Nondisclosure Agreements (NDAs)

Game concepts and ideas are not protected by copyrights and trademarks. This means the developer must protect them as trade secrets, and a nondisclosure agreement helps do this. Basically, an NDA states that what you are discussing with another party is to remain a secret, thus enabling the concepts to be considered trade secrets. If you discuss your concept with someone who hasn't signed an NDA, the concept loses its trade secret status and becomes public domain. So if you want to protect your ideas, don't discuss them with anyone without having an NDA signed.

The two common types of NDAs are unilateral and mutual. A unilateral NDA is used when you are discussing your game concept with someone who is outside of the game industry, such as an independent investor. This protects any ideas you discuss with him or her, because he or she doesn't have secrets—you do. A mutual NDA is used when people in the industry are discussing ideas with each other, such as when a publisher discusses game concepts with an independent developer. This protects the information revealed by both parties. In instances like this, the publisher is likely to provide the NDA.

The catch is that most publishers are reluctant to sign any type of NDA with external developers. This is because publishers review hundreds of games a year; there is a risk they might have a game similar to the one being pitched already in production or in the concept stages. You can always ask them, but chances are they will not sign one. Of course, this creates a dilemma for any developer pitching an idea, but in all likelihood, if a publisher is not interested in your game, they will tell you and won't be interested in copying it.

2.7.4   Development Contracts

Development contracts between a publisher and an external developer outline what responsibilities each party has to the other. These contracts cover all the issues involved in the developer–publisher relationship, including financial terms, elements of the project, asset deliverable and advance payment milestone schedules, IP ownership, marketing plans, distribution plans, and obligations of each party.

The financial terms define the payment schedule and royalty structure. The developer's advances are usually divided into a series of payments that are tied to milestone deliverables. The specific milestone content and deadlines will be detailed in the developer's obligations section of the contract. In addition, specific submission and approval guidelines are set forth for each deliverable.

One of the most important items covered in the contract is the transfer of IP rights from the developer to the publisher. This means the developer relinquishes all rights to the game's code, characters, textures, story, concepts, and anything else that goes into creating the game. It might also cover any proprietary tools the developer creates to streamline the game development process, such as scripting tools, texture editors, or software plug-ins. If the game is based on an existing license, such as a movie, detailed guidelines of how the developer can utilize the license are included.

Development contracts also discuss other contingencies, such as who is responsible for QA testing, localization, publicity, and ancillary rights (such as movie and television deals). Also, as with employee–consultant agreements, information is included on how disputes between the parties will be arbitrated. The publisher is responsible for finalizing the publishing contract, although the developer will need an attorney to review it before signing.

WORKING WITH LICENSORS

Stuart Roch, Executive Producer
Activision

When thinking of schedule concerns in particular, ample consideration must be taken on the producer's part to send approval packs off much sooner than they would normally feel necessary. When dealing with a movie licensed game, a producer needs to factor in the longer turnaround time that is a result of active film production schedules, especially when the directors are integral to the creative process.

On Enter the Matrix™, Warner Bros. approved many of the assets, but in most cases they did so for legal reasons rather than creative ones. Since the Wachowski brothers were so involved with the creation of the game, Warner Bros. allowed them responsibility for the majority of the creative approvals, leaving Warner Bros. the time to help us more with the business side of the game production.

Enter the Matrix was even more unique than other licensed games because the Wachowski brothers were so supportive of the game from the start, thus giving us a near all-access pass to the film production. By having a nontraditional and completely complementary relationship with the Wachowski brothers, they opened doors for us that we wouldn't have even been able to approach otherwise. Whether it was working with the primary talent, the costume designer, the visual effects team, or even just bouncing ideas off the brothers themselves, the personal Wachowski touch meant we had a closer collaboration with the film production than had ever been attempted up to that time.

■ 2.8 Licenses

Games based on licenses, such as Spider-Man™, James Bond™, or the NFL®, are becoming more common each year. The allure for publishers to secure well-known licenses is the ability to build upon an audience that is already familiar with the brand, which generates higher awareness for the game and translates into higher sales. For example, it is easier to market an adventure game based on Harry Potter™ than to market one featuring an unknown character and universe. A Harry Potter game immediately means the game will feature Harry and his friends, wizards, amazing adventures, mythical creatures, and a host of other magical characters. An unknown character does not have any immediate associations, so players must be educated on what the elements are.

A producer is not normally involved in the actual process of securing the interactive rights to a license; instead, the producer is usually assigned a project with a specific license already attached. This means the producer must plan for the impact this has on production, particularly on the design, schedule, and asset creation.

Depending on how the licensing deal is structured, the licensor may be either minimally involved in the actual game production or extremely involved in determining the game design, assets, and features. At a minimum, it is likely the licensor has approval rights over the general game concept and key assets, since their main concern is to protect the integrity of the license. For example, it is unlikely that a developer making a game based on a Disney cartoon would be allowed to create content that would get an M rating, as these titles are geared toward children; thus, a game will never involve Mickey Mouse™ going on a shooting rampage. These approvals need to be clearly spelled out in the licensing agreement, and the producer must account for these approvals in the schedule. You don't want to hold up production on a title because you forgot to schedule two weeks to receive final approval from the licensor on the game concept.

In addition, there may be a bible that clearly spells out what can and cannot be done with characters and settings based on a license. It might detail what types of clothing the character wears, what actions he or she can perform in the game, what other characters from the universe can appear in the game, and so on. The producer needs to get this information during preproduction so it can all be accounted for and integrated properly into the game. Overall, the producer must be proactive about working with licenses, so establishing a good relationship with your licensing contact is the first step to ensure that approvals, concepts, and assets are signed off on in a timely fashion.

Create a schedule for the licensor that shows when assets and builds will be sent for approval and indicates the deadline for receiving approval so that the licensor has a better idea of how these approval cycles impact the game's schedule. If you can be proactive about getting the licensor everything they need, you are more likely to have a positive working relationship with them.

LICENSOR APPROVALS

Jamie Fristrom, Creative Director

Torpex Games

When working with a licensor, time must be added to the production schedule for receiving approval on all these materials, and the licensors usually will take as much time as they can. You can have clauses in the contracts that limit how much time they have to approve something; if you don't hear something from them by the deadline, it is "deemed approved," and you can move on with production.

Sometimes you'll find yourself working with two licensors: for example, a movie based on a book or comic. The approval rights will be divvied up between the licensors, or you'll have to submit everything to both parties.

Your licensor probably will leave actual gameplay mechanics or design documentation up to you, but they'll still want to see regular builds of the game so they can see how things are progressing. There are probably many things you just can't do with their character. For example, he or she might not be allowed to kill anyone, which affects the game design. This can be challenging, but it sometimes helps you to be creative and do things that haven't been done before in games.

■ 2.9 Console Manufacturers Approval

Games published for proprietary hardware platforms, such as consoles or cell phones, must be submitted for approval to the appropriate third-party manufacturer, such as Sony, Microsoft, or Nintendo. In most cases, the publisher or developer will want to get the game concept approved by the third-party manufacturer before production begins on the game. For example, both Sony and Microsoft require a concept proposal to be approved by them before development begins on a title. If the developer skips this step in the process, they might find that the fully developed title is rejected outright before it is even submitted for final approval and manufacturing.

These manufacturers also have a standard set of technical requirements that each product must meet in order to be approved for release. These requirements are listed in detailed documentation and cover all aspects of the game, such as how to word specific pop-up messages, how to set up the friends list, and so on. The developer must fulfill all of these requirements, or the game will fail the approval process. These requirements must be built into the development process so they can be implemented and tested along with the other game features. The console manufacturers will assign an account manager as the main point of contact to help the developer navigate the submission process. The manufacturer might also have gameplay feedback on how to improve the game to best show off the specific features of the gaming platform. Refer to Chapter 14, "Testing and Code Releasing," for more information on the console submission process.

■ 2.10 Chapter Summary

The relationship between developers and publishers can be very complex, yet one cannot exist without the other. In order for a game concept to become a full retail product, developers and publishers must work together to make this happen. Developers have more distribution options available today than they did 20 years ago, so it is easier for independent developers to thrive in today's game market. However, publishers are better able to market and distribute games to a wider audience, which is necessary in order to recoup investments in multimillion-dollar games. This chapter discussed how to pitch a game to a publisher and how to establish a good working relationship between the developer and the publisher.

The next chapter discusses the roles on a game development team. Once you have a solid game concept, the right team needs to be assembled. The type of team you put together depends on the scope of the game. Will you need a large team with a robust management structure, or can you get a better job done with a small team of people who have multiple roles?

■ 2.11   Questions and Exercises

1. What elements should a developer include in a pitch to a game publisher?

2. Why is it important for developers and publishers to maintain a good working relationship?

3. What are the differences between an independent game developer and one that is owned by a publisher? What are the pros and cons of each?

4. What does it mean to vet a developer? What type of information is needed in order to vet a developer?

5. Discuss how the publisher is involved in the development process when working on a game with an independent developer.

6. Pick a recently released game and research the publisher and the developer. Include a company history for both. For the publisher, include information on previously released games, revenues, and company size. Define what type of game would be best to pitch to this publisher. For the developer, include information on the size of the team, whether they are independent, and previously released titles.

7. What are the benefits of using a work-for-hire contract for an external vendor who is contributing work to a game?

8. What is the purpose of a development contract?

9. How does an NDA affect something that is a trade secret?

3 Roles on the Team

■ 3.1 Introduction

To better understand the production cycle, it is important to know what types of roles are normally found on a game development team. The roles vary from team to team, depending on the project needs, the company size, and the scope of a project. For example, for a mobile phone game, the team might be four people who all fulfill multiple roles on the project. For a next-generation console game, the team might have more than 80 people, with each person assigned a specific role on the project.

This chapter discusses the general roles on a development team and how the teams are organized. In addition, information is presented on nonproduction roles, such as sales and marketing. For more in-depth information on roles and job descriptions, please refer to *Get in the Game!: Careers in the Game Industry* (2003) by Marc Mencher.

WORKING ON A GAME DEVELOPMENT TEAM

Wade Tinney and Coray Seifert

Large Animal Games

If you are working in game production, you need to have a deep understanding of games and why people play them. It's amazing to us how many people who don't play games apply for jobs at a game company. Would you apply for a job at a film studio if you didn't watch movies on a regular basis? One must not only play games but also think critically about them. If you don't understand interactivity and how a given set of choices affects a player's game experience, it's unlikely that you'll be able to effectively contribute to the development team. This ability to think critically about gameplay is especially important for producers and designers.

Aspiring game developers must also be able to interact constructively with other members of a creative team. Gone are the days when a commercial game could be created by a single person. It is now imperative for developers to understand the importance of teamwork in creating a successful product. Even team experience from other creative industries is a good start; if you have experience working collaboratively on a film project, for example, or even on a school project, that experience can help prepare you for the game industry.

In addition, you must have the discipline to complete your tasks within tight deadlines, without handholding, and, in many cases, with fewer resources than you would really like. Frequently, smaller development teams depend on each member to wear many different hats and to do whatever it takes to get the game done. This can include designing parts of the game, making decisions on budgets and schedules, or even creating art assets. If you are able to quickly adapt to situations like these, you will be right at home making games.

■ 3.2 Production

Production roles run the gamut from production coordinator to executive producer. People involved in game production are focused on managing and tracking the game's development and are the main intermediary between the development team and anyone external to the team, even studio management. Those in production roles should keep the team happy, motivated, and productive on the project. Production people are not usually responsible for actually creating game assets, as their main responsibility is to efficiently manage the people creating the content. This management keeps the team's time focused on actually completing game tasks instead of tracking schedules, dealing with personnel issues, managing external vendors, negotiating contracts, proofreading marketing copy, and anything else external to creating game content.

Three basic production roles exist, although the names may vary from company to company:

- Executive producer
- Producer
- Associate producer

Not all of these roles are necessary for every project, which means that the responsibilities shift for each role, depending on the needs of the project.

3.2.1 Executive Producer

An executive producer (EP) is usually a producer with 5 to 10 years of production experience. EPs most often oversee multiple projects, and their main function is to ensure that the game development process is running smoothly and efficiently. They are focused on broader production tasks—researching hardware and middleware needs, establishing employee training programs, negotiating contracts, evaluating external vendors, and other duties that will benefit current and future projects.

An EP normally reports to the studio vice president or chief executive officer (CEO). He or she manages multiple producers and works with the producers individually to evaluate and implement solutions for potential problems on the projects. EPs are not involved with the day-to-day operations of the development team and do not communicate with the project leads on a regular basis, as that is the producer's responsibility.

3.2.2 Producer

The producer is typically a developer with three to five years of production experience who has worked as an associate producer on several game titles. The producer is usually in charge of a single game and the entire development team for that game. The producer is one of the most visible people on the project and is the team's representative to anyone outside the team. His or her primary responsibility is to make sure that the game is delivered on time, on budget, with all the expected features, and at the highest quality possible, while keeping the team focused on and enthusiastic about their work. Although a producer is heavily involved with the project leads in making creative decisions, the main focus is on facilitating the development process, not on dictating the creative content and game features.

The producer reports to an executive producer or studio vice president and works closely with marketing, sales, operations, public relations, studio management, creative services, legal, third-party console manufacturers, and external vendors. Also, a producer manages the game development plan, communicates it to the team, tracks it, and neutralizes any risks to the plan. Basically, a producer steers the development team toward completion.

Producers can focus on different areas, depending on the needs of their projects and how their development teams are structured. The most noticeable division in production roles can be seen when comparing a publisher producer with a developer producer (DP).

A DP directly manages an internal development team. He or she works closely with the art, engineering, design, and quality assurance leads on the project. As a core team, the DP and leads work together to create the development plan and update it as necessary;

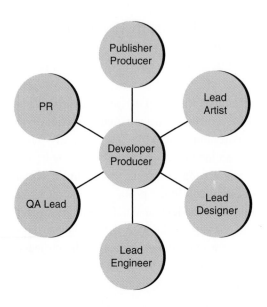

❙ **FIGURE 3.1**   Developer producer's main project contacts.

the DP is also involved in the day-to-day production of the game. If working for an external publisher, the DP will communicate on a regular basis with the publisher producer (PP). Figure 3.1 is a diagram of a DP's main points of contact.

A PP represents the publisher's interests and usually works with external developers. Rarely do PPs manage the actual development team; instead, they oversee other departments that are not directly involved in the internal game development cycle, such as sales, marketing, quality assurance, and localization. A PP can manage multiple projects, especially if they are not all scheduled to be released at the same time. Figure 3.2 is a diagram of the PP's main points of contact.

There are several types of producers one may encounter on a project, such as a creative producer or a project manager. The type of producer depends on the project, the team size, and the needs of the company.

3.2.3 Associate Producer

An associate producer (AP) typically has one to three years of experience and may have started out in an entry-level development position, such as a quality assurance tester or production coordinator. The AP's primary responsibility is assisting the producer with any production-related tasks. A more experienced AP can also be in charge of producing a major aspect of the game, such as localization, music and voiceover, cinematics, or open beta tests.

I FIGURE 3.2 Publisher producer's main project contacts.

The AP reports directly to the producer and may be one of several on a project. They interact with the team on a day-to-day basis and may also be tasked to help the art, design, and engineering leads when necessary.

3.2.4 Background and Training

Because producers have a variety of backgrounds—some started out in game development and worked their way up, and others worked in a different industry and transferred to game development—there are no set guidelines for what skills a producer must possess. Some producers are more technical than others and work most effectively when focusing on ways to push the technology during game development; others may be more effective at guiding the design features of the game. However, anyone working in a production position must have the following characteristics:

Strong leadership skills: These abilities include motivating teams and individuals, negotiating conflicts, building a consensus, and providing the guiding vision of the game from beginning to end.

Effective communication skills: All communication must be clear, diplomatic, and timely. These skills include the ability to deliver bad news in a sensitive fashion, give constructive feedback, and answer any questions in a forthright manner.

Highly developed organizational skills: These skills include creating schedules, delegating tasks, and tracking all the fine details of the project. Knowledge of project management principles is extremely useful.

Desire to work with (and for) others: Overall, a producer is there to serve the team and not the other way around. The team is actually creating the content for the game, and the producer must create a working environment that allows team members to be at their most productive. The producer must always be available to listen to complaints, suggestions, and questions from the team and deal with them in a positive and open-minded fashion. Production is not a fit for someone who does not enjoy working with people.

While there is some training available for game producers, these programs are few and far between. However, there are several areas a producer can concentrate on to build up his or her skills:

Knowledge of the game industry: Keep up-to-date with the latest industry technology and trends, talk with other developers, and play games.

Project management training: Take some classes in project management or better yet, become a certified project manager or scrum master.

People management training: Learn how to effectively manage and motivate people. There are numerous books and classes that can provide valuable information on how to manage a diverse group of people. See Chapter 4,"Teams," for some ideas.

Public speaking experience: Become more confident when speaking at team meetings by taking a public speaking class. Also, Toastmasters (www.toastmasters .org) is a nonprofit organization that helps people practice public speaking and leadership skills.

PRODUCER SKILLS

Stephanie O'Malley Deming, Producer
Xloc

A producer must be a good diplomat and have the ability to communicate with people on all different levels, from a texture artist to the vice president of the studio. A producer must figure out what motivates each person on the team and use this knowledge to get people excited about their tasks. Good organizational skills and the ability to multitask are musts.

Someone who wants to be a producer should start at the bottom, as a production coordinator, assistant designer, or QA tester, and work their way up. Gain as much hands-on experience as you can, because experience counts for an incredible amount. Being in the trenches helps you understand how and why decisions are made and allows you to foresee potential issues in the production schedule. It also gives you the ability to knowledgeably converse with and lead the developers on your team and ensure that the best decisions are made for the design, engineering, and art aspects of the game. After you become a producer, you have many different experiences to pull from and can understand which processes will work best.

■ 3.3 Art

Artists are responsible for creating all of the graphic assets for the game—characters, cinematics, vehicles, buildings, and levels. As technology improves, the quality of the assets must match the advancement, especially for next-generation hardware. These machines have more memory, processing power, and storage space, which gives the artists the opportunity to create highly detailed objects, realistic-looking terrain and water, and special effects for explosions and weather that are comparable to those found in the real world.

Artists work closely with the designers on the objects, worlds, and cinematics that are needed and also work with engineering to determine how to utilize the technology most effectively in the art production pipeline. If a large number of art assets needs to be created, artists are likely to outnumber other team members by two to one. Each team might have different titles for the art positions on a development team. The basic art positions are as follows:

- Art director
- Lead artist
- Concept artist
- World builder or level designer
- Asset artist
- Animator
- Technical artist
- Marketing artist

3.3.1 Art Director

The art director's main function is communicating the artistic vision to the team. This person is skilled in all aspects of creating digital art and is responsible for ensuring that all of the artistic assets relate to each other within the game. An art director is a very skilled and respected artist who has 5 to 10 years of work experience. Not all projects will have an art director on the team.

3.3.2   Lead Artist

The lead artist works closely with the art director to ensure that the artistic vision is maintained throughout the development process. The lead manages the quality of the art assets and the day-to-day tasks of the team and is a go-between for the art director and the art team. This facilitation allows the art director to focus on the creative aspects of the game instead of managing personnel. If the team has no art director, the lead artist assumes the responsibility for defining the artistic vision. The lead artist is an experienced and respected artist with at least three to five years of game development experience.

3.3.3   Concept Artist

Concept artists are visionaries. They are responsible for creating concepts of all of the art assets before they are produced. They are skilled in 2D art, traditional drawing and painting methods, and sometimes 3D art. They work directly with the art director in creating and documenting the artistic vision of the game.

3.3.4   World Builder or Level Designer

The world builders or level designers are responsible for building the geometry and creating the textures for the game world. They are skilled in 2D and 3D art, and have an understanding of level design. In some companies, this position is considered to be a design position, as the gameplay is heavily impacted by the way the game world is mapped out.

3.3.5   Asset Artist

The asset artist has 2D and 3D art skills and is responsible for creating the assets that appear in the game world. These assets include such things as characters, weapons, vehicles, props, user interface screens, and any other necessary game assets. Some asset artists will specialize in a particular type of asset, such as vehicles.

3.3.6   Animator

Animators are responsible for creating all the in-game and cinematic animations. They need to be skilled in traditional 2D and 3D animation. However, 3D animation is more desirable for game development, especially to take advantage of the latest technology.

3.3.7   Technical Artist

Technical artists manage the technical side of asset creation, such as creating collision volumes, making sure that objects are exported correctly, and applying physics attributes to an object. They will work closely with engineering on the art tools and art pipeline and, therefore, need to have enough technical knowledge to communicate with engineers.

3.3.8 Marketing Artist

Marketing artists create all the marketing assets for the game. These activities include taking game screenshots, assembling gameplay videos, and creating high-resolution art, packaging, and anything else that marketing needs to promote the game. These artists are usually skilled in 2D art, with some knowledge of 3D art.

3.3.9 Background and Training

The background and training required for a game artist is well-defined. In general, an artist must possess artistic skill and be able to express this skill in traditional artistic media such as painting, drawing, and sculpting. Another critical component is the knowledge of how to use 2D or 3D software to create assets. Most universities or art schools offer classes on how to use the software, so this hurdle is not difficult to overcome.

Knowledge of the game industry is also beneficial for artists, as technology is always changing, affecting how art can be used in the game. If artists keep up with these changes, they can bring this knowledge to the games on which they work and continue to improve the graphics as the technology evolves.

Finally, artists should have strong communication skills because they will be communicating with designers, engineers, and production personnel on a team. Effective communication makes everyone's job easier.

ART SKILLS

Carey Chico, Art Director
Pandemic Studios

Game artists must have a strong background in working with a blank piece of paper, as this is essential in getting the mind activated. Artists should also have an understanding of how to draw using traditional drawing methods, such as pen and ink. They must also learn the tools of the trade, which include 2D painting and 3D content-creation tools. Finally, they must have technical knowledge. This can't be overstated: The game industry is extremely technical, and it is essential that artists can communicate with technical and creative people.

One way to start working as a game artist is to get involved in a modding community. The modding community will use level editors for a particular game to create new game assets, levels, and missions. Once the mods are completed, the creators usually offer them as free downloads. There are several level editors (such as the Unreal Engine) readily available, which aspiring game artists can use to develop and demonstrate their skills. The modded levels can be the beginning of a game art portfolio that can help someone get their foot in the door at a developer.

■ 3.4 Engineering

Engineers are involved in every aspect of the game—graphics, animation, scripting tools, physics, user interface, sound, and more—and are responsible for creating all the code that makes the game work. They must start with design documents, define the necessary functionality, write code that creates the functionality, and then revise the functionality based on feedback. They also work closely with the art team to determine the technical art needs for the game.

Game engineering is much different from engineering business software, especially with regard to the high priority placed on creating an *entertaining* software package. Game engineers usually have a passion for games and understand the unique skills required for this position. Game engineers must be able to work well with creative types, managers, and other engineers on a project so the team can realize the vision of the game. The basic engineering roles on each game project are as follows:

- Technical director
- Lead engineer
- Engineer

3.4.1 Technical Director

The technical director is a counterpart to the art director. The technical director must be knowledgeable of the latest technology and determine how it can best be used in the game code. Technical directors focus some of their time on research and development and are ultimately responsible for setting the coding standards, determining which technologies are used in the game, coding and maintaining libraries, and so on. Not all projects have a technical director. A technical director must be a skilled engineer with at least 5 to 10 years of experience.

3.4.2 Lead Engineer

The lead engineer is responsible for managing the day-to-day tasks of the team. The lead also works closely with the technical director to determine what technologies are needed for the game. The lead may or may not have a chance to actually create code for the game, as it depends on how busy he or she is managing the engineers. If there is no technical director on the team, the lead engineer is responsible for setting the technical standards of the game. A lead has three to five years of experience, general knowledge of all areas of game technology, and good communication skills.

3.4.3   Engineer

"Engineer" is a general title for a role that can have many variations within a development team. Many game engineers are well versed in several areas of programming but will probably choose to focus on one or two specialties. However, engineers need to be flexible enough to move out of their specialized areas to work in other areas if needed.

Some basic engineering roles on a development team are as follows:

Networking engineer: The networking engineer is responsible for creating multiplayer code. This person works closely with the multiplayer designer to ensure that all the necessary gameplay functionality is supported.

Sound engineer: The sound engineer focuses on creating the sound engine for the game. This person works closely with the sound designer to make sure that the sound engine can support the desired sound features for the game.

Graphics engineer: The graphics engineer is responsible for creating the graphics code. This person works closely with the technical artist on the art tools and art production pipeline.

Tools engineer: The tools engineer is responsible for creating the proprietary tools used during game development. These tools include scripting, lighting, exporters, localization tools, and any other tools that can be coded to streamline the game production pipeline. This person will work with many different people on the team to get an understanding of what tools are needed.

AI engineer: The AI engineer focuses on the artificial intelligence (AI) behaviors in the game. This person works closely with the design team to identify the behaviors and functionality that are needed for the characters in the game.

3.4.4   Background and Training

Many game engineers have a degree in computer science, although a fair number of game engineers are self-taught. Whatever path taken, game engineers require knowledge in programming languages, operating systems, compilers, debuggers, and application programming interfaces (APIs). After being educated in these basic areas, engineers must continually educate themselves in the latest technology and understand how this technology impacts their work. Game technology is constantly changing, and new gaming platforms are guaranteed to emerge every three to four years.

As with artists and production personnel, engineers should also have knowledge of the game industry and a desire to make and play games. Additionally, they need to have strong communication skills, the ability to work in a team-based environment, and the ability to get along with a variety of personalities.

ENGINEERING SKILLS

Tobi Saulnier, President
1st Playable Productions

Game software is becoming more complicated and sophisticated in terms of lines of code and complexity of math. This means that engineers must have a broader and deeper understanding of it than typically feasible for someone who is purely self-taught. Two of the most basic areas that game engineers work on are the core game engine and the game code that runs on top of the core features provided by the engine.

An engineer working on the core game engine for a console game needs to be a good assembly coder and comfortable working with hardware and compilers. The areas they might work on include rendering, effects, physics, and lighting. The focus is on getting the code to run more quickly and getting more graphics piped through the memory on some very idiosyncratic systems. This person should also have an understanding of CPU and memory usage—specifically for game engines—and be comfortable crossing the boundary between software and hardware. An engineer in this position will need to have a high threshold for frustration, because if working with new hardware (which is often the case in game development), the compilers and other tools will be buggy and not mature. And by the time the compilers *are* mature, the hardware will change.

An engineer working on game-specific code must understand and be able to implement game state management, character-handling algorithms, AI, and other behaviors into the game. This area is becoming quite complex as well, especially with the next-generation platforms with so much processing horsepower available. An engineer in this position must be able to work with changing specs, because many of the behaviors he or she is implementing will be tuned throughout the production process. These changes often are identified only after enough of the game is playable that some play-testing can be done and the designers realize that the behaviors are not creating a fun experience.

Large games will have niche areas, such as networking and sound programming, that become big enough that an engineer can work just on one of these specific areas for the entire project. Other engineers are needed to work closely with design and art as writers for AI scripts, shaders for artists, or to create tools that speed up production bottlenecks. These engineers have a technical background but work largely with the nonsoftware creative people on the team, so it is useful if they have some art or design experience themselves.

Basically, a company is looking for an engineer who is very adaptable with a strong engineering background as a foundation. It is important that an engineer be a quick learner to be able to change what he or she is focused on, either to adapt to what a particular game needs or to be able to help with an area that becomes the critical path for a particular project. Depending on the team size, for example, the engineer may be coding UI for one project and then move on to coding the animation system on another project. In addition, engineers must be able to work with other people's code and, of course, write code that other people can work on. Games often require code that is modified from project to project, which means that different engineers will be working on the code base. With the newest systems, it would be quite unusual to be able to have the luxury of building the game from the ground up.

■ 3.5 Design

The game design team is responsible for developing, documenting, and scripting the core concept for a game. This concept can originate with the design team, creative director, studio management, publisher, or a combination of these and other team members. The design process varies from company to company, as each has its own procedures and role definitions.

Designers have a broad range of responsibilities on a development team, such as designing the game's control scheme, creating the characters' backgrounds and personalities, and designing the combat system. Ultimately, they are responsible for creating a compelling and immersive gameplay experience. To accomplish this goal, designers must work closely with artists and engineers to determine how to utilize art and technology to best bring the game to life.

Designers are involved in the game production process from start to finish. In preproduction, they are brainstorming and prototyping potential gameplay ideas and then documenting the ones that will work best within the game's limitations. During production, they are implementing the game design, which includes scripting missions, writing dialogue, and play-testing. Their duties also include incorporating feedback and redesigning certain aspects of the game when necessary. In addition, designers must work cooperatively with the other team members throughout the development process. The basic design positions on a development team are as follows:

- Creative director
- Lead designer
- Designer
- Writer

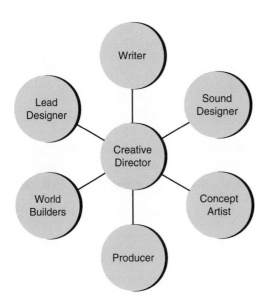

FIGURE 3.3   Creative director's main project contacts.

3.5.1   Creative Director

Each development team will interpret the role and responsibility of a creative director differently. Normally the creative director is responsible for communicating the overall creative vision to the team and ensuring that this vision is carried through to every aspect of the game.

To be successful at this position, the creative director must interact with many different team members. Figure 3.3 is a diagram of the types of interactions a creative director might have on a project. The interactions revolve around the members who are directly responsible for generating creative assets. The creative director ensures that the environments, characters, music, dialogue, and gameplay all work together to form a cohesive whole. It is important to note that the creative director does not assume the role of the art director, but rather works closely with the art director in determining the look and feel of the game. Not all projects have creative directors. Someone in this position usually has 5 to 10 years of work experience and lead design experience on several shipped titles.

3.5.2   Lead Designer

The lead designer is responsible for managing the day-to-day tasks of the design team and acting as a go-between for the creative director and designers. The lead designer directs the design team in documenting the design concepts, prototyping gameplay, implementing design features, balancing gameplay, and redesigning features as needed. If the team has no creative director, the lead designer is responsible for communicating the creative vision. A lead designer usually has at least three to five years of design experience.

3.5.3 Designer

"Designer" is a general title for a role that has different functions on a team. The designer is responsible for creating, prototyping, implementing, and balancing different areas of the game, depending on his or her expertise. A few types of designers on a team are as follows:

Systems designer: This person designs the system components within the gameplay. Examples include the scoring system, the combat model, the controller scheme, and the character creation system.

UI designer: This person designs the game's user interface including how the UI screens will function and fit together in the game.

Level designer: Also known as a world builder, this person creates the level layouts for the game. Some developers consider this to be an art position rather than a design position. In some instances, the designer creates the level designs on paper and then an artist builds the levels.

Scripter: This person places the interactive objects and enemies in the levels. Essentially, he or she controls how many enemies a player will face, where the gameplay challenges appear in a level, how nonplayer characters will interact with the player's character, and so on.

3.5.4 Writer

The writer is responsible for creating the story elements, characters, and dialogue for the game. The writer interacts closely with the lead designer and/or creative director to ensure that these elements are in keeping with the game's creative vision. The writer also writes marketing and PR copy, website content, the manual, and anything else that needs to be written related to the game. Writers must have experience in creative writing and writing for interactive media.

3.5.5 Background and Training

As with producers, no clearly defined guidelines exist regarding the skills a designer must possess. Designers come from a variety of backgrounds with no standard job path. Designers need strong communication skills, both written and verbal, because they must clearly communicate abstract creative concepts to an entire team of people and guide that team in making those ideas concrete. Designers are familiar with a variety of game theories and play many games. Ultimately, they must be open-minded and have a sense of what the player finds fun and entertaining.

DESIGN SKILLS

Clint Hocking, Creative Director
Ubisoft

Game design is such a new field that there isn't really a specific path toward it. You need to be able to see both the system design aspect and the experience design aspect of the job. As far as I know, there is no really effective way to receive training in both of these things.

The best advice I can give to anyone who wants to be a game designer is to get a broad education. Go to a good liberal arts school, or a good engineering school where interdisciplinary study is emphasized. Get a degree in computer science with a minor in fine art or the inverse. While you're studying, work on games and play games. Design pen-and-paper role-playing games, board games, card games, web-based games, or text adventures. Make an independent film to learn how to work in disparate situations with small teams of people with diverse artistic and technical talents. Anything you can do to get a broad range of experience working with both technical and creative people is going to be useful.

After doing a little bit of work in the mod community and releasing a level for an Unreal mod called Strike Force, I got my start in the game industry as a level designer on the first Splinter Cell™. One level ended up being selected to go to E3, where we received a lot of recognition, and my other level ended up being the OXM demo level for the game.

During Splinter Cell's development, the game designer left the project at the alpha deadline, and I was asked to take over for him. The writer also left the project, and because I have a master's degree in creative writing and had been working quite closely with the writer, I was asked to take over that job too. When we started working on Splinter Cell: Chaos Theory™, I took on the dual role of lead level designer and scriptwriter. About halfway through, I also took on the role of creative director. It's been quite a roller coaster, and I've been very lucky to be in the right place at the right time.

On development teams, the roles of the various designers depend upon and are defined by their specific talents. I have been a level designer, a lead level designer, a game designer, a writer–designer, and a creative director. I have worked with designers who are very methodical and process oriented, designers who are very creative, and some who are very technical.

Currently I am in preproduction as a creative director. I work directly with the lead programmer, the producer, and the marketing manager. Underneath me are the creative leads, the game designer, art director, lead level designer, writer, and so on. So at the high level the creative director has a lot of influence over the game concept, and at the next tier, the game designer has as much influence as the other creative leads. In smaller projects, the game designer might be equivalent to the creative director.

A level designer is responsible for delivering a level, a scripter is responsible for delivering working code, a writer–designer is responsible for delivering script. "Pure" game designers might be responsible for working with focus tests to deliver focus test reports and then communicating with level design about what the reports mean, and then for delivering documentation that illustrates the follow-up plan to the producer or creative director. Certain designers, like a creative director, lead level designer, or game designer, will be responsible for playing the game constantly and delivering regular evaluations of the content, comments and criticism, and tasks to the level designers so they can improve their levels.

Usually, the most senior creative person on the project will have a lot of influence in the early stages. In the beginning there is a lot of freedom to be creative, but the further you move along, the less freedom you have and the more constraints you adopt. Toward the end of the project, the creative lead has almost no say, and in the last days before shipping, the lead programmer is the one who runs everything. In a sense, influence migrates from creative to technical over time at a pace dictated by the producer.

As a general rule, the best designers—whether leads or not—all have one thing in common. They are all able to see the systems, content, and experience (or whatever aspect of the design they are focused on) from the perspective of the player. The best designers are able to let go of the specific direction they have for the experience and design in such a way as to facilitate the player's ability to express *himself* or *herself* in the interactive space. Unlike other creative fields where the creator has a lot of authorial control over his or her creation, game designers do not create *specific experiences*; they are *enablers* who create the possibility for people to engage in a meaningful set of experiences. It's difficult to understand this and let go of your authorial control, but it's critical to being a good designer.

■ 3.6 Quality Assurance Testing

Quality assurance (QA) testers are a vital part of the game development process and are involved in play-testing and finding defects in the game. Testers usually begin their work in the production phase, after playable game builds are available. They are involved in the development process until the end and are often the last people to finish working on the game. Testers work closely with all members of the development team and are a good resource for testing prototypes and new features. The basic testing roles include the following:

- Lead QA tester
- QA tester

3.6.1   Lead QA Tester

The lead QA tester works closely with the producer and other leads on a project to evaluate the game's features from a testing point of view. For example, if the game is going to feature 50 variables for creating a character, the lead QA tester will estimate how long these variables will take to test and then most likely suggest that the number be greatly reduced to save on testing time. This recommendation might be because testing combinations of different variables can quickly eat up valuable time, which is needed for testing other areas of the game. The lead QA tester also determines, along with the producer and leads, when the game is ready to be code released.

The lead QA tester is responsible for writing the game's test plan. To do this, he or she must know exactly how every part of the game functions so these details can be included in the test plan. Finally, the lead QA tester manages all the testers and assigns them specific areas of the test plan to check. A lead QA tester should have two to three years of experience as a QA tester.

3.6.2   QA Tester

QA testers are responsible for checking the game's functionality against the test plan, testing new features and prototypes, and finding defects in the game software. In addition, they check that the game meets all of the console manufacturer's technical requirements. They spend the majority of their workday actually playing the game and, therefore, have informed opinions on the overall fun factor.

3.6.3   Background and Training

There is no formal training for a testing position. In general, testers are people who enjoy playing games and have the ability to analyze problems and determine their cause. Testers should have good written and oral communication skills so they can clearly describe a bug to a developer. Lead testers should also have good organizational and communication skills as they are responsible for managing a team of people.

Because testers are exposed to all aspects of game development, the testing department is a good entry point into the field.

■ 3.7   Team Organization

The team hierarchy can be organized in several ways, depending on the team size and the roles to be filled. Small companies might have a single person fulfilling multiple roles on a project, such as producer–lead designer, and large companies might have a person with a single, clearly defined role, such as UI artist or AI engineer. Whatever the team size, a clear hierarchy must be established so people know with whom they need to talk to get information.

Figure 3.4 depicts a general organization chart for a typical small team with a producer–lead structure. The producer manages the art, engineering, design, and QA leads, and the leads manage the rest of the development team. With the team organized in this fashion, it is still possible for a single person to fulfill multiple roles, even though it may cause some conflict. For example, Wade Tinney is a producer–lead designer at Large Animal Games. He sometimes finds his producer side disagreeing with his designer side, especially if it means adding more time or money to the project.

Figure 3.5 is an organizational chart for a larger team. This structure still follows the producer–lead model, but now specialized areas are evident in each discipline. In a structure like this, a network engineer reporting to the lead may be in charge of several other network engineers. Also, an associate producer is included on this team to assist the producer with the day-to-day management of the production tasks.

Figure 3.6 shows an organizational chart for a team headed up by an executive producer and directors in each discipline. This structure is likely to be more common for larger development teams. With this particular structure, both the producer and creative director report directly to the executive producer. The producer is in charge of managing all the team personnel, and the creative director is in charge of managing the creative vision of the game. This reporting structure might be different for each development team.

This structure also indicates that the leads are the intermediaries between the directors and the rest of the team. In addition, a production coordinator might be added to assist the associate producer with day-to-day tasks. This is especially helpful if the associate producer is managing several areas of the game, such as localizations and the voiceover recordings.

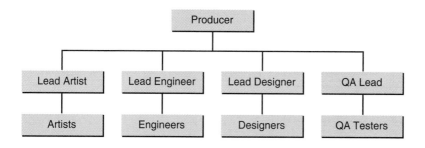

FIGURE 3.4 Small team with producer/lead structure.

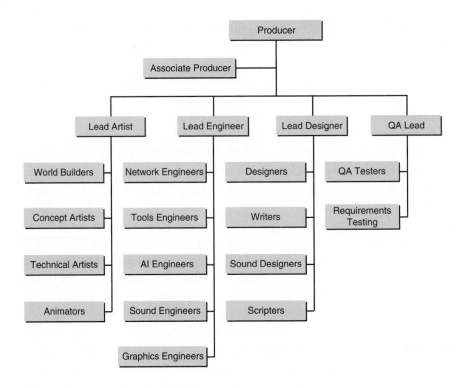

FIGURE 3.5   Large team with producer/lead structure.

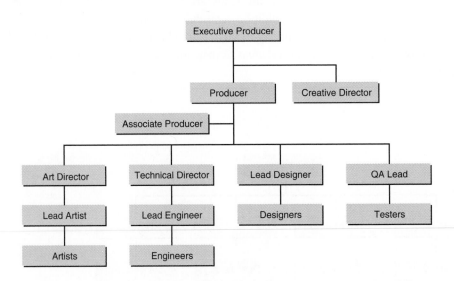

FIGURE 3.6   Team with executive producer structure.

LEARNING TO WORK ON A TEAM

Tracy Fullerton, Assistant Professor
University of Southern California

The University of Southern California (USC) School of Cinema–Television is very good at training people to work collaboratively on creative projects. Collaboration is a cornerstone of their filmmaking program and is deeply ingrained in the production process they teach. In the Interactive Media Division of that program, we have built on that tradition. The idea is not to make a huge project your first time out, but rather you work on several small projects and prototypes that revolve around different types of games. It is challenging, but the participants become very limber in understanding how games work. In the intermediate classes, students work on larger projects that are team based. On the advanced projects, the teams are even larger, and each person works in a specialized area.

This process has a reality to it, in that as students get to the advanced projects, they really have to start selling themselves to the person who is the producer or director on the project in order to be chosen for the position. This methodology also has a practical base, because when students get out in the real world, they need some skills in pitching and speaking with others who may not be knowledgeable in the specific language of game development. That's one of the things emphasized in the interactive program—this sense that students can work together and function collaboratively so they don't just walk out with a game they made all by themselves, but rather walk out with a game made in collaboration with a number of other people.

■ 3.8 Corporate

Any full list of game credits includes recognition of all the corporate people who are integral to creating and launching a successful game. People in these roles are usually working for the publisher, and are responsible for creating the packaging, marketing campaign, sales plan, and anything else that supplements the actual game. These people normally communicate with the producer and are treated as external members of the development team. These departments include the following:

- Marketing and public relations
- Creative services
- Sales

3.8.1   Marketing and Public Relations

The main responsibility of the marketing department is to market the game to the target consumer. Their challenge is building a compelling marketing campaign around the game's features, story, and gameplay experience that entices players to buy the game. To be most effective, marketing should be involved with the game during pre-production. This involvement gives them the opportunity to suggest features and other ways to make the game more marketable. For example, they might suggest using licensed music from a popular band, casting celebrity voices, or adding some unique new gameplay features.

Public relations is responsible for generating publicity for the game through websites, magazines, and television spots. This process includes setting up interviews with the development team and organizing press tours for the game. In addition, they create unique publicity events to get players to ask questions about the game. Marketing and public relations work together closely to ensure that they are presenting a unified vision of the game to the target audience. Please refer to Chapter 15, "Marketing," for more information.

3.8.2   Creative Services

Creative services works closely with the marketing department to create the packaging and manual for the game. After the look and feel of the packaging is decided, creative services generates the necessary assets, creates the final layout, and coordinates the printing of all the materials.

Because the producer is more familiar with the game than someone in the creative services department, the producer is expected to provide the manual text, screenshots, and other game assets for the printed materials. See Chapter 15, "Marketing," for more information on the process for creating the packaging and the manual.

3.8.3   Sales

The sales department is responsible for selling the game to retail stores, such as Wal-Mart, EB Games, and Best Buy, as well as online providers, such as IGN's Direct2Drive. They also determine whether special editions of the game can be created to increase sales. For example, a special edition of the game may be created that includes game-related merchandise, a strategy guide, and other premiums.

3.8.4   Background and Training

If you are interested in obtaining a position as a sales, marketing, or PR person in the game industry, it is useful to have a degree in business or marketing. You can apply for junior-level positions in these departments after graduating from college and work your way up into a higher position. People who do well at these positions possess strong communication skills and understand the business aspects of the game industry. It helps to play games and understand how each game appeals to the target audience.

If you are interested in a creative services position, you will want to study graphic design, layout, and desktop publishing. Strong writing skills are also useful for writing manuals, box, and website text.

■ 3.9 Chapter Summary

With so many people involved in creating games, the producer must understand everyone's roles and responsibilities on the team. This chapter presented general overviews of the production, art, engineering, design, testing, and corporate roles on a team and briefly discussed the background and training necessary for these roles.

With a clear understanding of team roles, the producer can decide on the appropriate team structure and production process to use when developing a game. The next chapter discusses team dynamics, including how to choose good leaders, build teams, and motivate people. Strong teams that work well together are the key to making good games.

■ 3.10 Questions and Exercises

1. What are the major roles that must be filled on every game development team? How are these roles similar and different?

2. What is the difference between a publisher producer and a developer producer? Who do they interface with during game development?

3. What are some ways to structure large game development teams?

4. How do marketing and PR fit into the game development production cycle?

5. Research the Internet for game development job postings and write up your findings on some of the specific position titles and the requirements for each. What skills should everyone on the team have regardless of whether they are a programmer, artist, producer, or tester?

6. Go to MobyGames (www.mobygames.com) and examine the credits for a popular big-budget game, and note the various roles involved. How many people are attributed to the various tasks in development? How many people are involved in marketing, sales, PR, or something else besides development?

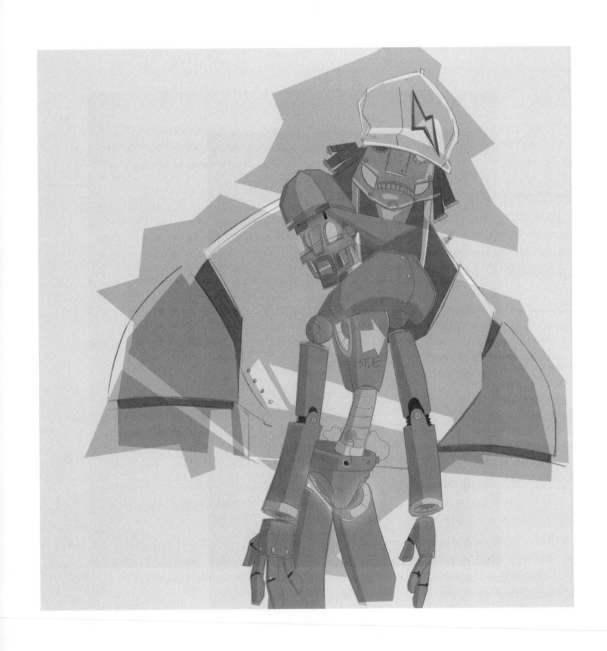

4 Teams

In this chapter:

- Project Leadership
- Picking Leads
- Team Building
- Team Buy-in and Motivation

■ 4.1 Introduction

Game development is a young industry—both in age of the average employee and in the age of the industry. This youth is reflected in the sense of immaturity that is commonly found in development teams. Some people have the misconception that working at a game company is all fun and games. Although this is the case to some degree, employees are still expected to act in a professional manner, which means showing up to work on time and taking responsibility for completing any assigned work. One of the major responsibilities of a producer is managing this young talent and ensuring that everyone makes a useful contribution to the game.

To be a strong and effective producer, you must develop your leadership skills so you can maintain the team's morale, take care of the team's needs, and keep everyone motivated throughout the game's development. Motivation can be a challenge as it requires managing many different personalities, helping people discover their strengths, and neutralizing any risks to team morale, such as shortened schedules, difficult personalities, and so on. The producer must take this responsibility seriously; otherwise, people will stop collaborating with each other and the quality of the game will suffer.

If the producer is committed to building and maintaining a strong team, many of the other risks on a project will be minimized, mainly because the lines of communication are open and people are aware of these risks much sooner in the process. Because of this awareness, the risks have less chance of snowballing into more serious problems. This chapter discusses some ways to build strong teams and maintain project momentum, even during stressful times.

HOW THE PRODUCER BUILDS A TEAM

Tracy Fullerton, Assistant Professor
University of Southern California

When I am a producer, I think of my role as being quite a bit about social engineering—making sure there is an environment in which people can do their best work, feel like they are contributing their best efforts, and have the necessary resources to do the work. Some other people will tell you that the producer's job is to get the project in on time and under budget. This is also very important, but I am more focused on making sure that the team and the processes are running smoothly. This involves a lot of walking around and talking to people, so I can see what people are working on and help facilitate their collaboration with others on the team.

The best possible way to manage the team is to make sure that every single person on the team, including the executives, feels a sense of authorship. Sometimes, not everyone wants everyone else to feel that sense of authorship; they want to make decisions on their own and dictate to everyone else, and that's where you can get into hairy situations. But the best situation is if you can keep people communicating and create a good atmosphere in which the executives feel like their input is important, and the artists, technologists, and designers feel like their opinions have an impact on the game.

RECOMMENDED READING, *THE ESSENTIAL DRUCKER*

Peter F. Drucker has written on the topic of management for over 30 years and is considered one of the foremost experts on management. He believes that in order to get the best work out of people, you must manage their strengths and present them ample opportunities for personal and professional development. *The Essential Drucker* (2008) is an abridged reference of his articles on management and is recommended reading for anyone who wants to become a better leader. The book discusses topics that focus on how to be a better manager, including making effective decisions and hiring good people.

4.2 Project Leadership

The producer is viewed as the team leader and is usually the official representative of the team to marketing, management, and anyone else external to the team. Additionally, the producer is directly responsible for the well-being of the project and everyone on the team, so he or she must be an effective and positive leader. If the team is headed by an ineffective or negative leader, then the team and the game are going to suffer. If you don't think you possess natural leadership qualities, don't worry. More than likely if you are a producer, you have already exhibited enough leadership qualities to be entrusted with a team and a game. If you are hoping to become a producer, you can develop any existing leadership qualities you already have. However, you will need to take the initiative to develop your skills, as companies rarely have training programs in place for such development.

So what is a leader? A leader is someone who presents himself or herself with confidence and has strong vision, values, and an appreciation for the people with whom he or she is working. He or she is able to pull together a group of people to achieve a shared vision and hold people accountable for their work. He or she is constantly projecting passion, enthusiasm, and a positive attitude about his or her work. Most important, a leader has the courage and initiative to take risks, make unpopular decisions, and do whatever is necessary to achieve the project goals.

A leader is defined more by what he or she does than by his or her assigned position on the team, which means that someone else besides the producer can be a leader for the team. It might be hard to pick out the leaders in your company, but if you think about it, someone will come to mind—like the well-respected artist who is always driving people to create the highest quality art.

The good news is that you can become a better leader if you work at it. The key is to have a good understanding of your personality and temperament so you can develop your natural leadership abilities. There are a few basic leadership archetypes—someone charismatic who inspires people to do the impossible, the strong silent type who leads by example, and a person who individually works with each member of the team to bring out his or her best qualities. Become familiar with your team and figure out which style or styles best fit you; you will find that different leadership styles work better for different situations. If you don't work to improve your leadership skills, you might find yourself in charge of a team that is demoralized, unhappy, and unproductive.

RECOMMENDED READING, LEADERSHIP

Project Leadership (2003) by James P. Lewis provides practical advice for someone in a leadership position on a project team. Several techniques are presented for improving your leadership skills.

The Leadership Challenge (2008) by James M. Kouzes and Barry Z. Posner is a research study of all types of leaders in different organizations. The findings are distilled into fundamental leadership practices.

On Becoming a Leader (2003) by Warren Bennis is considered to be a leadership primer with in-depth information on leadership characteristics and what you can do to develop these characteristics for yourself.

The 7 Habits of Highly Effective People (2004) by Stephen R. Covey is a respected resource for self-improvement, presenting seven main areas of growth that will have a positive impact on your interpersonal relationships.

■ 4.3 Picking Leads

As discussed in Chapter 3, "Roles on the Team," people in lead art, design, engineering, and quality assurance positions are not normally content creators. Instead, they manage the content creators and provide leadership and guidance for the project. The most effective leads have expertise in their fields and strong people skills, which means they can advise people, such as the producer or junior team members, on what techniques and processes are needed to get the desired result. For example, an art lead who is knowledgeable about the technical limitations of console hardware can converse intelligently with both art and engineering about the tools that are needed to create realistic terrain. In addition, the art lead helps the art team to successfully complete their project tasks by managing the schedule, providing useful feedback, answering questions, arranging for tutorials in new techniques, defining the art production pipeline, and performing other duties. The lead engineer and lead designer provide the same types of services to the engineering and design teams, respectively.

Strong leads are an invaluable asset for any producer. If the producer can depend on the leads to manage the day-to-day art, engineering, and design tasks, he or she can concentrate on the other aspects of the project, such as coordinating localizations, managing external vendors, dealing with the marketing and legal departments, updating senior management on the project status, and providing the leads and team with the necessary resources to do their jobs. If a lead is not as strong in one area as another, the producer must provide training for the lead to improve in that area in order to avoid problems down the line. For example, a lead designer who is a talented designer but not easily approachable cannot manage the design team effectively. The other designers might be reluctant to come to him or her with concerns for fear of being yelled at or rudely dismissed. If a lead designer continues acting this way, even with proper coaching and training, the producer may consider replacing him or her with someone who may not be as talented a designer but has much better people skills.

When choosing leads, there is a tendency to appoint someone who is talented and has successfully shipped a few games. The benefit of doing this kind of appointment is that an expert is readily available to offer technical or artistic guidance to team members. However, this person may not be prepared for the management and administrative responsibilities of the position. He or she goes from being a well-respected content creator to someone who has to start managing people, schedules, and office politics, and he or she may have little interest in accepting a lead position because of these types of tasks. He or she might prefer to remain a content creator and lead the team in a more unofficial capacity.

In fact, a lead should not be the most artistically talented or technically gifted person on the team. You want to keep these talents doing what they do best—creating high-quality assets for the game. If you move these high-quality content creators to lead positions, they won't have time to create content, and the quality of the game will be less than it could be. You may also find the production schedule suffers if you remove one of your most prolific asset creators to a position where he or she does not create.

When picking leads, focus on choosing the best managers for the job, not the most technically skilled person. People with strong management abilities have a tendency to be organized, work well with others, possess strong communication skills, be knowledgeable in their field, and have earned the respect of their peers. It is easier to help someone improve his or her knowledge of artistic and technical techniques than it is to train someone to be a better people person, so keep this in mind when picking leads on the project.

Ineffective leads who do not improve upon their weaknesses can put a project at risk. How many times have you heard someone on the development team complain about how ineffective or useless their lead is? If this complaint is common and is not addressed immediately, the people under this lead will stop asking questions, pointing out risks, and making progress on the game. Instead, they will quickly lose interest in their contribution to the game and watch things on the project slowly erode as communication breaks down between the team members.

In some cases, a producer might not have the authority to replace an ineffective lead who did not respond to coaching. In such instances, a liability is created around which the producer has to work. The producer might decide to take on part of the lead's role and provide the management or technical skills the lead is lacking, or may unofficially grant lead status to a junior member of the team who shows a lot of promise as a future lead. If you are stuck with a lead who becomes a liability, try to deal with the situation without further alienating any of the team members who are under this lead.

EFFECTIVE LEADS

Jamie Fristrom, Creative Director
Torpex Games

An effective lead can't just be an expert in his or her field; he or she also has to possess strong people skills and the ability to be a leader. People skills determine how effective his or her management style is for getting people to do what they've been asked to do. It is common for people to get promoted to a lead position based on their talent alone, but they often don't have the leadership skills for the position. If a lead cannot correctly manage the people under him or her these people will not progress in their skills or careers and will become frustrated, which contributes to low morale and puts the project at risk. If someone is not working out as a lead, it is fine to put him or her back in their old role. This was done a few times at Treyarch without any big problems.

It is better to promote people who exhibit natural leadership skills instead of assuming it is something that can be learned. There have been situations in which someone is promoted to a lead position, and it is evident within six months that this person is not suited for the job. At this point, it is probably too late to train him or her to be a lead, so your choices are to replace him or her with someone else, appoint a co-lead, or hope that he or she can finish the job without putting the project at substantial risk.

■ 4.4 Team Building

Team building is a critical part of the game development process and often one of the most neglected. There is a common misconception that assigning a group of people to work together creates a team, which is definitely not the case. A *group* consists of individuals whose work is directed by someone who is head of the group. A *team* is made up of a group of people who are working together toward a common goal and are holding each other mutually accountable for the outcome, which is a big difference from a group. To have strong teams, the teams must be built carefully and supported throughout the project.

As the project leader, one of the producer's main responsibilities is to build a strong team by any means necessary. This task is not for the faint of heart nor for those who are timid around people. For one thing, you must be able to deal effectively with many different types of personalities and get them all working in harmony with each other. You need to deal with your team as both individuals and a team by creating the best working environment you can for the individual while still doing what is best for the team.

Also, a producer takes some risk in getting people to participate in "team-building" activities, especially because such activities can best be described as "corny" or "cheesy." However, if the producer makes no attempt to build a team, he or she will never have a team, just a group of people doing work as directed by their lead or producer—meaning no sharing of ideas, no collaboration, no sense of ownership or pride in the project, and no passion—which can lead to less than stellar games that don't register on consumers' radar. This section discusses some simple team-building techniques that have been proven to be effective in a game development environment.

BUILDING A STRONG TEAM

Wade Tinney and Coray Seifert
Large Animal Games

At Large Animal, we are committed to building a strong team that works well together. Although it may be easier for the 12-person company than it is for larger companies with hundreds of employees, team building can be effective at a company of any size if there is a commitment to do it.

We want everyone working at Large Animal to feel a strong sense of creative ownership of the games we make. The fact is, everyone on the team has a deep impact on the game, and the finished product is a reflection of their collective effort. Great ideas can come from anyone, and we want everyone on the team to feel comfortable sharing their thoughts with everyone else. Also, we find that people enjoy themselves the most and do their best work when they are excited about the material, and they like to do lots of research to get to know the content with which they're working. For example, when we worked on RocketBowl, we took the whole team bowling so they could figure out other gameplay mechanics that would work well with bowling. These sorts of "field trips" are not only a great way to stimulate new ideas about the game you're working on, but they also give people a chance to establish rapport with each other outside of the office—another important aspect of building strong teams.

Effective team communication is important even when it's not directly about the games we are building together. At Large Animal, we all eat lunch together almost every day and discuss the latest movies, games we've been playing at home, and other outside interests. We also play board or card games, which is a great excuse to interact with each other in situations that don't solely revolve around work. Not only do these analog games often give us ideas and insights into the digital ones we make, but it's amazing how much you can learn about your fellow team members and their individual strengths by sitting across the game table from them. Otherwise, we might never have known that our lead programmer, Yossi Horowitz, has such an incredible poker face. We believe that the most efficient team communication is built on a rich shared vocabulary of jokes, references, and memories. Conversations about work are just much more fun to have with someone with whom you enjoy having *non*work conversations.

We want everyone to have an understanding of how the individual tasks they are working on fit into the big picture of that game. One thing we do to encourage this is by starting each morning with a short team meeting. We spend about 25 minutes talking about what everyone did the day before, what people are working on today, and whether there are any roadblocks that will prevent that work from being completed. We learn a great deal about each other's work patterns from hearing everyone talk about their tasks. Occasionally, someone won't realize there is a problem they can help with until they hear about it in the meeting.

4.4.1 Role Definition

People on the development team have a strong desire to contribute and want to know exactly what their role is on the team. Conflict is generated if roles are not clearly defined. For example, if there are two lead artists on a large development team, and they have not defined the areas each of them is overseeing, confusion results. Artists on the team won't know which lead to go to with questions or problems, and the leads themselves won't know how to definitively allocate any new art responsibilities, which might result in features and assets being unfinished when the game ships. The artists and the leads will become increasingly frustrated with this situation, leading to less efficient and lower-quality work and possibly conflict between the leads and the artists.

This frustration can also occur if a junior programmer does not specifically understand what his or her tasks are on the project. If the lead engineer tells a junior programmer to work on the user interface but never states exactly what the expectations are, the junior programmer won't know whether he or she is supposed to be leading a task force to get the UI designed, prototyped, and implemented, or whether he or she is supposed to merely implement the tasks he or she is given (but at the same time he or she might not know who is responsible for assigning the tasks).

These situations can be remedied by clarifying people's roles. James P. Lewis, author of *Team-Based Project Management* (1998), has developed a simple role-clarification exercise that can be done at the beginning of the project and should also be done during the project whenever new people are added or there seems to be role ambiguity. This is also a good exercise for the producer and leads to do during preproduction so that everyone is clear on who is responsible for which aspects of the project.

The exercise begins with each person answering the following four questions:

- How does the company see your role on the team?
- How do you see your role on this team?
- What resources do you need in order to effectively carry out your role?
- What do you need to know about other people's roles in order to do your job better?

Each person writes answers to these questions and comes prepared to discuss them in a meeting. Each person begins by presenting his or her answers, and then everyone discusses them and comes to an agreement on how that person's role is best defined.

Ten to 20 minutes should be allocated to each person. If you do this for a large team, schedule a few separate meetings instead of trying to have a single meeting that lasts for hours. At the end of the meeting, role definitions can be typed up for each person and then posted on the team website and displayed in the team rooms. Figure 4.1 is an example of a spreadsheet that can be used to organize this information after the exercise is completed.

4.4.2 Cross-Training

Cross-training is a method where people on the team are trained in disciplines they haven't worked in before. For example, have an artist follow an engineer for a day and learn how to code features for the art tool. Or have an artist spend the day testing the game with the QA department and learn the ins and outs of testing, logging, and regressing bugs. Once people spend some time in someone else's role, they are more appreciative of that person's role on the project.

This practice might even lead to improvements in the process. For example, if an artist walks an engineer through the process of importing a level into the game and then has the engineer do it, the engineer might realize there is a way to improve the current set of tools to make this easier for the artist. A designer with some basic training in how to create 3D levels will gain a greater understanding of how to document his or her level designs on paper so they are more easily translated into 3D spaces by an artist.

Cross-training is a good way to integrate new people into the team as well. During their first week, they can spend part of each day shadowing an artist, engineer, or designer. Shadowing can help them more quickly become part of the team and learn what people's roles and responsibilities are on the project.

RECOMMENDED READING, MANAGEMENT

The Tao of Coaching (2009) by Max Landsberg offers several solid coaching exercises accompanied by examples that are fun to read and easy to understand.

The Mythical Man-Month (1995) by Frederick P. Brooks Jr. is a well-respected book that contains important insights about the human cost of software development. This book is highly recommended for anyone working in software development.

Marcus Buckingham and Curt Coffman, authors of *First, Break All the Rules: What the World's Greatest Managers Do Differently* (1999), researched managers at several companies to determine what qualities great managers possess.

Peopleware: Productive Projects and Teams (1999) by Tom DeMarco and Timothy Lister is geared toward team leads and managers who head up software development teams. It offers a lot of practical advice for building teams, picking the right leads, and increasing productivity.

Role	Organization Expectations	Role on Project	What do I need from others?	What do I need to know about others?
Producer	– Get project done on schedule – Meet quality standards of project – Lead and motivate the team – Carry vision of project to management, marketing, and external people	– Lead the team in getting the project done on time – Schedule and track progress – Interface with management on behalf of the team – Hold the vision of the project and communicate to team – Motivate the team – Deal with personnel issues – Order the necessary resources for the team – Set up production processes – Work with marketing and PR – Work with leads on management and communication skills – Coordinate localizations – Work with external vendors – Be knowledgeable about what everyone is doing on the project and the progress they are making – Keep team informed of progress and up-to-date on any project changes – Set up and maintain team website – Indentify risks, red flags, and solutions	– Notification of any risks or red flags – Information on how each person is doing on the project and how he or she performing in his or her role – Information on what resources each person needs to get his or her job finished – Assistance with communicating information to the rest of the team	– What each person's special skills are on the project – What each person needs on the project to get his or her work done – Understanding of engineering, art, and design limitations

I FIGURE 4.1 Example of a role definition spreadsheet.

4.4.3   Seating Arrangements

Seating arrangements can impact the strength of the team. If you have all of the engineers, designers, and artists sitting in separate groups, getting communication to flow between the groups is difficult. If like disciplines are sitting together, they will have a tendency to focus solely on the assets they are creating for the game, instead of taking into consideration what the other disciplines are contributing as well. Situations will arise in which artists complain about engineers, engineers complain about designers, designers complain about artists, and so on. Team morale will suffer, as an "us" versus "them" mentality develops within the team.

While artists, engineers, and designers might prefer to group themselves by discipline, with the reasoning that it is more conducive to consulting with peers on a technical or artistic issue, such grouping does nothing to build the team. A better seating arrangement is one in which those working on similar features are grouped together, so they can be in immediate contact with other people working on a similar functionality for the game. For example, grouping level artists, graphics engineers, and scripters together creates a cross-functional team within the team that handles all aspects of creating a playable level in the game. Even though those people are in different disciplines, they are dependent on each other's work to successfully get something up and running in the game. You can also seat the animators and the engineers working on the animation system together, which helps streamline the feedback process.

In addition, think about the personality types that are sitting near each other. If possible, make sure that positive and enthusiastic people are seated throughout the team rooms. These people bring a natural positive energy to the team and really get people excited about what they are working on. They also help mitigate the negative energy from people who have a tendency to complain.

The team might object to switching around the sitting arrangements, especially if they are not used to doing so. In addition, they may be concerned about the increased noise level in an environment where people are encouraged to talk with each other. To keep the working environment productive, inform people that any meetings lasting more than a few minutes and/or consisting of three or more persons must be conducted in areas outside the team room so as not to disturb others. You can also invest in noise-canceling headphones for everyone on the team. This way, people can feel more comfortable in the open environment.

4.4.4   Team Meetings

Team meetings are also a good opportunity to enhance team building. As discussed earlier in this chapter, team meetings are a great way to introduce new team members and become more familiar with existing team members. Team meetings are primarily a venue for discussing the progress of the game and to provide a forum for team members to raise questions and concerns. As development teams get larger, this regular forum will be more important to team members who are not privy to the day-to-day happenings with everything on the project.

Provide a complete project update in each meeting. Discuss what progress has been made in the overall game plan, what marketing and PR events are being planned, how things are progressing with getting approvals on licenses, the current status of any hardware requests, and anything else that happened in the past week on the project. This information helps people gain an understanding of the game as a whole and see how their work fits into the big picture. The team's morale will be boosted to hear how much work was accomplished in the past week.

Team meetings are also a good opportunity to discuss any rumors circulating about the project or the company. If there is no truth to the rumors, make it clear in the team meeting. If there is some truth to the rumors, set the team straight on exactly what the situation is. Clarifying is much better than allowing people to start basing decisions on rumors that have grown out of control. Also discuss any upcoming milestones and potential schedule changes. If people are reminded a few weeks in advance of an impending milestone, they may start working more efficiently to avoid crunch time before the milestone is due. If the schedule changes for any reason, such as shortened or extended deadlines, inform the team about it and explain the reasons why. The team has a vested interest in the game and has a right to know when there are any changes to the plan.

Establish a regular meeting time so that the team meeting becomes a fixture in the team's mind. Jot down notes during the week of items to discuss in the next team meeting. People will come to rely on the team meeting as a resource for useful information. It also doesn't hurt to occasionally provide some cookies or doughnuts during the meeting.

4.4.5   Team Website

A well-maintained team website or wiki functions as the central source of information about the project and is a great team-building resource. The website is a living repository for design documents, prototypes, task lists, pictures of team members, and any other project-related materials. The website should be well-organized so that people can easily find the information they need. Types of information to include on the website are as follows:

- Design documents
- Technical documents
- Meeting schedules
- Meeting minutes
- Weekly status reports
- Marketing updates
- Process guidelines

- Vacations and absences
- Key milestone deadlines
- Milestone deliverable descriptions
- QA testing plans
- Contact information (phone numbers and personal email addresses)
- Forms (expense reports, change requests, and so on)
- Names and tasks for each team member
- Prototypes
- Development schedules
- Play-testing guidelines
- Important announcements (new team members, schedule changes, and so on)

Storing this information in a publicly accessible place allows the team members to be as informed as they choose to be about the project. Some people will rarely visit the team website; others will make it their home page and check it on a daily basis. The team website is also a great tool for educating new people about the project or for directing management to the most current set of design documents.

To make the team website an effective tool, always keep it up-to-date. Then the team can rely on the website for the most current project information. This practice also ensures that everyone on the team has equal access to all the information—not just the few people who constantly check in with the leads on the status of the project. The minute the team realizes the website does not contain the latest information, they will stop using it as a development tool and instead rely heavily on the producer and leads to directly supply them with the necessary information.

■ 4.5 Team Buy-in and Motivation

Team buy-in and motivation are important elements of a strong team. If the team feels ownership or has buy-in, it is more effective and produces higher quality work. People who are highly motivated and passionate about the game will also not mind putting in extra work when necessary to make the project the best it can be. If you take advantage of their passion and implement mandatory crunch times for an extended period, you will demotivate the team, which is likely to result in lower-quality work and a group of unhappy people.

When people believe their feedback, opinions, and concerns are being considered when making decisions about the project, they will buy into the project objectives. This support also comes about when people can clearly picture the project's success in their minds, which means the game ships on time to great reviews and is a number one best-seller for months. If people can visualize and share this success, they are more than willing to work on a project for six months to two years to make this success a reality.

If people on the team are not motivated or don't have buy-in, you can have a serious problem. Having just one or two unhappy persons on the team who are visibly unmotivated or vocal about their dissatisfaction with the project can quickly lead to trouble for the other members. When this happens, the producer must deal with the situation as soon as possible in order to prevent damage to the overall morale of the team.

4.5.1   Warning Signs

Unhappy employees will exhibit warning signs that show their discontent with their working situation. If you see any of these warning signs, address them quickly in order to head off serious problems. These warning signs can include:

Excessive or unplanned absences and tardiness: Do employees show up and leave work on time? Are they taking a lot of sick days? Do they request time off at the last minute? While absences can be related to personal issues at home, they also might indicate that an employee is unhappy with his or her work situation. If an employee's personal life is impacting his or her ability to do work, he or she should notify his or her manager in order to arrange a temporary work solution. However, if an employee is generally unhappy with work, he or she may be looking for employment elsewhere, which could explain why he or she is absent or tardy. There are many reasons why employees could be looking elsewhere, and if you take some time to figure out what these reasons are, you may be able to prevent a star employee from defecting to a competitor.

Lack of commitment: Do employees readily commit themselves to a long-term assignment (for example, working for the next six months to create the networking infrastructure for a game)? Are they hard to pin down about future vacation plans? If you feel that someone is not committed to being on the team for the long term, you need to find out why.

Complaints: Do employees overtly complain about management or other team members? For example, "This guy isn't useful, he doesn't know anything about . . . ." Proactive complainers eventually move to another company; the less proactive ones won't, but their complaints will create a negative work environment. This in turn will create more dissatisfied employees.

Lack of effort: Are employees productive? Do they miss deadlines or not care if they are late? Do they use their time efficiently? Or do they spend time away from their desks, chatting with other employees? Note that this behavior can also indicate that employees are overwhelmed by their tasks and are wasting time because they are unsure of how to tackle their work and so they waste time in the hopes that the problem will go away. On the other hand, this may indicate that the employee's workload is not sufficient and they don't have enough work and responsibilities to keep them busy for eight hours a day.

Apathy: Are employees actively involved in the project, or do they just come to work and put in their eight hours without any comment? If people are not excited about the project they are working on or the role they have on the project, they will become apathetic and less effective. Additionally, if people have been extremely involved in the past but suddenly become apathetic, you can bet that some specific incident has triggered this. Apathy can quickly spread throughout the team if it is not addressed.

Unfulfilled requests: If an employee has requested tools that let him or her do his or her job better (like a new computer), but the request is not addressed in a timely fashion (or at all), the seeds of dissatisfaction will be sown. If the request is something that can be easily fulfilled, it is a great way to build goodwill with employees and show them that management cares about their needs. If the request cannot be granted for whatever reason, take time to explain the reasons why to an employee and discuss whether any compromises can be made.

By the time these warning signs manifest themselves, the situation may be difficult to salvage and turn into something positive. A producer who is constantly gauging the mental health of the individuals on the team might catch some of these warning signs sooner, before the situation gets too out of control. The producer must know the employees and their work habits. For example, some people who are constantly late might just be really bad about waking up on time.

TEAM MORALE

Stuart Roch, Executive Producer
Activision

If your development team is demoralized, you're certainly going to know it. Productivity can sag; team members will seem less jovial than you remember them being; sick and personal time might increase; and you'll hear about the water cooler grumbling through underground channels. The trick of the proactive producer is to make sure that the team doesn't get demoralized to begin with. Managing a project correctly from the start and being organized with a regular schedule and feature reviews can make the difference.

When a team is demoralized, there is often very little you can do to lift it out of that. Offering financial bonuses has little effect, as do pep talks in the regular team meetings. The thing that gets a team demoralized, more often than not, is a project that is significantly behind schedule, causing a death march, or a product that just isn't fun, causing a general malaise rather than passion from the core team. When the project is behind, producers will have to deal with the demoralized team in many different ways, depending on the situation, with the understanding that at that point, there might be little that can be done to get the team fully energized again.

4.5.2   Addressing the Warning Signs

If you spot any of these warning signs, you'll want to talk with the employee about it right away. One of your responsibilities as a manager is to ensure that your employees are satisfied and productive. If you ignore these signs, the problems will only get worse and the employee may end up lowering team morale or leaving the company altogether. Someone who is having personal issues that affect his or her work should be dealt with differently than someone who has work-related issues. But you need to find out the cause of the problem so it can be properly addressed. Ask the employee leading questions to pull him or her into a conversation about the issue, but don't get confrontational or make accusations. Good starting points for a conversation include questions like "What would you do in this situation?" or "How do you think the project is going?" The employee's answers will reveal useful information about why he or she is unhappy and what can be done to improve the situation.

Keep communication open in order to spot and address these signs. If someone keeps coming to you repeatedly about the same issue, it is likely that the root of the issue has yet to be addressed, so you need to do some additional investigating to figure out what the real problem is. Keep in mind that you can't fix everyone's problem no matter how hard you try; some people will never be satisfied with what you do. However, many employees will appreciate the efforts you put forth to address their issues and create a pleasant working environment for them.

4.5.3   Showing Appreciation

Another way to improve morale and to create a more pleasant working environment is by showing your appreciation to the team on a regular basis. This feedback lets them know you view them as people, not just resources on your project schedule, and that you are aware of the sacrifices they are making to create a great game. Even though some of these gestures seem small and silly, they do not go unnoticed, even if no one on the team comments on them. Some examples of simple gestures that mean a lot are as follows:

> **Provide food during crunch time:** If people are working late, buy them a healthy dinner. If working on the weekend, have lunch catered. Also, go to Sam's Club and stock up on candy, pretzels, and other snacks (healthy ones, too), so there is

something for people to nibble on during the day. The team appreciates the free meal, and there is less downtime if food is available at the office.

Celebrate monthly birthdays: Once a month during team meetings, bring in a cake or ice cream to celebrate birthdays for that month. People always find this activity fun and like knowing who is celebrating a birthday with them.

Celebrate project milestones: The development team works hard to hit milestones on time, so show your appreciation by bringing in a cake to celebrate or by providing free movie tickets to the team. Better yet, give the team a few hours off during the day so you can all go see the movie together.

Host a launch/ship party: When a project is complete, organize a final activity to celebrate the project's success. If there is enough money in the budget, arrange to take the entire team out for a nice dinner.

Say thank you: Remember to tell your team "thank you" for a job well done. This acknowledgment can be done in the team meeting, via email, or both. This simple gesture lets the team know their work is appreciated.

4.5.4 Sharing Vision

If the team collectively understands the vision of the game, they will have a better idea of how their work contributes to the game as a whole. Therefore, it is important to keep the team informed of the game's vision, especially when this vision changes. A shared vision means the team understands the overall goals of the game, the game's major features, how the storyline and characters fit, and who the target audience is. For the team to best understand these things, the producer needs to inform the team when critical decisions are made and the reasoning behind these decisions. Knowing this information helps them to adjust their work so that it fits within the new vision of the game.

Strong, clear, and open communication is key to establishing a shared vision with the team. A simple way to do this during preproduction is to post the initial game concept and vision on the website. Continue building on this concept with design documents and prototypes so the team can participate in the game's evolution from concept to gold master.

During production, set aside time during the weekly team meetings to demo the latest version of the game. Point out new elements that were added to the game since last week and call out who contributed these elements to the game. As the game gets more stable, arrange for the team to play-test the game and participate in multiplayer sessions. Additionally, publicly post key information about the game in the team rooms. This information should include concept art, mission summaries, control schemes, and anything else that helps communicate what the game is.

■ 4.6 Chapter Summary

Teams come in many shapes and sizes, but remember that individual people make up the teams, and producers must have the ability to deal with the individuals and with the team as a whole. If people on the team are not happy and productive, the team won't be either. The producer must focus a good portion of his or her efforts on building and maintaining strong morale and high motivation on the team. This is done by picking strong leads, engaging in team-building exercises, and quickly addressing any warning signs of disgruntled employees. The producer must have strong people and project-management skills and be a good communicator. The next chapter describes some ways to foster good communication on a project and use communication as a tool to improve interactions on the team.

■ 4.7 Questions and Exercises

1. Discuss the qualities of a good leader.

2. How do you pick a good lead engineer, lead artist, or lead designer?

3. What are some team-building methods? Be sure to include examples.

4. What types of information should be included on the team website? Why?

5. What are some warning signs of low employee morale? How can this be addressed?

6. Create teams of people and assign them one of the following roles on the team: designer, artist, producer, engineer or QA tester. Have each person on the team answer the role definition questions and then discuss them with each other.

5 | Effective Communication

In this chapter:

- Written Communication
- Oral Communication
- Nonverbal Communication
- Establishing Communication Norms
- Communication Challenges

■ 5.1 Introduction

In the numerous postmortems published by *Game Developer* magazine, communication is often cited as something that needs to improve during the game development process. But what exactly does improving communication mean? How do people know whether communication is bad in the first place? What is good communication? These are hard questions to answer, because everyone has a different way they prefer to receive information, which means certain forms of communication are more effective for some people than others. People might think they're communicating something clearly, only to later find that there was a miscommunication with the other person.

As a producer, it is your responsibility to foster good communication on the team and ensure that everyone is receiving the correct and necessary information in a format they understand. Types of communication happening on a daily basis during any project are written (email and meeting notes), oral (meetings), and nonverbal (body language). This chapter discusses some general ways to improve in these areas of communication and some simple ways to deal with communication challenges.

■ 5.2 Written Communication

During game development, written communication is usually the producer's primary form of conveying information. How many emails do you send and receive in a single day? For most producers and leads, it can be upwards of 100 or more, which is a lot of information to read and digest in a single day. Each email interaction must be clear and concise, so that you don't spend all day at the computer handling your email instead of interacting with the team on a more immediate level. Here are a few guidelines for writing clear and effective emails:

- Use informative subject headings.
- Put the most important information at the beginning.
- Keep the wording concise.
- Include specifics, especially for deadlines and other important information.
- Set up mailing lists to reduce internal spam.
- Use the high-priority label sparingly, or else people will ignore its importance.
- Use correct grammar and write in coherent sentences.
- Use bulleted lists to quickly convey major points.
- Use a font that is large and easy to read.

Many of the preceding guidelines also apply when writing other types of documentation, such as meeting notes or status reports. In addition, create a standardized format so that people can better understand the information being presented. In some instances of written communication, especially if the information is critical, you need to follow up with people in person to confirm they got the email, notes, or report and are interpreting the information correctly. This follow-up takes only a few minutes to do, and if the information is vital, the time spent is worth the investment.

■ 5.3 Oral Communication

Oral communication is the most effective form of communication, especially if you need to discuss sensitive topics (such as bad news) or get the team motivated to complete a milestone. Communicating with someone face-to-face is more personal because people can interact with you and get their questions or concerns addressed immediately. However, it can also be unreliable, since oral communication is open to interpretation, and some people are guilty of "selective hearing" and take away only the information they choose to.

Meetings, be they formal or informal, are one of the main forms of oral communication for a producer. So make the most of each of your meetings. From a process standpoint, set an agenda, take notes, and write down action items for each meeting.

For meetings to be effective, you have to think ahead about what needs to be said and how it can best be communicated. For example, if you are discussing some major gameplay changes with the team that just got handed down from management, don't start off the meeting by complaining about management and how ridiculous these changes are. Instead, focus on the positive aspects of the changes and present the reasons these changes were made to the team diplomatically. You don't have to sugarcoat the reasons; just be sensitive to how this information is presented so you don't rile people up unnecessarily—people are likely to respond better to positive rather than negative communication.

Also, make sure that you understand what people are telling you. Communication is a two-way street, and if you misunderstand one of your team members, it can reflect poorly on you. Active listening is a technique that ensures you have a better understanding of what you are being told. This technique is not easy to do effectively the first time, but you will become more skilled with practice. Active listening means you are actively engaged in what the person is telling you and show this engagement by occasionally rephrasing what the person said to you. You don't need to rephrase everything he or she tells you; that would become an annoyance to the person trying to talk, and he or she might feel you are just parroting back his or her words instead of listening to him or her. Instead, focus on rephrasing the key points of what he or she telling you. For example, if someone is complaining about a coworker, you can say something like, "So, let me make sure I understand this. Joe is giving you a hard time because he thinks you are behind on your tasks, when in reality, Sam is behind, which is impacting your work." If you are correct, the person will show agreement and continue with his or her conversation. If you are incorrect, the person will tell you the information again, possibly in another way, until you rephrase back to him or her what he or she needs to hear.

This can work in the reverse as well. If you are presenting information to someone, such as changes to the production schedule, wrap up the conversation by asking what the changes are and how these will impact the person's schedule. It isn't difficult to get someone to rephrase what was said to him or her, and if he or she is incorrect, tell him or her the information in a different way until you are satisfied he or she understands. In most cases, you should also follow up conversations relating to key information and decisions with an email. This way, a written record is always available for reference.

When you are orally communicating with someone, keep in mind these basics:

- Don't mumble; be clear in your enunciation.
- Don't talk in a low voice, especially during meetings.
- Don't use swear words.
- Don't talk over people; have conversations with people.
- Pause every once in awhile, so that people have a chance to say something.

◼ 5.4 Nonverbal Communication

What you communicate nonverbally has just as much impact as what you say. For example, how many times have you gone to ask someone a question and he or she acted like you disturbed him or her from something important (even if he or she was surfing the

Internet at the time)? You feel like you are intruding, even when you have a valid, work-related question to ask, and you are apt not to approach that person again until absolutely necessary. Also, how often have you caught someone in a bad mood, for whatever reason, and he or she takes it out on you just because you happen to be around? What about people who don't take you seriously, who turn everything into a joke and act like you don't know anything? Incidents like these are not pleasant, are often annoying, and can impact how you perceive people at work.

As a producer, you must be especially aware of how your nonverbal cues come across to the team. As their leader, you must always be accessible for any question (no matter how small), be able to turn a negative into a positive (and not the other way around), and act in a decisive manner (even when asking people for help). You don't have the luxury of being moody, disinterested, or fake to anyone—behaving like that will quickly diminish any respect or authority you have with the team.

For example, if you are in an office, don't keep your door shut all the time. If you are in a cubicle, don't constantly have your headphones on. Both of these things indicate that you are unavailable and don't want to be disturbed by anyone. This indication can be off-putting to team members who feel more secure in knowing you are always available to them. Remember that one of your main responsibilities as the producer is to serve your team, not the other way around.

If someone approaches you to talk and you find him or her annoying, don't roll your eyes or sigh; instead, act like you are ready to talk to him or her and fix whatever problem he or she is having. A friendly "hello" goes a long way, so when you walk through the team rooms, smile, stop by people's desks, and look at what they are working on. Showing genuine interest in what the team is doing will be appreciated.

Because nonverbal cues are so important and people each have a preferred method of giving and receiving information, it is useful to read some books on psychology to better understand people. In addition, much information exists about different personality types and how they interact with each other, which is useful to understand when managing large groups of people with diverse personalities. For example, the book *Type Talk at Work* (2002) discusses how the 16 Myers-Briggs personality types are likely to function in a working environment. The authors discuss effective ways to communicate, set goals, build teams, and so on with each personality type. Keep in mind that personality types are stereotypes, so don't expect everyone to fit neatly into a single category.

■ 5.5 Establishing Communication Norms

Communication norms are guidelines that everyone subconsciously or consciously adheres to when interacting with each other. These norms are formulated in several ways: they can emerge naturally over time; they can be defined up front; or they can be triggered by a problem that needs a solution. An example of a norm that emerges naturally is making it a habit to stop by your boss's office first thing each morning to give a brief update on what you plan to accomplish for the day. If you miss a morning of chatting with your boss, you both might feel that something is off but can't quite put your finger on it. An example of a norm that is defined up front is when your boss *requires* you to stop by his or her office at 9 A.M. each morning and update him or her on what you plan to do throughout the day. If you don't do this, the boss will want to know why you missed your standing appointment with him or her. And, finally, if there is an issue on your project that puts the ship date at risk, your boss might institute a policy in which you have to submit a task list to him or her each morning; this norm is often established as a solution to a specific problem.

Establishing communication norms for your team can help foster good communication among them. Also, involving the team in defining a set of norms is a great team-building activity—everyone has a say in what the norms are and everyone agrees on the final list. After a set of norms is established, other norms will naturally evolve that will improve the overall communication between team members, leads, the producer, and studio management.

Conducting a meeting to establish some communication norms is simple. Get the whole team in the room, ask people to discuss some of the communication issues they are having on the project, and establish what areas need improvements. When people define the communication issues, they can more easily formulate a set of norms. After the problems are defined, explain to the team what norms are and ask them to brainstorm on what guidelines will work for them. When they have offered all their ideas, have everyone participate in narrowing down the ideas and defining the norms. Here are some examples of team communication norms:

- Know who the point of contact is for your questions.
- Be considerate of other people's time.
- Don't mumble or be a low-volume speaker.
- Don't yell or raise your voice.
- Be constructive with criticism; don't complain.
- Act professionally toward your peers.

COMMUNICATION AND GAME DEVELOPMENT

Jamie Fristrom, Creative Director
Torpex Games

I have read several books on producing movies and television shows, as these resources offer advice that is applicable to game production. What I've found interesting is that film and television are mature industries, and accordingly, they've developed a shorthand that allows them to effectively schedule and hit their dates. It is a simple matter of what shots are needed and what characters are in these shots. They don't need a really heavy scheduling system with Gantt charts or Microsoft® Project, because they already have a system in place that makes production easy for them.

We will eventually get to this point in game development, where we will have a similar shorthand, with the production of characters, levels, and other assets following a standardized process, no matter what the game. We would still need to block out the production plan, but if we had shorthand and common practices, it would be much easier to accurately estimate when a game will be finished.

■ 5.6 Communication Challenges

Communication challenges are to be expected in any situation, but clear communication will certainly alleviate many challenges. Some basic areas where extra care must be taken with communication are resolving conflict, delivering bad news, and giving effective performance feedback.

5.6.1 Resolving Conflict

Conflict happens on any project, so don't be surprised when you see it on your project. Some basic causes of conflict are personality differences, miscommunication, and disagreements over how things should be done or over what things should be done. As a producer, you will be involved in conflicts and will need to mediate conflicts between other team members. Don't be afraid of confrontations, because conflict will not escalate if it is dealt with in a timely and assertive manner.

One of the main points to keep in mind when there is conflict is that you should not attempt to resolve the conflict when emotions are running high. You or the other person might say something that is regretted later, and the conflict becomes worse. For example, if a feature is cut from the game for schedule reasons, and you find out a few days later that your lead designer has instructed the designers to continue working on it, don't confront him or her while you are still visibly angry. Give yourself some time to cool down, and then deal with the situation. The same applies when you are mediating conflict between other people—they should only discuss the situation after each of them has cooled off.

Before discussing the conflict with the other party, take some time to figure out exactly what the conflict is. With the previous example, the conflict could stem from the designer misunderstanding that the feature was cut from the game, the designer disagreeing with this decision, or the designer disrespecting and trying to undermine your authority. Whatever is bothering him or her, make sure that you fully understand it and formulate ways to deal with it.

When you finally meet with the other person to resolve the conflict, start by stating the facts of the conflict. Follow these guidelines as a starting point:

- Don't generalize the situation by saying words like "always," "never," and "constantly." Stick to the facts and don't interpret or embellish.

- Don't assume you know what the person's motivations are for doing something. There are many reasons why people act the way they do, and you won't know why until you ask the person.

- Don't confuse issues and personalities. For example, if someone misunderstands what you say, don't assume it is because the person is stupid.

- Don't resolve conflicts publicly. If someone acts improperly during a meeting, don't reprimand him or her there; instead, deal with the situation privately after the meeting.

After you lay out the facts, describe the tangible impact this situation has on the project, so the person has a better understanding of the cause and effect. Give the person a chance to respond and then let the person know what needs to be done to remedy the situation. Show him or her how an improved situation will be a benefit to him or her and the project. Using the preceding example, the conversation might go like this:

> The team agreed to cut the feature from the game because there was not enough time to implement it. This decision was communicated to the team in the team meeting and via email. On Wednesday, I found out from another designer that you instructed the designers to continue working on it. This direction has caused them to get behind on their design documentation for the UI, and now UI engineering is held up until the documentation is complete. [Give the person a chance to respond. He or she may apologize, state why he or she wants to keep the feature in, or have an emotional reaction. No matter what he or she does, be prepared to assertively state your solution to the problem. However, you will want to tailor your response appropriately to the situation.] The designers need to get the UI design documentation finished, so please have them work on that until it is completed. If you feel strongly about this feature, we will schedule a meeting to discuss it again with the leads; maybe we can put in a scaled-down version or replace another feature.

Of course, every situation is different, but this format presents a good guide for keeping the conversation focused on resolving the conflict. If the person has an emotional reaction during this meeting, tell him or her you can't continue the discussion and will set up another time to talk with him or her.

5.6.2   Delivering Bad News

There may come a point during game development when bad news must be delivered to the team. Things such as project cancellations, layoffs, and key people leaving the company might fall into this category. Although it seems daunting to be the one responsible for telling people the project got canceled, the ship date was pulled in, or someone was fired, it's not so bad if you do it with honesty and compassion. First and foremost, be honest about why something is happening. You don't have to get into the nitty-gritty details, but do provide the context of the decision and answer any and all questions as honestly as you can.

Second, be sensitive about how the news is delivered. Even though something bad might be happening—such as layoffs—don't overemphasize the negative aspects. People will feel bad enough already for their friends who may be let go. Instead, discuss the reasoning behind the layoffs, what steps were taken to minimize the impact, and what is being done to take care of the employees who have to find new jobs.

Finally, deliver bad news in a timely fashion. People have a natural instinct for sensing when things aren't quite right, and they will start jumping to their own conclusions about what is going on. In cases like this, the rumors are sometimes much worse than what is actually happening, and by the time you actually address the problem, morale could be at an all-time low. Concern among the team that something bad is going on at the studio is likely if you see groups of people whispering in the hallway or by the coffee machine. As a producer, it is your responsibility to address these concerns quickly and confirm what the problem is. If there is not a problem, and rumors have started circulating about something, call a team meeting and ask the team what their major concerns are. Discuss the issues and make sure that the team is satisfied with the results of the discussion by following up with people afterward.

DELIVERING BAD NEWS

Stuart Roch, Executive Producer
Activision

As long as you have an existing relationship with the team of talking to them straight and being honest with them, delivering bad news might not be as scary as it seems. Although no one on the team likes to hear bad news, such as their project being delayed, they look to the producers to be there to deliver such news and answer any questions in good times and in bad. Keeping the team informed at all times by communicating all types of project news might be difficult, but this communication is a necessary part of the job and should be handled in an honest and straightforward fashion.

5.6.3   Giving Effective Feedback

Most companies give annual performance reviews to let employees know which areas they excelled in and which areas could use some improvements. These performance reviews are an excellent learning tool for the employees, especially if they are working toward a promotion or want to improve their skill sets. Providing feedback to employees at other times during the year is also important (even when it is not a formal review) because it is not really fair to assess the employee only once a year. Employees who are provided with regular feedback will become stronger and more skilled. Also, regular feedback is critical if the employee is having problems with his or her work habits or quality of work.

To fairly assess each employee, the producer and the appropriate lead must be involved in the feedback process, as well as anyone else the employee reports to directly. In this fashion, the employee gets a well-rounded assessment of his or her project contributions and more constructive feedback. Most employees look forward to receiving feedback on their work because they want to make sure they are doing a good job or improving in areas of weakness.

Here are some general guidelines for giving effective feedback:

- Base feedback on personal observations, not on what people tell you about someone. If team members have given you feedback on another member, you should consider the information in making your own observations, but not merely repeat the feedback as you heard it.

- Give feedback often and in a timely fashion. If you see that an employee is under-performing, don't wait until the annual performance review; talk with him or her as soon as possible. Similarly, providing immediate positive feedback on a task well-done will strengthen your relationship with the employee.

- Be specific with feedback. Don't just tell an employee he or she needs to improve his or her work habits; cite specific examples of his or her bad work habits and then offer suggestions on how to improve them.

- Focus feedback on behaviors and not on individuals. For example, instead of telling someone he or she is difficult to approach with comments, tell him or her that because he or she constantly interrupts and cuts people off, he or she makes it difficult for people to talk to him or her.

- Be constructive with feedback, not destructive. You don't want the employee to feel bad about what he or she did in the past; you want the employee to understand what he or she must work on for the future.

- Whenever possible, offset negative feedback with positive feedback. With this balance, the employee can see that you are not "out to get him or her," but in fact see his or her strengths as well. This approach lends credence to your feedback. However, be careful not to overuse this method, as the employee will be conditioned to expect negative feedback each time you start a conversation by giving him or her positive feedback.

Keep in mind that even negative feedback can be delivered in a constructive way. You don't want the person to come away from the meeting feeling like he or she has been picked on. But he or she should come away with a clear understanding of what things he or she needs to improve.

■ 5.7 Chapter Summary

Communication is a large part of any team effort, and good communication helps build a stronger team. Because communication comes in several forms—written, oral, and nonverbal—it is important to understand how to use each of these forms effectively. This chapter presented an overview of how to do that, along with some practical tips to enhance communication. The chapter concluded with some guidelines on how to handle specific communication challenges.

■ 5.8 Questions and Exercises

1. What are some ways written communication can be improved?
2. Describe the active-listening technique.
3. Why is it important to be aware of nonverbal communication?
4. What are communication norms and why are they important?
5. Pair up people in groups of two. Have them role play the communication challenges described in Section 5.6.

6 | Game Production Overview

In this chapter:

- Production cycle
- Preproduction
- Production
- Testing
- Postproduction

■ 6.1 Introduction

The production process begins with defining the initial game concept and ends with creating a gold master of the final game code, with everything else happening in between. The process differs from project to project, which is one reason why game production can be challenging to manage. One developer might have a small team of 15 people working on a web-based game, but another developer might have more than 100 people working on a next-generation console game based on a well-known movie license.

Regardless of the size of the team, scope of the game, budget, or other variables, a basic framework exists for the overall production process. The process can be broken down into four broad phases: preproduction, production, testing, and postproduction. Within each of these phases, several goals must be accomplished before moving on to the next phase. The successful completion of each phase directly affects the successful release of the game.

■ 6.2 Production Cycle

Figure 6.1 serves as an overview of the basic production cycle. Specific game production tasks, such as recording voiceover, creating character models, and debugging multiplayer code, are not indicated, as these tasks will vary from project to project.

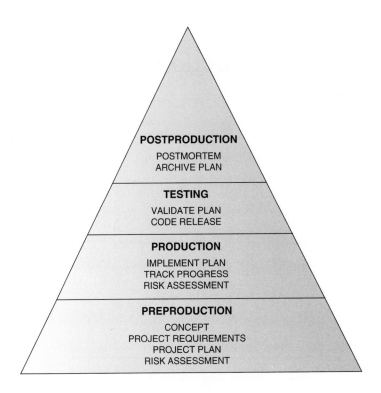

POSTPRODUCTION
POSTMORTEM
ARCHIVE PLAN

TESTING
VALIDATE PLAN
CODE RELEASE

PRODUCTION
IMPLEMENT PLAN
TRACK PROGRESS
RISK ASSESSMENT

PREPRODUCTION
CONCEPT
PROJECT REQUIREMENTS
PROJECT PLAN
RISK ASSESSMENT

FIGURE 6.1   Basic game production cycle.

The diagram depicts the general goals of each phase and how the success of each phase builds upon the completion of the previous phase. As you can see, detailing the project plan in preproduction is important as it provides a solid foundation upon which to build the game. A project that does not define a plan in preproduction is likely to encounter several problems that could have been avoided or prepared for in advance.

It is important to note that this diagram outlines a very basic view of the game production cycle and that some games, especially as the stakes get higher, will go through an iterative production process with numerous production cycles. For example, if you plan to create a working proof of concept for your game—a fully polished playable level—you will want to include a few game development cycles in the overall production process, with the first cycle consisting of preproduction, production, and testing of the prototype; the second cycle focusing on the core set of features and assets for the game; and a third cycle creating and adding any "glitz" features and assets, such as extra levels. Figure 6.2 is a diagram of multiple production cycles for a single project.

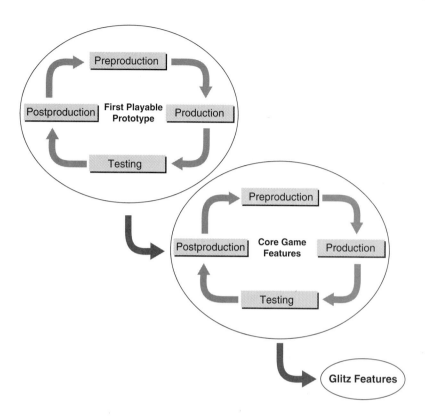

I FIGURE 6.2 Multiple production cycles for a single project.

■ 6.3 Preproduction

Preproduction is the first phase in the production cycle and is critical to defining what the game is, how long it will take to make, how many people are needed, and how much everything will cost. Preproduction can last anywhere from one week to more than a year, depending on how much time you have to complete the game. One rule of thumb is that preproduction requires about 10 to 25 percent of the total development time of a game. So if you are working on a six-month project, preproduction will last from a few weeks to a month. If you are working on a two-year project, preproduction will last anywhere from two to six months.

The overriding goal of preproduction is essentially to create the game plan, which is a road map for finishing the game and releasing code. The plan must include information on the game's concept, the features and constraints that affect this concept, the basic technical and design documentation, and finally, how much it will cost, how long it will take, and how many people and with what skills will be needed. Preproduction can be broken down into the following components: game concept, game requirements, and game plan.

6.3.1   Game Concept

James P. Lewis, author of numerous books on project management, suggests thinking about the concept as finding a solution to a problem. Therefore, a game concept that starts off as a question presents a problem to be solved. Would it be fun to play cowboys and Indians in space? What would it be like to race concept cars? After the game's initial concept is determined, usually by studio management or your publisher, it is passed on to the development team as a problem to solve.

Many concepts start off fuzzy, and the core development team must then flesh them out so that everyone can easily understand what the goals of the product are and what major gameplay elements are needed to support and strengthen it. For example, if you are working on a realistic tactical military shooter, it would not fit within the game world to use fictitious alien technology. The concept also defines the game genre and hardware platform, as these decisions will shape how the concept grows. When the concept is determined, you must clearly communicate it to the rest of the team, so they understand and can get excited about it. This communication can be done by defining a mission statement.

A mission statement gets everyone excited about the game on which they are working. The mission statement answers what is going to be done and for whom it is being done. Short and sweet, something that everyone can remember, the mission statement is the team's "elevator speech." The whole team should be involved in defining and shaping the mission statement, giving everyone a stake in the project. This sense of ownership is imperative to building a strong team. Keep in mind that the mission statement doesn't need to state how these things will be done, as the how will be addressed when the project plan is put together.

After determining the initial concept, the next step is to add the basic gameplay elements. Initial thoughts on the gameplay mechanics, the control scheme, the genre, the story, the characters, and other hooks that will set the game apart from the competition should be included. Prototyping the elements helps to further define the game experience. Prototypes can start off on paper, and as the ideas develop more fully, playable prototypes will be created. If possible, try to create a polished prototype that will be representative of the final gameplay experience.

As these concepts are further detailed, conduct a risk analysis to determine the game production's biggest risks. At this point, several unknowns exist, so it will be difficult to determine specific risks. However, if a few constants are already defined, like the team size or technology, they can be used as the basis for an initial risk analysis. If you don't take time to define the development risks, you are likely to encounter unexpected problems on the project that could have been minimized if they were identified as risks early on.

After the concept is fully defined and a prototype is created, you will pitch it to studio management and the publisher. This pitch provides them the opportunity to see how the team has planned to create a solid game from the initial concept. They will likely have feedback on the pitch, which will need to be incorporated by the team. If they like what they hear, they will approve the game for further preproduction. When this approval occurs, the producer will organize an official project kick-off to present the fully approved concept to the team.

Chapter 7, "Game Concept," discusses the concept phase in more detail. After the concept is defined, the next step is to figure out the game's requirements.

6.3.2 Game Requirements

Game requirements include the basic art, design, and engineering features that must be supported, any constraints on the project, and basic technical and design documentation. The features must all fit within the established concept and mission statement.

The team members should be involved in determining the core feature set and prioritizing the other features so they can develop a sense of ownership of the game. The feature set should include some unique elements that set it apart from other games. One way to do this is by having the team brainstorm "must have," "want to have," and "would be nice to have" features, discuss them, and then create a final prioritized feature set. Chapter 9, "Game Requirements," presents one method for doing this.

Constraints should be considered when determining the feature set priorities. For example, everyone may agree that building a new graphics engine is a "must have" feature, but if there is not sufficient time to build the engine, this feature will be dropped down to a "would be nice to have" feature, and the team must figure out other ways to achieve the graphics goals for the game.

After the feature set is defined and fits within the constraints, the milestones and deliverables for each milestone are defined. Some projects are scheduled around monthly milestones, and other projects are scheduled around first playable, alpha, and beta milestones. Either method will work, as long as the deliverables expected at each milestone are clearly defined and published to the team. Deliverables refer to elements in the game, such as art assets, technical features, and level scripting, that demonstrate gameplay and the look and feel of the game universe.

While the feature set is being defined, technology is researched to figure out what works best for the proposed game. This includes looking at the hardware constraints, exploring middleware solutions, and evaluating any suitable internal technologies. In addition, thought must be given to what tools are needed to create the game assets and the best way to establish a production pipeline.

As all of these elements become more defined, the team must create some basic technical and design documentation focusing on the core aspects of the game. As illustrated in Figure 6.2, games can have several production cycles, so this documentation must focus on fleshing out the current production cycle. The documentation details are added to the core features as preproduction continues, so that by the time production begins, everyone has the information they need to begin their work. Finally, conduct a risk analysis at this stage to determine the game's biggest risks so far.

When the game requirements are determined, all the decision makers in the process should review and sign off on them. This includes studio management, the publisher, and even marketing. Along with the development team, these groups also have a stake in the project and want to make sure that their best interests are considered during the requirements phase. As people review the documentation, they will have feedback that will likely affect the constraints. It is a good idea to centralize all the feedback, determine what can be incorporated, and then send the revised plan for everyone to review again.

It may be difficult to get everyone on board with the requirements, especially if the groups are at different geographical locations. In cases like this, the producer will want to schedule a time and place where everyone can meet together (either in person or via conference call) to come to a consensus and finalize the requirements. Refer to Chapter 9, "Game Requirements," for more information.

6.3.3   Game Plan

The game plan is where all of the information is pulled together to show how everything will be accomplished. The producer spearheads the effort to prepare the budget, schedule, and staffing needs for the game, but he or she must work with the team to determine them. If the producer does not consult with the core development team, especially when it comes to schedule and staffing, it will be hard to get the team members to buy into the game plan. This is especially true if the schedule is extremely aggressive and the producer is counting on everyone to work at their highest level of productivity. Refer to Chapter 10, "Game Plan," for details on creating budgets, schedules, and staffing plans.

When the budget, schedule, and staffing plan are assembled, the team reviews them to make sure they can achieve the desired game requirements. If not, the plan or the game requirements might need to be amended. In fact, both the game requirements and game plan should be updated whenever something changes on the project. Don't forget to conduct another risk analysis and have all the stakeholders review the plan as well.

6.3.4   Preproduction Checklist

Figure 6.3 is a preproduction checklist you can use to track your progress during this phase.

PREPRODUCTION CHECKLIST	Y / N	NOTES
CONCEPT		
Is initial game concept defined?		
Are platform and genre specified?		
Is mission statement completed?		
Are basic gameplay elements defined?		
Is prototype completed?		
Is risk analysis completed?		
Is the concept pitch ready for approval?		
Have all stakeholders approved the concept?		
Is project kick-off scheduled?		
GAME REQUIREMENTS		
Are "must have," "want to have," and "nice to have" features defined?		
Are constraints defined and accounted for in feature sets?		
Are milestones and deliverables defined?		
Has technology been evaluated against the desired feature set?		
Are tools and pipeline defined?		
Is basic design documentation completed?		
Is basic technical documentation completed?		
Is risk analysis completed?		
Have all stakeholders approved the game requirements?		
GAME PLAN		
Is budget completed?		
Is initial schedule completed?		
Is initial staffing plan completed?		
Have core team members approved the schedule and staffing plan?		
Have all stakeholders approved the game plan?		

I FIGURE 6.3 Preproduction checklist.

■ 6.4 Production

The production phase is when the team can actually begin producing assets and code for the game. In most cases, the line between preproduction and production is fuzzy, as you will be able to start production on some features while other features are still in preproduction. This start of the production phase is also affected by any checks and balances that the publisher or studio management has in place. For example, the team might be unable to begin full production until a playable prototype has been created and approved.

If everything is planned for during preproduction, the production phase should have no surprises; of course, this is rarely the case. After your team has started full production, there is a good chance that some feature or asset will need to be added, changed, or removed. However, if you have a tiered implementation strategy that focuses on getting the core features and assets completed first, it is easier to plan for unexpected changes.

The production phase is focused on content and code creation, tracking progress, and completing tasks. In addition, risk assessment is ongoing during production, so you are prepared for any unexpected events that negatively impact the game's production cycle. Production is loosely categorized into the following components: plan implementation, tracking progress, and task completion.

6.4.1 Plan Implementation

Plan implementation requires the producer to communicate the final plan to the team and provide them all the tools and resources needed to implement it. Make the plan publicly available to the team in a format that is easily accessible, such as a team website or designated area on the network. Include all the documents created in the preproduction phase, with the schedule and milestones in a clearly visible place. It is also helpful to post hard copies of key deadlines throughout the team rooms.

When the plan is communicated to the team, the producer must be vigilant about keeping everything in the plan up-to-date. If a feature design, milestone deadline, or asset list changes, it must be accurately noted in the game plan and communicated to the team, studio management, and possibly the publisher. Making these changes in a timely manner is important, because everyone is using the project plan as the main point of reference. If the plan is not updated throughout the production process, it is likely that features will be overlooked or the wrong features will be implemented.

Feature creep, when features are continually added to the project during the actual production phase, often occurs because things are changing on a regular basis. Someone will think of a great idea for the game and will want to add it to the feature set without thinking of the impact this will have on the game's schedule or resources. Feature creep is not good for the project as a whole because every time a new feature is added, more resources must be allocated to design it, implement it, create assets for it, and test it. This means that the resources already in use will be stretched to the limit and adding extra features may cause the game to miss an all-important code release deadline. If feature creep is not controlled during production, the game will quickly run out of time and resources.

After the game plan is implemented, art, design, engineering, and testing are even more dependent on each other for completing tasks. The artists may be in a holding pattern if they are waiting on design for the details of a specific level design. The final deadline for the cinematics may be at risk if the cinematics team is waiting for final voiceover files from the sound engineer. As the producer, you are responsible for working with your leads to quickly resolve any task dependencies. In some situations, the cinematics team might be able to do other work while waiting for the voiceover files, and so on. Tracking progress helps the producer and leads identify bottlenecks in the production process.

6.4.2 Tracking Progress

Tracking progress against the game plan is critical to knowing where the game is at any given time in production. If you don't have a plan to track against, your game will quickly get out of control, and you will find yourself in an unpleasant situation. If you, as the producer, don't know how much longer it takes to complete a feature, or how much of the feature is already completed, how can you know whether the game team is on track to meet their deadlines?

Progress tracking does not have to be complicated. In fact, the more complicated it is, the more unlikely people will do it. For example, you might decide to track the progress in Microsoft Project, and if you are an expert in using this software, it will be very easy for you. However, if you don't know how to use the tracking features in Microsoft Project, you might avoid tracking the progress altogether. In any case, you must implement a method that will work for you and the team, as they also need to be aware of what progress has been made. One simple way to do this is to create checklists or to track tasks in Microsoft® Excel®.

6.4.3 Task Completion

Task completion in most areas of game development is fairly straightforward, especially when the work results in a tangible asset, as with art and design assets. Determining when engineering tasks are completed is difficult, since there are no hard indicators regarding when a piece of code is complete, especially when bug fixes can always be made to the code.

Defining exit criteria is a good way for a producer or lead to more accurately determine when a task is complete. Exit criteria are conditions that must be met before a task is deemed finished. For example, a design document is complete after it is written and approved; a character model is complete after the artist adds the final texture to it.

The exit criteria must be easily understood by everyone, especially the person who is actually doing the task. For a task that is difficult to define criteria for, the producer can meet with the appropriate team member and lead so everyone agrees on the exit criteria. If you are an independent developer working for a publisher, the exit criteria for the major milestone deliverables must be clearly spelled out in the publisher–developer agreement.

6.4.4 Production Checklist

Figure 6.4 is a production checklist you can use to track your progress through the production phase.

PRODUCTION CHECKLIST	Y / N	NOTES
PLAN IMPLEMENTATION		
Is game plan clearly communicated to team?		
Is game plan in publicly accessible place?		
Can plan be easily updated with changes by producer?		
Does everyone on team have the necessary resources to do their work?		
Is process in place for controlling feature creep?		
Is risk assessment happening on a regular basis throughout production?		
Is process in place for managing task dependencies?		
PROGRESS TRACKING		
Is there a game plan to track progress against?		
Is process in place for producer to track all task progress?		
Is progress posted in visible areas in the team rooms?		
TASK COMPLETION		
Does each task have clearly defined exit criteria?		
Are these exit criteria publicly available to the team?		
Are all stakeholders in agreement on what the exit criteria are?		

| FIGURE 6.4 Production checklist.

■ 6.5 Testing

Testing is a critical phase in game development. This is when the game gets checked to ensure that everything works correctly and that there are no crash bugs. Testing is ongoing during the production process, as the quality assurance (QA) department will check milestone builds, new functionality, and new assets as they become available in the game. After beta, when all the game assets and features are fully implemented, the main focus of the development team will be fixing bugs and creating new builds for QA to test. The testing phase can be considered as two parts: plan validation and code release. Chapter 14, "Testing and Code Releasing," contains more detailed information on the testing process.

6.5.1 Plan Validation

The QA department's main responsibility is to write the test plan for the game and validate the game against this plan. The test plan is based on the assets and functionality outlined in the game plan. If the game plan is not updated, QA cannot create the appropriate test plans. The producer and leads work closely with the QA department to make all the necessary information available to write accurate test plans. In addition, the QA department works with the development team to educate them on the testing process and how to use the bug-tracking software.

The game must be validated in all areas and, depending on the size of the game, this can require a significant amount of testing time. For example, if working on a PC game that is localized into two languages, the QA testers need to check several PC configurations, with different operating systems, sound cards, and video cards. In addition, they must check each of the localized versions on these configurations.

The QA department is not only responsible for finding bugs, they are also responsible for regressing bugs that the development team has fixed. Usually a bug is not considered closed until the QA department has rechecked the bug in the game and verified that it is fixed.

6.5.2 Code Release

After a game has been thoroughly tested, the QA department will start the code release process. The code release process is different from normal QA testing in that they are looking at code release candidates (CRC)—builds that the development team considers ready to ship. At this point in production, all of the major bugs are fixed, the functionality is working as designed, and all the game assets are finalized. The game just needs one last set of checks to confirm that it is ready to be shipped to the manufacturer.

The producer must schedule time in the schedule for the code release process so that QA has sufficient time to make the final checks on a game. The time for this will vary, depending on the size of the game and the size of the QA department. Ideally, there is enough time for QA to run through the entire test plan on the CRC, which could take as little as a day or as long as a week. If they can complete the entire test plan and are confident everything checks out against the plan, the game is considered code released, and the disc can be shipped to the manufacturer for replication. Refer to Chapter 14, "Testing and Code Releasing," for more details on this process.

If you are working on a console title, you will also need to submit the game to the console manufacturer for approval, as they have their own checks and balances for each game. If they do not approve a game, it is not manufactured until the problems are corrected and the game is resubmitted for approval. There is a chance that even if the developer's QA department code releases a game, it may not be approved by the console manufacturer. However, developers are usually given an opportunity to resubmit builds for approval until they get the final sign-off.

6.5.3 Testing Checklist

Figure 6.5 is a checklist to be used for the testing phase of a game.

TESTING CHECKLIST	Y / N	NOTES
VALIDATE PLAN		
Is test plan written?		
Is game plan updated for QA?		
Has test plan been updated with any changes to the game plan?		
Are testing milestones accounted for in the schedule?		
Is bug-tracking software available for the testers and development team?		
Are all areas of the game tested?		
Are all bugs regressed and closed?		
CODE RELEASE		
Has development team submitted a final code release candidate?		
Is there sufficient time in the schedule for QA to complete the test plan on the code release candidate?		
Has QA approved the product for code release?		
CONSOLE ONLY: Has code-released game been submitted to console manufacturer for approval?		
CONSOLE ONLY: Has console manufacturer approved game for final replication?		

▌ FIGURE 6.5 Testing checklist.

■ 6.6 Postproduction

After the game is code released and approved for manufacturing, the game development process needs to be wrapped up before it is officially completed. Many times, this step is forgotten or ignored, which is unfortunate. This is when the team can relax, prepare a closing kit for future projects, and review the pros and cons of their recent game development experience. The postproduction phase consists of two things: learning from experience and archiving the plan.

6.6.1 Learn from Experience

Learning from experience is the best way to improve the game development process for future projects. One way to do this is by conducting a postmortem at the end of a project. A postmortem is a chance for everyone to review the good and bad on a project and to propose solutions based on these experiences for future projects.

As a producer, you plan to conduct "mini" postmortems at key points during development, such as alpha and beta. It is never too late to learn something about improving the process, even mid-project. The "Postmortems," section in Chapter 14, "Testing and Code Releasing," provides details on how to conduct and publish a postmortem.

6.6.2 Archive Plan

After the game is code released, it is archived for use on future projects. This is done by creating a closing kit. This kit contains all the design documentation, source code, source art, final game assets, final music files, and everything else that was used to create the game.

Closing kits are necessary because the publisher may want to create a special version of the game to be bundled with a piece of hardware, or the development team might want to reuse the code or assets for another project. Closing kits are especially useful if your team works on a franchise and wants to base the next iteration of the franchise on the previous game's source code.

6.6.3 Postproduction Checklist

Figure 6.6 is a postproduction checklist for tracking your progress.

■ 6.7 Chapter Summary

The game production process can be challenging for a producer to manage, but if it is approached methodically, these challenges can be minimized. This chapter presented an overview of the general game production process from the producer's point of view.

POSTPRODUCTION CHECKLIST	Y / N	NOTES
LEARN FROM EXPERIENCE		
Is postmortem completed?		
Is postmortem published to the entire development studio?		
ARCHIVE PLAN		
Is closing kit completed?		

FIGURE 6.6 Postproduction checklist.

General information was given about preproduction, production, testing, and postproduction on a project. These areas are presented in more detail in subsequent chapters in this book.

■ 6.8 Questions and Exercises

1. What are the four main phases in the game production cycle and what is the main purpose of each one? How many production cycles will occur during game development?

2. What are the key phases of preproduction? What is the main purpose of each one?

3. What are the key elements of the production phase? What is the significance of each?

4. What are the key elements of the testing phase? What is the significance of each?

5. What are the key elements of the postproduction phase? What is the significance of each?

6. Pick a popular game and discuss the main phases of production as it goes from concept to release.

7 | Game Concept

■ 7.1 Introduction

Preproduction starts with defining the game's concept. After all, you can't start working on a game until you have some idea of what the game's goal is and what the final game will look like when it is completed. An initial concept starts with a broad idea—what would it be like to race concept cars against each other—and then more details are added to narrow the concept and create a vision for the game. Elements such as the hardware platform, genre, and key features are defined, along with more specifics on what the game world is like, the character designs, and the gameplay mechanics. After all of this is defined, anyone presented with the game information should understand the goals of the game's concept.

Rarely does the producer alone determine the initial game concept and the general game design, unless he or she is funding a game development team and has final authority over all game design decisions. In reality, game design is a collaborative process, and the producer's main role is to manage the development process and make sure that all the key elements of the design are completed. A lead designer or creative director usually manages the creative process to ensure that all of the game's elements support the initial concept. In some cases, if you try to manage both the creative and production process, you can find yourself in a dilemma when you have an idea for a cool feature but need to cut it for production reasons. Additionally, if you assume some of the lead design responsibilities without strictly defining this in your role as producer, the other team members—particularly the lead designer—might be frustrated if they do not understand the reasoning behind your creative authority on the project.

Of course, there are instances where the producer is also the main creative leader, and this can be a successful way to structure as a team, as long as everyone understands what your role as producer–director entails. The key is to define the creative and production management responsibilities clearly, so that people are assured that both aspects of these areas are being expertly handled in the game development cycle. After the roles are clearly defined for preproduction tasks, you can start working on the game's concept.

Remember that when a team collaborates on a creative project, people are never in 100-percent agreement. If you spend your time trying to get everyone to agree on everything about the game, little progress will be made. People can spend too much time disagreeing with decisions and so no final decisions are made. If people are in disagreement on how a certain element functions in the game, don't waste time trying to convince the dissenter that the idea is good. Instead, spend the time prototyping the idea, get some actual gameplay feedback on the fun factor, and make adjustments or change the functionality based on this information.

This chapter presents an overview of what game elements are defined in the concept phase. In order to demonstrate some of the key points, a sample game will be used throughout this chapter and subsequent chapters discussing the game development process.

■ 7.2 Beginning the Process

At the beginning of the game development process, the team will likely consist of a producer, lead designer, lead engineer, and lead artist. This core team is responsible for taking a concept and turning it into a game design. This means determining the concept, platform, genre, gameplay mechanics, character designs, and any other key game elements.

If you are working for a publisher-owned developer, the publisher will likely assign your team specific games to work on, including the platform, genre, and initial concept. With this basic information, the core team needs to define all the other elements of the game. If you are working for an independent developer, your core team will come up with the initial concept and further define it. Regardless of where the initial concept originates, there is still plenty of creative work for the team to do.

When determining the initial concept, there are several factors to consider, including your target audience, player motivation, genre, and platform. Each of these has a significant impact on how the game concept will be shaped and defined into a full gameplay experience.

7.2.1 Motivation

As a developer, it is important to be aware of what motivates someone to play a game in order to create a game experience that will satisfy the target audience. While there are many reasons why someone is motivated to play games, they can be roughly categorized into four types: challenge, social interaction, fantasy, and emotion.

Challenge is found in all games, even fairly simple games targeted toward children. Risk and reward are intertwined in games, and there must be some chance of failure, however slim, in order for a game to feel rewarding. Some gamers value the challenge above all, pursuing the thrill of beating a difficult game and achieving various goals.

Social interaction is found in numerous cooperative games, and is also a hallmark of massively multiplayer online (MMO) games. Players who enjoy social interaction see gaming as an opportunity to socialize with friends, enjoy themselves, and have a good time while rocking out to a Guitar Hero® game or conducting a World of Warcraft® raid. Even if the attempt doesn't end in victory, there's still fun to be had.

Fantasy, in this context, doesn't refer to a category of games involving dragons and elves; instead, it addresses wish fulfillment, regardless of setting. Some players like to explore various fantasies, such as being a star athlete, a heroic soldier, or a risk-taking fighter pilot. In many cases, games that cater to this audience are prized for their attention to detail, as this helps immerse the player further in the game world. For instance, games like IL-2 Sturmovik™ are heavily researched, featuring authentic planes and uniforms, as well as a broad range of real-world planes that respond in a realistic manner to player input.

Emotion is elicited in different ways. Some games, such as the Resident Evil® series, evoke dread and terror during gameplay; Psychonauts™ was considered an extremely funny and cleverly written game; and Call of Duty® 4: Modern Warfare™ is well regarded for its exhilarating gameplay. Players who value emotion are more likely to focus on a game's production values, such as voice acting, music, graphics, and story, than the core gameplay.

7.2.2 Target Audience

The target audience consists of the group of people who will enjoy your game. Often, developers make the mistake of trying to appeal to everyone, but this is patently impossible. Even the most popular games only succeed in pleasing a fraction of the entire gaming population. Typically, companies perform market research in order to determine the target audience, and calculate the probability of a game's success on the results of that research. A niche game that will cater to only a few thousand gamers isn't going to receive the same budget as a mainstream title with broader appeal.

There are millions of video game enthusiasts around the world, and dividing them into categories is a difficult task. However, there are two broad classifications that can help when discussing the people who play games: hardcore gamers and casual gamers.

Hardcore gamers are passionate devotees. They're involved and informed; they read game industry magazines and websites; they post on message boards; they're opinionated about publishers and developers; and they keep up with current events in the game industry. For hardcore gamers, it's not enough to play a game—they feel a sense of accomplishment when beating a game. They enjoy overcoming obstacles and are frustrated by easy games.

Casual gamers play for fun and are more likely to enjoy a game's production values (such as story) or the thrill of exploration than the experience of overcoming difficult challenges. When a game ceases to entertain and becomes frustrating, casual gamers move on to something else; they're unlikely to keep playing despite repeated failures.

Hardcore and casual are broad ways to categorize a game's potential audience, but in order to create a well-defined and quality gameplay experience, the developers need to have a more in-depth understanding of their target market. Game audiences have significantly changed since the early days, and now there is a much larger market for games.

During the early days of the game industry, the target audience consisted primarily of young males. However, gaming has become a form of mainstream entertainment. According to *Essential Facts about the Computer and Video Game Industry 2009*, published by the Entertainment Software Association in 2009, the industry's target audience has shifted considerably. According to the publication:

- 60 percent of gamers are male.
- The average age of a gamer is 35.
- 25 percent of gamers are over 50.
- The average adult gamer has been playing for 12 years.
- 68 percent of American households play video games.

Clearly, the audience is no longer what it was.

However, the industry isn't keeping up with the evolving customer demographic. *The Virtual Census: Representations of Gender, Race and Age in Video Games*, published by SAGE Online Publications in 2009, reports that women and minorities have been underrepresented as characters in games.

Though African-Americans and Latinos make up 12.3 percent and 12.5 percent of the U.S. population, respectively, and despite the fact that minority youths play video games more often than Caucasians, African-Americans account for 10 percent of video game characters, and less than 3 percent are Latino. While the figures for African-Americans seem promising, the virtual census goes on to note that if sports games are removed from the equation, the number of African-American characters drops dramatically, and many of those remaining are criminals.

Women fared no better; the study found that 90 percent of major characters and 85 percent of secondary characters are male, leaving women with 10 percent and 15 percent, respectively. As the audience continues to expand, and as more and more women and minorities enter the game industry, this paradigm will begin to shift, making for more inclusive representation. Developers who are aware of the potential markets stand a better chance of creating a game that can appeal to a more diverse audience.

The work on the initial concept should not take more than a few weeks. Any longer than that and you will lose valuable preproduction time and any creative momentum the team has built up in anticipation of working on a new project. One of the first things the team will participate in is a brainstorming session.

Brainstorming

Brainstorming sessions are an opportunity to involve the team in generating a large number of ideas about the game. You can brainstorm about the initial game concept, the basic gameplay mechanics, the game's setting, or what the characters will look like. Well-managed brainstorming sessions are also a great team-building exercise because they allow everyone to offer their opinions about what makes a fun game. The core team is involved in the brainstorming session, or you can open it up to other people within the studio; it depends on how many ideas you want to generate in the sessions.

Before organizing a brainstorming session, familiarize yourself with guidelines for how to effectively manage one. If the session is not managed properly, it will not yield useful information, and the participants might feel frustrated by their experience. Some common complaints of an unsuccessful brainstorming session are as follows:

- The session lost focus and did not provide useful information.
- Participants' ideas were not listened to.
- No new ideas were generated.
- Participants felt used when the final decisions had no relationship to their initial input.

These mistakes can be avoided if a few guidelines are followed when setting up and conducting the session. Prepare for the session beforehand:

Clearly define the purpose of the session: If the purpose is to think of names for the game's main character, make sure that everyone involved in the session knows this. Also, define who's running the session and who's taking notes.

Get the right group of people involved in the session: In some cases, it isn't conducive to have 50 people involved. You might need to have several smaller sessions on different topics or be selective about who is invited. For example, if you are brainstorming on what graphics features to include in the game, you will need to have more artists and engineers and fewer designers.

Have everyone prepare for the session beforehand: Let people know what topic they will be discussing so they can do some preliminary research. They might want to find out what the competition did, what technologies are available, or sketch out some ideas. This way, everyone is already thinking about the topic before the session, which makes the time spent brainstorming more productive.

During the actual session, establish a set of norms to follow during the session. The purpose of these norms is to create an environment in which people feel comfortable throwing out their ideas. Some basic norms are as follows:

Do not criticize anyone or any ideas during the session: When someone throws out an idea, don't start picking it apart right away. The purpose of the session is to generate information, not to eliminate it.

Do not start discussing an idea during the session: Write each idea on the board and then move on to the next one. The session will quickly lose focus after people start discussing an idea in detail, and you will miss opportunities to generate other great ideas.

When ideas stop flowing, be prepared to generate more: If people start running out of ideas in the session, look at the ideas already generated and start expanding on them or prepare some thought-provoking questions to ask to get the conversation started again. For example, "What does our competition do that we aren't doing?" or "How can we avoid the problem of _____?"

After the ideas are generated, spend some time with the team grouping them together into like-minded ideas and then prioritize them. From this, generate a report of the results of the brainstorming session and add it to the meeting notes. The higher-priority ideas are assigned to specific people for follow up and research. Be very clear about the action items generated in each brainstorming session and include these in the meeting notes. If you don't follow up on any of the ideas generated, people will feel that their participation was a waste of time. Some of the topics to be brainstormed might include the genre, platform, and initial game concept.

Schedule the brainstorming session as one of the first tasks for preproduction, so you can get everyone's ideas out in the open. Try to get as many brainstorming sessions completed and documented as possible in the first week of the project. The longer you put off the brainstorming session, the longer it will take to determine the game's initial concept. Ideally, each brainstorming session is managed by someone who has a neutral stance on the topic addressed. This way, his or her attention can be focused on running the session effectively and taking notes. When each session is completed, publish the notes within 24 hours. Also, each action item generated should take no more than a few days for the assigned person to complete.

7.2.3   Initial Concept

The initial concept can be generated by anyone—the publisher, the producer, the lead designer, or any other team member. The initial concept does not need to be detailed but does need to present a compelling goal for the game to achieve. This is also sometimes referred to as the game's *hook*. This hook provides the basis for all game decisions and is something the marketing department can communicate easily to the target audience when the time comes.

Initial concepts usually start off as a question to be answered. What if zombies existed and were living in outer space? What if animals had humans as pets? After the initial concept is determined, decisions are made that shape what the final version of the game will be like.

Here is an example of the initial concept for a game called Justice Unit:

Can a group of misfits come together as the Justice Unit and save the world from super villains?

7.2.4 Genre

A game genre is a category based on the type of gameplay that's experienced; while books and movies are often categorized based on the kind of story and/or setting they feature, games typically don't follow this pattern. For instance, a novel about sorcerers and mythical creatures might be classified in the genre of fantasy, but a game with similar subject matter might be defined as a role-playing game (like Final Fantasy® XII), a strategy game (such as The Lord of the Rings™: The Battle for Middle-Earth™), or a first-person shooter (like Dark Messiah of Might and Magic™).

Some genres are played more on particular platforms. For example, first-person shooters are quite popular on the Xbox 360® but rare on the iPhone®; by contrast, puzzle games are seldom released on the Xbox 360, but the iPhone offers many of them. The following are some common genres, but it's important to note that many games blend genres to create new types of gameplay. For example, Deus Ex™ is a hybrid of adventure game, role-playing game, and first-person shooter, while Brütal Legend™ is a third-person action/adventure game with elements of real-time strategy.

Adventure

Adventure games feature quests in which the player must use the inventory of items gathered along the way to solve puzzles of varying degrees of complexity. Solving the puzzle allows the player to progress to the next area. These puzzles might consist of decoding messages, locating and using specific items, locating devices that unlock doors, or reaching difficult-to-find areas. Adventure games are known for their comparatively slow pace and cerebral nature. In recent years, the genre has declined.

Fighting

Fighting games allow players to control a single combatant on the screen; typically, the player faces off against a computer-controlled opponent or another player. Using martial-arts maneuvers (which may include kicks, punches, attacks with weapons, blocks, throws, and combination moves), the characters battle until one of them is dispatched; some games, like the Mortal Kombat® series, feature particularly gruesome finishing moves. Fighting games, also known as fighters, were initially 2D games with static backgrounds, but the genre evolved to include 3D characters and interactive 3D backgrounds.

Fitness

Fitness gaming, also known as exergaming, requires the player to move around. These games promote exercise and an active lifestyle, but there's not much evidence to indicate that they actually improve one's health. The most successful of these is Wii Fit™, which has sold over 20 million units.

MMO

Massively multiplayer online (MMO) games can include numerous genres, but typically MMO games are role-playing games (known as MMORPGs). These are RPGs in which hundreds or thousands (or even millions) of players explore vast worlds online. They can gather into groups or play solo, but group play makes it easier to perform complex quests, explore dangerous territories, or battle powerful enemies. In some MMORPGs, players battle against each other, whereas in others, they are prohibited from doing so and can only battle computer-controlled opponents. The MMORPG usually doesn't feature an endgame state, instead allowing the player to continue to grow in power until he or she reaches a threshold of some kind (such as the maximum number of levels). The most successful MMORPG is World of Warcraft, which features over 11 million subscribers. Another MMO type is the MMOFPS (massively multiplayer online first-person shooter), a relatively small genre including games like MAG™ and Huxley: The Dystopia®. In these games, large armies of hundreds of players battle in teams against one another.

Music

Music games allow the player to interact with music through rhythm or melody or a combination of the two. The Guitar Hero and Rock Band® series require the player to play instrument-shaped controllers, including guitars and drums, which are played in rhythm with icons on the screen while songs play. Other games, like SingStar®, have the player sing along to the music being played. The DanceDanceRevolution® games feature large pads that the player must dance on, moving his or her feet to the rhythm of the icons displayed on the screen.

Platformers

Platformer games require the player to jump through the environment, leaping from one platform to another. Along the way, the player must collect items and defeat enemies. Some platformers, like Super Mario Bros., are 2D, but more recent titles, like Ratchet & Clank Future: Tools of Destruction are 3D.

Puzzle

Puzzle games require the player to solve a series of puzzles in order to progress. Typically, these games don't include much of a narrative, and protagonists are fairly rare. Successful puzzle games feature a fairly simple structure that the player can grasp quickly, along with complex interactions that take time to master. Tetris®, for instance, requires the player to manipulate simple blocks that fall from the top of the screen; the game's pace accelerates over time, increasing the difficulty, but the core concept never changes. Many popular iPhone and mobile titles are puzzle games.

RPGs

Role-playing games (RPGs) are heavily influenced by the most popular of their pen-and-paper antecedents, Dungeons & Dragons™. In an RPG, the player controls a group of heroes (or, occasionally, a single character, as in Morrowind® and Panzer Dragoon Saga™) who explore the world. Often, the characters in a group have skills that complement one another, such as a warrior (good at combat but unable to use magic) and a wizard (good at magic but fairly useless in battle). These characters progress through combat, becoming more powerful, sometimes growing in number as new members are added to the team. As they kill more enemies, they acquire more wealth, which can be used to acquire new items and abilities. Often, RPGs feature epic storylines, which are frequently delivered through elaborate cinematics. Though many RPGs are set in a world of fantasy, there are also horror RPGs (Parasite Eve™), sci-fi RPGs (Mass Effect™), and so on.

Serious

Serious games are not designed to entertain; these simulations seem gamelike, but are designed to educate the participant, explore real-world concepts in a virtual setting, and/or market a product or service. The subject matter can include topics such as health care, war, religion, politics, or economics. Schools, medical institutions, and branches of the military have all used serious games as training tools.

Shooters

Shooters are just what they sound like: The player must shoot his or her way through levels populated with a large number of enemies. Most early shooters, such as Doom and Quake®, were known for their frantic pace; later games, such as Rainbow Six®, stressed cautious, strategic gameplay. In first-person shooters (FPSs), such as Halo®, we see through the eyes of the protagonist. In third-person shooters (TPSs), such as SOCOM, we see the character on the screen, though sometimes just from the waist up. The TPS features a wide perspective, which makes it easier to judge the distance between the character and obstacles or foes.

Simulations

Simulations allow the player to explore real-world situations, but unlike serious games, they're built purely for entertainment. Valued for their authenticity, simulations permit the gamer to explore fantasy situations such as managing a major league baseball team, winning a high-speed race, or running a huge city. Many of these games are built around the economic challenge of governing or managing complex systems, such as an ant colony (SimAnt™: The Electronic Ant Colony), a theme park (RollerCoaster Tycoon®), or a family (The Sims™). Some of these games veer away from simulating real-world events, such as racing games in a sci-fi setting (Wipeout™).

Strategy

Strategy games are most often built around a clash of armies, whether the setting is modern, futuristic, or fantastic. Typically, the player looks down at a huge battlefield, where troops, weapons, creatures, vehicles, buildings, and/or factories are placed. These resources are managed as the player tries to wipe out the opposing force. Initially, most strategy games were turn-based, like chess—one player moved, then the other, until one side was destroyed. Each player had time to plan his or her actions and make decisions. Real-time strategy games (RTSs), in which both players move simultaneously, have become more popular. In an RTS, the players race against each other to dominate the field, which means that some resources (such as soldiers) will receive more attention than others. This form of triage creates a very tense atmosphere.

Survival Horror

Survival horror games are unique in that the genre is defined primarily by mood, theme, and atmosphere. The developers strive to create a sense of trepidation and shock by limiting the player's resources, using darkness to obscure creatures and objects, and deliberately making it harder to see what's around the corner through the use of fixed camera angles. Though some of these decisions would be judged as poor design in another genre, fans of games like the Resident Evil® series consider these to be attractive elements of survival horror. Lately, titles such as Resident Evil 5 have focused more on action than the tension-building aspects of earlier installments.

The genre affects the design of the game. Here is an example of how the genre shapes the game, using Justice Unit as an example:

Fighting game: If Justice Unit were a two-player fighting game, it might feature a roster of superheroes and villains from which to choose. Selling points could include unlockable characters, combination moves, and possibly a crossover with a licensed property, such as an existing comic book hero.

Real-time strategy: As an RTS, the game would feature an army of superheroes fighting against waves of alien invaders.

Role-playing game: As a first-person RPG, the player takes on the role of a single character, fighting evil in a superhero universe of masked villains and crime fighters.

At some point during the concept phase, the game genre will be defined. The designer might combine several genres, improve on an existing genre, or even try to create a new genre. Also, ideas for the genre can be discussed in the brainstorming session.

7.2.5 Platform

The platform also needs to be considered when defining the game concept. For example, games designed for a cell phone will not feature cutting-edge graphics or technology. Cell phone games are less complex and easy to complete when the player only has a few minutes to spare. A PC game has cutting-edge graphics and a more complex controller scheme, and gameplay requires a much longer time commitment.

When games are released on multiple platforms, consider which game design elements work best with each platform and tailor the design accordingly. With next-generation consoles, players expect a game that caters to their platform of choice rather than playing a game designed for a PC that's been ported to an Xbox 360, and vice versa. Here's an example of how the design for Justice Unit would change for different platforms:

PC: A PC-based version of Justice Unit would feature customizability as a primary feature, enabling the player to create new enemies, maps, and mission types.

Nintendo DS™: As a DS game, Justice Unit would be a simple, easy-to-learn FPS with a layout similar to Metroid Prime®. The player would progress through several levels, fighting bank robbers and super villains.

Xbox 360: As an Xbox 360 game, Justice Unit is an explosive action title featuring fast-paced action sequences and team-based multiplayer. Key selling points include the immersive first-person perspective, dozens of multiplayer modes, and a story-driven single-player campaign.

7.2.6 SWOT Analysis

A SWOT analysis, which stands for *strengths*, *weaknesses*, *opportunities*, and *threats*, identifies the strengths and weaknesses of your game's concept, market opportunities, and any threats that might impact the game's success.

Begin an initial SWOT analysis by identifying a game that is potential competition. It can be a game with a similar genre or comparable gameplay features, a game that appeals to your target audience, or a game based on similar licenses. After you've determined who the competition is, analyze its strengths and weakness. Use this information to compare your game's strengths and weaknesses against the competition's. When you can clearly define your game's strengths and weaknesses, you are able to figure out ways to exploit or neutralize them accordingly. This information contributes to a solid game design and provides the basis for the game's marketing strategy.

Strengths and weaknesses are internal influences that you have some control over. Threats and opportunities identify external influences on the project that are beyond your control. For example, your game might be a launch title for a new platform—a *strength* since you could choose to develop for another platform. This is also an *opportunity* since the console manufacturer will cross-promote your game when marketing the new console platform. Conversely, if you are working on an MMO that doesn't offer any unique features that set it apart from World of Warcraft, that is a *weakness* since you have some control over the game content and feature set. However, if you are working on an MMO that is in a unique setting but it ships the same day that World of Warcraft releases an expansion pack, this is a *threat* since you have no control over the release dates for other games.

Here is a list of topics to start thinking about when doing your SWOT analysis:

Strengths	Weaknesses
• ICore features	• Lack of team experience
• Innovative features	• Lack of competitive features
• Player capabilities	• No innovation
• Unique selling points (USPs)	• Platform choice
• Production values	• Poor company reputation
• Licensing tie-in	• Financial issues
• Price points	• Schedule and deadlines
• Appeal to demographics	• Resource availability
• International appeal	• Lack of team morale
• Potential revenue streams	• Poor leadership
• Marketing tie-ins	
• Franchise tie-ins	
• Console bundle potential	
• Multiplatform potential	
• Team experience	
Opportunities	**Threats**
• Political influences	• Lifestyle or industry trends
• Competitors' strengths	• Technical innovations
• Competitors' release dates	• Market trends
• Waning market demand	• Competitors' weaknesses
• Loss of key staff	• Globalization
• Loss of financial backing	• Target market
• Technical innovations	• Niche target markets
	• Partnerships
	• Middleware trends
	• Release dates

SWOT ANALYSIS			
The primary competition for Justice Unit is PostMortal, a first-person shooter set in a superhero universe.			
INTERNAL FACTORS		**EXTERNAL FACTORS**	
Our Strengths	**How to Exploit**	**Our Opportunities**	**How to Exploit**
Compared to rival PostMortal, Justice Unit features a strong multi-player experience, including a customizable multiplayer avatar, dozens of gameplay types, and several maps.	Emphasize these features in the marketing plan.	Justice Unit will launch at the same time as the movie sequel, which will garner additional attention for the game.	Cross-promote game and movie. Create a separate story for the game that intersects with some plot points in the movie.
Our Weaknesses	**How to Neutralize**	**Our Threats**	**How to Neutralize**
Justice Unit features a free-roaming, nonlinear single-player experience, which will not deliver the same thrills as the linear, heavily scripted PostMortal.	Downplay this feature in the marketing plan and focus on the multiplayer features.	PostMortal is scheduled to release two months before Justice Unit and this may have a negative impact on sales—people may buy the PostMortal superhero game instead of Justice Unit.	Build early buzz about the player's ability to play as his or her favorite character from the Justice Unit. Sponsor an enemy contest, where the winner gets to meet the cast of the movie and get an advance copy of the game.

❙ FIGURE 7.1 SWOT analysis form.

Figure 7.1 is a form that can be used to conduct a SWOT analysis. When doing the analysis, it is equally important to define how you are going to exploit any strengths or opportunities and neutralize any weaknesses or threats. The SWOT analysis will become part of the game plan and is updated throughout production.

The SWOT analysis should be completed during the first few weeks of preproduction so everyone on the team has a full understanding of the competition and challenges, as this will affect the choices for the game's feature set and development strategy. Appoint one person to head up this analysis, such as an associate producer or even the producer. This person needs to get input from the development team and the marketing department.

7.2.7 Competitive Analysis

In addition to a SWOT analysis, you will also want to conduct a full competitive analysis of all current and future competition. This competitive analysis is especially important if you are pitching a game to a publisher. By presenting a competitive analysis as part of your pitch, you demonstrate that you know the market and how you can differentiate your game from the others.

A competitive analysis contains some information that is similar to the SWOT analysis. For example, the competitive analysis will highlight the strengths and weaknesses of the competitor's game. In addition, this analysis will list other pertinent information such as sales figures (if available), average review scores, and any key features that really make it stand apart from other games. All of this information helps give you a better idea of how strong the competition is and what you need to do in order to present your game in the best light. Figure 7.2 is an example of a competitive analysis spreadsheet.

7.2.8 Documentation Standards

Because a lot of documentation is generated during preproduction, developers must employ some type of documentation standards in order to create useful documents that people will read. Through direct presentation of content, good sentence structure, and an appropriate choice of words, developers can create game documents whose meaning is understood immediately. Documents that are structured and legible are far more likely to be read by the development team.

All content must be verified for accuracy, because any misunderstandings will result in additional work for the development team. For example, one segment of the game features a scripted scene where a character climbs a ladder, so an animation artist creates a ladder-climbing sequence for that scene. Later, it may be discovered that the scene begins with the character crouching near a manhole. The ladder climbing actually was supposed to take place off-camera, because there was no time to create a vertical shaft. In this instance, a little more time dedicated to verifying the exact content of that cut-scene would have saved time and effort.

When writing an enemy description, a story synopsis, or a breakdown of missions in a game, the designer should be presenting content with the audience in mind. This means that there is no room for intrusions, observations, or opinions in the document.

Organizing the content of the manuscript effectively will also improve the chances that the developers are actually going to read it. It is important to consider the elements that make a document easy to read: good use of white space, paragraph breaks, and accentuated headings.

7.2.9 Approval

After the basic concept information is defined and a SWOT analysis is conducted, put together a summary document and present it to all interested parties for approval. If the publisher likes the direction you are going, they might make a few minor suggestions and let you continue working. However, if the concept is veering away from what

Game	Developer	Publisher	Platforms	Est. Release Date	Game Summary	Features	Avg. Review	Sales Figures
PostMortal	Funtime Studios	A-1 Publishing	Xbox 360, PS3	Oct-09	PostMortal is a new IP about superheroes. It is a third-person action adventure game and the player assumes the role of Avenger Boy. Other superheroes will be in the game, but the player controls only a single hero throughout the game. The game features traditional costumed superheroes in a 1950s world setting. Avenger Boy will band together with the other heroes to battle Dr. No Good.	• Avenger Boy is the main player character. • New IP that has no cross-over appeal. • Limited multiplayer modes, although it will have a small online co-op campaign. • Traditional third-person action adventure; uniqueness is based on settings and characters. • Each character has one unique super-power they can use against the enemy. They will help in the game if their assistance is requested by the player.	n/a	n/a

FIGURE 7.2 Sample competitive analysis spreadsheet.

the publisher envisioned, they might request major changes and ask you to present to them again. If you are working on a two-year development cycle, plan to schedule this initial approval meeting about two to three weeks after starting preproduction. If working on a six-month project, try to have this meeting about one week after starting preproduction.

Getting approval at this stage is important, as it can save you work. If you continue to define the concept and write up design documents, you might find that your team spent months putting together all this information, only to find that it is not what the publisher or studio management envisioned. And since they are footing the bill for game development, it is best to make sure the team is delivering the type of game they want.

Schedule a meeting for all of the stakeholders and present the information you have so far. Involve other key members of the team in this meeting so they are on hand to answer any questions, and so they can hear the feedback firsthand. Be sure to take accurate notes at the meeting, post them for the team to review, and follow up on any action items.

DESIGN CONSTRAINTS

Clint Hocking, Creative Director
Ubisoft

The best constraint to take into account when creating a concept and initial design is to *not think about features and content*. You need to define what your game is *about*, not how many levels you have or how many guns you have and what their alt-fire is. You need to know what your game is *about* in the broadest strokes, and you need to be able to represent that with some kind of simple system diagram. You don't need to know what it's about in terms of its *story*; you do need to know what it's about in terms of its *systems*. That concept needs to be beautiful and elegant, because it is the foundation of your entire game. When you are confident that your high-level concept is strong, then you can start to think about the mechanics and dynamics that support the high-level concept. Your features and content should then flow naturally out of those mechanics and dynamics. If you do it this way, you should not have problems limiting your content and features to a meaningful set. Ideas are cheap, but harmony among ideas is really hard to achieve. If you start with a random collection of good ideas and try to build a concept from the bottom up, you will not have a harmonious whole. If you start with a vision of the whole and then support it robustly with the systems that it requires, then you probably will not have to worry about limiting yourself for schedule or resources.

On Chaos Theory™ I worked very closely with the marketing manager to understand the needs of the audience and to communicate his vision of the game. There was a definite synthesis of ideas that took place there. The concept of Chaos Theory—of small actions having potentially large repercussions—as well as the Closer Than Ever system in the game and the systems that support them came about through lengthy discussions between design and marketing (and others). They arose from both the need to have expressive, unified, and robust systems, as well as from the need to differentiate the title from the competition and strengthen the franchise and the brand where it was weak. The game's marketing bullet points are concepts like tension, freedom, cinematic quality, and meaningful choices. These come from that initial collaboration between marketing and design. Some people take shots at that idea and say that makes me a marketing-driven designer and that designers who design for the market are simply rehashing the same old proven designs and not bringing anything new. Those people compare the bullet points mentioned previously with the more standard bullet points of "20 different weapons," "three playable races," "five different alien worlds." Design needs to work closely with marketing, if only to make sure that marketing understands what your game is actually about so they can communicate it and help create the need for more meaningful, less-derivative games.

■ 7.3 Defining the Concept

After the stakeholders have approved the initial direction of the concept, your core team continues to define the concept. During this phase, the team starts detailing the specifics about the game mechanics, setting, characters, storyline, and major features. Technical limitations should be loosely considered, but don't censor any ideas on perceived limitations at this point. Instead, focus on creating and prototyping a fun game. When these elements are ready for review, the engineers can fully assess the technical limitations. Although they might not be able to implement what was originally designed, they can take a look at what was intended and come up with some alternative ways to do this within the technical constraints.

During the concept definition phase, the lead designer and lead artist need to produce several deliverables. They will most likely create these deliverables themselves, especially if there are not other resources available. The types of information defined during this phase include the following:

- Mission statement
- Game setting
- Gameplay mechanics

- Story synopsis
- Concept art
- User interface
- Audio elements

On a two-year development cycle, plan to spend about one to two months defining the initial concept. On a six-month cycle, plan to spend about one to two weeks on this.

7.3.1 Mission Statement

The mission statement defines the major goals of the project. James P. Lewis, author of *Project Planning, Scheduling, and Control (2001)*, believes that a mission statement answers these two questions:

- What is going to be done?
- Who is it being done for?

If you can't clearly answer these two questions, it will be difficult to formulate a mission statement that concisely sums up the essence of the game. Good mission statements act as the measuring stick for all the ideas considered for the game. If the idea enhances the mission statement, it is likely a good fit for the game. If the idea goes against any aspect of the mission statement, it should not be in the final version of the game. After a mission statement is defined, publicly post it for the team, studio management, and the publisher.

Involve the core team in a brainstorming session to determine what the mission statement is. Spend a few hours brainstorming and try to finalize the mission statement by the next day. After it is determined, each team member has a better idea of what direction to take for his or her preproduction deliverables.

For example, the mission statement for Justice Unit is:

Justice Unit is a mass-market superhero game with streamlined controls. It is intended for fans of comic books and superheroes who want to experience the larger-than-life adventure of being a hero.

7.3.2 Game Setting

The game setting influences the look and feel of the game, such as the environment, objects, location, character designs, and any other elements that are part of the game universe. The game can have a setting, such as science fiction (Halo), real world (Ghost Recon™ 2), fantasy (Final Fantasy series), or historical (Call of Duty).

The lead designer has some ideas about what settings work well with the initial concept and can work with the lead artist to determine the look and feel of the setting. The lead designer can write up a description of the setting, and the lead artist can create concept art to show what the setting looks like. This might take a few days or weeks to complete, depending on what other assets these team members are generating. The setting might evolve based on other decisions made about the story, characters, and gameplay mechanics.

The setting for Justice Unit is:

The game is set in a classic world of fiendish villains and gun-toting thugs. The player's team consists of oddball heroes with superpowers. In a universe full of straight-faced heroes and villains, the Justice Unit is a group of bizarre misfits with strange powers and wacky personalities. Justice Unit is part parody of and part tribute to the classic superteams of the 1960s, complete with improbable origin stories and larger-than-life villains.

7.3.3 Gameplay Mechanics

Gameplay mechanics encompass many of the actions the player does or experiences in the game. The mechanics make up the bulk of the design documentation as the functionality of the different gameplay systems is detailed. Some of the systems that fall under this category are as follows:

- Challenges for the player (such as end-level bosses and puzzles)
- Player rewards (such as points, extra weapons, and special items)
- Learning curve (How fast can the player learn the basics and start having a fun experience?)
- Control scheme (How will the player use the controller or keyboard?)
- Player actions (such as running, jumping, and casting spells)
- Multiplayer elements

This doesn't list all the necessary gaming systems for any one game, but it is a good starting point for determining which areas of the game need more details. The systems are defined before pitching the game to the publisher.

The lead designer will take point on generating the bulk of the design documentation. He or she works with the other leads and producer to make sure that all the necessary elements are defined and work with the approved concept. At this stage in production, the documents will outline a vision for how each of the gameplay systems might work, without providing minute details. The functionality requirements will be worked out after the overall gameplay mechanics are approved. If working on a two-year development cycle, it might take the lead designer two to four weeks to produce these gameplay documents.

As an example, the multiplayer game mechanics for Justice Unit are:

Justice Unit features two multiplayer modes. In Justification, two teams of up to eight players (16 total) square off against each other in objective-driven battles. In Vindication, up to 16 players can play in every-man-for-himself free-for-all battles.

7.3.4 Story Synopsis

Story is becoming increasingly important in games. Not only do players want compelling gameplay, they are also interested in a compelling story. A good story is the difference between a good game and a great game, because the story helps to further immerse the player in the game world. The details of the story don't need to be fully defined in the concept phase; this is something the writer can work on while the designer finalizes the design documents. However, the synopsis must present a storyline that integrates the game setting, gameplay mechanics, and characters into a cohesive entertainment experience for the player.

The story synopsis for Justice Unit is:

When marketing executive Mark Ferrier was struck by lightning during a presentation, he developed astonishing powers. At first, he kept these to himself, but after witnessing the Justice Unit in a pitched battle with the villainous Wire Hanger, he joined in their defense. The Unit recruited Ferrier, who chose the name BulletPoint. Along with Montezuma, Ice Queen, Major Malfunction, and The Caribou, he fights crime and those who commit it.

7.3.5 Concept Art

As the saying goes, a picture is worth a thousand words. Concept art shows what the visual elements of the game will look like before any art assets are produced for the game. Concept art can be appreciated by anyone, from studio management down to the team, and since everyone is looking at the same thing, it is a useful tool for communicating the game's vision. Any core preproduction team must include a concept artist who can start sketching out some of the team's ideas. The concept artist will work mainly with the lead artist and lead designer on what the characters, levels, and objects look like in the game. There should be a process in place, managed by the lead artist, for the team to give feedback. Concept art can take several weeks to produce, depending on how much needs to be generated and how detailed it is.

7.3.6 User Interface

The player interacts with the game world through the user interface (UI), which consists of on-screen elements. The UI allows the player to glean information about the game world and the status of his or her character(s). If well designed, the UI can make it much easier to play a game because the player will be able to rapidly assess the situation and respond accordingly. A poorly designed UI makes it harder for the player to figure out what needs to be done or what resources are available; this can frustrate the player and ruin a good game.

The UI should be fairly simple, requiring a minimum number of keystrokes or button presses. It should display pertinent information at a glance, alert the player of significant threats or condition changes (such as impending character death), provide

CONCEPT ART

Carey Chico, Art Director
Pandemic Studios

In the past, game development teams were not very big, and technology was a limiting factor to creating realistic-looking game worlds. Now that teams have gotten larger, and we can create huge, believable worlds, game developers have taken on a concept art paradigm that's derivative of the film industry—we concept out all the assets before creating them for the game.

The main reasons concept art is important and will become more important when creating assets for next-generation technology are as follows:

- It helps the artistic vision to be carried all the way through to the final assets that appear in the game.

- The artists can work and rework assets on paper, when the cost is much lower, and then only create the actual assets when everyone agrees on what will appear in the game.

- Outsourcing art assets will become more common as the volume of assets needed for next-generation titles increases, so clearly defined concept art will ensure that the assets look consistent with the game, no matter where they are created.

feedback for actions taken (like displaying a diminishing number of bullets in a gun), and remain consistent throughout the game.

7.3.7 Audio Elements

Audio is a critical part of the game, as it helps immerse the player into the game world. Think about the Silent Hill® series of games—would they be as creepy if you played with the sound and music turned down? The lead designer might want to work with a sound designer for a few days to come up with an initial plan for voiceover, sound effects, and music. The sound designer can advise on which audio elements work best with the proposed setting, story, and gameplay mechanics.

The audio overview answers questions such as the following:

- Will each character have a unique voice?

- How do the characters' voice cues function in the game (for example, help for the player, comic relief, or character development)?

- What types of music work best with the game (such as licensed heavy metal songs, an original orchestral score, or instrumental techno music)?

- Where in the game will the music play (for example, only in the UI shell or real time in gameplay during climatic battles)?
- What types of sound effects will work best in the game?

■ 7.4 Game Programming Basics

One of the key things that sets games apart from other types of software applications is the game loop. The game loop is responsible for managing the game world, regardless of whether the user has provided input. For example, the game loop will update the enemy movement in the game, check for victory–loss conditions, and update the game elements throughout the game world, even if the user has not provided input. The complexity of the game depends on the technology: Simple Flash®-based games may feature a simplistic game loop where the game tracks the input, updates the game elements, and then checks for victory–loss conditions. More complex games will feature collision detection, interaction with nonplayer characters (NPCs), multiple players, and real-time graphics rendering, among other things.

C++ is one of the more popular languages used in game development, along with Java and C. Lua and Python are also used, although they are not as popular. Some prominent engine developers have created custom languages for games based on their engines, such as Epic Games' UnrealScript™ for the Unreal® Engine.

There are also numerous APIs and libraries to choose from that will take care of key programming tasks in the game, such as AI pathfinding, graphics rendering, and sound processing. The choice of which ones to use is based on the target game platform. Some libraries allow for cross-platform development, which streamlines the development pipeline.

■ 7.5 Prototyping

Prototyping is a key component of game development, especially during the preproduction phase. Prototyping allows the team several opportunities to validate new gameplay features and anything else that is not well-defined (such as a tools pipeline). In game development, a prototype is an early and playable version of a proposed game mechanic or idea. The prototype does not necessarily have to be playable in digital form; in some cases, gameplay can be prototyped with existing board games, a deck of cards, or a pencil and paper mock-up; these are usually referred to as "low-fidelity" prototypes. These types of prototypes may not always contain playable and dynamic elements. Eventually, "high-fidelity" prototypes will be created. These are usually software based and provide both a dynamic and working model of the proposed system and a better representation of the gameplay experience. However, you can identify and solve many potential issues in low-fidelity prototypes before proceeding to a high-fidelity one.

There are several goals that can be accomplished during prototyping. Exploratory prototypes are used to investigate new ideas, identify requirements, or research alternatives. Experimental prototypes are used to validate system requirements (such as what weapon statistics work best to balance the weapons in the game). These two types of prototypes are likely to generate work that is discarded along the way, but this shouldn't be viewed as a waste of time or money. While much of this prototyped work may not be used, the lessons learned about the strengths and weaknesses of the concepts are worth the effort. Prototyping may also lead to other ideas that are implemented in the final version of the game. If there is some reluctance to spend time on work that will be discarded, operational prototypes can be used. These consist of an initial prototype that is refined in iterations until it becomes a final working version that ships in the game.

Other things to consider before beginning work on a prototype (especially a software one) are the primary objectives and the target audience. For example, a prototype that demonstrates a vertical slice of gameplay entails implementing elements that provide a representative sample of the final gameplay experience. This includes key gameplay mechanics with proper play balancing, polished art assets (including UI, key character models, and a playable level), representative audio assets, and key demonstrations of technology innovations (such as physics-based gameplay). A vertical prototype is strongly recommended when shopping a game to a publisher.

Will the prototype be focused on a specific feature and viewed only by members of the development team? For example, is the lead engineer working on a prototype of the new animation system in order to work out kinks in the engineering and art pipeline? This type of prototype does not need the same level of detail and polish, can be put together with placeholder assets, and can contain functional issues that can be addressed later.

While the prototyping process can be roughly categorized into phases, these phases may not have a distinct beginning and end, especially during iteration. The process normally begins by defining what is being prototyped. Next, a low-fidelity prototype is created based on these initial requirements. The team will iterate on this prototype. Iteration involves a cycle of specifying the requirements, designing something that meets these requirements, evaluating the results, and starting the cycle over again. There could be several iterations on a single prototype; the number is likely dependent on how much time there is in the schedule.

Once the team is satisfied with the results, they may decide that the feature or idea is not feasible and discard the prototype, or they may find a new idea they want to prototype instead, or they may decide to move forward to the next phase of creating a high-fidelity prototype. This prototype will also go through some iterations until the team is happy with the results. Once this happens, the prototype specifications are frozen and a final version is built on these specifications.

Prototyping can occur at any phase in the development cycle, and the team should plan to prototype as much as possible. Tight schedules and deadlines may prohibit much prototyping toward the end of the production phase, so plan to take advantage of the unscheduled blocks of time that occur in preproduction. It is better to spend a day or two (or even a week) prototyping key features of the game than to spend several weeks implementing a feature that ends up not working as expected in the game. If this happens, there is little time left in the development schedule to tweak or redo the feature, and the game may end up shipping with the feature as is. It is common to work on multiple prototypes at once—some prototypes may be more complicated (such as a vertical game slice), while others may be simpler. Don't hold back from prototyping something, especially if there is time in the schedule. The prototyping phase is ongoing during preproduction and is headed up by the lead designer or possibly the producer.

CREATING PROTOTYPES

Tracy Fullerton, Assistant Professor
University of Southern California

One of the most important things a game prototype gives you is the ability to understand the player's experience immediately. A prototype also makes an idea tangible and, therefore, creates something that is much easier for team members to speak about and work on from their own perspective. People tend to butt their heads together most when they are speaking in the abstract, so you will see designers and programmers butting heads. They might actually be saying the same thing, but because they don't have a prototype or something concrete to reference, they don't even realize it.

I am a strong believer in paper prototyping and don't like students to write up any game specifications until they have some form of prototype. From the moment you come up with an idea, you can begin to model the core mechanics and the underlying structures. Those early paper models—and you might have to build two or three to understand all the systems—will be used to build digital prototypes. After these are created, people can start defining specs.

Truly innovative design comes from asking wild and impertinent questions and spending small amounts of time and money on proving whether these questions will provide interesting and provocative answers. Paper prototyping is something a dedicated designer can do on his or her own time. A designer can usually complete a prototype, enlist play testers, and make changes, all in a short amount of time. It's a fantastic experimental method for asking these kinds of interesting questions. For example, right now I am working on a game where the central question we're trying to understand is "How can you make a game about the journey of spiritual enlightenment?"

It is very important that the technology team be a part of the creative team, but it is equally important that technology doesn't drive the experience design. This means the designers have to understand and respect the technical limits of the platform with which they are working, but creatively they don't have to live within those limits the same way that technologists do. Designers need to understand the technical limitations well enough to work around them or to use them as a springboard for some type of creative twist that doesn't restrict the game but actually makes the game better. One of the best ways to do this is to have the technologists play the paper prototypes. Again, when the idea is tangible, people can talk about it, and out of the discussion comes the true essence of what the designer was trying to do with that feature or technique. This means the technologists don't have to just blindly implement the feature; they are actually part of the process of discovering what the feature is really about. Being part of the process makes it easier for the technologists to implement the essence of the feature.

■ 7.6   Risk Analysis

Risk assessment is an ongoing process, and the producer must be constantly aware of what the biggest risks are for the game, even after production begins. Doing an initial risk assessment in preproduction that involves all the project stakeholders is a good way to identify and start preparing for risks.

Risks are things that *could* go wrong on a project, such as a key team member leaving mid-project, not getting the graphics pipeline completed in time to begin production, or an external vendor missing his or her final deliverable date. When the risks are identified, prioritize them and plan mitigation strategies. Keep in mind that all risks are not equal. Although some risks might have a higher probability of occurring, the impact may not be as severe as a risk that has a low probability of occurring.

Steve McConnell's book *Rapid Development (1996)* contains an excellent chapter on risk management and is recommended reading for anyone who wants to learn more about this. As he points out in his book, a project utilizing risk management is not as exciting to work on because there is little need for people to run around putting out fires. Instead, everyone can focus on getting the game done because risks have already been identified and planned for in the schedule.

His approach is divided into two parts: risk assessment and risk control. During risk assessment, the core team needs to do the following:

- Identify risks that could impact the project.
- Analyze each risk's likelihood of occurring and the impact it could have on the project.
- Prioritize each risk beginning with the ones with the most impact.

There are numerous potential risks on any given game that can affect the ship date, the quality of work, the scope of features, and the cost. When doing the risk assessment, brainstorm as many risks as possible and then prioritize them accordingly. Your biggest risks are the ones that have a high probability of occurring and will have the biggest impact on the project. Figure 7.3 is a basic classification grid for four levels of risk. More risk levels can be added as appropriate for your project. Risks that fall into categories 1 and 2 are considered critical risks and must have solutions in place to manage them if they occur.

The second part of McConnell's risk management strategy involves risk control. After the risks are identified and prioritized, the team needs to do the following:

- Create a management plan for neutralizing or removing the most critical risks. Make sure the plans for each risk are consistent with the overall project plan.
- Implement the proposed plans to resolve the risks.
- Monitor the progress toward resolving the known risks.

In addition, any new risks must be identified and controlled throughout development by using the same process of risk assessment and risk control discussed previously.

Risk management is the responsibility of everyone on the team, although the producer should spearhead the effort to identify risks and solutions. The initial in-depth

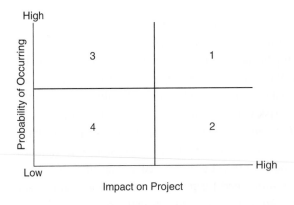

FIGURE 7.3 Risk classification grid.

IDENTIFYING RISKS

Stuart Roch, Executive Producer
Activision

If I can get onto a project early enough, I'm a big fan of proactively identifying any game features or new technology that pose a scheduling risk. After I've identified these particular risks, I set lifeboat milestones to launch if things start running behind schedule. The idea is to have your plan A and plan B worked out ahead of time so you don't have to scramble and make reactive decisions if things go wrong. After you identify your at-risk features and set your plan B milestones, it's important to follow up regularly to help the at-risk features along and identify the warning signs if things aren't going as planned. If handled correctly, this method will help keep the risky features on everyone's radar, thus maximizing their chances of success and in a worst-case scenario reducing the impact of the feature cuts if the original goals aren't met.

risk assessment meeting should happen after some of the major game elements have been defined. This way, there is a better idea of which elements are risky. Spend one day defining the risks with the team and one or two days creating a risks resolution plan, and then publish this plan to the team. Figure 7.4 is an example of a risk analysis spreadsheet.

■ 7.7 Pitch Idea

After the concept documents, prototypes, and risk analysis are complete, the producer schedules a pitch meeting with the publisher and studio management. Be prepared to present all aspects of the game to them, including the risk analysis. The project leads should attend as well, so they can answer any questions within their areas of expertise.

The pitch meeting might last two to three hours. Plan an agenda and include a break in the middle so that people have a chance to take a break and refresh themselves (you don't want people falling asleep in the meeting). Make sure that all presenters are enthusiastic about the game and can communicate this enthusiasm to the meeting attendees. People who are poor public speakers should not be presenting in the pitch meeting. Make sure that someone is taking notes during the meeting so that all the feedback is accounted for.

Risk	Probability of Occurring	Impact on Project	Risk Classification	Mitigation Strategies
Licensor who owns Justice Unit IP may not deliver feedback and approvals in a timely fashion. If they don't approve content of gold master, console sub-mission process will be delayed, which may impact the ship date.	HIGH	HIGH	1	• Schedule kickoff meeting with licensor early in preproduction to review the project goals and schedule constraints. • Work out defined approval process that both parties agree to. • Deliver game assets on a regular basis in preproduction to get feedback and approval before production begins. • Once playable builds are available, deliver builds on a regular basis for licensor to review. • If possible, include caveat in contract that if they don't respond with written feedback in 10 days, the item will be considered approved. • Establish good working relationship with licensor contact and try to include them in the development process whenever possible; make them feel like they are part of the team and have ownership in the game.
Design might be able to create a workable gameplay system where the superhero powers are balanced equally against each other.	LOW	HIGH	2	• Focus on prototyping the core superhero powers for each character to limit the number of variables that must be balanced. • Work with engineering to get a digital prototype up and running as quickly as possible. • Create a system that allows variables to be easily changed and tested in gameplay. • Continue brainstorming ideas for superpowers until the core features are proto-typed and approved.
During the two-year development cycle, some employees may leave the company.	HIGH	LOW	3	• Train at least two people to handle specific tasks on the project. • Schedule time for hiring and training new people mid-project. • Focus on creating a positive working environment to increase employee retention. • Be aware of any sudden changes in employees' work habits so you can identify at-risk people and improve their job satisfaction before they start looking elsewhere. • Require everyone to document the work they are doing and to check all assets into source control system at the end of each day.
Initial game concept art may not accurately depict what the Justice Unit characters will look like in the game.	LOW	LOW	4	• Concept art will be based on character design bible provided by the licensor. • Feedback from licensor can be quickly implemented until they are satisfied with the concept drawings. • Make sure the artists get all available character concept art from the movie.

FIGURE 7.4 Risk analysis spreadsheet.

After the presentation, the publisher and studio management might love exactly what you've shown them and will give you the green light to continue with those ideas in preproduction. It is more that likely that they will have feedback on certain elements of the game and will want this feedback incorporated before they greenlight your project for the next phase of preproduction. Either situation is a positive outcome for all the hard work the team has done so far. In extreme cases, they might decide to shelve the project or ask you to go back and reconceptualize it. If this happens, be sure that you understand exactly what they didn't like about the pitch and what areas need major changes.

■ 7.8 Project Kickoff

When the idea is approved by all the stakeholders, schedule a formal project kickoff. The kickoff is a great team-building exercise because it provides an opportunity for all the team members to come together and talk about the project. It is also a great way to welcome any new team members who might be added at this phase in development. Consider having a team lunch or a group outing as part of the kickoff, so that people can also casually socialize with each other and get to know their teammates.

Additionally, if you are working on a console title, you will need to submit this initial concept to the console manufacturer for approval. They might request changes to the concept as well. If they reject the concept entirely, you might be able to revamp it and resubmit for approval. However, there is a small chance they could reject the concept and not allow you to resubmit a revised concept, but this does not normally happen.

■ 7.9 Concept Outline

Figure 7.5 is a summary of each step that must be completed in the concept phase. This is based on a two-year development cycle.

■ 7.10 Chapter Summary

The importance of the concept phase in preproduction cannot be overstated. This concept is the foundation the game is built on, and if the concept is weak or is not fully defined before beginning the next phase, there might be major elements missing from the game that are not discovered until the team is well into production. This chapter discussed some of the major areas that must be defined and approved by the project stakeholders before preproduction continues. These areas include the initial concept, gameplay mechanics, setting, characters, and audio elements. Information was also

Initial Concept	Resources	General Timeline	Est. Start	Est. End	Tasks
Brainstorming	Producer runs sessions, team participates	1 week	1-Oct-07	5-Oct-07	Brainstorm initial concepts for game, including genre and platform.
Initial Concept	Lead designer	1 week	8-Oct-07	12-Oct-07	Review brainstorming notes. Define initial concept, genre, and platform. Incorporate feedback from team.
Competitive Analysis	Producer, marketing	2 weeks	15-Oct-07	26-Oct-07	Review current and potential competition, complete SWOT analysis based on initial concept.
Approve Initial Concept	Producer runs meeting, leads attend	2–3 days (2–3 weeks after preproduction begins)	29-Oct-07	31-Oct-07	Present initial concept, with genre and platform, for approval. Initial competitive analysis completed. Incorporate management feedback.
Define Concept	**Resources**	**General Timeline**	**Est. Start**	**Est. End**	**Tasks**
Mission Statement	Producer runs sessions, team participates	1–2 days	1-Nov-07	2-Nov-07	Define mission statement for the game.
Game Setting	Lead designer, lead artist	3–5 days	5-Nov-07	9-Nov-07	Define game setting, including look and feel.
Gameplay Mechanics	Lead designer	2–4 weeks	12-Nov-07	6-Dec-07	Create general overview of how major game elements will function: challenges, rewards, learning curve, control scheme, audio elements, multiplayer.
Story Synopsis	Lead designer, writer	3–5 days	10-Dec-07	14-Dec-07	Create game's backstory, character biographies, and general outline of how the story unfolds in the game.
Concept Art	Lead artist, concept artist	3–5 weeks	12-Nov-07	7-Dec-07	Create concept art for game setting, characters, and objects.
Audio Elements	Lead designer, sound designer	2–4 days	17-Dec-07	21-Dec-07	Create general overview of how voiceover, sound effects, and music will be presented in the game.
Prototyping	Lead designer, producer	4–6 weeks	12-Nov-07	21-Dec-07	Prototype major game elements.
Risk Analysis	Producer runs sessions, team participates	2–3 days	19-Dec-07	21-Dec-07	Assess risks on project, determine resolution strategy, and publish to the team.
Pitch Idea	Producer, leads	2–3 days (2–3 months after approval of initial concept)	2-Jan-08	4-Jan-08	Present all major gameplay elements to management for approval and incorporate their feedback.
Project Kickoff	Producer	1 day after management approves pitch	7-Jan-08	8-Jan-08	Meet with team to celebrate the concept approval. If working on console title, submit game concept to console manfacturer for approval.

FIGURE 7.5　Outline of concept phase.

presented on prototyping and risk analysis, which are an integral part of the process as well.

After the concept is firmly established, the characters, setting, and story need to be fleshed out. The next chapter discusses dialogue.

■ 7.11 Questions and Exercises

1. What are some common complaints about the brainstorming process? How do you conduct a successful brainstorming session?

2. What are the key phases of the concept phase? What is the main purpose of each one?

3. How do you define and categorize risks on a project?

4. What are the goals of prototyping? What types of prototypes can be created?

5. What are the differences between a SWOT analysis and a competitive analysis? What is the main purpose of each one?

6. Think of a game concept and do a competitive analysis for it.

7. Do a SWOT analysis for a fictional game.

8. Do a risk analysis for a fictional game.

8 Characters, Setting, and Story

In this chapter:

- Story Development
- Gameplay
- Characters
- Setting
- Dialogue
- Cinematics
- Story Documentation

■ 8.1 Introduction

The development of a game's story can be the work of a single developer or a team. Writers, story designers, narrative designers, creative directors, lead designers, and game designers can all contribute to the process, as can producers, project leads, quality assurance testers, marketing coordinators, studio managers, and those affiliated with the game's publisher. As a consequence, it can be difficult to describe the process of story design, as it varies from company to company. For the sake of brevity, we'll use the term "writer" when describing a developer who works on story content.

■ 8.2 Story Development

During preproduction, the writer creates the concept for the game's story. This can precede or follow the design of the gameplay. In some cases, the game will be designed and levels will be built before the story designer is even brought on board the project. Other times, the game will begin with a story outline, and characters and events will be determined before game design begins.

Regardless, the writer must consider several factors during the concept development stage. He or she will need to deal with brand management, publisher input, game design, fan base, and licensing.

A cursory examination of game store shelves will reveal that the majority of published games are either sequels, remakes, spinoffs, or adaptations. Given that the typical game is in some way linked to other media (a previous game, a movie, or a comic book), it's important that the writer make sure that his or her game maintains a consistent tone with predecessors. He or she will need to research major themes, events, characters, and tropes, so that his or her game doesn't deviate from the other installments. Sometimes, of course, deviating is a good thing; Resident Evil® 4 established a new direction for the series, leaving behind Raccoon City, STARS, zombies, Umbrella Corporation, and the fixed third-person camera angles. The game was also a huge hit, so it's possible to successfully forge a new direction; but it still behooves the writer to do the necessary homework before writing dialogue or story documents.

The publisher is responsible for the distribution and marketing of the game, and may also be financing the project. The golden rule applies: The one with the gold makes the rules. Many games are heavily influenced by publisher input, and it's good for the writer to understand this going in. Members of the publishing team may request rewrites or changes from the development team.

■ 8.3 Gameplay

As a general rule, the story doesn't influence the gameplay; it's usually the other way around. The writer may be a part of the design team or a contractor brought in to work on a project for a few months, but either way, he or she will probably spend a great deal of time working with the game's designers. Once the design team has established the parameters of core gameplay, the writer can begin to contextualize content by creating story documents, integrating the narrative into the gameplay experience.

For example, the design team may have settled on a single-player character with a pair of sidekicks who provide information and resources. This decision has created a set of parameters that the writer can now work with—one hero and two supporting characters. The three of them might converse during cinematics or during briefing sequences, allowing the writer a place to include expository dialogue and character development at the same time.

It's also likely that the level design of a game will impact the story design significantly. If the game is a linear shooter, the writer might be able to construct a narrative that places scripted dialogue at key moments, knowing that the player will have to pass through Section 1 before reaching Sections 2 and 3. On the other hand, if the game is a nonlinear role-playing game, the writer will have to find another way to deliver the story to the player because there will be no way to predict the order in which the player will visit various parts of the game world.

■ 8.4 Characters

Much like people in real life, there are two levels to the characters in a video game: We know them based on the actions they take and the things they say. On a game development team, there are typically two different groups of people working on these two aspects of character identity.

Designers and artists work on the scope of the character's actions. Designers write the documents that outline the various actions that a character can take (run, jump, move, shoot, blow up terrorist base, rescue princess), and artists create the animation sequences that make these actions possible. In some games, the actions are relatively limited (you run, you jump, you shoot); in others, there are myriad choices (such as in Morrowind®, where you can run, jump, fly, buy and sell clothing, go on a religious pilgrimage, become a noble and build your own stronghold, master the art of potion making, save the kingdom, or assassinate good people for money).

Another aspect of character action is the computer-controlled allied character, sometimes referred to as the AI (artificial intelligence) teammate. Programmers and designers work together to create AI teammates; the designers document the desired behavior, and the programmers create the code. If you've ever played a game in which you commanded a squad of computer-controlled allies, then you know how important it is that they respond swiftly and precisely. If the AI is subpar, then the character's actions will probably disappoint and annoy the player, resulting in irritation, and no amount of smooth animations or clever dialogue will make the character useful.

Writers and designers work on the scope of the character's words. The choice of words, along with the delivery of the voice actors, can tell us a lot about who these characters are, what they feel, and what they believe. Lines of dialogue don't just deliver information and exposition; they also convey the character's attitude toward circumstances, and they reveal the way that he or she relates to other characters.

It's possible to write good dialogue for a character who doesn't respond the way the player wants (due to bad design or sloppy animations), resulting in frustration on the player's part. It's also possible to write bad dialogue for a well-designed character, which can also be frustating, though often is more easily forgiven.

Once the game is released, actions are shared by the developers and the players. For example, the developers show the character taking action during cinematic sequences, and developers can frame the player's actions, restricting the types of behavior that are possible (you can't kneecap people while playing Super Mario Bros.®, and you can't hug prostitutes in Grand Theft Auto IV™). Players take it from there, using the resources available to further define what a character does (and, by extension, what he or she is). The more freedom the developer affords the player, the more ownership the player has over the character's actions.

The result of these words and actions is a reaction of some kind on the part of the player. The character's actions and words may transform him or her into someone that the player likes or despises; he or she might elicit humor or irritation; or the player might identify him or her as cool, obnoxious, or clichéd.

When character development is executed properly, something human is found within the character. He or she becomes more than an archetype, or a stereotype; he or she becomes more alive somehow. The game's protagonist doesn't need to be heroic, but he or she must be well-defined if you wish to elicit emotion.

Then there is the question of established identity. As a developer, it's important to determine, from the beginning, what kind of identity is being created. Is the character a well-defined persona, like Lara Croft from the Tomb Raider™ series? Or is the character easily recognizable but mute, like the cipher from Grand Theft Auto III™? Perhaps the character is a blank slate, like the protagonist of Oblivion®, whose race, gender, and profession can be chosen by the player.

The development team must now figure out how to convey this persona. Will the character's identity be reflected in his or her appearance? For example, will the butt-kicking hero appear as a large soldier in an imposing suit of armor, like Master Chief from the Halo® series? Or will he or she be a bespectacled scientist wielding high-tech weaponry, like Gordon Freeman from the Half-Life® series?

Voice and interaction can also convey a great deal about a character. Domasi "Tommy" Tawodi, the hero of Prey™, is sarcastic, irritable, and impatient; shortly after the game begins, he argues with his grandfather about living on the reservation, then tries to pressure his girlfriend into leaving town with him, and subsequently gets into a bar fight with two men. We can tell a lot about him from his words and interactions. However, over time, Tommy matures, risking his life in an attempt to rescue others and defeat the extraterrestrial menace.

There numerous other techniques that can be used to further define individual characters:

- Mannerisms: How does your character behave when angry or surprised or confused?

- Turns of phrase: What unique sayings or catchphrases does the character employ?

- Opinions: How does the character feel about the situation, or others, or himself or herself?

- Role: Who is the character in this game: the hero, the mentor, the ally, the villain, the victim?

Relationships can also define characters for the player. Choose two of the main characters in your game. How do they feel about one another? How does their interaction reflect this relationship? How do their words and actions support this relationship?

In many books and movies, characters evolve over time. This isn't always the case in games. In fact, many characters start and end in the same place, even across multiple games in a series. Events may transpire, and the character's situation may change, but he or she remains the same, responding in the same way, sequel after sequel.

If the character is to evolve, it must be in a believable manner. Tommy, the aforementioned hero of Prey, watches as someone close to him is brutally murdered and his girlfriend's life is placed in jeopardy. Worse, the entire world is threatened by an unbelievably powerful force. Tommy's transformation from ill-tempered brawler to heroic champion is rendered more credible by the events that force him to change. His identity is well established early on, but the reasons for his evolution are compelling, so we can accept his change.

Ultimately, the more effort the developers put into establishing and fleshing out the characters, the more immersive the game.

■ 8.5 Setting

The setting encompasses the entirety of the game world, even the parts that aren't visible on-screen. This can include a game's geography, religion, politics, culture, races, languages, technology, and magic. In a game that's set in the real world, fleshing out these elements isn't necessary; there's no point in coming up with a new history for the United States when it already exists, so the developer simply needs to research the material. However, if the setting is imaginary, such as a far-future dystopia or a medieval fantasy, then the setting needs to be fleshed out thoroughly.

A well-envisioned and meticulously detailed world helps the player to maintain the suspension of disbelief, resulting in a more immersive experience. This has the added benefit of helping the developers as well; once the game world is fully defined, it's easier to create storylines, missions, quests, and goals, as well as characters, creatures, organizations, and obstacles. All of these elements will be more grounded in a virtual world, and will therefore be more consistent.

For example, BioShock™ combines a nostalgic art deco style, the Objectivist philosophy of Ayn Rand, the notion of a failed utopia, and the eerie visuals of a city at the bottom of the sea to create a unique and fully realized setting.

■ 8.6 Dialogue

Writers give their characters personality through their choice of words. When writing a game, it's important to ask yourself what your written words reveal about a character. Could another character say these words?

Often, less is more; long-winded chatter and extended scenes can cut into gameplay, interrupt action sequences, or lengthen cinematics to the point of tedium. To combat this problem, it's always a good idea to read scripts out loud, particularly in a group, to see how the dialogue actually sounds when it's not just words on a page.

Variety is invaluable. If characters begin to repeat themselves, particularly when giving instructions to the player, it can become extremely aggravating. Whether a character needs to repeat a command, warning, observation, or question, it's essential that the writer come up with several variants and alternates so that the player doesn't hear the same word or phrase again and again. This variation also helps to maintain the immersion (because the player isn't constantly reminded that it's just a game).

■ 8.7 Cinematics

Cinematics are noninteractive sequences that can be entertaining, informative, dramatic, or suspenseful. Prerendered cinematics are rendered and animated by a team of artists and tend to have graphics far superior to that found in-game. By contrast, scripted cinematics are typically created using a scripting editor and have graphics that are more or less the same as gameplay.

Before creating a cinematic, it's important to outline the goals. Why is the player watching? Is the sequence intended to elicit a mood, such as apprehension, surprise, amusement, or awe? Or is it designed to inform the player about the world and its characters? Is the cinematic intended to show off some stunning visuals or perhaps some pyrotechnics?

Whatever the case, once the concept for each cinematic has been determined, it's time to write the screenplay. In some cases, this is preceded by storyboarding, but typically storyboarding follows the screenplay.

Once the screenplay has been written, reviewed, and revised, it should be recorded. Since this is just a placeholder, there's no point in paying for voice actors, voice directors, and sound studio personnel, so the dialogue should be performed in-house, by game developers (who, ideally, will audition and be selected), local students, or some other inexpensive source.

After the placeholder dialogue has been recorded, it's time to integrate it into the flipbook animatic.

The flipbook animatic begins with storyboards. These are still images, sketched by a concept artist, that communicate action and motion from one scene to the next. Arrows may show the movement of characters or objects, or changes in the position of the camera (such as zooming in). Storyboards can be captioned with notes and lines of dialogue, which can help when evaluating the flow of a cinematic sequence.

When the storyboards are finished and the script is ready, a flipbook animatic can be constructed. The flipbook animatic is a sort of slideshow in which a developer creates a video consisting of storyboards, shown in sequence, with music or voice acting dubbed in. These can be created with any movie-making software, such as Adobe® Premiere® or Windows Movie Maker™.

The flipbook animatic is a rudimentary rough draft of the cinematic, but it serves various purposes. It gives the development team an idea of how the cinematic will feel when images are matched up to sound, music, and voice; it can help to contextualize the action more effectively than words on a page or a verbal description; and it allows the developers to estimate the length of the cinematic.

Once the flipbook animatic is reviewed, it's likely that many problems will be found, requiring another round of rewrites and more placeholder dialogue. After this process has been repeated enough times, the developers can move on to the creation of the rough animatic.

The rough animatic is a video file that serves as a second draft for the cinematic. It conveys the basic camera angles and movements of characters, objects, and vehicles; typically, it uses objects like blocks, spheres, and mannequinlike stick figures to indicate locations and movement. Once this blocking phase has been completed, the artists can add more detail to each subsequent iteration until the cinematic is complete.

■ 8.8 Story Documentation

A game's dialogue is more than just words on a page. It's a design document, and its format needs to reflect the development process. By understanding the way that a game is produced, you can ensure that the dialogue is structured in a way that makes it useful instead of something that slows down the workflow.

The classic movie script format isn't really useful for video games. This passive format (passive because the audience doesn't participate in the action) doesn't address the interactivity of games, and it's formatted for a different kind of production. Movie scripts feature wide margins, lots of white space, the Courier New font, and frequent use of all caps—this makes it easier to locate content in a hurry while filming, and it facilitates the addition of notes or the revision of dialogue on the fly. Games aren't made the same way, so the format isn't useful at all. Furthermore, all that white space adds up to the Hollywood rule of thumb regarding script length, which is that one page of script equals one minute of film time; if applied to games, this means that a 10-hour shooter would require 600 pages of dialogue. Hard to carry that script around in your backpack, don't you think? Besides, scrolling through hundreds of pages while searching for one line of dialogue can be extremely tedious (and rest assured, dialogue will need to be revised over and over again; if the first draft is deemed a success and recorded immediately, then something has gone wrong, and the game's story will not be well received).

When developing a format for your dialogue, consider your various audiences: designers, producers, audio personnel, voice actors, and scripters. Any format used for the documentation of dialogue should take all of these developers into consideration.

Designers will have some degree of input over the story and dialogue; furthermore, throughout the development process, parts of the game will doubtless change, including level design and character rosters, which will impact the dialogue.

Producers manage schedules and budgets. The better a writer's documentation, the easier it is for the producer to glean important data, such as total line count, total text-on-screen, or total lines of dialogue for a specific character.

Audio personnel, including sound designers, sound directors, and sound programmers, work with the game's audio component, and are thus closely linked to the work of the writer. The writer should be aware of the game's parameters with regard to voice acting (How many actors?), special effects (Will there be radio futz?), and prototyping (When should the script be ready for placeholder recording?).

Voice actors (and directors) transform lines on a page into the spoken word; by considering the way they work, the writer can make their job easier. Dialogue should be accompanied by notes that explain how the character feels, what the character is going through, where the action is taking place, and what kinds of effects will be added to the dialogue.

Scripters place voice cues in the game by means of a scripting editor. While the writer may not be a part of that integration process, he or she should understand how the process works.

Once all of these elements have been studied by the writer, a format can be created that addresses all of the above concerns. Typically, a spreadsheet is ideal for the documentation of dialogue. For example, programs like Excel® and OpenOffice.org Calc™ allow the writer to arrange text alongside various fields that contextualize the dialogue. The spreadsheet should include the name of the character, the name of the actor, the line of dialogue being spoken, the context (such as "in the middle of a firefight" or "telling a dirty joke"), the inflection (such as "loud and angry" or "muttering quietly"), the location where the dialogue is being spoken, any applicable effects (such as echo or radio futz), and the file name for the audio file.

If the writer and the other developers working on the story are familiar with all of the moving parts, they'll be more likely to create an emotional, story-driven game. Anticipating problems before they arise will allow the team to deliver a more polished experience.

■ 8.9 Chapter Summary

Story, setting, and characters are a key way to make a game stand apart from other games. There are many things to consider when developing these elements, including genre, target audience, technology, and budget. You need to develop a game world that makes sense for the game being made and for the people who will play the game. Currently, there is no standard set of guidelines for creating the story, setting, and characters, but this chapter outlined some basics on how to approach this creative process.

After the concept, chapters, and setting are firmly established, the next phase of preproduction, determining the game requirements, begins. The next chapter discusses the deliverables that are generated during this phase, such as core feature set, milestones, and design documentation.

■ 8.10 Questions and Exercises

1. When working with an existing IP, what does the writer need to research in order to make sure the game is consistent with the elements already established in the IP?

2. What does the writer need to consider when creating a game character?

3. How can relationships with other characters impact the player's character?

4. What types of elements need to be considered when developing a game setting?

5. Why doesn't a classic movie script format work well for documenting a game's story?

9 Game Requirements

In this chapter:

- Define Game Features
- Define Milestones and Deliverables
- Evaluate Technology
- Define Tools and Pipeline
- Documentation
- Approval
- Game Requirements Outline

■ 9.1 Introduction

When the initial concept deliverables are completed and approved, the team needs to determine the game's requirements. The requirements detail how the concept will be turned into a real game. Decisions are made about the main project goals, the core feature set, and the milestone deliverables. In addition, the core technology and production pipeline must be established. Finally, all documentation needs to be written and finalized. After these items are completed, you will have a clear idea of what needs to be done to create the game. These items are then used to further determine the budgeting, scheduling, and staffing needs for the game.

■ 9.2 Define Game Features

During preproduction, everyone has an idea about what cool features can be included in the game. Obviously, you can't include every single feature request: Some won't fit with the game's vision; the team won't have enough time to get everything in; or the technology cannot support the functionality. Therefore, you need to prioritize the features into different tiers for implementation. For example, tier one features are the core features of the game; tier two features add value to the core features; and tier three designates features that would be nice to include. Ideally, all the tier one features are included, and you might find time to add many (or all) of the tier two features. Usually, the tier three features are considered for the next version of the project and will not make it into the final game.

To begin, involve the team in a brainstorming session about what features should be included in the game. Conduct these sessions over the course of two to three days. Brainstorm about multiplayer features, single-player features, gameplay mechanics, sound, and any other aspects of the game. Gather all the feature ideas in a single list and then categorize them by type. Doing this will help the producer and leads to better prioritize the features. Some categories to consider are as follows:

Process: These features revolve around improving the development processes. This includes improving the formats of the design documentation, establishing an approval process for multiplayer levels, and setting up mini-tutorials to teach people how to use the development tools.

Production: These features involve improvements to the tools and technology used to make the game. Examples include adding cut-and-paste functionality to the scripting tool, improving how destructible objects function in the game, and adding enhanced lighting functionality to the art tools.

Gameplay: These features consist of gameplay elements that will directly impact the player's experience and be visible to the player. This includes the ability of the player to control vehicles, functionality for changing options on-the-fly, and the ability of the player to customize his or her avatar.

You could also create categories around specific gameplay elements, or by discipline, or any other grouping that will help you get a better handle on the types of features being requested. Figure 9.1 is an example of what this categorized master feature list looks like.

After this list is generated and categorized, the producer sends the list to the leads and asks them to each assign a priority to every feature on the list. The leads should base their priorities on the known project constraints. For example, if the game is a *time to market* game, the final code release deadline is the main constraint, and all of the core features must be doable within the limited time on the project. If the game is a sequel to a best-selling franchise, the constraint is to create a game that lives up to its predecessor, so more time might be added to the schedule to ensure that the game has all the key features.

The leads also need to consider the overall art, engineering, design, and testing concerns when assigning priorities. For example, the lead artist might be tempted to assign the highest priority to all the art feature requests and a lower priority to all the design feature requests. However, if the lead artist does not fairly consider the overall game needs, the game might end up with stunning graphics but so-so gameplay.

Category	Feature
Gameplay	Dynamic missions objectives.
Process	Mission review process should also include multiplayer levels.
Process	Establish a system for circulating design documents and updates to documents to the team.
Gameplay	Easy-to-understand user interface.
Gameplay	Replayable missions.
Production	Improve physics so explosions look more realistic.
Gameplay	Ability for player to customize character appearance.
Production	Support cut-and-paste functionality in scripting tool.

| FIGURE 9.1   Categorized master feature list.

Experienced leads will know how to strike a balance among the art, design, engineering, and gameplay needs on a project.

After each lead has assigned a ranking to the features (with 3 being highest priority and 1 being lowest priority), collect all of the data and add it to the master feature list. Include a column for each person's rankings and make the last column an average of the rankings. After calculating the average ranking, use this value to sort the entire list. Figure 9.2 is an example of what the feature ranking spreadsheet will look like after sorting it by the average ranking.

After this is completed, schedule a meeting with the leads to discuss the results. This meeting might last a few hours, as you will need to go through each feature, assess its overall ranking, and finalize whether it is a "must have," "like to have," or "nice to have" feature. Even though everyone might not be in 100-percent agreement about the rank for each feature on the list, this exercise provides a good way to garner consensus on the features that are most important for the game. When the meeting is over, publish the final ranked feature list to the team. This feature list will provide the basis for defining the milestones and deliverables.

■ 9.3   Define Milestones and Deliverables

After the core features are determined, the producer can put together initial documentation on the milestones and deliverables. Milestones mark a major event during game development and are used to track the project's progress. They provide the team smaller, more manageable goals to work toward and can be easily defined by listing what deliverables are expected for each milestone.

Category	Feature	Prod.	Art	Design	Eng.	QA	Average
Gameplay	Dynamic mission objectives.	3	3	3	3	3	3
Process	Establish a system for circulating design documents and updates to documents to the team.	3	3	3	3	3	3
Gameplay	Easy-to-understand user interface.	3	3	3	3	3	3
Process	Mission review process should also include multiplayer levels.	3	3	3	2	3	2.8
Production	Improve physics so explosions look more realistic.	2	3	1	3	1	2
Gameplay	Replayable missions.	2	2	2	1	2	1.8
Gameplay	Ability for player to customize character appearance.	1	2	3	1	1	1.6
Production	Support cut-and-paste functionality in scripting tool.	1	1	3	1	1	1.4

Rankings:

3 = MUST HAVE

2 = LIKE TO HAVE

1 = NICE TO HAVE

FIGURE 9.2   Feature ranking spreadsheet sorted by average ranking.

FEATURE CREEP

Clint Hocking, Creative Director
Ubisoft

Part of the problem is that features are not discrete. Basically, any new feature could be called an improvement or a bug fix for an existing feature, so there can be no rigid definition of when the rule has been broken. My feeling is that if you design correctly, this should not be a problem. If you start with a concept for the entire game and then you specify the mechanics and dynamics that support that concept, you won't be in a feature hunt. You won't be looking to copy random sexy features from other games because your game won't be a random collection of features; it will be a unified whole. That's pretty idealized, and there's no way any game development is going to work like that, but it's a good place to start. Limit your scope to what is *meaningful* under the creative concept of the game. Anything outside that (even if it's awesome) is feature creep.

Each development team will have a different set of milestones to mark the game's progress. Some teams establish monthly milestones, and other teams work toward bigger milestones every few months. When working on a two-year development cycle, a common set of milestones is as follows:

First playable: This is the first major milestone for the game. It contains representative gameplay and assets. Often, it is based on the prototype that was created in preproduction. This milestone is usually scheduled to occur 12 to 18 months before code release.

Alpha: At this milestone, key gameplay functionality is implemented, assets are 40 to 50 percent final (the rest are placeholders), the game runs on the correct hardware platform in debug mode, and there is enough working that you can start to get a feel for the game. Features might undergo major adjustments at this point, based on play-testing results and other feedback. Alpha occurs 8 to 10 months before code release.

Code freeze: At this point, the game is code complete, and the engineers are only fixing bugs from this point forward. No additional features are added so that the code has time to stabilize and the critical bugs can be identified and fixed. This milestone happens about three to four months before code release.

Beta: By beta, the game is code and asset complete. Art, design, and engineering only focus on fixing bugs that are listed in the bug database. No new assets are generated, no new features are coded, and no changes are made to existing features and functionality unless it is identified as a bug. Beta occurs about two to three months before code release.

Code release candidate: At this milestone, all the bugs have been addressed and the developers are confident that the build is ready to be shipped or submitted to the console manufacturer for approval. The code release candidate is tested against the QA test plan, and any crash bugs or other critical issues are fixed as necessary. The team is not actively making any fixes. The first code release candidate should be ready for QA testing about three to four weeks before the code release date. Figure 9.3 is a table with more details about each of these development milestones.

After you have determined which milestones to include in the production schedule, define in as much detail as possible what the expected deliverables are for each one. Doing this is important so that there is a clear way for the team to determine whether the milestone is completed. If nothing is defined, how will the team know whether the milestone is completed? This list is also useful for the QA department, since they know exactly what parts of the game need to be checked for functionality. These lists are also a great way to track the game's progress to ensure that nothing important is omitted.

A simple way to define the milestones is to establish a list of deliverables for each one. These lists can be started in preproduction and updated as information about the game is defined. Include information about what is completed and ready for testing on each aspect of the game. If an asset or feature is not 100-percent complete, state what should be completed and viewable in the game for each milestone delivery, as some items are so large they might span several milestones before they are fully complete. Use categories such as the following:

- Characters, objects, levels
- Cinematics
- Gameplay features
- Engineering features
- UI
- Sound
- Localization
- Scripting
- General

You might not be able to fill in all of the information at the beginning of the project, as there are many decisions still to be made, but fill in what you can. After the initial lists are established, send them to the leads for review so they can check that the

	First Playable	Alpha	Code Freeze	Beta	Code Release	Third-Party Submission—CONSOLE ONLY
Time Frame	12–18 months before code release	8–10 months before code release	3–4 months before code release	2–3 months before code release	First code release candidate available to QA 3 weeks before final code release deadline.	Submit code release candidate at least 8–12 weeks before desired ship date.
Engineering	Basic functionality for a few key features are in to demonstrate very basic gameplay.	Key gameplay functionality is in for all game features. Features work as designed, but may be adjusted and changed based on feedback. Game runs on target hardware platform.	Code complete for all features. Only bug fixing from this point forward. No new features are added, unless approved by senior management.	Code complete; only bug fixing from this point forward.	Full code freeze. During this phase, only crash bugs can be fixed. Critical bugs can be fixed with approval.	Code final. If submission is rejected, only specific bugs as requested by the third party will be fixed for resubmission.
Art	Two to three key art assets are created and viewable in the build. The assets demonstrate the look and feel of the final version of the game.	Assets are 40–50% final, with placeholder assets for the rest of the game.	Assets are 80–90% final, with placeholder assets for the rest of the game.	All art assets are final and working in game. Only major bug fixes from this point forward.	Full art freeze. No art fixes, unless it is to fix a crash bug.	Art final. If submission is rejected, only specific bugs as requested by the third party will be fixed for resubmission.
Design	Basic features are defined, key gameplay mechanics have basic documentation, and there is a playable prototype if possible.	All design documentation is completed. Feature implementation is in progress. 40–50% of design production tasks are completed. Major areas of game are playable as designed.	Game is 80–90% playable. Play-testing feedback is being incorporated.	All design assets are final and working in the game. Only major bug fixes from this point forward. Minor gameplay tweaks can be done, based on play-test feedback.	Full design freeze. No design fixes, unless it is to fix a crash bug.	Design final. If submission is rejected, only specific bugs as requested by the third party will be fixed for resubmission.

| FIGURE 9.3 Common development milestones.

	First Playable	Alpha	Code Freeze	Beta	Code Release	Third-Party Submission– CONSOLE ONLY
Sound	The sound of the game is determined, including voiceover, music, sound effects. Samples are available to communicate the sound vision of the game.	40–50% of sound effects are in and working. Voiceover design is in progress, placeholder VO files are recorded. Music in process of being composed.	Final voiceover is recorded and in game. Final music is in game. Sound effects are 80–90% implemented.	All final sound assets are in and working in the game.	Full sound freeze.	Sound final. If submission is rejected, only specific bugs as requested by the third party will be fixed for resubmission.
Localization	Work with publisher to determine which languages are needed. Select localization vendor and send them design documents and first playable. Define localization pipeline.	Work with vendor to determine asset delivery schedule. Send glossaries, cheat codes, walk-throughs to vendor. Test localization pipeline to ensure translations are displayed correctly.	Final text and VO assets are sent for translation. Translations are completed and returned to developer for integration.	Final language assets are integrated into the game. Linguistic testing is complete. Send builds to appropriate age rating boards to secure final rating.	Full localization freeze.	Localization final. If submission is rejected, only specific bugs as requested by the third party will be fixed for resubmission.
Production	Basic game requirements and game plan are completed.	Full production has begun. The game requirements and game plan are fully completed and approved. If working with licenses, all licenses are secured and an approval process is in place.	Localizations have started. Manual is in process of being written. Marketing assets are being generated.	Localizations are complete; only bug fixes from this point forward. Manual is complete. External vendors are finished with work. All approvals for licenses are secured. Development team can start rolling off project.	All production tasks are completed. If submitting game to console manufacturer, the submission forms are filled in and ready to go.	Production final. Only managing submission process.
QA	Can test game against the first playable milestone deliverables defined in the game requirements phase.	Game is now playable as a full game, although there are some rough edges and holes in some of the functionality. Play-testing can begin. Can test against the alpha deliverables expected for this milestone.	Test plan is 100% complete. Full game functionality can be tested and debugged. Play-testing continues. Can test against the code freeze milestone deliverable list.	All aspects of game can be fully tested and debugged. Some play-testing continues in order for design to put the final polish on the game.	Test code release candidates for any crash bugs that will prevent the game from shipping.	Testing continues on submission candidate(s) until game receives final approval.

FIGURE 9.3 (Continued).

goals for each milestone are attainable. Publish these lists to the team so they clearly understand the expectations for each milestone. Also, get into the habit of checking the lists for updates on a regular basis. However, don't make changes to a set of milestone deliverables that are due in a few days; that is, don't add things to the alpha deliverable list one week before the milestone is due. Figure 9.4 is an example of a partial deliverable list for the Justice Unit alpha milestone.

■ 9.4 Evaluate Technology

During the game requirements phase, the lead engineer is evaluating the technology needs of the project. Decisions must be made on the game engine, art tools, scripting tools, AI systems, physics systems, and other technical elements that are needed to provide the desired game functionality. The technology used will depend on the schedule, the resources, the desired features, and the quality of these features. For example, if the main goal of the game is to have cutting-edge graphics, the lead engineer will spend some time evaluating what graphics technology is necessary.

The lead engineer must also research how this technology will be obtained: Will it be coded by in-house engineers, or will an existing software package be licensed and modified for use in the game? There are pros and cons to each choice, although larger games will probably use a combination of in-house technology and licensed technology.

The benefits of creating the technology in-house are that it is owned by the studio and, therefore, has no licensing fee; in-house experts are readily available to fix bugs and add feature enhancements; and the technology can be specifically tailored to the game. One drawback is that the engineers have to spend valuable development time reinventing the wheel for basic technical functionality (such as physics, AI, and animation), meaning that they have less time to focus on game-specific functionality. Also, using a team of in-house engineers to code basic functionality, such as a physics system, might be more expensive in the long run rather than licensing a middleware solution, such as one of the products by Havok™.

The main benefit of licensing an existing technology is that it provides a basic framework for common technologies, meaning the engineers can focus on game-specific functionality. The drawbacks can be costs (especially if the budget is small), limited technical support from the vendor, and the need to alter the code to fit the game's functionality. However, these drawbacks might be worth the trouble if licensing saves time and/or money during the development process.

After the lead engineer has researched the available technologies, he or she will make a recommendation to the producer. The producer can use this information when creating the budget and schedule and will work closely with the lead engineer to determine the best technology solutions for the game.

JUSTICE UNIT

Alpha Deliverable for March 30, 2007

Last Updated February 10, 2007

Levels

- The following levels are asset complete, with gameplay scripting:
  - Justice Hall
  - Villain's Lair
- The following levels have basic geometry and are viewable in-game, but have no gameplay scripted:
  - City Hall
  - Office Complex

Characters

- The following characters are asset complete:
  - BulletPoint
  - Montezuma
- The following characters are viewable in-game, but don't have final textures:
  - Caribou

UI

- UI color scheme and font are final and approved
- UI flow is prototyped in Flash®
- Basic UI screens are implemented and functioning:
  - Start screen
  - Profile screen
  - Options screen
- In-game UI has placeholder art with basic functionality for:
  - Health bar
  - Inventory

Sound

- Placeholder VO cues and sound designs are implemented for the following levels:
  - Justice Hall
  - Villain's Lair
- Sound designs completed for remaining levels in the game

Engineering

- Scripting tools completed and functioning
- Art tools completed and functioning
- Networking APIs are implemented
- Build process finalized and in place

FIGURE 9.4   Partial alpha deliverable list for Justice Unit.

■ 9.5 Define Tools and Pipeline

In addition to evaluating which technologies will be used for the game, the lead engineer will work with the other leads to define the production pipeline. The production pipeline refers to the series of steps needed to get code and assets working in a playable version of the game. It must smoothly incorporate the tools, assets, and production needs of the game. It is very rare that an asset can be created and be instantly usable in the game; the asset might need to be converted to a specific file format or compiled into the code. The game is not instantly playable with the new updates and assets; the engineers have to compile the code and build a new executable first. Key things to consider when defining the pipeline are the following:

What tools and software are needed? Software tools are needed to convert the file formats, and source control software must be used to check assets in and out of the build. Decisions must also be made on which compilers and coding languages are used.

Can the pipeline support two-way functionality? The pipeline should support functionality both for assets to be converted for game use and for game assets to be converted back into their original source assets. This allows asset changes to be made more readily.

What is the critical path? Are there any bottlenecks? Make sure that no one person has a disproportionate amount of work in the pipeline and becomes a bottleneck for getting assets converted. Also, limit the number of steps in the pipeline; assets should be viewable and playable in a build as quickly as possible.

When does the system need to be fully functioning? In order to create a playable build of the game with the correct assets, the pipeline must be functioning. Partial functionality is usable for a few months, as long as it does not prevent people from creating assets and seeing them in the game.

How are assets managed and tracked in the system? Decide which source control software to use to ensure that people check out assets before working on them. Everything should be kept under version control to prevent multiple versions of a file from causing confusion in the pipeline.

Which areas of the system can be automated? Automate as much of the pipeline as possible in order to reduce time and human error.

After these questions are answered, the leads can determine which pipeline will best work for the game. *The Game Asset Pipeline (2004)* by Ben Carter is an excellent resource for more details about setting up a production pipeline. For example, the production pipeline for Justice Unit requires the artists to create their character models in 3ds Max®, convert them to a proprietary file format, and check them into the build.

The build is set up so the artist can copy over the model to a build of the game on his or her personal development kit and instantly see how it looks in the game. However, in order for the character model to be fully viewable in an official build, the engineers must create a new build and publish it to the team.

CREATING THE PIPELINE

Carey Chico, Art Director
Pandemic Studios

One of the necessities of game development is a solid tools strategy. You must have a core group of engineers who are dedicated to tools programming on your team. They can enhance the proprietary tools that are part of your pipeline by upgrading features, fixing bugs, and adding new features based on the game development needs.

This is important because much of what we battle during game development is tools not working or being too slow. Because efficient game production depends on creating assets quickly, the developers are constantly thinking of ways to use tools to speed up the asset production pipeline—especially if the same type of asset is being created over and over. The longer it takes an artist to get an asset from source art to an asset that can be seen in-game, the less they want to deal with the process and the lower the quality.

The art director and technical director can work together to create an efficient production pipeline for the art assets. There are several things to consider when defining how the pipeline should work. For one thing, make sure that the pipeline is not bottlenecked by a single component in the process. For example, if the process is heavily dependent on 3ds Max, the pipeline is front-loaded for art, and everyone will have to go through an artist to see something working in the game. All pertinent people on the team must be able to access, manipulate, modify, and change the content in the game simultaneously or equally. This spreads development risk and provides multiple pipelines to complete the job.

Make sure that the number of steps in the pipeline are as few and bug free as possible. Don't have nontechnical artists doing lots of technical things in the pipeline in order to get their assets working in the game. The artists are likely to make mistakes and will need to go back and redo the assets. This slows them down. The pipeline should be focused on speeding up the development environment.

Make sure that the data going through the pipeline is manageable in a fast and efficient way. If the pipeline begins with a nodule of data that has information added to it as it progresses in the pipeline, figure out how mistakes can be corrected along the way instead of having to start the process from scratch. It also helps to limit the tools used in the pipeline. For instance, don't mix 3ds Max and Maya®; pick one. Additionally, keep the number of data conversions to a minimum.

Another key thing is a two-way pipeline. Anyone should be able to easily convert from one set of data to another. For example, if an artist needs to create a cinematic of two people walking around in a scene, he or she exports all the necessary art assets into After Effects®, creates the scene, and then reexports this back into the game.

Finally, automate communication of when steps are completed in the pipeline. It might seem very simple to remember to tell the person waiting on your data that you are finished with it and he or she can start working on it. However, communication will break down because people are not effective at maintaining it. People get busy and completely forget that someone else is waiting to be told the asset is ready. Therefore, the more ways this communication can be automated, the more efficient the pipeline is. If an artist checks something into Visual SourceSafe®, an email can automatically be sent to the appropriate person that states what was completed.

■ 9.6 Documentation

As preproduction comes to a close, documentation must be completed for all major elements of the game. This includes art, design, and technical documentation. If the documentation is not clearly written or doesn't provide the desired information to the target audience, people might not read it. If this happens on your project, it is your responsibility as the producer to work with the documentation writers to create something that is useful for the team. If the team is not reading the documents because of some other reason—they don't have time or they think they already understand how a feature works—you need to set aside a time for everyone to meet and read through the documentation together.

Each development team will have a different format for design, art, and technical documentation. The key is to have a format that is easy to read and provides clear information about how the game works. There are several books on game design that discuss how to format design documents in detail. These same lessons can be carried over to art and technical documents. *Game Design Workshop: Designing, Prototyping, and Playtesting Games (2004)* by Tracy Fullerton, Christopher Swain, and Steven Hoffman is a good resource to consult about writing effective documentation.

Consider having different document formats for different audiences. The documentation needed by the development team must include all the details of each gameplay feature. The idea is that any member of the development team can consult the documentation for clear directions on how a feature is supposed to work in the game. The design documentation is the definitive resource for any game design questions, so if a feature design changes, update the documentation to reflect this. Documentation for studio management should focus on the overall gameplay mechanics, key features, and how these fit together to provide the overall gameplay experience to the player.

Even if the feature has a working prototype, some type of documentation is needed as a written record of how the feature works. For one thing, not everyone will have access to the prototype or be able to get it working correctly; if there is documentation, they can read through it to understand how the feature works. Additionally, the QA department usually uses design documentation when writing the test plan. For example, if an artist creates a working prototype of the game's shell and does not document the functionality, it will be difficult for QA to write an accurate test plan to check that all the buttons, boxes, and screens are working correctly in the game. You cannot expect QA to load up the UI prototype on a computer and then play through the game and compare the actual game UI screens with the screens in the prototype. This creates additional work for them, work that they don't really have time for; they might miss a large chunk of functionality if they forget to click on a button.

9.6.1 Design

The design documentation details how all the features will function in the game and includes the following:

- UI
- Multiplayer
- Character backgrounds and dialogue
- Scoring
- Mission designs
- Control scheme
- Player actions
- Storyline
- AI
- Weapons, special objects, power-ups
- Voice recognition

The documents need to provide enough detail that an engineer, artist, QA tester, or another designer can read them and understand how to implement the feature as

WRITING DESIGN DOCUMENTS

Clint Hocking, Creative Director
Ubisoft

The best practice for writing useful design documents is to keep them short, precise, and technical—like this sentence. Additionally, all design documentation should follow the exact same standards and formats. This should be rigidly enforced. There is a time and place for your artists and designers to be creative—within documentation is *not* one of those places. You have a cover page, a table of contents, and three double-spaced pages—every page beyond that halves the number of people who will read the document. If people are not reading documentation, a producer or associate should first enforce document formatting to make sure that the documents are short, precise, and technical. If they are, and documents are still not being read, they should gather people together into meeting rooms and read the documents out loud to them. They will learn to read them on their own very quickly. Finally, as far as getting people to understand what's in a document—if it is short, precise, and technical, and it has been read, then the designer and the implementer need to communicate. Simple as that.

designed. After the feature is implemented according to the specs in the documentation, it can be play-tested and adjusted as necessary. The documentation must be updated with any changes, as it is the central written resource for the game design.

It is useful to create a comprehensive list of all the documentation and prototypes that must be generated for the game. This list can be used as the basis for the design tasks for the production schedule. Refer to Chapter 10, "Game Plan," for more information on creating a schedule.

9.6.2 Art

Art documentation is also necessary during preproduction. The types of art documentation created by the lead artist and/or art director are as follows:

- Style guide
- Asset list
- Tools instructions

The style guide details the look and feel of the universe, objects, and characters in the game. It includes concept art, color palettes, and other visual examples of what the finished game will look like.

The asset list is a comprehensive list of every art asset that must be created for the game. This includes character models, levels, cinematics, textures, and any other visual elements in the game. As with features, prioritizing the art assets into three tiers ensures that the most critical art assets are completed first, and then additional assets are added as time allows. The art asset list can also be used as the basis for the art production schedule.

Tools instructions are technical documents that provide information on how to use the art tools in the production pipeline, such as the lighting tool, the level-building tool, or the cinematics conversion tool. This documentation should be written in conjunction with the engineers who are programming the tools.

CREATING ART DOCUMENTATION

Carey Chico, Art Director
Pandemic Studios

Preproduction is a time when *everyone* can discuss the game design and artistic vision and make compromises; many ideas can be explored and considered for concept art and prototyping. There are also several art tasks that must be completed before full asset production can begin. The core art team should comprise an art director, concept artist, and asset artist. The goal is for the art director to envision what the game will look like and then have the concept and asset artists create different sets of assets to support the vision. From these assets, the final look and feel can be determined, and work can begin on the art bible.

The art bible details concept art and other references for the art assets in the game. It demonstrates to the team and the publisher what the game is going to look like. While the art bible is being created, art assets can be prototyped, added to the engine, and viewed in the game. This process allows the art director to get a clear idea of what works and what doesn't work in the game. A large part of creating this bible is research; if the game is set in World War II, the art team will want to research locations, weapons, uniforms, and anything else that will evoke that time period.

The art director works closely with the lead designer to determine how to develop the art direction around the story content. The story content will have a direct effect on what the art director's final artistic vision of the game will be.

Also during preproduction, the art director works with the lead engineer on what features are needed for the art asset production pipeline. This includes making decisions on what shaders will be used, what the polygon limits are, what types of environments the engine will support, and so on.

9.6.3 Technical

Technical documentation is written by the lead engineer and discusses things such as the following:

- Coding standards
- Technical design
- Tools instructions

Documentation on the coding standards includes specifics on coding conventions, hardware and software specifications, naming conventions, technologies used (including middleware), file types, data layout, and any other technical information that is necessary for developing the game. The documentation should also provide an overview of what all the functions and data do and how they interact with each other.

Technical design documentation is the counterpart to design documentation. The engineers will read through the design documents and provide technical information on how the features will be coded for the game. This documentation is disseminated to the appropriate engineers on the team for implementation.

Tools instructions provide information on how to use the tools. For example, an engineer and designer will work together to document how the scripting tools work. These tools instructions must be updated when any changes are made to the tool functionality; otherwise, the documentation will quickly become unhelpful and even obsolete.

CREATING TECHNICAL DOCUMENTATION

Tobi Saulnier, CEO
1st Playable Production

Part of the lead engineer's responsibility on a project is to put together a technical design document (TDD) that describes the software systems that are needed to produce the game, for both existing systems and systems that need to be developed. They are usually working on this document in parallel with the game design document (GDD) being written by designers.

A detailed GDD is extremely useful for the engineers when they start working on the TDD, as it assists them in identifying the list of in-game features and the needs of the art and design pipelines required to develop those assets and integrate them into the game. If some areas are missing from the GDD, this can cause problems for engineering, resulting in either an important feature not being included in the upfront software planning or the engineers not fully understanding how a feature is expected to work. For example, if one of the bosses (the enemy at the end of a level or mission) does not have a detailed description of his or her expected behavior, the engineers will not know how much time to plan for implementing his or her AI, or the boss once implemented will not behave as the designer envisioned.

Detailed examples and mock-ups should be included in all documentation, as words alone often can't fully define what the desired functionality is. Use of references from other games is extremely helpful, especially for complex concepts like camera behavior and art style. For example, if you are describing how the camera will move in the game, include reference examples of the desired and undesired camera movements. It is also useful to mock up a reference movie of how the character will move through the game world.

A final note is that the TDD should be user-friendly, which in this case means easily reviewed by art and design, not just other software engineers. Writing the GDD and TDD is usually an iterative process, which means the information from each affects the other. For instance, the memory planning in the TDD will impact things like the number of levels or the number of unique AI. Having all disciplines involved in reviewing each document will help catch anything that is forgotten and more quickly sync up the game design with the technical restrictions.

■ 9.7   Approval

After the game requirements are defined, present them to the stakeholders for approval. As with the concept phase, the stakeholders might have feedback they want implemented before they sign off on the requirements.

You don't need to wait for all the requirements to be defined before seeking approval. Instead, schedule regular meetings to present completed required deliverables for approval. This allows you to stagger the deliverables. If there is feedback to include, you can take a few days to implement it and then resubmit it for approval. This keeps the process going during preproduction, and bottlenecks are not created in the process while waiting for management approval.

■ 9.8   Game Requirements Outline

Figure 9.5 is a summary of each step that must be completed in the game requirements phase. This is based on a two-year development cycle.

■ 9.9   Chapter Summary

On a two-year development cycle, the game requirements phase will take about two to three months to complete. However, this phase will not have a hard start and end date;

Step	Resources	General Timeline	Tasks
Define game features	Lead designer	1–2 weeks	Core features are defined. Secondary and tertiary features also defined.
Define milestone deliverables	Producer	Ongoing. Each milestone deliverable list completed about 4 weeks before the official milestone delivery.	Define the main project milestones and the deliverables that are needed for each milestone. Rough milestone estimates based on desired ship date.
Evaluate technology	Lead engineer	4–6 weeks	Evaluate the technology needs for the game and make a recommendation.
Define tools and pipeline	Lead engineer works with other leads	2–3 weeks	Define the production pipeline that will produce a playable build with updated assets.
Create concept art	Lead artist	2–3 weeks	Generate concept for key characters and settings in the game.
Design documentation	Lead designer	6–8 weeks	Document the key features in the game, including prototypes where possible.
Art documentation	Lead artist	6–8 weeks	Document the artistic look and feel of the game, generate asset lists, and write up instructions on how to use the art tools.
Technical documentation	Lead engineer	4–6 weeks	Document the coding standards, technical design, and tools instructions for the game.
Risk analysis	Producer	Ongoing during requirements phase	Assess risks on project, determine resolution strategy, publish to the team.
Approval	Studio management, publisher	2–3 months after requirements phase begins	Present all major gameplay elements to management for approval and incorporate their feedback.

FIGURE 9.5 Outline of game requirements phase.

you might need to design an additional feature during production, revamp the pipeline, or start production on some aspects of the game while completing preproduction on other aspects.

The goal of the game requirements phase is to more fully flesh out the design, art, and technical needs of the game. This includes writing the documentation; making decisions about the tools, pipeline, and milestone deliverables; and conducting a risk analysis. All of this information will be used to create the game plan in which all of these tasks are scheduled and a budget is created. The next chapter presents details on what tasks to complete during the game plan phase.

■ 9.10   Questions and Exercises

1. What types of features will be defined during the game requirements phase? Discuss what each type contains.

2. What are the key milestones during a game development cycle? How are they defined?

3. What is the production pipeline and what are some key elements that are necessary for a successful production pipeline?

4. What types of art, design, and technical documentation are written during the game requirements phase?

5. Conduct a brainstorming session for potential features for a fictitious game. Include representatives from art, engineering, design, QA, and production. Once the session has concluded, create a ranked feature list that has everyone's input.

6. Write up a sample alpha deliverable list for a fictitious game.

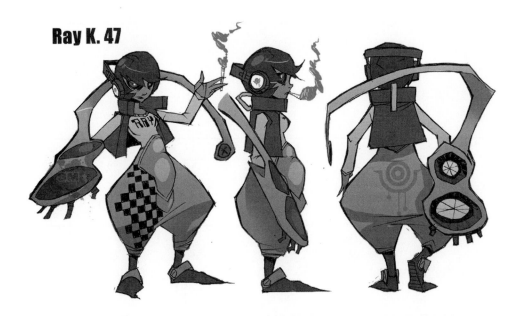

Ray K. 47

10 Game Plan

In this chapter:

- Dependencies
- Schedules
- Budgets
- Staffing
- Outsourcing
- Middleware

■ 10.1 Introduction

After the game requirements are determined, the game plan is created. The game plan defines the following:

- What work must be done
- What order the work is done in
- Who will do the work
- When the work must be completed

All the information generated during the requirements phase is needed in order to make an accurate game plan. There are many useful project management books that provide detailed information on creating project plans. Most of these techniques are applicable to game development, although some modifications might be necessary. *Project Planning, Scheduling, and Control* (2001) by James P. Lewis is recommended reading, as it provides practical and easy-to-understand information about creating project plans and managing projects.

Keep in mind that the game requirements might change after the initial game plan is completed. For example, the plan might show that the game will be too expensive to make, and thus some of the requirements will need to be adjusted to lower the cost. After the initial game plan is completed, expect to make changes to it during production. In order to create a solid game plan, it is important to understand the dependencies of the schedule, budget, and staffing plan.

■ 10.2 Dependencies

If the budget, schedule, and staffing needs are not planned during preproduction, you cannot manage these elements efficiently during the development process. In some cases, the feature set of the game might need to change in order to accommodate a change in schedule, such as a request by the publisher to accelerate the release date. Therefore, factoring in the allotted time (schedule), the available staff and budget (resources), the feature set of the game (features), and the quality that is expected (quality), such as next-generation graphics, is extremely important when putting together your game plan.

Figure 10.1 illustrates this dependency between the schedule, resources, features, and quality. If one of these factors changes, it will affect the other three factors. If all of these factors are constantly changing during the development cycle, the project is never stable and is always at risk. One of the producer's biggest challenges while managing the game development process is striking a balance between the schedule, resources, features, and quality. As stated throughout this book, all development teams are different and never have exactly the same processes in place or risks to mitigate, but the producer's ultimate goal is still releasing a quality game on time and on (or under) budget. If the producer carefully controls the balance among the schedule, budget, and staffing, there is a much higher chance this goal can be achieved.

When working on schedules, budgets, and staffing plans, you must keep these dependencies in mind at all times so that your game plan is accurate. The schedule is a good starting point because a lot of information is generated during preproduction that can easily translate into a robust schedule.

FIGURE 10.1   Dependencies among schedule, resources, and features.

■ 10.3   Schedules

A schedule lists each task to be completed, estimates of the task duration, who is doing the task, and what tasks are dependent on the given tasks. Consider using some type of scheduling software, as this makes tracking the tasks easier. Scheduling software enables the user to plug in new tasks and dates to see how changes affect the overall schedule. Microsoft® Project is a popular scheduling software that is useful in creating detailed schedules. Even if dates and deliverables shift, the schedule's basic task list will essentially stay the same unless the feature is cut from the game. For example, the level-building section of the schedule outlines each task needed to build a level. It might include creating a concept, prototyping, building basic geometry, creating textures, polishing the assets, and bug fixing. The important thing to note is that even though dates may change, the same tasks need to be completed.

Game development schedules can be extremely frustrating to create and track. For one thing, feature creep runs rampant in game development, which makes it difficult to create an initial schedule and use it throughout the game development process. On a two-year development cycle, feature creep has a huge impact; people will see a feature functioning in the game and figure there is plenty of time to change or add functionality to make it better. It is helpful to schedule small milestones along the way so you can keep better control of the features being implemented and additional feature requests.

When creating the game development schedule, there might be a tendency to become overwhelmed by the thought of scheduling six months' to two years' worth of work at the beginning of the project. How can anyone know all of the tasks that need to be done? Don't let this prevent you from creating a useful schedule as early in the development process as possible: Even if the schedule changes, which it will, it is much better to have an initial baseline schedule of the estimated work than to have nothing to compare against the actual schedule changes. For example, if there is no schedule and the publisher tells you the game has to ship three months earlier, how will you know which tasks need to be cut from the schedule or how many people need to be added to the team to accomplish this goal?

Involve the entire team in creating the schedule. Generally, if people are just told to complete all their work by a specific deadline, with no explanation on how this date was determined or why this date is important to the project, they are less likely to take the date seriously. Because they don't have full knowledge of what the impact is when they miss their deadlines, they might treat the due date as more of a guideline than a deadline. When this happens, the schedule can quickly get out of control.

If the team is involved in creating the schedule, they have more ownership over their tasks and treat the deadlines more seriously. Also, each person best understands how much work he or she can accomplish in a day and can better inform you how long it will take to complete each of the assigned tasks. Team members are also able to point out areas where critical tasks are missing and identify high-, medium-, and low-risk areas on the schedule.

10.3.1 Creating a Schedule

Creating a schedule will take some time, especially during preproduction when many game elements are not final. The producer can expect to spend several days or even weeks putting together a complete schedule and will continue to update it throughout production. Although time-consuming, a schedule is not too difficult to put together as long as you stay focused on the actual tasks to be completed. Avoid creating a schedule based on what you *think* needs to be done rather than what *actually* needs to be done.

One way to properly determine which tasks to complete is to determine exit criteria. Exit criteria are a predefined set of conditions that must be fulfilled before a task is deemed completed. Exit criteria mainly consist of tangible assets that are easily defined. For example, the exit criteria for the concept phase includes the following:

- Initial concept
- Competitive analysis
- Pitch presentation
- Risk analysis
- Concept approval
- Project kickoff

When all of these deliverables are completed, the concept phase is fully complete. Involve the team in determining exit criteria for each phase of production, with the final exit criteria being an approved gold master that can be manufactured and shipped to stores.

CREATING AN ART SCHEDULE

Carey Chico, Art Director
Pandemic Studios

The art director and lead artist will be able to provide estimates for each art task and define what the final deliverables will be for each task. As you create the art schedule, break down the tasks into smaller tasks that can be assigned to individual artists. In addition, it is helpful if you schedule groups of artists to work on similar assets and appoint someone as the point of contact for this group. For example, you could have one group working on all the character and vehicle models on the game and another group working on all the destructible objects in the game.

10.3.2   Initial Schedule

An initial schedule is created in preproduction and communicated to the development team in order to plan for key dates. Start the scheduling process by listing all the major exit criteria for each area of the game: production, approvals, art, engineering, design, audio, localization, QA, external vendors, and marketing. More exit criteria can be added as development progresses.

After these criteria are determined, fill in estimated dates. Figure 10.2 is an example of an initial production schedule. Major exit criteria are listed for each phase of the game, and eventually deadlines are assigned to each one. The overall goal of the game plan is to adjust the project factors (resources, features, schedules, and quality) in order to hit the ship date. From this submission date, you can determine a general time frame for the first playable, alpha, code freeze, beta, and code release candidate dates, which can help you better gauge the work to be completed for each milestone.

Although the initial production schedules provide a good guideline for the overall development process, a more detailed schedule must be created as information is confirmed. This detailed schedule contains subtasks for all the main tasks listed in the initial schedule. The exit criteria for detailed tasks are based on deliverables from the concept and requirements phases:

- Tiered master feature list
- Milestone deliverable lists
- Art documentation
- Design documentation
- Technical documentation

These deliverables include detailed information on how many levels, characters, and objects must be created, which engineering features will be coded, how much voiceover needs to be recorded, and everything else about the project. In order to best determine all the little things to do, it is helpful to break down these large deliverables and tasks into smaller ones.

10.3.3   Work Breakdown Structure

Work breakdown structures (WBSs) are useful for breaking down large tasks into smaller ones. By breaking down a large task into specific, incremental tasks, a master task list is created. The WBS process initially involves the producers and leads, with input from the team as needed. Here is a sample WBS process for determining what tasks are necessary to create a shippable level:

Justice Unit	Estimated Date	Notes
"Languages: English, German, French, Italian, Spanish"		
Production		
Concept phase completed		
Requirements phase completed		
Initial game plan completed		
First playable		
Alpha		
Code freeze		
Beta		
Pre-cert submission to Microsoft		
Code release candidate		
Certification submission to Microsoft		
Approvals		
Concept Approval		
Requirements Approval		
Game Plan Approval		
License Approval		
Console Manufacturer Approval		
Design		
Deliverables Completed for Concept Phase		
Deliverables Completed for Requirements Phase		
Detailed Documentation Completed for Game Features		
Character and Story Documents Completed		
Voiceover Scripts Completed		
Mission and Scenarios Designed		
Mission Prototypes Scripted		
Play-testing		
Final Missions Scripted		
Art		
Deliverables Completed for Concept Phase		
Deliverables Completed for Requirements Phase		
Prototypes Completed		
First Playable Level Completed		
Special Effects Completed		
UI Completed		
Cinematics Completed		

FIGURE 10.2   Sample of an initial production schedule.

Engineering		
Deliverables Completed for Concept Phase		
Deliverables Completed for Requirements Phase		
Art and Design Tools Completed		
Production Pipeline Completed		
Engineering Prototypes Completed		
All Major Gameplay Features Implemented		
Code Freeze		
Audio		
Sound Designs Completed		
Sound Prototypes Completed		
Placeholder VO Recorded		
Final VO Recorded		
Final Music Implemented in Game		
Localization		
Determine Localization Needs		
Organize Assets for Translation		
Integrate Assets		
Functionality Testing		
Linguistic Testing		
QA		
Test Plan Completed		
First Playable Testing Completed		
Alpha Testing Completed		
Play-testing Completed		
First Code Release Candidate to QA		
Code Release		
Cinematics (External Vendor)		
Deliver Initial Specs to Vendor		
Storyboard from Vendor		
Animatic from Vendor		
Rough Cut from Vendor		
Final Movie from Vendor (no sound)		
Movie to Sound Designer		
Final Movie Ready for Game		
Marketing		
Demo Build		
E3 Build		
Preview Code for Journalists		
Review Code for Journalists		

FIGURE 10.2 (*Continued*).

1. The producer and leads meet and define the specific tangible steps that are needed to create a level and mission from start to finish. All departments are involved—production, art, design, engineering, and QA.

2. During the meeting, the group brainstorms about every possible task to be completed for a level. Describe tasks in the present tense, with an active verb. For example, "design initial level layout." This helps the group determine the tangible tasks to be done.

3. The tasks are grouped together by department and then placed in rough chronological order.

4. Durations are set for each task by the appropriate lead. (Art lead provides art estimates and so on.)

Figure 10.3 is an example of a WBS to create one shippable level for Justice Unit.

10.3.4   Detailed Schedule

When the WBS is completed, have the team double check it to ensure that no tasks were forgotten. This task list is then added to the project schedule; dependencies are added; and the actual team members are assigned their tasks. They must assess the original duration estimated by the lead. Each task should be no more than three to five days in duration. Ideally, each task takes one to two days. If the task owner agrees with this estimate, the number stays as is. If the task owner disagrees with the estimate, he or she provides an updated estimate that is added to the project schedule. This process gives team members more ownership of their tasks, instead of feeling like they are just assigned an arbitrary deadline that must be achieved no matter what.

If there is some difficulty in determining how long a task will take, the lead should make an educated estimate based on experience. Don't leave the duration for any task blank, as this will not give a true picture of the overall schedule. Accurately estimating tasks is very subjective and improves with experience. It is good to build some extra time in the schedule to accommodate any work that takes longer than originally estimated. Some people like to add this extra time on a per-task basis, although this is not recommended as it does not give an accurate picture of the overall schedule. However, adding some slack at the end of the schedule provides a good padding for accommodating any task overruns.

One technique to use for estimating tasks is called time-boxing. A time-box is a fixed period of time during which someone attempts to complete a well-defined task. The task should have each of its requirements prioritized from highest to lowest, so that the most critical work is completed first. To use this technique, assign start and end dates to a given task, assign someone to work on it, and then measure how much is completed in the allotted time. After the agreed-upon period of time is over and the feature is not fully implemented, assess the work that is completed and determine whether further work should be

Art Tasks (Villain's Lair)	Duration
Create prototype	5 days
Implement prototype feedback	1 day
Create level geometry	20 days
Add placeholder textures	3 days
Fix first round of bugs	3 days
Create destructible objects	2 days
Add final textures	10 days
Create player reference map	.5 day
Create special effects	2 days
Optimize level for budget constraints	5 days
Polish map	5 days
Fix final round of bugs	3 days
Design Tasks (Villain's Lair)	**Duration**
Design initial level layout	2 days
Design initial mission scripting	2 days
Script prototype	.5 day
Play-test prototype scripting	.5 day
Implement prototype feedback	1 day
Script first pass of mission scripting	5 days
Script first pass of multiplayer scripting	2 days
Review scripting	1 day
Script second pass	5 days
Verify all supporting files are tagged correctly	1 day
Create localization tags for in-game dialogue	1 day
Polish scripting	3 days
Fix final round of bugs	2 days
Sound Tasks (Villain's Lair)	**Duration**
Create sound design	3 days
Implement sound design prototype	2 days
Implement prototype feedback	2 days
Complete first pass of sound implementation	3 days
Polish sound	2 days
Fix final round of bugs	1 day
QA Tasks (Villain's Lair)	**Duration**
Play-test prototype	1 day
Test geometry and terrain navigation	7 days
Check textures	2 days
Test initial scripting	1 day
Test second-pass scripting	1 day
Final test all level geometry and textures	5 days
Final test for mission scripting	1 day
Approvals (Villain's Lair)	**Duration**
Approve initial layout	1 day
Approve initial art prototype	1 day
Approve initial design prototype	1 day
Approve sound design	1 day
Approve final level, scripting, and sound	1 day

FIGURE 10.3 WBS for completing Villain's Lair level.

done, whether the work done already is good enough, or whether the feature should be cut because the effort already put into it indicates the feature will take too long to implement in the given schedule. This method can help you maintain more control over the schedule, instead of just letting a feature continually run over schedule.

For example, if the lead engineer makes an educate estimate of three weeks to implement normal mapping into the graphics pipeline, check with the engineer on a regular basis to check his or her progress. At the end of three weeks see how much normal mapping functionality is implemented. At this point, the feature might be good enough to ship, or further work might be needed. If you are going to have the engineer invest more time in the feature, determine a new set of feature priorities and define a new time-box.

When durations are assigned to the schedule, add in time for sick days, holidays, and vacations. You can't assume that everyone will be in the office every single workday. Also, don't schedule overtime. This is a bad practice and will quickly cause you to have an unhappy and, therefore, unproductive team. Instead, limit the scope of the project so that everything can be completed in a reasonable amount of time. In fact, all the task durations should be based on accomplishing about five to six hours of work during a normal eight-hour workday. The other two to three hours per day account for time people spend checking email, going to meetings, and dealing with general non-task-related work.

Keep in mind that task dependencies and assigned resources can dramatically affect a schedule. For example, if it takes several days to get the prototype approved, level production comes to a standstill, valuable time is lost, and a bottleneck is created. Additionally, if someone is overloaded with too many tasks, he or she cannot keep up the same pace of work as others involved in the level production process and will cause delays. So it is important to make sure that the correct dependencies and resource allocations are included in the schedule. The importance of this is best shown in Figures 10.4, 10.5, 10.6, and 10.7.

Figure 10.4 is a detailed level production schedule for Villain's Lair. This does not include any task dependencies or assigned resources. Based on this schedule, all the art, design, sound, QA, and approval tasks will take 15 days to complete.

Figure 10.5 is the same level production schedule with assigned resources. Now that resources are assigned, you can see it takes 63 days to complete the work. This increase happened because there is only one artist, one designer, one sound designer, and one tester available to do all the work, and they can only work on one task at a time. If the tasks were assigned to multiple artists and designers, the time could be reduced.

Figure 10.6 is the same level production schedule with just the task dependencies added. Now the scheduled time has increased to 77 days. This is because there are several tasks that are on hold until another task is completed. For example, under the QA section, you can see that QA has more than three weeks of nonproductive time between tasks 36 and 37. In an actual game development environment, several levels would be in production at once, so it is likely that QA would be testing another level during these three weeks.

	ⓘ	Task Name	Duration	Start	Finish	Predecessors	Resource Names
1		⊟ **Villain's Lair Level Production**	**15 days**	**Mon 2/19/07**	**Fri 3/9/07**		
2		⊟ **Art**	**15 days**	**Mon 2/19/07**	**Fri 3/9/07**		
3		Create prototype	5 days	Mon 2/19/07	Fri 2/23/07		
4		Implement prototype feedback	1 day	Mon 2/19/07	Mon 2/19/07		
5		Create level geometry	15 days	Mon 2/19/07	Fri 3/9/07		
6		Add placeholder textures	3 days	Mon 2/19/07	Wed 2/21/07		
7		Fix first round of bugs	3 days	Mon 2/19/07	Wed 2/21/07		
8		Create destructible objects	2 days	Mon 2/19/07	Tue 2/20/07		
9		Add final textures	10 days	Mon 2/19/07	Fri 3/2/07		
10		Create player reference map	1 day	Mon 2/19/07	Mon 2/19/07		
11		Create special effects	3 days	Mon 2/19/07	Wed 2/21/07		
12		Optimize level for budget constraints	10 days	Mon 2/19/07	Fri 3/2/07		
13		Polish map	5 days	Mon 2/19/07	Fri 2/23/07		
14		Fix final round of bugs	5 days	Mon 2/19/07	Fri 2/23/07		
15		⊟ **Design**	**5 days**	**Mon 2/19/07**	**Fri 2/23/07**		
16		Design initial level layout	2 days	Mon 2/19/07	Tue 2/20/07		
17		Design initial mission scripting	2 days	Mon 2/19/07	Tue 2/20/07		
18		Create initial prototype scripting	2 days	Mon 2/19/07	Tue 2/20/07		
19		Implement prototype feedback	2 days	Mon 2/19/07	Tue 2/20/07		
20		Script first pass of mission scripting	5 days	Mon 2/19/07	Fri 2/23/07		
21		Script first pass of multiplayer scripting	2 days	Mon 2/19/07	Tue 2/20/07		
22		Review scripting	1 day	Mon 2/19/07	Mon 2/19/07		
23		Script second pass	5 days	Mon 2/19/07	Fri 2/23/07		
24		Verify all supporting files are tagged corr	1 day	Mon 2/19/07	Mon 2/19/07		
25		Create localization tags for in-game dialc	1 day	Mon 2/19/07	Mon 2/19/07		
26		Polish scripting	3 days	Mon 2/19/07	Wed 2/21/07		
27		Fix final round of bugs	2 days	Mon 2/19/07	Tue 2/20/07		
28		⊟ **Sound**	**3 days**	**Mon 2/19/07**	**Wed 2/21/07**		
29		Create sound design	3 days	Mon 2/19/07	Wed 2/21/07		
30		Implement sound design prototype	2 days	Mon 2/19/07	Tue 2/20/07		
31		Implement feedback	2 days	Mon 2/19/07	Tue 2/20/07		
32		Complete first pass of sound implementa	3 days	Mon 2/19/07	Wed 2/21/07		
33		Polish sound	2 days	Mon 2/19/07	Tue 2/20/07		
34		Fix final round of bugs	1 day	Mon 2/19/07	Mon 2/19/07		
35		⊟ **QA**	**7 days**	**Mon 2/19/07**	**Tue 2/27/07**		
36		Play-test prototype	1 day	Mon 2/19/07	Mon 2/19/07		
37		Test geometry and terrain navigation	7 days	Mon 2/19/07	Tue 2/27/07		
38		Check textures	2 days	Mon 2/19/07	Tue 2/20/07		
39		Test initial scripting	1 day	Mon 2/19/07	Mon 2/19/07		
40		Test second-pass scripting	1 day	Mon 2/19/07	Mon 2/19/07		
41		Final test all level geometry and textures	5 days	Mon 2/19/07	Fri 2/23/07		
42		Final test for mission scripting	1 day	Mon 2/19/07	Mon 2/19/07		
43		⊟ **Approvals**	**2 days**	**Mon 2/19/07**	**Tue 2/20/07**		
44		Approve initial layout	2 days	Mon 2/19/07	Tue 2/20/07		
45		Approve initial art prototype	2 days	Mon 2/19/07	Tue 2/20/07		
46		Approval initial design prototype	2 days	Mon 2/19/07	Tue 2/20/07		
47		Approve sound design	2 days	Mon 2/19/07	Tue 2/20/07		
48		Approve final level, scripting, and sound	2 days	Mon 2/19/07	Tue 2/20/07		

❙ FIGURE 10.4   Level production schedule with no dependencies or assigned resources.

Figure 10.7 is the same level production schedule with both the assigned resources and task dependencies added. Now the work requires 81 days to complete. This time could be slightly reduced by assigning another artist and designer on the project for a few days.

Work breakdown structures and detailed schedules must be created for every aspect of the project. If the producer and leads commit to making this happen, the schedules can be very useful to everyone on the team. Also, after spending all this time creating the schedule, put an equal amount of effort into tracking and updating it.

If you are working on a two-year development cycle, don't try to create a detailed scheduled for the entire two-year process. Instead, concentrate on creating detailed schedules for each project milestone as needed. This gives you more flexibility with the schedule, and adjustments can easily be made when necessary.

	0	Task Name	Duration	Start	Finish	Predecessors	Resource Names
1		⊟ Villain's Lair Level Production	63 days	Mon 2/19/07	Wed 5/16/07		
2		⊟ Art	63 days	Mon 2/19/07	Wed 5/16/07		
3		Create prototype	5 days	Mon 4/9/07	Fri 4/13/07		Artist 1
4		Implement prototype feedback	1 day	Tue 5/15/07	Tue 5/15/07		Artist 1
5		Create level geometry	15 days	Mon 2/19/07	Fri 3/9/07		Artist 1
6		Add placeholder textures	3 days	Mon 4/30/07	Wed 5/2/07		Artist 1
7		Fix first round of bugs	3 days	Thu 5/3/07	Mon 5/7/07		Artist 1
8		Create destructible objects	2 days	Fri 5/11/07	Mon 5/14/07		Artist 1
9		Add final textures	10 days	Mon 3/12/07	Fri 3/23/07		Artist 1
10		Create player reference map	1 day	Wed 5/16/07	Wed 5/16/07		Artist 1
11		Create special effects	3 days	Tue 5/8/07	Thu 5/10/07		Artist 1
12		Optimize level for budget constraints	10 days	Mon 3/26/07	Fri 4/6/07		Artist 1
13		Polish map	5 days	Mon 4/16/07	Fri 4/20/07		Artist 1
14		Fix final round of bugs	5 days	Mon 4/23/07	Fri 4/27/07		Artist 1
15		⊟ Design	28 days	Mon 2/19/07	Wed 3/28/07		
16		Design initial level layout	2 days	Thu 3/8/07	Fri 3/9/07		Designer 1
17		Design initial mission scripting	2 days	Mon 3/12/07	Tue 3/13/07		Designer 1
18		Create initial prototype scripting	2 days	Wed 3/14/07	Thu 3/15/07		Designer 1
19		Implement prototype feedback	2 days	Fri 3/16/07	Mon 3/19/07		Designer 1
20		Script first pass of mission scripting	5 days	Mon 2/19/07	Fri 2/23/07		Designer 1
21		Script first pass of multiplayer scripting	2 days	Tue 3/20/07	Wed 3/21/07		Designer 1
22		Review scripting	1 day	Mon 3/26/07	Mon 3/26/07		Designer 1
23		Script second pass	5 days	Mon 2/26/07	Fri 3/2/07		Designer 1
24		Verify all supporting files are tagged corr	1 day	Tue 3/27/07	Tue 3/27/07		Designer 1
25		Create localization tags for in-game dialc	1 day	Wed 3/28/07	Wed 3/28/07		Designer 1
26		Polish scripting	3 days	Mon 3/5/07	Wed 3/7/07		Designer 1
27		Fix final round of bugs	2 days	Thu 3/22/07	Fri 3/23/07		Designer 1
28		⊟ Sound	13 days	Mon 2/19/07	Wed 3/7/07		
29		Create sound design	3 days	Mon 2/19/07	Wed 2/21/07		Sound Designer 1
30		Implement sound design prototype	2 days	Tue 2/27/07	Wed 2/28/07		Sound Designer 1
31		Implement feedback	2 days	Thu 3/1/07	Fri 3/2/07		Sound Designer 1
32		Complete first pass of sound implementa	3 days	Thu 2/22/07	Mon 2/26/07		Sound Designer 1
33		Polish sound	2 days	Mon 3/5/07	Tue 3/6/07		Sound Designer 1
34		Fix final round of bugs	1 day	Wed 3/7/07	Wed 3/7/07		Sound Designer 1
35		⊟ QA	18 days	Mon 2/19/07	Wed 3/14/07		
36		Play-test prototype	1 day	Fri 3/9/07	Fri 3/9/07		Tester 1
37		Test geometry and terrain navigation	7 days	Mon 2/19/07	Tue 2/27/07		Tester 1
38		Check textures	2 days	Wed 3/7/07	Thu 3/8/07		Tester 1
39		Test initial scripting	1 day	Mon 3/12/07	Mon 3/12/07		Tester 1
40		Test second-pass scripting	1 day	Tue 3/13/07	Tue 3/13/07		Tester 1
41		Final test all level geometry and textures	5 days	Wed 2/28/07	Tue 3/6/07		Tester 1
42		Final test for mission scripting	1 day	Wed 3/14/07	Wed 3/14/07		Tester 1
43		⊟ Approvals	10 days	Mon 2/19/07	Fri 3/2/07		
44		Approve initial layout	2 days	Mon 2/19/07	Tue 2/20/07		Management
45		Approve initial art prototype	2 days	Wed 2/21/07	Thu 2/22/07		Management
46		Approval initial design prototype	2 days	Fri 2/23/07	Mon 2/26/07		Management
47		Approve sound design	2 days	Tue 2/27/07	Wed 2/28/07		Management
48		Approve final level, scripting, and sound	2 days	Thu 3/1/07	Fri 3/2/07		Management

FIGURE 10.5   Level production schedule with assigned resources.

10.4 Budgets

After the initial schedule is created, you can start creating the budget. The budget must be within reason for the quality, scope, and schedule so that the game will make a profit when it is released. The publisher also watches the bottom line closely to ensure that development costs are justified and that they have made a profitable investment in your game. Ultimately, the producer is responsible for managing the costs. If the game development is poorly planned, it will require more time or more personnel, and thus cost more money, resulting in lower profit margins. If the game development is efficiently planned, it is easier to identify areas where there is cost-saving potential.

To determine the likely profitability of the game, the publisher creates a profit-and-loss statement (P&L). A P&L, which measures the overall profit and loss of

	❶	Task Name	Duration	Start	Finish	Predecessors	Resource Names
1		⊟ Villain's Lair Level Production	77 days	Mon 2/19/07	Tue 6/5/07		
2		⊟ Art	73 days	Fri 2/23/07	Tue 6/5/07		
3		Create prototype	5 days	Fri 2/23/07	Thu 3/1/07	44	
4		Implement prototype feedback	1 day	Tue 3/6/07	Tue 3/6/07	45	
5		Create level geometry	15 days	Wed 3/7/07	Tue 3/27/07	4	
6		Add placeholder textures	3 days	Wed 3/28/07	Fri 3/30/07	5	
7		Fix first round of bugs	3 days	Wed 4/11/07	Fri 4/13/07	37	
8		Create destructible objects	2 days	Mon 4/16/07	Tue 4/17/07	7	
9		Add final textures	10 days	Wed 4/18/07	Tue 5/1/07	8	
10		Create player reference map	1 day	Wed 4/18/07	Wed 4/18/07	8	
11		Create special effects	3 days	Wed 4/18/07	Fri 4/20/07	8	
12		Optimize level for budget constraints	10 days	Wed 5/2/07	Tue 5/15/07	9,10,11	
13		Polish map	5 days	Wed 5/16/07	Tue 5/22/07	12	
14		Fix final round of bugs	5 days	Wed 5/30/07	Tue 6/5/07	41	
15		⊟ Design	69 days	Mon 2/19/07	Thu 5/24/07		
16		Design initial level layout	2 days	Mon 2/19/07	Tue 2/20/07		
17		Design initial mission scripting	2 days	Mon 2/19/07	Tue 2/20/07		
18		Create initial prototype scripting	2 days	Wed 3/7/07	Thu 3/8/07	17,4	
19		Implement prototype feedback	2 days	Tue 3/13/07	Wed 3/14/07	46,36	
20		Script first pass of mission scripting	5 days	Wed 3/28/07	Tue 4/3/07	5	
21		Script first pass of multiplayer scripting	2 days	Wed 3/28/07	Thu 3/29/07	5	
22		Review scripting	1 day	Wed 4/4/07	Wed 4/4/07	20,21	
23		Script second pass	5 days	Thu 4/5/07	Wed 4/11/07	22,39	
24		Verify all supporting files are tagged corr	1 day	Wed 5/16/07	Wed 5/16/07	12	
25		Create localization tags for in-game dialc	1 day	Wed 5/16/07	Wed 5/16/07	12	
26		Polish scripting	3 days	Thu 5/17/07	Mon 5/21/07	23,24,25	
27		Fix final round of bugs	2 days	Wed 5/23/07	Thu 5/24/07	42	
28		⊟ Sound	29 days	Tue 3/6/07	Fri 4/13/07		
29		Create sound design	3 days	Tue 3/6/07	Thu 3/8/07	45	
30		Implement sound design prototype	2 days	Wed 3/7/07	Thu 3/8/07	4	
31		Implement feedback	2 days	Tue 3/13/07	Wed 3/14/07	47	
32		Complete first pass of sound implementa	3 days	Thu 4/5/07	Mon 4/9/07	22	
33		Polish sound	2 days	Thu 4/12/07	Fri 4/13/07	23	
34		Fix final round of bugs	1 day	Fri 4/13/07	Fri 4/13/07	40	
35		⊟ QA	58 days	Fri 3/9/07	Tue 5/29/07		
36		Play-test prototype	1 day	Fri 3/9/07	Fri 3/9/07	18	
37		Test geometry and terrain navigation	7 days	Mon 4/2/07	Tue 4/10/07	6	
38		Check textures	2 days	Wed 5/2/07	Thu 5/3/07	9	
39		Test initial scripting	1 day	Wed 4/4/07	Wed 4/4/07	20,21	
40		Test second-pass scripting	1 day	Thu 4/12/07	Thu 4/12/07	23	
41		Final test all level geometry and textures	5 days	Wed 5/23/07	Tue 5/29/07	13	
42		Final test for mission scripting	1 day	Tue 5/22/07	Tue 5/22/07	26	
43		⊟ Approvals	66 days	Wed 2/21/07	Wed 5/23/07		
44		Approve initial layout	2 days	Wed 2/21/07	Thu 2/22/07	16	
45		Approve initial art prototype	2 days	Fri 3/2/07	Mon 3/5/07	3	
46		Approval initial design prototype	2 days	Fri 3/9/07	Mon 3/12/07	18	
47		Approve sound design	2 days	Fri 3/9/07	Mon 3/12/07	30	
48		Approve final level, scripting, and sound	2 days	Tue 5/22/07	Wed 5/23/07	12,26,33	

❙ FIGURE 10.6   Level production schedule with task dependencies.

a game, is a spreadsheet that compares the development, marketing, packaging, and distribution costs for the game against the projected sales. If the projected sales numbers increase, the better chance there is of making a profit. For example, if it is determined that 20,000 copies can be sold, the budget will be smaller than for a game that is predicted to sell 500,000 copies. The P&L is used to run different profitability scenarios to determine a reasonable balance between costs and potential profits.

Because the schedule, budget, and staffing plan are dependent on each other, the budget can change markedly depending on what your schedule and staffing plans are. Therefore, when you create an initial budget, be prepared to make adjustments to it and the other elements as necessary. After the budget is established and approved, manage the costs closely so you don't find yourself grossly over budget.

There will be instances when unexpected costs arise—for example, you need to buy three new computers and three copies of 3ds Max—so don't panic when this happens.

	o	Task Name	Duration	Start	Finish	Predecessors	Resource Names
1		⊟ Villain's Lair Level Production	81 days	Mon 2/19/07	Mon 6/11/07		
2		⊟ Art	77 days	Fri 2/23/07	Mon 6/11/07		
3		Create prototype	5 days	Fri 2/23/07	Thu 3/1/07	44	Artist 1
4		Implement prototype feedback	1 day	Tue 3/6/07	Tue 3/6/07	45	Artist 1
5		Create level geometry	15 days	Wed 3/7/07	Tue 3/27/07	4	Artist 1
6		Add placeholder textures	3 days	Wed 3/28/07	Fri 3/30/07	5	Artist 1
7		Fix first round of bugs	3 days	Wed 4/11/07	Fri 4/13/07	37	Artist 1
8		Create destructible objects	2 days	Mon 4/16/07	Tue 4/17/07	7	Artist 1
9		Add final textures	10 days	Wed 4/18/07	Tue 5/1/07	8	Artist 1
10		Create player reference map	1 day	Mon 5/7/07	Mon 5/7/07	8	Artist 1
11		Create special effects	3 days	Wed 5/2/07	Fri 5/4/07	8	Artist 1
12		Optimize level for budget constraints	10 days	Tue 5/8/07	Mon 5/21/07	9,10,11	Artist 1
13		Polish map	5 days	Tue 5/22/07	Mon 5/28/07	12	Artist 1
14		Fix final round of bugs	5 days	Tue 6/5/07	Mon 6/11/07	41	Artist 1
15		⊟ Design	79 days	Mon 2/19/07	Thu 6/7/07		
16		Design initial level layout	2 days	Mon 2/19/07	Tue 2/20/07		Designer 1
17		Design initial mission scripting	2 days	Wed 2/21/07	Thu 2/22/07		Designer 1
18		Create initial prototype scripting	2 days	Wed 3/7/07	Thu 3/8/07	17,4	Designer 1
19		Implement prototype feedback	2 days	Tue 3/13/07	Wed 3/14/07	46,36	Designer 1
20		Script first pass of mission scripting	5 days	Wed 3/28/07	Tue 4/3/07	5	Designer 1
21		Script first pass of multiplayer scripting	2 days	Wed 4/4/07	Thu 4/5/07	5	Designer 1
22		Review scripting	1 day	Fri 4/6/07	Fri 4/6/07	20,21	Designer 1
23		Script second pass	5 days	Thu 4/12/07	Wed 4/18/07	22,39	Designer 1
24		Verify all supporting files are tagged corr	1 day	Tue 5/22/07	Tue 5/22/07	12	Designer 1
25		Create localization tags for in-game dialc	1 day	Wed 5/23/07	Wed 5/23/07	12	Designer 1
26		Polish scripting	3 days	Thu 5/24/07	Mon 5/28/07	23,24,25	Designer 1
27		Fix final round of bugs	2 days	Wed 6/6/07	Thu 6/7/07	42	Designer 1
28		⊟ Sound	35 days	Tue 3/6/07	Mon 4/23/07		
29		Create sound design	3 days	Tue 3/6/07	Mon 3/12/07	45	Sound Designer 1
30		Implement sound design prototype	2 days	Wed 3/7/07	Thu 3/8/07	4	Sound Designer 1
31		Implement feedback	2 days	Thu 3/15/07	Fri 3/16/07	47	Sound Designer 1
32		Complete first pass of sound implementa	3 days	Mon 4/9/07	Wed 4/11/07	22	Sound Designer 1
33		Polish sound	2 days	Thu 4/19/07	Fri 4/20/07	23	Sound Designer 1
34		Fix final round of bugs	1 day	Mon 4/23/07	Mon 4/23/07	40	Sound Designer 1
35		⊟ QA	63 days	Fri 3/9/07	Tue 6/5/07		
36		Play-test prototype	1 day	Fri 3/9/07	Fri 3/9/07	18	Tester 1
37		Test geometry and terrain navigation	7 days	Mon 4/2/07	Tue 4/10/07	6	Tester 1
38		Check textures	2 days	Wed 5/2/07	Thu 5/3/07	9	Tester 1
39		Test initial scripting	1 day	Wed 4/11/07	Wed 4/11/07	20,21	Tester 1
40		Test second-pass scripting	1 day	Thu 4/19/07	Thu 4/19/07	23	Tester 1
41		Final test all level geometry and textures	5 days	Tue 5/29/07	Mon 6/4/07	13	Tester 1
42		Final test for mission scripting	1 day	Tue 6/5/07	Tue 6/5/07	26	Tester 1
43		⊟ Approvals	71 days	Wed 2/21/07	Wed 5/30/07		
44		Approve initial layout	2 days	Wed 2/21/07	Thu 2/22/07	16	Management
45		Approve initial art prototype	2 days	Fri 3/2/07	Mon 3/5/07	3	Management
46		Approval initial design prototype	2 days	Fri 3/9/07	Mon 3/12/07	18	Management
47		Approve sound design	2 days	Tue 3/13/07	Wed 3/14/07	30	Management
48		Approve final level, scripting, and sound	2 days	Tue 5/29/07	Wed 5/30/07	12,26,33	Management

FIGURE 10.7 Level production schedule with assigned resources and dependencies.

You might be able to reallocate some money in the budget for these items without increasing your overall budget. If that doesn't work, you might be able to reallocate actual computers from another project in the studio and use them temporarily. Just remember to be as cost conscious as possible when these things happen.

10.4.1   Creating a Budget

Budgets consist of all the costs associated with the project, including personnel, overhead (rent, utilities, and taxes), hardware, and software. Determine all of these costs up front so there are no surprises during the development process.

When creating the budget, refer to the game requirements and schedule to determine what costs to plan for. These documents provide guidance on how much you need to spend on certain areas of the game. Don't automatically assume that the cheapest item is the best solution, as this will ultimately affect the quality of the game. For instance, if the game needs to be completed in one year and be of top quality, you probably don't want to cut corners on the personnel and hire entry-level people. You probably want to spend money on more experienced people who can work effectively within the tight schedule. However, if you have several years to complete a game, you might want to hire some entry-level people and train them on the job so they can be experienced people for the next project.

These types of decisions are best made by taking all of the game elements into account. By this point, the major goals of the game are approved and the requirements are defined, so you have a good idea of whether the game is a budget title or a AAA one. Additionally, the game requirements indicate which technology is being used, so you have an idea of what the hardware and software needs are. The schedule defines how much time you have and how many people you need. Of course, each project will have a different budget depending on the game requirements, but there are general things to be planned for in each budget.

Start by creating a list of all the major line items that must be accounted for in the budget—this includes both personnel and other major costs. Figure 10.8 lists some of these line items.

Next, just as you did with the major tasks in the schedule, break them down into smaller line items. Use the information on the schedule to determine all the personnel needs and the information from the requirements to determine all the hardware and software needs. Figure 10.9 is an example of the personnel needs broken down into smaller line items.

Personnel Costs
Art Personnel
Design Personnel
Engineering Personnel
Production Personnel
QA Personnel
Audio Personnel
Other Major Costs
Hardware
Software
IP Licensing Fees
External Vendors
Food
Shipping
Office Supplies
Overhead (HR benefits, insurance, office space, etc.)

FIGURE 10.8 Major budget line items.

Art Personnel
Art Director
Lead Artist
Concept Artist
World Builder
Asset Artist
Animator
Technical Artist
Marketing Artist
Design Personnel
Creative Director
Lead Designer
Designer
Writer
Engineering Personnel
Technical Director
Lead Engineer
Networking Engineer
Sound Engineer
Tools Engineer
AI Engineer
Gameplay Engineer
Production Personnel
Executive Producer
Producer
Associate Producer
QA Personnel
Lead QA Analyst
Tester

FIGURE 10.9 Breakdown of personnel needs.

After determining all of the line items, create your budget. Figure 10.10 is a sample budget for the personnel costs on a project. In this example, the number of each type of personnel is indicated in the "Number" column, which is then multiplied by the "Monthly Rate" and "Number of Months" needed on a project. All of these costs are added for the grand total.

Figure 10.11 is a sample budget for the other costs on a project. In this example, the "Number" column is used to indicate multiple purchases of a given item, such as 10 computers. The "Number" column is multiplied by the "Rate" column to determine the total cost for each line item. These, in turn, are added for the grand total.

After the development budget is determined, it can be added to the publisher's P&L statement to determine whether the title will yield a profit. If not, you will be asked to make adjustments to the budget and schedule until they are satisfactory.

Production Personnel	Number	Monthly Rate	# of Months	Cost
Producer	1	$8,000	24	$192,000
Associate Producer	3	$6,000	18	$324,000
Art Personnel				
Lead Artist	1	$10,000	24	$240,000
Technical Artist	1	$8,000	24	$192,000
Concept Artist	2	$6,000	10	$120,000
World Builder	10	$6,000	12	$720,000
Object Artist	3	$6,000	8	$144,000
Texture Artist	4	$6,000	12	$288,000
Marketing Artist	1	$6,000	12	$72,000
Animator	3	$8,000	8	$192,000
Engineering Personnel				
Lead Engineer	1	$10,000	24	$240,000
Networking Engineer	2	$8,000	16	$256,000
Graphics Engineer	4	$8,000	18	$576,000
UI Engineer	1	$8,000	12	$96,000
AI Engineer	4	$8,000	18	$576,000
Sound Engineer	1	$8,000	12	$96,000
Tools Engineer	3	$8,000	18	$432,000
General Engineer	5	$8,000	18	$720,000
Engineer	2	$8,000	12	$192,000
Design Personnel				
Lead Designer	1	$8,000	24	$192,000
Designer	4	$6,000	18	$432,000
Sound Designer	1	$6,000	12	$72,000
Writer	1	$6,000	6	$36,000
QA Personnel				
Lead QA Analyst	1	$8,000	24	$192,000
Tester	20	$6,000	10	$1,200,000
GRAND TOTAL	**80**			**$7,792,000**

Based on a 24-month development cycle.
Monthly rates are for example only; they do not reflect actual rates.

FIGURE 10.10   Sample budget for personnel costs.

10.4.2   Managing a Budget

As with the schedule, you will need to track your budget during the development process. The same person who is appointed as the schedule tracker is also a good candidate to be the budget tracker. Any budget expenditures should be noted on a weekly, or at least a monthly, basis.

Hardware	Number	Rate	Cost
Computers	80	$3,000	$240,000
Console Development Kits	40	$10,000	$400,000
Controllers	60	$100	$6,000
Graphics Cards	80	$300	$24,000
Software			
Perforce®	76	$750	$57,000
3ds Max	19	$4,000	$76,000
Photoshop®	4	$600	$2,400
Microsoft Project	5	$1,000	$5,000
Unreal Engine™ 3	1	$1,000,000	$1,000,000
Visual C++®	23	$3,000	$69,000
Licensing Fees			
Justice Unit Royalty	1	$500,000	$500,000
External Vendors			
Voiceover	1	$250,000	$250,000
Music	1	$50,000	$50,000
Cinematics	1	$300,000	$300,000
Localization	4	$50,000	$200,000
Other			
Travel	24	$1,000	$24,000
Food	24	$500	$12,000
Shipping/Postage	24	$200	$4,800
GRAND TOTAL			**$3,220,200**

Based on a 24-month development cycle.
Rates are for example only; they do not reflect actual rates.

| FIGURE 10.11   Sample budget for other costs.

The studio's or publisher's accounting department will also be involved in watching the budget. They keep records of all the expenditures on the game—salaries, hardware purchases, and costs of external vendors—and will allocate all of these things against your game's budget. They are a good source of information if you need to find out the total amount spent on the game at any given point.

Keep detailed records for any expenditures. Each studio has a different process for paying expenses, so check with the accounting department and studio management on what forms need to be filled out to make purchases, pay a vendor, or hire new team members. For example, when paying an external vendor, you might need to get an invoice and detailed statement of work from the vendor. After receiving this, you might need to fill out a check request form and submit it to accounting for payment. The form probably will ask for general information about the expenditure, such as whether it was budgeted and what part of the budget it is applied to. After all the paperwork is received, accounting will cut a check and mail it to the vendor.

If you find that the project is going over budget, don't ignore the problem; it's not going to go away. Instead, take time to reassess your game plan and determine whether there are any adjustments that can be made to the schedule, staffing, or scope of the project.

■ 10.5 Staffing

The schedule details what work needs to be done, and the staffing plan determines who will do it. When these elements are combined and the resources are added to the schedule, it determines when all the work is completed. Therefore, it is important to understand the strong dependencies between the staffing plan and schedule. The staffing plan is also affected by budget; if you need to hire additional people to complete the work, you need to have money in the budget to do this. If you can't afford extra people, you will need to reduce the scope of work so that the people you do have available can complete it on time and at budget.

Your staffing plan is largely based on what tasks must be completed. For example, if the game requires 10 character models and five levels, you are going to need several artists to complete this work. If the game is utilizing brand-new technology, you'll want to have enough engineers on the project to prototype, code, and debug it. It is helpful to add or subtract people to the schedule to determine the effect this has on the deadlines. After you find a good balance between the tasks to be completed and people needed, you can fully define your staffing plan.

In general, the preproduction phase will include a small group of people who will be on the project until the end. During production, people will roll on and off the project as needed. By beta, the team will again be reduced to a small group of people who will bug fix and code release the game. All of these staff changes will be reflected in your production schedule. Figure 10.12 is an example of a partial staffing list for a game with a two-year development cycle. The information was pulled from the schedule and contains an overview of the amount of time people are needed for the project.

■ 10.6 Outsourcing

Outsourcing work to an external vendor is a good way to save time and possibly money on the project. You might want to use an animation house to create the game's introductory movie so that your artists can focus on creating in-game content.

Role	Duration	Notes
Lead Artist	24 months	Need for preproduction, production, code release.
Concept Artist	10 months	Need for preproduction and part of production.
World Builder 1	12 months	Need for production.
World Builder 2	12 months	Need for production.
World Builder 3	12 months	Need for production.
Texture Artist 1	8 months	Begin after first round of levels are geometry complete.
Texture Artist 2	8 months	Begin after first round of levels are geometry complete.
Lead Designer	24 months	Need for preproduction, production, code release.
Designer 1	18 months	Need for production.
Scripter 1	8 months	Will start after first round of levels are built and textured.
Scripter 2	8 months	Will start after first round of levels are built and textured.
Producer	24 months	Need for preproduction, production, code release.
Lead Enginer	24 months	Need for preproduction, production, code release.
Engineer—Multiplayer	16 months	Need to start right after preproduction.
Engineer—Tools	18 months	Need to start right after preproduction.
Lead QA Analyst	24 months	Need for preproduction, production, code release.
Tester 1	10 months	Part-time for alpha, full-time at code freeze.
Based on a 24-month development cycle.		

FIGURE 10.12   Example of a partial staffing list.

Obviously, using an external vendor saves time for the internal development team since they are not responsible for completing a given section of work. Money is saved if the vendor can do something more quickly and/or cheaper than the internal development team, such as voiceover recordings.

There are many types of game development services you can outsource without impacting the quality or schedule of the project. These areas involve design and art assets, as these tend to be discrete sets of tasks that are not dependent on work from several parts of the team. Other things to outsource include the following:

- Cinematics and animation
- Motion capture
- Voiceover
- Music
- Sound effects
- Writing
- Localization

Outsourcing engineering tasks is not recommended, as the engineering tasks are more dependent on each other. Code merges can also be time-consuming, making it difficult to test outsourced code on a regular basis. Additionally, an engineering vendor will need access to source code, which is highly confidential, and will need to set up a development environment that exactly matches what the internal engineering team is using.

Before contacting an external vendor, clearly define the scope of work to be outsourced. The earlier work can be scoped out, the more prepared the vendor is to accurately estimate the workload and complete it on time. Also, provide as much information as needed to the vendor about the game, as this will help them plan their work better. For example, if hiring an external vendor to compose music for the game, it is helpful to show them concept art, playable prototypes, the style guide, and anything else that can help them get a good idea of what the game's vision is and what music will best fit with this vision.

As with any project, there are pros and cons to working with external vendors. Overall, using a vendor can save time and resources during the development process, making it more likely for the game to be finished on time. Another benefit is that the team can concentrate solely on their tasks for the game and spend additional time play-balancing features, fixing bugs, and polishing the assets so the game is the best it can be. If you select vendors that are highly specialized in one area, their quality of work will be high and will contribute to the overall quality of the game, leaving the team to concentrate on the areas they do best.

There are a few drawbacks to working with a vendor, such as the extra costs involved. But if the project is large and complex, the cost of an external vendor might be worth the time and resources saved by the internal development team. Another drawback is that the developer loses the flexibility to shift project deliverables and internal deadlines around. When working with a vendor, the developer must be organized and confident in the team's ability to meet key milestone dates. The developer must provide the vendor with necessary assets when needed. For example, a cinematics vendor might need to have the final character models to complete the final version of the movies. Providing this information requires the developer to think months ahead in the production cycle in order to give accurate estimates to the vendor.

Another big risk to outsourcing is that the vendor might not meet their deadlines. This can severely impact the project if the deadlines are extremely tight. In order to mitigate this risk, be sure to allot ample time in the schedule for finding a vendor. Additionally, after you get the vendor's schedule, add some padding to it so there is some slack if needed. It is never a good idea to schedule a vendor's deadline at the same time as a major milestone. For example, don't have a vendor deliver final cinematics or music on the beta date; plan to have it delivered at least a week ahead of time.

If the vendor is running behind schedule and all necessary assets and documentation have been provided to them by the development team, you have a problem. In order to avoid this, schedule regular milestones for the vendor as well. They should get into the habit of making deliveries every week or every few days, depending on the work to be done. If the vendor misses any of these deadlines, it is a red flag that they might be in jeopardy of missing the final and most important deadline.

In some cases, the vendor might be good at convincing you everything is fine, and then they miss the final deadline by a long shot. If the situation is this bad, you might need to cut your losses and look for another vendor to complete the work or bring the work in-house and assign someone on the development team to finish it. This is not an ideal situation, as it means people need to work overtime to complete the work.

10.6.1 Communication

After an external vendor is hired, the key to a good relationship is effective communication. If the developer and vendor do not establish the communication pipeline up front, information will fall through the cracks, and key details will be missed. Poor communication might also impact the vendor's ability to meet proposed deadlines, especially if necessary information from the developer is not received on schedule.

Most external vendors will have a project manager who is responsible for managing the vendor's part of the development process from beginning to end and acting as the primary contact for the developer.

It is important to designate a single person from the development team to be the primary contact for the vendor's project manager. These two must communicate on a daily basis, even if it is just to provide a brief status update on what went on that day with the project. If more people are involved in the communication chain, it is likely that confusion will occur. If it is necessary to have a few people from the development team in touch with the vendor, such as the person who is handling all the voiceover for the game, the lines of communication must be clearly delineated so confusion does not exist about team members' responsibilities.

The internal development contact is responsible for delivering all the necessary assets and resources to the vendor and must inform the vendor of any changes to the schedule that affect the vendor's deadlines. If the vendor is not informed of a schedule delay that affects their work, you might find yourself paying extra money to the vendor because they received the assets late and had to work overtime or hire more people in order to meet the deadline. If the vendor is flexible, unforeseen schedule changes can be accommodated.

■ 10.7 Middleware

In the game industry, middleware has become an all-encompassing term for an out-of-the-box software package that can be modified for use in a game. Middleware is used for game systems, such as AI, animation, physics, rendering, and networking. For example, developers can license Havok Physics™ and modify it for use in their game instead of programming something from scratch. Cross-platform game engines, such as Epic's Unreal Engine 3, are considered middleware, as well as other third-party tools used for such development tasks as modeling, texturing, bug tracking, and project management.

One of the biggest benefits of middleware is that the developer can theoretically spend more time creating and polishing unique features of the game rather than creating a generic but necessary feature, such as lobby support for an online game. If the developer is familiar with the middleware technology (for example, they used it on previous games), it is usually an easy decision to use it again on another game. However, if the developer is not familiar with the middleware, they need to plan for a learning curve that may initially slow down development time as the team gets up to speed on how to work with the technology.

The biggest drawback to working with middleware is likely to be cost—you will need to pay a licensing fee (and sometimes royalties) to the middleware provider, which, depending on the product, can be several hundred thousand dollars. However, you may find the cost justified after putting together your game plan. Many middleware providers price their products competitively and provide excellent technical support to make it easier for developers to decide to use middleware.

Once the license is in place (and in some cases before), the middleware vendor will provide a software development kit (SDK) that includes the APIs, tools, and documentation. Most middleware providers offer technical support and will help work through any technical issues the team encounters while they are integrating the middleware technology into the game's production pipeline.

After the middleware is integrated into the game, the vendor may request a build of the game in order to check how their software was implemented. They may have a formal set of technical requirements that the game needs to fulfill before they will approve the middleware implementation in the game. This ensures that the technology is working as intended and that no surprises will occur when the game releases. The approval process can be a benefit for the developer, because testers who are familiar with any common problems that may occur when implementing the middleware will check the game and flag any issues that need to be addressed. Be sure to include time in the production schedule for this approval process.

USING MIDDLEWARE

Amanda Rubright, Producer
Aspyr

If you are considering using middleware, definitely make this part of your initial planning phase of a project. If you decide middleware is not the way to go, you need to know up front so you can be sure to allocate time and resources to creating what it is the project needs internally.

The benefits of using middleware are great when it comes down to time and efficient use of a product that you know has a proven track record. We often choose to use middleware when development from scratch doesn't make sense due to time constraints and the potential risks that may be encountered during development. Also, outsourcing some of the not-so-fun tasks makes your developers happy because it allows them to focus on the fun side of development!

Both parties benefit equally—it's usually more cost effective to utilize middleware than it is to develop a system from the ground up. Proven, working systems are always less risky than creating something new that needs to be developed and debugged.

In my opinion, there really aren't many disadvantages—only in worst-case scenarios. Sometimes the cost is high and unfamiliarity with the product can cause issues. Technical support can sometimes put the production schedule at risk if the vendor does not respond quickly to questions. However, this is usually not the case. By conducting due diligence of the vendors you want to use and by soliciting recommendations from your industry peers, you can mitigate many of these disadvantages and risks. We're a small industry so we are our best resources.

One of the main things to keep in mind when using middleware is that licensing fees must be paid to the middleware provider. Most of the licenses are tied to an actual title and/or platform. For instance, if you were working on PS3™ and Xbox 360® versions of the same game, you might need to secure a license for each platform, or you might be able to purchase one license that covers all the platforms for the game. You may even need one for additional languages, depending on what the licensing agreement covers. In some cases, you may also need to pay royalties to the vendor for each copy of the game sold, so be sure to thoroughly understand the licensing costs when conducting due diligence. If you work on a sequel to a game, it is likely you would also need to secure a new license. However, some vendors will allow you to use the license at no extra cost if you are releasing additional content for the main SKU of the game. Some vendors do cut deals if you are doing multiple titles and multiple platforms, but all platforms and SKUs still need to be licensed.

Typically the publisher pays for the licensing, but this ultimately depends on the project. Who pays what depends on the contract between the developer and publisher. For example, if the developer is shopping for a publisher, it's likely they will need to front any middleware licensing fees. In this case, it's possible for the developer to ask the publisher to reimburse these fees during contract negotiation, or the developer may include them in the completion budget they request from the publisher.

The negotiations for the vendors I've worked with usually take little time. Usually, you get the licensing agreement from the vendor, have the legal department review it, sign it, and return it with a check to the vendor. Once they get the check, the vendor will release the SDK so your team can begin working with it. In some cases, they will provide the SDK before the contract is finalized, which is very useful if the team is working on a tight deadline.

Integration of middleware is typically where you may see issues. How familiar is your team with this middleware? Have they used it before? How will it work with the title it is being used for? What is that middleware's support system like? Will they be available to guide you through integration/issues? The reality is that the experience and talent of your development team will dictate the types of issues that will occur with integration.

If you run into problems, you can get technical support from the middleware vendors. Most all of the middleware vendors I've worked with have provided fantastic support. Demonware, Quazal, and Unreal all have tech support websites that contain information on their product. They also have support email, which is very useful for getting questions answered. They have all been very responsive and helpful in answering development and integration questions. More often than not, all issues can be resolved via email, but sometimes a call is required for more in-depth issues. In some cases, middleware vendors will send integration specialists out to you; for example, Punkbuster will send an integration developer out to the site to work with your team to integrate their anti-cheat software.

Once you have integrated the middleware into your game, you may need to submit it to the vendor for approval. This is mainly to check that your implementation is correct. The approval time will vary, so find out about this up front so you can build it into your production schedule. Because they know the team is already working on a tight deadline, the vendor will be as flexible as possible about setting up the approval process. Most middleware approvals can occur concurrently with game development as they will not be looking to approve the same things your publisher would be. They may also want to sign off on the packaging to make sure that their logo and legal text are used correctly (and as contractually agreed to).

Step	Resources	General Timeline	Tasks
Create master schedule	Producer	Happens in parallel with requirements phase	Create project schedule with main milestones and break down each milestone into major art, design, engineering, and QA tasks. Add in sections for any localization, voiceover, or other outsourced work. Include sections for third-party approvals.
Create detailed schedules for core features	Producer	Happens in parallel with requirements phase	As design, art, and engineering determine requirements, create schedules for major features to determine scope, cost, and resources for desired features.
Determine budget	Producer	Happens in parallel with requirements phase	Make educated assumptions about estimated costs and create an initial budget.
Determine staffing needs	Producer	Happens in parallel with requirements phase	Make educated assumptions about estimated staffing needs and create an initial staffing plan.
Determine outsourcing needs	Producer	Happens in parallel with requirements phase	Based on staffing needs, team expertise, and budget, make an educated guess about which areas of the game will need to be outsourced.
Research and select vendors	Producer	Happens in parallel with requirements phase	Research potential vendors to get an idea of cost, quality, and dependability.
Approval	Studio management, publisher	Happens in parallel with requirements phase	Present budget, schedule, and staffing plan to management for approval.

FIGURE 10.13 Outline of game plan phase.

■ **10.8   Game Plan Outline**

Figure 10.13 is a summary of each step that must be completed in the game plan phase. This is based on a two-year development cycle.

■ **10.9   Chapter Summary**

The game plan is a critical component of preproduction as this pulls together all of the requirements and shows how the work is going to get done on time. The schedule, budget, and staffing plan are the key components, and all of these factors will fluctuate during production. However, if you spend time in preproduction creating an in-depth game plan, you have a better idea of what factors can be adjusted when changes happen during the development process. This chapter discussed the basics of determining the schedule, budget, and staffing plan and ways you can define these for your game plan. After the game plan is completed, you have a clear idea of what to expect during production.

The next chapter begins the discussion of what happens during the production phase, such as asset creation, making builds, and testing. If you put together a solid plan during preproduction, hopefully there will be no unexpected surprises during production.

■ **10.10   Questions and Exercises**

1. What is the purpose of a game plan?
2. What is the purpose of creating an initial production schedule?
3. What are the elements that must be included in a useful schedule? How do these elements impact the schedule?
4. What are the pros and cons of outsourcing and what types of things can be outsourced?
5. Research middleware to use for one aspect of a fictitious game (such as engines, UI, or AI). Which middleware is the best choice, taking into consideration the project's schedule, budget, and staffing?
6. Put together an initial schedule for a fictitious game.

11 Production Cycle

In this chapter:

- Design Production Cycle
- Art Production Cycle
- Engineering Production Cycle
- Working Together

■ 11.1 Introduction

When preproduction is completed, you will have a clear idea of the game that is being made, how to make it, who is going to do the work, and how much time you have to do it. It is important to note that there is not a definite point where preproduction ends and production begins. The transition will be gradual. For instance, while art and engineering begin working on the features outlined in the core design documentation, design is still busy designing the actual mission scenarios that appear in the game. Also, art will begin production on some assets, while still prototyping others. Engineering begins coding the game but might still be working on technical prototypes for some of the minor features.

What's important about production is that the team can start implementing the plan and watch the game take shape. So even though some small details are still being worked out, production can begin after the major aspects of the game are defined and approved. The main tasks occurring in production are implementing the plan, tracking the game's progress, and finishing the game. It is the producer's responsibility during production to manage these tasks smoothly and deal with any surprises or problems.

Every producer hopes that they have planned for every possible contingency during preproduction, and production is where this plan is put to the test. However, on a game that takes two years to develop, it is a bit optimistic to think that a plan made in January 2010 will be completely valid 18 months later in July 2011. Games change and grow with time, and a plan made more than a year ago might not take into account the hot new graphics feature that marketing wants added to the game. The producer must be constantly vigilant about the game's progress during production, so that high-risk areas are identified and corrected and high-priority feature requests can be accommodated when necessary.

During production, the producer's day-to-day tasks will involve interfacing with the leads and team on a daily basis, assessing the game's progress, evaluating gameplay, working with QA, keeping management happy, providing assets to marketing, working with external vendors, approving milestones, filling out paperwork, and a host of other things. Each day will be different; on some days, there may be several fires to put out, and on other days, you can spend your time catching up on work. Whatever the day brings, be prepared to get the production back on track so the game ships on time.

Of course, the art, design, engineering, and QA departments are also busy during production. Each discipline is working hard on their assigned tasks. Individuals can complete some tasks on their own or with help from someone in their discipline, but other tasks will require multiple people and disciplines to complete. If the team is enthusiastic and has high morale, getting them to work well with each other won't be difficult. They will become involved in each other's work, offer feedback, and work together to make the game the best it can be.

■ 11.2 Design Production Cycle

By the time production begins, design has completed documentation for the major parts of the game. They spend their day implementing gameplay into the build, tweaking existing gameplay features, and providing feedback to the artists and engineers on their work. In addition, a designer might be writing all of the dialogue for a game and working with the producer to organize the voiceover shoot.

The design production cycle also involves a lot of iteration and feature evolution. After a feature is implemented in the game as originally planned, the designer will continue to tweak and polish the implementation until it is perfect. This includes how the control works, scoring, dialogue, UI buttons, and anything else that needs to be tweaked when a playable version is evaluated. In some cases, a feature might be redesigned if necessary. A feature redesign is not something to be taken lightly and will need approval from the producer and leads before it is done.

Play-testing is also a large part of the design cycle. As gameplay mechanics start functioning in the game, the designers conduct play tests to determine whether a feature is fun or whether more work is needed. Ideally, people outside of the development team can be play testers, so that the designer can get unbiased feedback. However, it is a good idea to involve the team when possible, as this builds camaraderie and gives people more ownership over the game. In some instances, publishers will conduct open beta tests in order to get information directly from the target audience about what works and what doesn't work in the game. The feedback is useful to the designers, as they are getting feedback directly from the players and don't have to guess what they want.

CONDUCTING PLAY TESTS

Clint Hocking, Creative Director
Ubisoft

You can do several things to create useful play tests. First, you need external people to participate in the play tests who can look at the game neutrally. You also need dedicated people to plan, schedule, monitor, record, and report upon these tests. You need to conduct the tests regularly from first playable until you reach the point where you don't have time to implement anything your testing might uncover anyway (which is literally at about the master date). You need to do the testing in small groups of three to six players, and you need to do dozens of different tests. You need to have each group test as much of the game as it is possible for them to test, and the people running the test group need to know exactly what they can and should test for in each test. They need to gather as much data as they can, and they need to know how to construct questionnaires and how to compile the data they gather into useful information. The information you get from 100 to 200 individual players is absolutely invaluable in terms of improving the overall quality of your title.

■ 11.3 Art Production Cycle

The art production cycle revolves around asset creation. Characters, vehicles, objects, weapons, environment, UI art, and cinematics are created during the production phase. Each artist has assigned deliverables to produce by specific deadlines. After the deliverables are completed and working in the build, the feedback starts coming in. As with design, art will then revisit their state. Because each game has numerous art assets, the lead artist also spends a lot of time tracking the asset creation and making sure the artists are getting feedback in a timely manner.

Prototyping is still being done at this point. Even though the list of assets is defined, concept art and prototyping is necessary for specific assets that are generated. Also, an animator will work with the producer on planning the motion capture shoot if one is necessary.

Art will spend time working with the engineers to refine the art production pipeline. Usually when art production begins, some of the proprietary art tools are still being coded by the engineers. Artists can often start creating assets even if the pipeline is not ready, especially if the source assets are created in a commercial software package, but they won't be able to view these assets in-game until the pipeline is complete. Be aware that any delays in getting the pipeline up and running has a negative impact

PROTOTYPING

Carey Chico, Art Director
Pandemic Studios

Prototyping is extremely important when creating art assets for a game. To this end, the art director and producer must commit to doing everything in their power to get prototypes of levels, models, special effects, and any other key art assets running in-game. One thing you can do, if the game's engine is not up and running, is to use a ready-made engine and level editor (such as the Unreal Engine™) to build a temporary world. If this is not possible, create a lot of concept art to convey the mood, feeling, and style of the game. Although concept art will not solve technical challenges, it can help define them when considering what technical art features need to be included in the game.

Prototyping and concept art also gets the team excited about the game. The more the team can see, the more they can share the vision of the game with each other. Completed concept art and prototypes can create a lot of excitement and positive energy on a project.

on the overall schedule. If these delays drag on for weeks, it is possible that milestones will be missed or marketing will not have viewable builds of the game for important conferences and trade shows.

■ 11.4   Engineering Production Cycle

During production, engineering is working hard to get the features coded and debugged in the game. If they are using middleware, they also work with a middleware vendor to get the code up and running. They will work closely with QA to identify crash bugs and test fixes. As with design and art, engineering will also implement any necessary changes based on feedback.

Additionally, engineering is responsible for making regular builds of the game and maintaining the production pipeline. If the build is not working, more than likely the lead engineer and his or her team will need to fix the problem.

Engineers might spend a lot of production time debugging and putting out fires. Technology never works the way it is expected to, so a feature that was originally planned for might need to be cut because the technology can't support it. Sometimes these problems are not realized until engineering begins production and is finally seeing how things will function in the game.

◼ 11.5 Working Together

GIVING EFFECTIVE FEEDBACK

Carey Chico, Art Director
Pandemic Studios

Giving effective feedback to an artist is not difficult if you answer two questions: Do you like it? and Why? Why is the cornerstone of useful feedback; if you can't explain why you don't like something, the artist will not understand the feedback and will not know what changes to make.

All feedback on art assets should go through the art director and not directly to the artist who created the asset. This way the art director can filter the feedback, so there is no confusion on what changes must be made. The art director can also rephrase the feedback so that it is diplomatic and provides useful information to the artist. This also prevents the lines of communication from getting crossed, especially in a situation where the lead designer and lead artist might have conflicting feedback.

Establish a good process for tracking all the feedback. For example, Alienbrain® and Perforce® force you to add a comment when you check in something, which is a good way to track what changes were made to an asset. You can also track these changes in a change control log or in a designated area on the team website.

It is important that everyone on the team works together toward a common goal. Art should be talking with design and engineering on a regular basis about the game, and so on. If you have a team in which art, design, engineering, production, and QA don't interact with each other, you might soon find that communication between the departments is rare, and that when it does happen, it's to complain about each other.

Feedback between art, design, engineering, and QA is valuable to the game and the team. If an engineer takes time to play some of the missions the designers have scripted, he or she might have some suggestions on ways to improve them or may discover a minor change he or she can make to the scripting tool that provides added scripting functionality to make the missions more fun. Constructive feedback is always welcome if delivered in a tactful and respectful manner.

During production, it is also important for the team to realize what the task dependencies are and how any delays affect the overall deadlines. People need to work closely together, especially if multiple departments are working on the same feature. Each team member should set aside a few minutes each day to check in with his or her or her coworkers about where they are with their work. Also, people should not be afraid to raise red flags or bring any concerns to their lead or to production.

USEFUL FEEDBACK

Clint Hocking, Creative Director
Ubisoft

Sadly, everyone is a critic, and because design is something everyone thinks they can do, everyone seems to think they are entitled to give feedback on the design and have that feedback be integrated. What is the best way for an artist, producer, designer, or manager to give feedback on code? The answer is: Go learn how to program, work your way up from intern to lead, and then conduct a thorough code evaluation and present that feedback in writing. Unfortunately, it is true that because design is so ill-defined and because we tend to not be rigorous we are subject to this kind of input in ways that programmers or producers are not. *This is our fault.* We need to develop and improve our methodologies and work on formalizing our field and developing ourselves and our abilities to the point where some guy off the street who happens to like Quake does not have a 50–50 chance of being as good or better than any working designer. Until we reach the level where there is a quantifiable skill set that is possessed only by designers, until we get past the "wouldn't it be cool if . . ." approaches to design, we will always be required to integrate feedback from people in other professions. That said, programmers and producers and artists out there have valuable design feedback. This is because they are engaged by design problems, they are analytical, and they know what they are talking about as much as your average designer. The best way for them to give their feedback is simply to be able to analyze and criticize the design in the same vocabulary as the designer. In other words, by coming to speak to me in my own language, you have shown that you understand my field. It's the same with art and programming and production.

It can be a challenge to get engineers, artists, and designers to effectively communicate with each other. We don't yet have a full formalized vocabulary for talking about and thereby facilitating design. This is a primary goal for modern game designers. Go read the books, lectures, or papers of Doug Church, Mark Leblanc, Harvey Smith, Chris Crawford, Raph Koster, Ben Cousins, Robin Hunicke, or basically any designer who is linked off of his or her website or blog. Then you will start to understand how to communicate with designers. Then you won't be coming to your designer and saying, "I think it would be cooler if . . . ." When you can do that, you will find yourself in one of two positions: You'll either find yourself talking to a designer who designs by saying "wouldn't it be cool if," in which case your project is probably in trouble, or you will find a designer who can communicate with you, in which case everyone wins. Designers need to be more thorough, and when they become more thorough, they will expect those who want to discuss design with them to be thorough as well.

Overall, production is a time filled with a lot of activity, and the team will grow to its maximum size. Things will be happening quickly, so everyone needs to be conscientious about getting their work done in a timely fashion. Production is also when crunch time becomes necessary, so be sure to keep an eye peeled for burnout or other potential personnel issues. Because so much is happening during production, it is also one of the most enjoyable times of the project if you have planned carefully during preproduction.

■ 11.6 Chapter Summary

Production starts after the game concept and requirements are defined in preproduction. If the game plan is detailed and well organized, production will go smoothly. During production, art, design, engineering, and QA are all focused on the same goal—delivering a high-quality and entertaining game. Each discipline will have different priorities for the game: art wants the game to look its best, design wants the game to play its best, and so on. But they all work together to strike a balance between each goal. These goals are influenced by all the play-testing and feedback that occur during production.

■ 11.7 Questions and Exercises

1. Describe what the designers are focused on during the production phase.
2. Describe what the engineers are focused on during the production phase.
3. Describe what the artists are focused on during the production phase.
4. What are some ways that people can improve their working relationships with others on the development team?

12 | Voiceover and Music

In this chapter:

- Planning for Voiceover
- Choosing a Sound Studio
- Casting Actors
- Recording Voiceover
- Voiceover Checklist
- Planning for Music
- Working with a Composer
- Licensing Music

■ 12.1 Introduction

Quality voiceover in a game is becoming an expectation of players. Players want to be immersed in a game world, and that means the characters must be believable and speak in a way that fits the game world. Great voiceover work adds to a game's appeal and makes a good game better. Conversely, poor voiceover work detracts from the game experience and makes a good game seem below average.

Because of this desire to fully immerse the player in the game world, voiceover work is also becoming more complex and, thus, more challenging to manage. There are more characters, more lines of dialogue, and more diverse uses of dialogue within the game. For example, Tom Clancy's Ghost Recon™ had about 600 lines of dialogue and about five unique voices, but four years later Tom Clancy's Ghost Recon 2™ had more than 2,500 lines of dialogue and more than 15 unique voices. These days, games such as Mass Effect™ and Grand Theft Auto IV™ have even more complex and challenging voiceovers to manage—hundreds of characters (some voiced by celebrities), tens of thousands of lines of dialogue, and dynamic voiceover systems so that the player doesn't hear the same voice cues over and over again.

If your game has thousands of lines of dialogue with numerous characters, work must start months in advance to write the script, secure a recording studio, audition actors, and record and process the voiceover files. As with all the other aspects of game development, the more you plan for these tasks, the more successful you will be during the voiceover process.

Music is also an effective tool for setting the tone of a game and makes the game world more immersive. The Silent Hill® series uses music and sound to great effect to enhance the creepiness of a world inhabited by demonic creatures. In some cases, music is one of the last things considered on a project, and the producer starts looking for a composer well after the game has started production. In other cases, music is an integral part of the entire game and is planned for during preproduction. For example, the Tony Hawk® series of games is known for licensing music from well-known bands. Licensing music on this scale requires planning and legal negotiations. If the licenses are not secured before the game is code released, the music track will likely be removed from the game.

Things to keep in mind for game music include technical considerations, budgets, schedule, and how music will be used in the game. In addition, you might want to license music instead of having original music composed.

This chapter will give a general overview of how to plan for and use both voiceover and music in your game.

■ 12.2 Planning for Voiceover

Initial planning for game voiceover needs to happen in the preproduction phase. In this phase, the goals of the voiceover design can be defined and any technical considerations for reaching these goals can be explored. If voiceover is an afterthought in the development process, it is more difficult, time-consuming, and costly to implement.

One thing to keep in mind when planning for voiceover is that you want to wait as long as possible before actually recording the final voiceover. Voiceover dialogue will change during the course of development. For example, during play-testing the designer might decide that adding a line of dialogue is necessary to make the mission objective more clear. This addition can be done more easily and cheaply if the final dialogue has not been recorded. However, having the basic plan outlined in advance but not implemented allows the team the flexibility to look for opportunities to improve the script with such revisions most efficiently. So even though you will not need to record the final voiceover until well after alpha, you must have the basic plan outlined to accommodate any last-minute voiceover changes.

12.2.1 Voiceover Design

Voiceover is one of the primary ways to bring the game characters and story to life for the player. For example, a good voiceover actor will be able to convey whether a character is human or alien, and uptight or carefree. Voiceover communicates information about a character's state of mind or a situation to the player. Is the character afraid, sad, in danger, or confident? Is the voiceover coming from a television broadcast or from another room?

Additionally, the voiceover design is the biggest determining factor of how much it will cost to get the desired voiceover effects. The design details how voiceover will be used in the game, how many lines of dialogue are needed, how many characters will have spoken parts, and which dialogue will have additional processing and effects. Usually the game designer and sound designer work together on the voiceover design to make sure that it is fully thought out and works for the game.

For example, when working on a massively multiplayer online game, the designers might decide that every nonplayer character must have several hundred spoken responses to different situations. If there are 100 characters in the game, the amount of dialogue can be well over 10,000 lines, which creates a huge amount of sound assets to record and track. After looking at the initial design and realizing there is not enough time or money to record this amount of dialogue, the designers can go back and revise the voiceover design accordingly.

The voiceover design will differ for each game, with the game genre being a major influence on some of the differences. For example, role-playing and adventure games usually have a large cast of characters and conversations going on between characters and, therefore, tend to have extensive dialogue. Games that are not story driven, such as racing games and some action games, usually have fewer speaking parts and use the dialogue to direct the player through the gameplay space or to create atmosphere.

12.2.2   Voiceover Script

A voiceover script is the main document that details all the dialogue to record for the game. A script that is well organized and contains all the necessary information for the actors, sound engineers, and development team goes a long way in making sure the voiceover process is problem free. The script should be the central location for any and all information about the dialogue, including filenames, audio effects, context, and inflection. If these elements are in separate documents, there are more assets to track, and it is likely that any updates to dialogue would not be carried over to every single document, which means mistakes are more likely to be made.

A spreadsheet is the best format for organizing the voiceover script because all the information can be clearly presented in a logical fashion. Another benefit of converting the voiceover script into a spreadsheet is the ability to use filters to sort the information in different ways. An actor or casting director will sort it by "character name." A sound engineer will want to sort it by "effects" to quickly see which files get effects. For these filters to work properly, all the information must be consistently labeled. Figure 12.1 is an example of how the voiceover information can be organized into a spreadsheet. Note that all the dialogue is listed in chronological order to show how the conversation flows between all the characters.

Line #	Character	English	Level	Type	SfX	Context	Voice Direction	Filename
1	Bad Guy #13	We're in the van, commander. We're going to lose the police on the interstate.	1	Mission Open	Radio futz	The bad guys are trying to outrun the police after they stole a museum artifact.	Serious	01_bg13_01.wav
2	BulletPoint	Sam, they're getting away!	1	Objective		BulletPoint has been monitoring radio chatter and knows what the bad guys are planning.	Serious, raised voice	01_bp_01.wav
3	Sam	I'll cut them off.	1	Objective		Sam received the update from BulletPoint and will cut off the bad guys on the highway.	Serious, calm	01_sam_01.wav
4	Civilian #3	Help me!	1	Nonplayer Character		This civilian got hit by the bad guys as they were trying to escape.	Scared, yelling	01_c3_01.wav
5	Sam	You'll be OK. I've called the ambulance.	1	Cinematic		Sam stops pursuit of the bad guys and aids the injured civilian.	Soothing	01_sam_02.wav

FIGURE 12.1 Voiceover spreadsheet.

The first column lists the line number. The line number is useful to have during the recording session so you can quickly reference any of the lines with an actor; this is especially useful if you need to rerecord a line or record a "pick-up" line. Just tell the actor which line numbers will have pick-up recordings. The second column lists the name of the character speaking the line. The third column lists the dialogue. The fourth column lists the level or area where this dialogue will be heard. The fifth column lists the type of information that is being conveyed; for example, is this banter between characters, information directing the player to a specific objective, or dialogue for the cinematics? This information is useful to note so you can quickly sort the voiceover script by dialogue type. The sixth column lists any special effects that need to be added during postprocessing, such as radio effects. The sound engineer will need this information to ensure that all the dialogue is processed with the correct effects. The seventh column provides context for the dialogue. The eighth column provides information on the voice direction of the line. These two columns are important for the actor. Even though the actors will have someone directing them at the shoot, these columns provide some basic information about what is needed and can help them prepare. Additionally, when the script is sent to be localized for any international versions, this information is necessary for the translators and localized voiceover actors. The ninth column lists the correct filename that will be used by the game.

If any of this information is missing or located in another file, it is likely that something will be forgotten and mistakes will be made. The most expensive problem that may occur is not getting all the necessary dialogue recorded at the voiceover shoot. It is time-consuming and expensive to book voiceover actors for each recording session, so if the voiceover script does not detail every line to record, some dialogue might be missed during the recording session, which means the actors would need to be called back at a later date to pick up any missed dialogue.

A traditional cinematic script format can also be useful, especially for actors recording dialogue for cut-scenes, but this format should not be primary for the script. The writer may have originally used this format to write all the in-game dialogue and cinematic cut-scenes, as it is a more familiar format and more readable during the writing process. This format is also useful for reviewing the dialogue because a group of people can easily get together, assign parts to each other, and read the lines aloud to check for pacing, content, mistakes, and so on. However, any dialogue written in a traditional script format must be converted to the master voiceover spreadsheet during the process, so the spreadsheet remains the main dialogue source document for the project.

12.2.3 Placeholder Voiceover

If there is time in the development cycle, recording placeholder dialogue and integrating it into the game is a great way to hear how the dialogue sounds in the game.

When listening to the placeholder dialogue, the designer and writer get a better idea of whether critical information is being clearly conveyed to the player. Also, they can hear how the dialogue sounds, understand the pacing, and figure out whether any additional dialogue must be written before the final voiceover recording.

Many members of the development team will be happy to be voiceover actors for a few hours, and the producer and writer can get some experience communicating with actors regarding what types of performances are needed. Placeholder dialogue should be done several weeks in advance of the final recording session to get the most benefit and make any adjustments to what is needed at the final recording session.

The other benefit of placeholder dialogue is working out any issues with the audio asset pipeline. Checks can be made on asset and memory usage, the filenaming convention, the file format of the in-game audio assets, and other things that affect the technical aspects of the audio. The placeholder files should have the same filename as the final voiceover files. In this way, the placeholder voiceover files can simply be replaced by the final voiceover files when they are ready. Additionally, the sound programmer and sound designer can make sure that they both understand how to work together to get the voiceover up and running in the game.

12.2.4   Schedule and Staffing

An initial voiceover schedule needs to be created early in preproduction so there is time to find a sound studio and schedule the recording session. As mentioned earlier in this chapter, plan the actual recording session to take place as late as possible during production, as the dialogue needs will change over the course of the project. Also, if dialogue is recorded too early in development, retakes might be needed down the line. These retakes can be costly, especially if the original actor is not available and all the dialogue needs to be rerecorded with a new actor to match the voice for the retakes.

If thousands of lines of dialogue need to be recorded, you probably will want to schedule multiple voiceover sessions to accommodate the needs of the project. Doing so will allow you time for any pick-ups on dialogue recorded in earlier sessions. The general rule of thumb is that 50 lines of dialogue can be recorded in an hour. A line of dialogue is usually considered to be one sentence or about 8 to 10 words.

In some instances, the cinematics team might need to get the final recorded dialogue earlier in development, so they have time to animate the characters to the dialogue and work on lip-syncing. In this case, you might want to schedule a session earlier in development just for recording voiceover used in the cinematics. You will need to work closely with the cinematics team to determine the best time for the cinematic voiceover recordings. If these recordings are done too late in the schedule, the

Task	Resource	Deadline
Initial dialogue written	Writer	~3–4 months before beta
Placeholder VO recorded	Sound designer	~3–4 months before beta
Send bid packages to sound studios	Producer	~3–4 months before beta
Book time for VO recording session	Producer	As soon as you have decided on a sound studio
Updated dialogue written	Writer	~6–8 weeks before sound shoot
Additional placeholder VO recorded	Sound designer	~6–8 weeks before sound shoot
Audition actors	Sound studio	~4–6 weeks before sound shoot (more time if casting a large number of actors)
Cast actors	Writer/producer/ sound designer	~4–6 weeks before sound shoot (more time if casting a large number of actors)
Final dialogue written	Writer	~2 weeks before scheduled sound shoot
Dialogue recorded	Writer/producer/ sound designer	~3–4 weeks before beta (more time if a large amount of dialogue is to be recorded)
Dialogue processed and ready for development team	Sound designer	~1 week before beta

FIGURE 12.2 Overview of voiceover schedule.

cinematics team might not have enough time to finish their work. Scheduling this recording correctly is even more critical when working with an external cinematics vendor because there is less control over their schedule.

Figure 12.2 is a general overview of the main tasks to schedule for the voiceover recordings. These time frames are based on recording 3,000 lines of in-game dialogue with 8 to 10 actors. The lead times should be longer if the game contains more dialogue and more actors.

Many variables can affect the schedule and should be taken into account when creating the schedule. Some of these variables include the following:

Number of lines of dialogue: More dialogue means more time is needed in the schedule.

Production schedule: When working on a six-month project, the voiceover process must be accelerated to get everything completed.

Amount of voiceover needed for the cinematics: Voiceover used in cinematics might need to be recorded sooner so the artists have time to animate to the dialogue.

Actor availability: Not every actor might be available when you want him or her; he or she could be already booked or on vacation.

Recording studio availability: The recording studio might be booked well in advance with other projects, so it is best to tentatively block out time with a studio a few months before your projected recording date.

Adding extra time into the schedule will help accommodate some of these unexpected factors.

Because organizing and running a voiceover shoot is time-consuming, designate one person to be in charge of this task. If there is not a huge amount of voiceover to record, this person will not be on this task full time. However, if there are 10,000 or more lines to record, or celebrity actors are being used, or multiple sound shoots need to be scheduled, this task could well be full time for one person to coordinate over the course of a few months.

This coordinator would be responsible for communicating with the writer, sound designer, recording studio, and anyone else involved in the voiceover process to ensure that all the tasks and deliverables are taken care of in a timely fashion. Usually, an associate producer or a sound designer can handle the management of this task. In some instances, such as when working with a large publisher, the publisher will take on the responsibility of coordinating these tasks. The key thing is that a single person is in charge and acting as the main point of contact.

■ 12.3 Choosing a Sound Studio

Finding a sound studio that is easy to work with and provides high-quality assets will make the voiceover work go more smoothly. A good sound studio will work closely with the development team to ensure that the final recordings are correct for the game. They will provide invaluable assistance in auditioning and casting actors, running the actual recording sessions, and delivering the audio assets in a timely manner. They may also provide additional services on request, such as voiceover direction, tracking, paying the union actors on the project, and special effects processing.

When choosing a sound studio, have a clear idea of what your needs are for the project. If you need to record only a few hundred lines of dialogue with a single actor, you might want to think about using a smaller studio and nonunion actors. If you are recording for a high-profile title with a large amount of dialogue and a number of actors, you might want to use a larger studio that has experience running sound shoots.

It is a good idea to talk with other people who have recorded dialogue for other games; they often will have a sound studio to recommend, and you can get firsthand knowledge of the pros and cons of a certain studio. A few questions to keep in mind when researching sound studios are as follows:

Do they have experience recording video game dialogue? Experience with video game voiceover will help them better understand what the voiceover needs are. Not having game-specific experience is not a major concern, as long as they are experienced in recording voiceover.

Are they a union signatory? Union signatories are authorized to pay union actors. If a studio is not a union signatory, you will have to hire a union payroll service or set up your game company or publisher as a signatory.

What types of recording equipment are available? Is the equipment, such as the microphones and mixing board, adequate to meet the quality expectations?

What software is used for editing? For example, if the game's sound designer is using Pro Tools® to edit the audio, he or she might want to use a studio that records with Pro Tools.

What size is the studio? If there is a need to record multiple actors at once, can the studio's recording booth accommodate this? If several people are present at the recording session—writer, producer, sound designer—is the studio large enough for all of them?

Are they set up for phone patch-ins? If someone must participate in the recording session but is unable to physically be at the studio, can they be patched into the session via phone? This ability is especially useful if you are working with a studio in another city.

What is the turnaround time for audio deliverables? How quickly can they turn around the audio after the recording session? This estimate must be included in the schedule. You might need to make this a deciding factor when choosing a studio if the project is on an accelerated schedule.

What options are available for receiving audio deliverables? Will the audio assets need to be burned to a CD and mailed to you, or can they be posted on an FTP site? Can the files be delivered in different file formats and with different compression schemes? Is the studio willing to use proprietary software to convert the files to the preferred file format for the game?

What are the rates? Studios usually charge hourly or daily rates for the actual time that actors will be recording in the studio. They also charge rates for processing the files after the recording session. In addition, rates are charged for the actors' time, and these rates will differ for each actor.

What additional costs are incurred? Examples of services that incur additional costs are auditioning and casting actors, directing actors, writing dialogue, and so on. Extra costs may also be incurred for discs, meals, postage, and so on.

How much advance notice is needed to book studio time? A studio might need to be booked several months in advance or only a week in advance. It is also good to know what the chances are for booking any last-minute, pick-up sessions.

12.3.1   Bid Packages

Sending bid packages to several sound studios gives you an opportunity to compare prices and services, enabling you to choose the best studio for your project. Getting multiple bids is also a good way to learn how much time the studios will need to record the voiceover and how responsive they are with questions.

Studios might have a preferred format for receiving bids, so check with them first to see whether they have specific bid forms you must use. If they don't have a specific form, find out what information is needed and create a form that will clearly present the key information the studio will need to calculate the bid. At a minimum, they will need to know how many lines of dialogue will be recorded, how many unique game characters will have dialogue, and how many actors will be used to record this dialogue.

Sending an estimated line count is very important when creating a bid package. This count is the basis of much of the studio's time and cost estimates. First, each studio might have a different method for determining line count, but generally you should count each sentence (about 8 to 10 words) as one line. Don't make the mistake of basing the actual line count on how many rows are used in the voiceover spreadsheet (see Figure 12.1), as this method might give an inaccurate count if an actor has a paragraph of dialogue listed in a single cell on the spreadsheet. A miscalculation in the line count makes it very difficult for the studios to accurately schedule the actors and determine costs.

For example, actors are booked for a maximum of four hours for a single recording session. If they exceed this four-hour period because the line count was much greater than planned, they will need to be rescheduled for an additional recording session, which incurs extra time and cost. Also, they might be unable to reschedule during the time you have already booked with the studio, which means the actor and studio both have to find another time to finish the session. This delay could put the game project's schedule at risk.

Other important information to include in the bid is how many unique voices are being recorded and how many actors are needed to record them. According to the rules of the Screen Actors Guild (SAG), a SAG actor is allowed to record up to three unique voices in a single recording session for a flat fee. If they do any additional voices, they must receive extra compensation. If you carefully manage the expectations for the character voices in the game, you can cast actors to do multiple voices, and thereby save money. For example, if you have a skilled voiceover actor do three minor roles in the game, you need to cast and pay for only one actor.

When casting for a major voice that will be heard throughout the game, you probably want to have the actor chosen for that role perform only that voice. This way the actor can focus on bringing the main character to life, and the voice will stand out as unique in the game. Additionally, the amount of dialogue for a major character in the game might require several recording sessions, which means there would not be time for the actor to record additional voices.

With regard to cost, another thing to keep in mind is that actors get paid for a four-hour minimum. So if the actor is only needed in the recording studio for one hour, he or she will still get paid for four hours of work. Because you have to pay for the actor's time anyway, it is a good idea to record as much dialogue as you can during the session, including alternate line reads and additional generic lines that can be used in the game (such as greetings, screams, and anything else that might prove to be useful later in development).

Other information to include in the bid request are as follows:

File processing: Indicate whether you want the sound studio to fully process all the files and remove pops, clicks, and other sound artifacts from the final audio files. Also indicate whether you will need any special effects processing for the files, such as radio futz.

Unique actor needs: For example, if you are looking for an actor who can do a certain accent or speak a specific language, include it in the bid request. Although this need will not affect the studio recording fee, it might affect the actor fee.

Union or nonunion: If the project requires union actors, additional union fees are added to the bid for the actors' time. Union versus nonunion actors is discussed later in the chapter.

File delivery formats: Indicate in what format the files are to be delivered. For example, you would need to specify uncompressed .wav files at 24 bit/96 kHz. If you want additional file formats, such as compressed 16 bit/44 kHz, indicate that as well. Also, detail how you want these files delivered—burned to a disc, uploaded to an FTP site, and so on.

Tentative schedule: Let the vendor know your schedule. Indicate when you will be able to deliver the final line count and final voiceover script and when you need to receive the final audio files. This planning will help the vendor manage their time. The vendor might have to speed up the turnaround time for the final audio deliverables to accommodate the game's audio schedule. If the vendor does not have the time or resources to take on a project with certain schedule constraints, they can let you know during the bid process.

Figure 12.3 is an example of a VO bid that would be sent to a VO vendor. In this example, the VO vendor will need to book the actors who are playing these same characters in the film. Securing celebrity voiceovers may add some additional time to the schedule.

Voiceover Assets

Any celebrity talent used? Include celebrity names in "Notes" column in table below.	Yes. The actors who play the main characters in the movie will also voice them in the game.
Union or nonunion (English version)	Union
Bit depth (ex: 8 bit, 16 bit, etc.)	16 bit
Sample rate (ex: 22 KHz, 44 KHz)	44 KHz
Channels (mono/stereo/5.1)	Dolby 5.1
File delivery formats	Uncompressed .wav files
Required processing (list any special effects needed)	Basic edits for pops and clicks, name files according to filenaming system provided by developer.

Character	Est. # of Lines	Male/Female	Age	Notes
BulletPoint	5,000	M	25	Need to get actor who is playing this character in the movie.
Melanie Cole	5,000	F	26	Need to get actor who is playing this character in the movie.
Caribou	3,000	M	24	Need to get actor who is playing this character in the movie.
Teacher	1,000	F	65	Actor needs to speak Chinese and English. The actor can also voice other characters in the game.
Sam	1,000	M	21	Actor can voice other characters in the game.
Woman #1	50	F	mid-40s	This actress will voice three characters.
Woman #2	75	F	early-40s	Voiced by same actress who does Woman #1.
Man #1	50	M	mid-40s	This actor will voice three characters.
Man #2	75	M	mid-30s	Voiced by same actor who does Man #1.

FIGURE 12.3   Example of a voiceover bid.

■ **12.4   Casting Actors**

Casting the correct actor for a role is one of the most important aspects of the voiceover process. If the correct actor is cast, he or she can go beyond recording lines of dialogue and add something extra to the character to really bring it to life. There are many elements to casting actors that you should consider to ensure you get the right person for the job.

12.4.1   Union Versus Nonunion

One of the first things to consider is whether you will hire union or nonunion actors. Your choice depends on the project's budget, the scope, and the schedule. Nonunion actors are cheaper, since there are no additional charges for union fees. However, talented nonunion actors are difficult to find. When using nonunion actors, even though you are saving money up front, you could end up spending more if it takes a long time to find suitable actors or if the actors need numerous takes to record each line correctly. If the project's voiceover needs are minimal, around a few hundred lines, using nonunion actors is not a big risk.

In the United States, union actors are members of the Screen Actors Guild (SAG), the American Federation of Television and Radio Artists (AFTRA), or sometimes both. Union actors are more readily available because they can be contacted through databases maintained by SAG and AFTRA. Costs for using union actors include the actor's normal fee, plus an additional percentage that goes directly to the union for the actor's pension and health benefits.

Additionally, union actors have very strict work guidelines and must be paid according to a fee schedule set by the union. For example, all union actors must be paid for a minimum of four hours of work, regardless of how long the session actually took. Also, union actors are limited to no more than three unique voices or characters per recording session. Any extra voices cost additional money.

Union actors are more expensive to hire, but this cost can be justified as they are certified professionals. If you are working on a large project and need to hire several actors, you might want to consider hiring union actors.

12.4.2   Celebrity Voices

In the last few years, the use of celebrity voiceovers has become very popular. Using celebrities lends a cinematic quality to the game and is useful for marketing and PR purposes. However, additional time must be added to the schedule because contracts need to be signed and approval might be required for the final voiceover files that appear in the game. Additionally, there might be restrictions on the actor's availability and how many hours of recording he or she can do. If using celebrity voiceovers, start preproduction for the voiceover process earlier so there is time to deal with any unexpected issues.

If you are using an internationally well-known celebrity, check with his or her agent to see how the celebrity's voiceover for the localized versions should be handled.

The publisher might be contractually obligated to use a specific voiceover actor who has been approved by the celebrity to dub his or her lines into other languages. This situation was the case with Bruce Willis, who voiced the lead character in Apocalypse™, a PlayStation® game published by Activision. He recorded the character's lines in the English version, and specific actors whom he had already approved recorded the lines in the localized versions.

WORKING WITH CELEBRITY VOICES

Stuart Roch, Executive Producer
Activision

We were fortunate that we worked as closely with the *Matrix* production team as we did. Getting AAA Hollywood talent into the recording studio for dialogue recording can be a real trick, but with the help of the film production, we were able to schedule time with the *Matrix* talent on days where they had a light shooting schedule or on days between their primary film commitments. Through the cooperation of the Wachowski Brothers and the *Matrix* production team, the scheduling of time with the primary talent for things like voiceover, motion capture, or digital photography went off without any problems. We recommend working with the film production office as closely as possible to ensure that the time you need to spend with the talent is organized, therefore making it as painless as possible for both the game development team and the actors themselves.

12.4.3   Preparing Character Descriptions

Character descriptions give a clear idea of who the character is and how he or she might sound. These notes are useful for actors auditioning for a particular role, as they don't have to guess who the character is and can focus on creating a voice that defines the character. The descriptions also help a casting directing further narrow the field on the type of actor needed for the role.

Figure 12.4 is one example of a character description template. Including a picture is invaluable as it gives a clear idea of the type of actor needed for the role. Other key information, such as gender, age, and ethnicity, is provided to further narrow the field. A brief description of the voice tone and speech patterns is helpful. The actor voicing the lines can use this information to determine how the character will sound. The last part presents information on where the character appears and his or her major role in the game. Generally, this type of description is useful for a game in which there is some freedom in how the lines are read.

Figure 12.5 is another example of a character description. This example takes a different approach in that detailed information is presented about the character's background

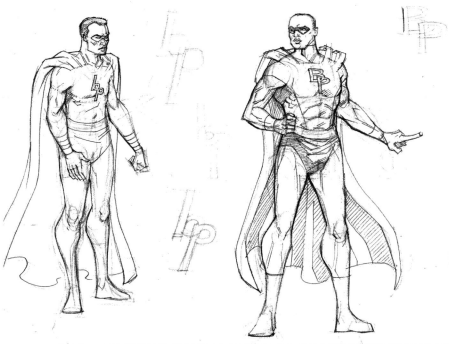

Name:	BulletPoint
Age:	25 years
Gender:	Male
Type:	Superhuman
Role:	Hero; member of Justice Unit
Voice:	Strong, confident voice
Speech Patterns:	BulletPoint is a marketing executive, and has a strong, clear voice that projects well. In conversation, he's long-winded and overanalytical, but in combat, he is quick and to the point. He tends to yell during fights, adopting a military tone of voice when giving orders.
Other Information:	*Player character
*New to the team; allows player to experience world of Justice Unit through his eyes	

FIGURE 12.4 Character description example.

and personality. This background information might not even appear in the game, but it presents a more fully fleshed-out character.

A voice description presents the character's tone of voice, speech patterns, and accents. The references section includes references to famous actors who have a voice similar to what the character should sound like in the game. These references are very helpful for the casting director and for actors.

Name	Ice Queen (real name Melanie Cole)
Background	Born in 1979, Melanie grew up in Virginia Beach, VA. Her father was an architect and her mother worked as a receptionist. An average student, Melanie studied at Tidewater Community College for two years before transferring to Old Dominion University, where she graduated with a degree in history in 2002. Melanie's parents died in 2004, when her sentience manifested itself. The freezing blast leveled three homes, killing a total of seven people. Horrified, Melanie fled, but was later apprehended by police. Later that day, her sentience erupted again, destroying the police station and killing several officers. BulletPoint and The Sensei were called in and were able to incapacitate Melanie. She was taken to Masada, where the Justice Division was able to train her in the use of her powers. Since then, Melanie has learned to control her sentience, and has proven herself a capable member of the Justice Division.
Personality	Melanie is extremely distant and has difficulty forming lasting relationships with people. Though she has fought beside the other members of the Justice Division for two years, she still refers to them by their code names and refuses to socialize outside of work. Members of the Division have joked that her most powerful offensive weapon is the Cold Shoulder. She still grieves for her family and feels a profound sense of remorse for the lives that she ended, even though she's aware that the deaths were accidental. Despite hundreds of hours of training, Melanie fears that she may lose control of her sentience, resulting in more innocent deaths.
Voice	Melanie's voice is low and firm. She only raises her voice when chastising or disagreeing with someone. She often sounds arch or condescending, particularly when explaining things to others, and can come across as callous when delivering bad news. She speaks unaccented English.
References	Gillian Anderson (*The X-Files*)
Sample Dialogue	"That's really too bad, but that's not our problem. We're here to apprehend Zomborg, and that's all I'm really interested in talking about." "What part of 'immediately' did you not understand? You were expected a while ago. Get in there and do your job." "I don't really have time to deal with this. The Division doesn't have time for this either. Suck it up, or quit."

FIGURE 12.5   Another character description example.

The sample dialogue section lists actual dialogue the character will be speaking in the game. Such samples can be used when the actors are creating audition tapes. A better judgment can be made on how an actor will sound for the role if he or she is auditioning with dialogue that will actually be used in the game, and if all candidates use the same dialogue.

This type of character description works well for major characters that need to be more defined. The detailed description is also helpful for characters that have appeared in previous incarnations of the game and have developed their personalities and backgrounds within the game universe.

12.4.4   Auditions

Auditions give you an opportunity to hear several different actors read for each character. Depending on how the auditions are set up, you will also have an opportunity to see how well the actors take direction, how wide their ranges are, and whether they are capable of doing multiple voices. The recording studio will handle the auditions or recommend a casting agency that does them.

If there is no time or money to set up a separate audition, the actor selections can be made by listening to an actor's voiceover reel. Doing so is not recommended, as it does not allow you to hear exactly how the actor is going to interpret your game's character. You will have to trust that the actor is right for the part based on nongame-specific information.

The basic audition process involves scheduling time for the actors to come to the studio to record some sample dialogue from the game. When they arrive at the studio, they are presented with character descriptions and a voiceover script. The voiceover director, if one is hired, will take them through the script and prep them for the audition. The actor will record the sample dialogue, and these lines will be processed and made available for the developer. The developer then will make final actor selections based on the audition tapes.

To successfully pick the right actor during the audition process, keep several things in mind. First, someone from the development team should be present either on the phone or in person at the auditions. Having someone from the team participate in the auditioning process is key, since he or she will be able to advise the voiceover director on what specific characteristics he or she is looking for from the actor. For example, if the character has a Russian accent, the developer can clarify whether this accent should be heavy, light, exaggerated, or more realistic. This way, when the developer is reviewing the auditions, they do not have to wonder whether the actor who used a light Russian accent is capable of doing a heavier, more realistic accent.

The other benefit of having someone from the team at the audition is that he or she will have firsthand experience of what it will be like to work with a particular actor. For example, the actor might need a lot of detailed direction, might be difficult to work with, or might not have a broad enough acting range for a pivotal character. All of this information is useful when making the final actor selections.

If someone from the team is not available to attend the audition, get feedback from the recording studio on the actors. Recording studios tend to work with the same group of actors over and over and will be able to give valuable feedback on an actor's ability to deliver what is being requested. They will also have feedback on how well the actor takes direction.

Second, make sure that the sample dialogue for the audition reflects the type of dialogue that actually will be in the final version of the game. If working on a realistic military game, include sample dialogue that reflects how soldiers speak. Also, the dialogue should include a wide range of emotions, volumes, and lengths. For example, include dialogue that is conversational, angry, shouted, whispered, happy, and so on. Also include short in-game comments—"area secured"—and longer dialogue made up of several sentences that might appear in a cinematic. This wide variety of sample dialogue will give you a better idea of how well the actor fits the character.

Third, don't be afraid to request that additional actors be called in for auditions. If you don't hear an actor who is suitable for the character you are trying to cast in the first round of auditions, call in another group of actors to audition. Recording voiceover is very expensive, and it is better to find the right person for the role instead of having to recast the part later.

Auditions should be done well in advance of the actual recording session so there is time to choose the actors and book their time. Refer to Figure 12.2 for a general timetable for the auditions.

12.4.5 Selecting and Booking Actors

After the audition tapes are complete and handed off to you for review, the final actor selections must be made. If several people have a stake in which actor is chosen for a particular role, you will want to listen to the tapes together and determine who to cast. This process can be frustrating and laborious, especially if everyone has different opinions as to what they are looking for in the character. This challenge is where the character descriptions become useful: If the descriptions are detailed enough, everyone should have a similar understanding of how the character will sound. If your team is not in agreement on the basic character description, you may find it difficult to agree on an actor.

Although your main focus is to get the right actor for the character, several other vocal qualities besides acting ability must be considered when evaluating the audition tapes:

Enunciation: The words must be clearly articulated and free of any mouth noises, such as pops, clicks, swallows, and lip-smacking. Also listen to how the sibilants sound; some actors pronounce words with an "S" or "P" that is too hard or soft. These types of speech patterns might be difficult to minimize in the recording session.

Breathing patterns: Listen to how the actor breathes when speaking. If he or she takes loud gulps of air when reading sentences, they will be audible in the recordings.

A good sound editor can minimize some of the breaths if they are taken during logical breaks in the dialogue.

Pitch: Determine whether the actor's pitch is a good match for the game. If the pitch is too high and squeaky or too low and gravelly, it will be difficult for players to understand key information. An actor with a wide range should not have a problem with pitching his or her voice appropriately. However, if his or her range is not very broad, it will be difficult for him or her to change the natural pitch of his or her voice.

Cadence: Listen to the rhythm of the actor's speech. Does it sound natural or like a sing-song voice? A character with an unusual cadence to his or her voice is not a problem. However, it can be problematic if the actor naturally has an unusual cadence.

When a final decision has been made for all the actors, communicate your choices to the sound studio. They will take this list and schedule the actors for the session. If you are scheduling the actors yourself, first schedule the actors on "avail" and then do the final booking after the recording schedule is confirmed with the sound studio. "Avail" means the actor is available for the recording session but is not fully committed; it is equivalent to penciling something in on a schedule. No money is owed to actors on avail. "Book" means the actor is fully committed to the session and will receive a payment, even if the session is canceled or rescheduled; essentially the actor has committed his or her time to the project and can't book any other jobs during this time period.

■ 12.5 Recording Voiceover

After the actors are booked and the studio time is scheduled, you are almost ready to record the actual voiceover. Recording voiceover can be a stressful process since there are many elements to prepare and finalize before the actual session. This stress is minimized if the voiceover spreadsheet is final and ready to go, all the actors are cast and scheduled, and the development team has prepared for the session.

12.5.1 Preparing for Recording Session

Because the actors are scheduled for a maximum of four hours at a time, use their time efficiently in the session. To maximize the actor's time, you must prepare several items before the recording session.

First, decide who will be directing the actors and which additional people will attend the session. Having multiple people at the recording session is fine, as long as there is only one person working directly with the actor. If you are working with celebrity talent, the publisher may want to have someone at the session as well, especially if they want to film the session for PR use. The development team might want to have several people present as well, such as the producer, a designer, a sound designer, and so on. The actual writer of the dialogue should attend the session as well, as he or she will be the best person to advise the voice director on the context and delivery of the lines. If the writer has experience directing voice actors, he or she might be able to direct the session.

Make sure the voiceover script (see Figure 12.1) is final and ready to go. The script must be sent to the recording studio in advance so they can prepare the scripts for the actors. The studio will break out the scripts by character. Bring the electronic version of this script to the recording session as well. If any dialogue changes are made, the script can be quickly updated with these changes. Additionally, if there are extra takes selected or additional lines added, the spreadsheet can be updated to reflect this.

The files from the actors' original auditions should be available for them to hear at the recording session. Such availability will quickly remind the actor of the voice that was created for the character and give the voiceover director a good starting point for discussing any voice changes with the actor. If several shoots occur at different times in the schedule, audio files from previous recording sessions must be made available to the actors so they can match the dialogue they have already recorded. The sound studio will have access to these files and can prepare them for the sessions.

Bring the latest version of the character descriptions to the sessions as well. These notes will refresh the actor's memory of the character and give the voice director concrete information on how to communicate the character to the actor.

Gameplay footage or a game trailer are also useful tools to show the actors what the game is about and how their voices will be used in the game. Don't bring a playable demo of the game; time spent setting up the demo and playing it should be spent actually recording dialogue. If gameplay footage is not available, be prepared to describe the general gameplay experience to the actor so he or she will have a better understanding of how his or her dialogue will be used.

Put together a pronunciation guide for key words that must be pronounced consistently. This guide is especially necessary for words that have been specifically created for the game, such as unusual character names and fictitious location names. Real-life words should also be included, such as foreign language phrases, international names and locations, and words that are commonly mispronounced. The pronunciation guide should include a phonetic spelling of the word. If there is time, audio files can be recorded of the correct pronunciation and played for the actor during the session.

Finally, have the most up-to-date schedule for each day of the recording session. This will help you track the actors' comings and goings and will make it easier for you to reschedule actors if necessary. For example, an actor might be booked for a four-hour session but complete everything in two hours. The schedule can be consulted to see whether any other actors can be scheduled at an earlier time to maximize the time in the recording booth.

12.5.2 Directing Actors

Professional voice directors can be hired to run the actual recording session. The advantage of using a professional is that he or she is well versed in working with actors to get the desired performance. The drawback is the expense. However, a professional director can be a good investment when recording thousands of dialogue lines with numerous actors because you are likely to get the needed performance the first time around and will not need to rerecord dialogue at a later date. Most sound studios can help you locate a professional director for your session.

If someone from the development team is going to handle the voice direction, make sure this person is an effective oral communicator. The director or acting director is responsible for making the actor feel comfortable and clearly communicating feedback to the actor. The director must be sensitive about giving the actor critique and direction so the actor does not get frustrated during the session. Most important, this person must remain positive and focused, even during a difficult session in which the actor is not responding to the directions given. Instead of getting frustrated, this person must devise different ways to direct the actor to the proper performance.

Some general guidelines for voiceover direction are as follows:

Let the actor warm up: Have the actor do a few dry runs of some of the dialogue to get him or her warmed up and ready to go. Sometimes the actor might not really be warmed up and relaxed until he or she is well into the recording session. In such cases, check the dialogue that was recorded at the beginning of the session and have the actor redo it if necessary.

Save all yelling until the end of the session: Inform the actor about any yelling or loud talking beforehand. Yelling tires out an actor's vocal cords, and he or she will want to schedule enough time in between voiceover sessions to rest. All yelling and screaming should be done at the end of a session so the vocal cords are not worn out at the beginning of the session.

Provide specific feedback to the actors: If you are requesting a retake or a pick-up, provide specific information to the actor about what needs to change. If the actor does not have specifics, he or she is likely to deliver exactly the same performance he or she gave the first time around. For example, he or she might not be enunciating clearly or the delivery might not match up with the intended emotion. Make this feedback clear to the actor so he or she can deliver the performance you want.

Don't stop the actor after each line reading; keep the flow going: Most actors can quickly run through an entire page of dialogue without a break and do two to three takes of each line of dialogue. For example, if the script has 20 lines of dialogue, the actor will read the first line three times (with each reading having a different inflection), then move onto the next line and read it three times (again with different inflections), and so on until he or she has completed the page of dialogue. This way of recording lines makes it easier for the actor to sustain the character he or she has created. If the actor has to stop after reading each line so the director can review the takes, it breaks the actor's concentration and will also take too much time to record the dialogue (meaning extra money is spent on the recording session).

12.5.3   Selecting Takes

During the voiceover session, actors do multiple readings, or takes, of each line, and the final take is selected from these choices. Accurately noting this information is important because the sound engineer and the sound editor are usually two different persons. The sound engineer is responsible for recording the session and handing this session off to the sound editor for processing. For the sound editor to know which take is the final, he or she needs script notes that track how many takes were recorded for each line and what was chosen for the final take. Each sound studio might have a slightly different way of doing this, so discuss their process of recording and selecting takes before the recording session starts. For example, some studios might label multiple takes for a single line as "1A," "1B," and "1C" with the number corresponding to the line number. Pick-ups recorded for this same line at a different time in the session would continue the pattern.

Alternative takes can be chosen for a single line; these should be indicated in the script notes as alternatives. You will also want to designate a way to distinguish alternate takes in the file naming convention. This way, the final take and the alternative take are easily differentiated. Keep in mind that studios charge for how many lines of dialogue they process and deliver, so if you end up adding many alternative takes, the cost might increase.

12.5.4   Audio Deliverables

After the dialogue is recorded and the takes are selected, the files are sent to the sound editor for processing. He or she will be responsible for preparing the file audio deliverables in the correct format and filename. As discussed earlier, define ahead of time which formats are needed, what special effects are needed, and what the filenames are. This will prevent confusion when the development team receives the files and starts integrating them into the game. Some studios will provide the raw data of the entire recording session upon request. This data can be useful if the sound designer needs to edit some of the files or if another take needs to be used.

■   12.6   Voiceover Checklist

Creating a checklist of the tasks that must be completed for the voiceover session can be helpful. Figure 12.6 provides an example.

Voiceover Checklist	Y/N	Notes
PREPRODUCTION		
Is initial voiceover design completed?		
Are initial character descriptions written?		
Is initial voiceover schedule completed?		
Is initial voiceover budget completed?		
Is file naming convention established?		
Is file management system established?		
Are file delivery formats defined?		
Are casting notes written with sample dialogue?		
Have bid packages been sent to sound studios?		
PRODUCTION		
Is sound studio selected?		
Has final decision been made on using union or nonunion actors?		
Have recording dates been tentatively booked with the sound studio?		
Is initial voiceover script written?		
Is placeholder dialogue recorded and implemented in the game?		
Are auditions scheduled?		
Are celebrity voices being used? Are they available for the tentative dates?		
Are final actor selections completed? Are they available for the tentative dates?		
RECORDING SESSION		
Are dates finalized and booked with the actors?		
Is the voiceover script final?		
Are audition files available for the actors to listen to?		
Is pronunciation guide final?		
Is game footage available to show the actors?		
Is voice director booked for the session?		
Are all final takes selected?		
POSTPRODUCTION		
Has sound studio edited the final takes of audio files?		
Are files delivered in the correct format? Are uncompressed versions available?		
Has the raw data from the recording session been delivered?		
Has voiceover script been updated with any dialogue changes and alternate lines?		

FIGURE 12.6   Voiceover checklist.

■ 12.7   Planning for Music

As with any other element in the game, music needs must be discussed during preproduction. You don't necessarily have to finalize the entire music plan at this point, but it is advisable to determine how much money you want to spend; decide whether you are going to license music, compose original music, or both; and tentatively put together a schedule for getting the music assets finalized and integrated into the game. Also, if you expect the music score to evoke a certain atmosphere, discuss this in preproduction to ensure that the music meshes well with the art and design elements.

12.7.1   Music Design

The sound designer will work with a lead designer or creative director to determine the music needs for the game. For example, if the game is an action/adventure game where the player spends a lot of time exploring the world and part of the time fighting the enemy, one type of in-game music can be used while the player is exploring, and another type of music can be used when the player is fighting.

When determining the music needs, consider which major areas of the game will need music:

- In-game
- User interface shell
- Cinematics

This can then be broken down within each category. For example, if using in-game music, is the music coming from an ambient source within the game world (such as a car radio), or is it constantly playing in the background? The UI shell might have one piece of music that continuously loops or several songs that cycle while the player is in the UI. The cinematics might be scored directly to the image, or several generic music loops can be composed and placed in the sound track by the cinematic artist.

After you have an idea of where music is going to be used in the game, estimate how many minutes of music are needed. Most composers charge by the minute when creating original music, and rates can vary from $300 a minute to upwards of $1,500 a minute. The rate depends on who the composer is and whether the music is recorded with live musicians or created digitally. Additionally, if live musicians are used, you might also need to compensate the musicians; your composer can work out the details with you and the musicians.

The amount of music varies for each game and might be budget dependent. For example, if you need 30 minutes of original music and can spend only $10,000 on music, you will need to find a composer who can do the job for around $300 a minute. On the other hand, you can reduce the amount of music needed for the game and spend money on a composer who charges more per minute. If you find a composer with whom you want to work, and he or she also wants to work with you, more than likely you both can agree on fair terms.

12.7.2 Schedule and Staffing

Whether you plan to license music tracks or hire a composer, you need to determine the music needs well before your game reaches beta. By beta, it is usually too late to commission a composer for original music because you will not be able to find someone who works on such short notice. If you do, it is unlikely the quality of the work will be as high as it could be, due to the limited time. It will also be too late to start negotiating with music publishers on which tracks you are interested in licensing.

Alpha is a good time to start approaching music publishers for licensed tracks or to send out bid packages to potential composers. If you hire an external composer, make sure the contract specifies that the work he or she is doing is a "work for hire." This means that your company, not the composer, owns the IP rights to the music. Refer to Chapter 2, "The Game Industry," for more information about work for hire.

If you have an in-house composer available to do work on your project, it can be tempting to manage this person without a formal deliverable schedule, since you can go speak to him or her any time you want. However, this is not recommended. As with any team member, the composer needs to specifically know what the deadlines are so he or she can plan accordingly. If he or she needs to deliver the final music mixes by beta, he or she must have scheduled milestones between preproduction and beta so he or she can hit the deadlines on time. The nice thing about having an internal composer is that he or she is readily available for any emergency music needs that arise on a project. Also, any work done by an in-house composer is fully owned by his or her employer.

As with voiceover, it is helpful to implement placeholder music during production to get a better idea of the final music needs and how things sound in the game. Just don't forget to remove any placeholder music before the game ships, especially if you are temporarily using licensed music to which you don't have the rights. Also, make sure that no early marketing footage of the game features any licensed music you don't have the rights to, as this can turn into a legal issue if the musician or his or her publisher finds out.

When putting together your music schedule, include deadlines for any music needed for marketing purposes. For example, marketing may need one to two minutes of music for an E3 game trailer. If the game is at an alpha stage, the final music might not be ready or the final tracks might not be legally licensed. In this instance, you want some placeholder music that marketing can use free and clear and that is similar to the final game music. If the final game is using an orchestral sound track, placeholder orchestral music can be used for the trailer. If you have already hired a composer or have an in-house composer, he or she can probably compose some music for this one-time marketing deliverable in one to two days.

After you have decided on a composer or finalized which tracks you are going to use, you need to determine the deadline for getting all the final music assets for the game. The composer should plan to deliver the final music mixes about one month before beta. If it is in the contract, the final music deliverable should also include the stems. "Stems" are the individual instrument tracks that exist within the final music mix. The stems can be used to compose variations for commercials, game trailers, or future games.

Plan to have all the music rights finalized and contracts signed about one month before beta. This ensures that everything is ready to go in time for the game's ship date. If you can't get a music track secured by beta, think about replacing or removing that track from the game.

Figure 12.7 is a general overview of the music deliverable schedule for a game. When the composer starts delivering music for you to listen to, you will want to schedule the specific deadlines for sending him or her feedback and getting the revised music tracks back for review.

12.7.3 Scheduling for Cinematics

If you have prerendered cinematics in the game and are using original or licensed music, you must consider the cinematic deadlines when creating the music schedule. For example, a composer who is creating original music for a set of cinematics needs to see a rough version of these cinematics before he or she can begin his or her work so he or she has a clear idea of how much music is needed and which events in the movie will be emphasized by the music.

Task	Resource	Deadline
Music design determined	Sound designer/sound engineer	Before production starts
Initial music deliverables defined	Sound designer	By alpha
Add placeholder music in the game	Sound designer	By alpha
Send bid packages to composers (if working with external composer)	Producer	By alpha
Start negotiating for music rights (if licensing music)	Producer	By alpha
First set of compositions delivered by the composer	Composer	~2–3 months before beta
Composer delivers final music mixes	Composer	~1 month before beta
Secure all final music rights	Producer	~1 month before beta
Implement all final music in the game	Sound designer	By beta

FIGURE 12.7   General overview of music deliverable schedule.

Usually, composers want to compose to picture so the music can be timed appropriately to key events in the cinematic. In order for this to happen, the composer needs to get a final and correctly timed cinematic, with voiceover and sound effects tracks, a few weeks before his or her final music deliverables are due. This allows him or her to tweak the final timing of the music track for the cinematics and correctly mix it to blend with the voiceover and sound effects.

If any edits are made in the cinematic after the final music is delivered, you have to send it back to the composer for the music to be retimed. Depending on how extensive the edits are, this can take some time because the composer will need to rearrange and remove parts of the music to fit within the new timing. If possible, avoid editing the cinematics after the final music, voiceover, and sound effects are completed, as this adds more time to the schedule and can put the project at risk.

If the composer is just delivering music loops that play as background music in the cinematic and is not relying on the music to punctuate key images in the game, the timing is not as critical. If any edits are made, the music will continue looping as necessary until the cinematic ends.

12.7.4 Bid Packages

Send bid packages to several composers during preproduction so you can get an idea of prices, how responsive they are, their music style, and how long it will take them to compose music for your game. Composers might have a preferred format for receiving bids, so check with them first for any necessary forms. In general, the bid packages must include as much information about the game's music needs as possible. Things to include are as follows:

- Grand total of how many minutes of music are needed
- How many different pieces of music are needed
- How long each piece of music must be
- Specifics on where each piece of music will be located in the game (UI, in-game, cinematics)
- Any sound, voiceover, and music mixes that are needed
- Format for music deliverables
- Final deadline for receiving all final deliverables

Figure 12.8 is an example of the information you should include in a bid package. This is a fairly straightforward way of organizing the music cues that are needed and the deadlines.

Music Cue	Length	Mixing Details	Location	Format	Notes	Deadline
Main theme	120 secs	Full Dolby 5.1 mix	UI	.wav	Main theme for the game; will be heard whenever players are in the UI shell screens. Must match the look and feel outlined in enclosed music vision document.	April 30, 2007
Loop 1	30 secs	Stereo	In-game	.wav	Heard in game as a looping piece of background music. Must match the look and feel outlined in enclosed music vision document.	May 30, 2007
Loop 2	30 secs	Stereo	In-game	.wav	Heard in game as a looping piece of background music. Must match the look and feel outlined in enclosed music vision document.	May 30, 2007
Intro cinematic	180 secs	Stereo; music + voiceover + sound effects. Music must be timed to picture.	Cinematic	.wav	Deliver final music, VO, and sound effect mixes on separate tracks.	June 30, 2007
Midtro cinematic	60 secs	Stereo; music only, background music. No timing.	Cinematic	.wav	Deliver final music, VO, and sound effect mixes on separate tracks.	June 30, 2007
Outro cinematic	90 secs	Stereo; music + voiceover + sound effects. Music must be timed to picture.	Cinematic	.wav	Deliver final music, VO, and sound effect mixes on separate tracks.	June 30, 2007

FIGURE 12.8   Example of music bid.

In addition, you will need to provide some documentation and samples on what you want the music to sound like. The music vision document should provide general information about the music genre, gameplay themes, and any other special considerations (such as regional flavor). It should also include samples of music from other games, sound tracks, bands, composers, or any other audio that can closely convey the look and feel you want for the game. After you send out the bids, follow up with each composer and make your final selection.

■ 12.8 Working with a Composer

Most likely your sound designer will be working directly with the composer. The producer is usually involved as a sounding board for opinions and might have final approval on the final music tracks for the game. The producer is definitely required to approve the deliverables and make payment to the vendor.

Before the composer can begin working on the music, he or she will need to get a much better idea of what the game is about. So send him or her a build of the game or a game trailer if a build is not available to play. In addition, concept art, character descriptions, and the storyline can also be helpful in conveying the look and feel of the game. The composer can review these elements, along with the music vision document, to determine the themes and inspiration for the music.

After the composer has these elements, he or she can begin roughing out the music tracks. Plan on several rounds of feedback between the composer and sound designer before the final music is ready. The composer will provide a rough audio mix of the initial music that can be reviewed by the sound designer to ensure that it is on the right track. This is where the feedback process begins.

The feedback process needs to be well-defined beforehand so that time is used wisely and the composer is not waiting weeks (or months) for feedback. It is important that all feedback is communicated in writing to all appropriate parties. If verbal feedback is provided via a conference call, write up the notes from the conversation and email them to make sure there is a written record.

Establish deadlines for when feedback will be provided and when it will be implemented. For example, when the composer delivers samples for review, he or she should expect to hear feedback within three days. If no feedback is given, he or she can assume that everything is fine and proceed with the next phase. After the sound designer has given feedback, the composer needs to determine when the next set of samples with the feedback incorporated will be ready for review. This deadline is communicated in writing to the sound designer.

Finally, when anyone is giving feedback, make sure that it is useful and constructive. It's not enough to say, "Eh, I really don't like this, but I can't put my finger on why," because that gives the composer nothing to work with. He or she won't know what to change in order to get it the way you want. Instead, be specific about what you don't like, even if you think it sounds silly. For example, "I really don't like the screeching at the end of the song; it's too shrill and may annoy the player. Maybe it can be toned down or replaced with something else." This type of feedback is much easier to work with. If possible, provide specific time codes on the areas of the music you are critiquing.

It is a good idea to gently remind composers of upcoming deadlines so they can be sure to deliver on time. They might get so caught up in doing the work that they forget their final deadline is in three days. This way, you can be sure that you have everything you need when you need it.

■ 12.9   Licensing Music

If you are licensing music, determine which bands you are interested in and start contacting their publishers. The publishers usually handle all negotiations for music rights. If it is a popular band, these negotiations can take some time, so start the process as soon as you can. Keep in mind that if you are licensing music, it is likely you will not be able to alter it in any way.

The contract might limit how many minutes can be used, how much additional mixing can be done on the track, or what other bands can appear in the game. The rights may cost a flat fee or may entail an advance against royalties on each copy of the game sold. You might also be able to get the band to record a special version of the song or even record an original song for use in the game.

The game publisher will likely have their legal department involved in the process as well. This way, the publisher can be sure that all the appropriate rights are accounted for in the agreement. The agreement should clearly define how the music can be used in the game, how the music can be used in marketing materials, and whether the music can be used on demos or game trailers. It should also detail whether the track can appear on a game sound track, which is becoming more common.

WORKING WITH A COMPOSER

Raymond Herrera, Co-owner and Executive Producer
3volution Productions

I have been playing games since I was 10 years old and have always wanted to blend music and games together. I started 3volution Productions along with my business partner, Laddie Ervin, to make this happen. We are involved in all aspects of audio and games: composing original music, licensing music, voiceover, and sound effects. Our gaming background makes it easier for us to work with developers in determining the music needs for the game. In some instances, the developer will know exactly what is required—15 songs for *x* amount of money. Other times, the developer is looking for some guidance on what music to include in the game—original music, licensed music, and so on.

The biggest factor in determining the music options for a game is how much money is available and how much music is wanted. If a lot of music is needed and the budget is limited, the developer can remix songs. Remixed songs are beneficial to the game and the band. The band now owns a remix and has worked with people they never thought they would work with, and the game gets a custom track and the ability to use the band's name without a high sticker price. When doing remixes, actual sounds and voiceovers from the game can be used to really tie it into the game. For example, 3volution used the team call-outs and the ammo sounds the player hears in the game for the Rainbow Six: LockDown® theme.

I believe that video games can benefit from using music the same way that movies currently do—select a hit song that can be used as an anchor and then remix it or license the original and feature it in the marketing campaign. This song can then be the feature on a game sound track, along with other music that is inspired by the game.

Another way to get quality music without spending a ton of money is by putting together a supergroup of musicians who work for a few days on creating and recording a song that exists only for the game. For example, for the WWE game 3volution worked on, there was a supergroup that consisted of me on drums, Shavo from System of a Down on bass, Wes from Limp Bizkit on guitar, B-Real from Cypress Hill on vocals, and DJ Lethal as the DJ. In some cases, marketing will pay to have a music video made for this song and played on MTV.

In order for us to make the most impact with music, we like to be involved with the game at the preproduction phase. This way, we can find creative ways for developers to make the most of their budgets. For example, if we put together a supergroup to record a song, marketing can be persuaded to have the money for this come out of their budget. This means the developers don't have to invest a lot of money in the music but still get a unique and high-quality song for their game. Also, if we are involved early on, we can make sure the music, voiceover, and sound effects are tightly integrated.

When first starting to work on a game, talk with the developers to find out what they need and what the attitude of the game is. Then talk to the marketing people. When talking with the marketing people, get them excited about all the cross-promotion opportunities—game sound tracks, iTunes®, bands going on tour and showing clips from the game, and music videos.

The process begins with a conference call between 3volution and all interested parties. When the initial meetings are completed, we create a guideline based on these discussions of what type of music will be created, the file formats, and any other notable details of the deliverable. This is sent to each and every person involved in the process—the publisher, the developer, marketing, and so on. This guide is useful because it holds everyone accountable to what was said and agreed upon. After that, all feedback is handled via email. Everyone is copied on the email chain so everyone has a chance to give their opinion. In addition, milestone deadlines are set up and scheduled with the developer. More time means better quality.

Music is the last thing that is worked on in the games. We are hoping this will change because music can be an integral part of making a game more effective and fun to play.

■ 12.10   Chapter Summary

Because voiceover and music are such noticeable parts of the game, recording quality voiceovers and effective music is important. As games get larger, voiceover becomes even more important and complex to include. Gone are the days of games with just a few hundred lines of dialogue recorded by developers; instead, thousands of lines of dialogue spoken by professional voiceover actors are now the norm. To make the most of the game dialogue, find a good sound vendor who will work with you on recording quality voiceover.

Using music effectively in games is not difficult to do. If you are able to define your music needs up front, you can determine whether you need to hire a composer to do original music or whether you can license music from a popular (or not so popular) musician.

This chapter discussed some of the key tasks that must be completed when managing game voiceovers. Information was presented on how to find a vendor, how to cast and direct actors, how to format the voiceover script, and how to select the work for the game. Additionally, this chapter discussed factors to consider when defining your music needs, how to prepare bid packages for composers, how to work with composers, and some basics on licensing music. These are the major areas a producer must be aware of when including music in the game.

■ 12.11   Questions and Exercises

1. Discuss some technical elements that must be considered when planning for voiceover.

2. Discuss the format of the voiceover script and why it is important.

3. What are some of the main tasks that need to be completed for a voiceover shoot? What is the typical schedule for including voiceover in the game?

4. What type of information should be included in a voiceover bid?

5. What are some guidelines for directing voiceover actors? Why are these important?

6. Create a fictious game and put together a sample voiceover bid.

7. Put together a sample character description to present to a voiceover actor.

8. Discuss some elements to consider when designing how music will be used in the game.

9. Discuss what needs to be included in a music bid package.

10. Discuss how to best work with a composer who is creating music for a game.

11. What are some limitations when licensing music?

12. Research a music vendor and create a music bid for a game.

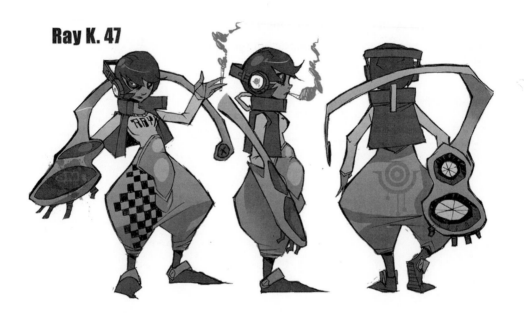

Ray K. 47

13 | Localization

In this chapter:

- Creating International Content
- Localization-Friendly Code
- Level of Localization
- Localization Plan
- Testing
- Localization Checklist

■ 13.1 Introduction

As international markets continue to grow, there are many opportunities for publishers to profit from localized games. It is now common practice for publishers to simultaneously release French, German, Italian, and Spanish versions of a game at the same time as the English version. Other languages, such as Chinese, Japanese, and Korean, are likely to be released a few months later, depending on the genre and content of the game. In addition, gamers in other countries continue to raise their expectations about what constitutes a quality localized title, and they want to have the same gaming experience as their counterparts around the world.

If not properly planned for, localization can be a frustrating and time-consuming process for the development team. However, if the development team starts planning for localizations in preproduction, many issues can be addressed and eliminated so that the localization process has minimal impact on the overall game development cycle.

This chapter presents an overview of how to plan a successful localization. The topic of localization is quite involved, and it is beyond the scope of this book to delve into specific details. For more information on localizations, please refer to *The Game Localization Handbook* (2004) by Heather Chandler.

■ 13.2   Creating International Content

When developing localized versions, consider how the game content may be received in other countries and try to develop content that is culturally sensitive. For example, if the game is going to be released in Germany, don't include references to Nazis; not only will the game be banned in Germany, this will also generate some bad publicity for the game. Be aware of how the game uses humor and slang, as these elements are difficult to translate and may end up making no sense in the translated versions. Figure out ways to tailor the content for international markets. For example, some sport titles include players from several different countries and the game will default to displaying the appropriate nationalities for each player—a French player will see a French sports team when the game initially starts, a German player will see a German team, and so on.

During preproduction, it is important to seek input from native speakers on the game design and story. A native speaker will be able to advise the team on potential red flags in the localized version and will also have advice on what type of content will best appeal to international players. There are many cultural issues to consider, so be sure to use whatever resources are available when developing content for the game.

■ 13.3   Localization-Friendly Code

Localization-friendly code is easy to localize. This means that text and other language assets can be easily swapped into the game and that build can be quickly compiled for testing. Localization-friendly code takes into account all technical, translation, integration, and testing needs. Even if localizations are not initially planned for, it is good practice to create localization-friendly code in case the publisher decides to localize the game at a later date.

Many factors are considered when planning for localization-friendly code, such as:

- How are language assets organized?
- What support is included for fonts and special characters?
- How are international keyboards supported?
- Does the game support subtitles?

If issues like these (and others) are planned for in preproduction, localization-friendly code can be easily created.

Retrofitting code to be localization-friendly is not recommended; it is time-consuming, challenging, and introduces a number of bugs. In situations like these, more time may be spent on retrofitting the code than on working with the current code to create a localization.

▌ FIGURE 13.1   Directory structure for organizing language assets.

13.3.1 Language Assets

Place all the language assets into a separate language-specific directory within the game. This makes the translation and integration process more efficient. Figure 13.1 is an example of one way to organize this for multiple languages. In each of the English, French, and German folders are subdirectories for "Audio," "Cinematics," and "Text."

Text Assets

Logically organizing the text assets in the game will save the developer time when the assets need to be organized and sent out for translation. Several things can make the text assets more localization-friendly. For instance, don't hard-code any of the in-game text. Instead, organize, integrate, and test with good organization; the developer will know exactly which files must be localized.

Art Assets

Avoid storing text in art assets whenever possible and use game code to display all the text instead. If text needs to be part of an art file, be sure to put the text in a separate layer on the source file so it can easily be replaced with translated text.

Voiceover Assets

As discussed in Chapter 12, "Voiceover and Music," it is important to define a file-naming convention that allows the voiceover files to be easily identified. The same goes for localized VO files—establish a naming convention that allows someone to quickly understand what language is used for any given VO file. Also, music, voiceover, and sound effects should be stored on separate tracks so that the dialogue can be easily replaced with translated VO.

13.3.2   International Characters and Fonts

The engine needs to be able to handle both uppercase and lowercase versions of special linguistic characters, such as ä, Õ, and Ç. Currently, Unicode is the standard for representing text characters, as it provides a unique number for every character regardless of the platform, software program, or programming language. This gives the game code the capability to display more than 65,000 unique characters, including Asian and Cyrillic. Keep in mind that if the language uses an Asian or Cyrillic font, the engine must be double-byte enabled and capable of displaying bidirectional text.

Choose a font that is easily read on televisions and computer monitors. Televisions display at a lower resolution, so don't choose fonts that will be difficult to read when they are displaying international characters. Keep in mind that some languages, such as Japanese, display better in larger fonts. However, make sure that the font size is not too large. If it is too large, there will be issues with overlap when displaying other languages.

13.3.3   User Interface

The user interface has many localization challenges. The text usually overlaps or is cut off, forcing the translator to come up with an abbreviation or an alternative translation that will fit the space better. Keep these things in mind when designing a localization-friendly UI:

Leave space in the UI: As a general rule of thumb, plan for localized text being about 25 to 30 percent longer than English text. Extra space must be designed in the UI to accommodate the longer words. This also ensures the UI screens don't have to be redesigned later on to display translated text.

Use scalable UI elements: If the UI buttons, drop-down menus, text boxes, and other elements can dynamically scale, localized text can be accommodated more easily.

Use icons: Using universally recognized icons is a good way to avoid localized text.

Support international date and currency formats: Display dates and currency in the appropriate formats.

13.3.4   Keyboard Input

For PC games, determine how the keyboard commands are mapped to the keyboard. If the keyboard commands are mapped by location (that is, the far left key on the bottom row will reload a weapon), make sure this key functions the same way on all international keyboards. Also, the manual writer for each language will want to make a note of the exact key when writing the manual, as the name of the key will be different in each country. If the keyboard commands are mapped directly to the keys (that is, ~ will switch the weapon the player is using), make sure that all versions of the keyboards have this key available. If not, it is necessary to pick a different key to map the command to for that language.

13.3.5 Other Technical Considerations

You must consider several other technical aspects when creating localization-friendly code:

Subtitles: Will the game have subtitling functionality? If so, the publisher might choose to subtitle the voiceover files for the localized versions instead of fully translating them.

Lip-syncing: How will lip-syncing be handled in-game and for prerendered cinematics? A common method is dubbing, in which the localized dialogue replaces the original source dialogue, and the animator attempts to match up the character's mouth movements as best as he or she can.

Compatibility between languages: If there is an online component to the game, users from different countries can usually play against each other. If this is the case, the different localized versions must be able to play with each other.

■ 13.4 Level of Localization

The extent to which game assets are localized can vary from project to project, depending on how many resources are available to invest in the localization and the likely return on the investment. The localization process is scaled according to the needs and expectations of the game. There are three main levels for localizing games:

Packaging and manual localization: Localizing the game's packaging and manual, commonly referred to as "box and docs," is one level of localization. The game code and language are unchanged from the original version, but the manual, packaging, and other supporting documentation are localized into the target language.

Partial localization: A partial localization means that only the in-game text is translated; none of the voiceover files are translated. This method is cost-effective, since time and money are not spent translating voiceover text, setting up recording sessions, and completing other tasks needed to localize voiceovers. In some cases, the voiceover files can be subtitled, but only if the code supports this feature.

Full localization: A full localization includes translating the text, voiceover, manual, and packaging. This can be costly and challenging if the game code is not localization-friendly and the assets are not well organized within the code.

■ 13.5   Localization Plan

Before localizing a game, work with sales to determine whether the projected sales point to a profitable localization. Start by figuring out how many assets need to be localized, how much the translations will cost, and how much development time is needed. This information is also necessary for any external vendors who want to bid on producing the localizations.

Figure 13.2 illustrates an asset overview form that is used to estimate the number of assets to translate. The developer fills in the requested information and then sends it to the translator for cost estimates. This form is a good starting point for collecting all the necessary information about the localizations. Since this form provides a general overview of the project and is filled out before the game assets are final, estimates will have to suffice.

13.5.1   Schedule, Budget, and Staffing

The localization schedule can be broken down into four major areas:

Organizing assets for translations: Include the time it takes to convert the text assets into a format that the translators can easily work with.

Translating: Include the time needed to translate and record localized VO.

Integrating translated assets: Include the time needed to integrate the art, text, and VO files, and compile the build.

Testing: This includes both functionality and linguistic testing.

Of course, each localized project will have a different schedule, but if localizations are planned for in advance and run according to schedule, expect to spend on average two to three months in production on the localized versions. Figure 13.3 is an example of an initial localization schedule with general estimates. Create this schedule in preproduction so the development team can prepare in advance for key localization tasks. As development continues, create a more detailed schedule to more accurately track the progress of the localizations.

Once the assets overview form and an initial schedule estimate are completed, a budget can be created. If using external translators, shop around for the best price.

Remember to include costs for all the development personnel needed; this usually includes a part-time engineer, part-time artist, part-time associate producer, and testers. The most significant development costs are likely to be testing, especially if the game is complex and content heavy. Designate a single person on the development team to manage all aspects of the localization, including any external vendors. If this person is the main contact for all localization queries, the process will progress more smoothly.

In-Game Text Assets	#	Delivery Format	Comments
Number of words to be translated			
Number of text files to be modified			
Art Assets			
Number of words in art assets			
Number of art assets to be modified			
Voiceover Assets			
Number of words in VO script			
Number of VO files to be modified			
Number of characters to record			
Total time of VO (min:sec)			
Cinematics Assets			
Number of words in cinematic script			
Number of cinematics to modify			
Number of characters to record			
Total time of lip-synced dialogue			
Total time of cut-scenes (min:sec)			
Printed Materials			
Number of words in manual			
Number of manual graphics to be modified			
Number of words in box text			
Number of box graphics to modify			
Other printed materials			

FIGURE 13.2   Asset overview form.

Task	Language	Resource	Duration	Start Date	End Date
Freeze English VO assets	French	Development team	1 day	July 5, 2009	July 5, 2009
Freeze English text assets	French	Development team	1 day	July 26, 2009	July 26, 2009
Organize VO assets for translation	French	Development team	3 days	July 6, 2009	July 9, 2009
Organize text assets for translation	French	Development team	3 days	July 27, 2009	July 30, 2009
In-game text translated	French	Translator	2 weeks	July 30, 2009	August 13, 2009
VO script translated	French	Translator	2 weeks	July 9, 2009	July 23, 2009
Actors cast for localized VO	French	Sound studio	1 week	July 9, 2009	July 23, 2009
Localized VO files recorded and processed	French	Sound studio	3 weeks	July 23, 2009	August 13, 2009
Text files integrated	French	Development team	1 week	August 13, 2009	August 20, 2009
Localized VO files integrated	French	Development team	1 week	August 13, 2009	August 20, 2009
Linguistic testing	French	Linguistic testers	4 weeks	August 27, 2009	September 17, 2009
Functionality testing	French	Functionality testers	3 weeks	August 20, 2009	September 17, 2009
Third-party approvals	French	Third-party publisher	6 weeks	September 17, 2009	October 29, 2009
Ship date	French	n/a	1 day	October 29, 2009	October 29, 2009

| FIGURE 13.3   Initial localization schedule.

■ 13.6   Testing

Testing is time-consuming because both functionality and linguistic testing have to be done for each language version. Additionally, all the versions need to be tested for compatibility between languages when playing multiplayer games. Time can be saved in the testing schedule if there are enough people to do concurrent functionality and linguistic testing.

13.6.1   Functionality Testing

Functionality testing checks for any bugs created by the localized assets that require a code change to fix. Ideally, if doing a straight asset swap, there should not be any functionality bugs introduced. However, if special characters and increased text length were not planned for, code changes might be needed to accommodate the localized assets.

Functionality testing can be handled by the same QA team that tested the primary version of the game, as they are most familiar with how to test the game functionality. While they may not speak the languages they are checking, they can still check for text overruns, incorrect language assets, and other functionality bugs. These bugs can be logged into the central bug-tracking database. Add a field to note which language is being tested so the database can be sorted by language if necessary. Functionality bugs found in the localized versions will be fixed by the team; it's possible that these bugs are also present in the primary version of the game as well.

13.6.2   Linguistic Testing

Linguistic testing checks all of the language assets in the game to make sure text is not overlapping, truncated, misspelled, or grammatically incorrect. It also checks that all the localized VO files play correctly. Linguistic testing should be done by native speakers, as they are best equipped to find errors in translation and context. There are several localization vendors that offer linguistic testing services.

In some cases, particularly for more complex localizations, the linguistic testers can be on-site with the development team. This speeds up the linguistic testing and bug-fixing process immensely since the linguistic testers can provide corrected translations right away. Advance planning needs to be done if linguistic testers will be traveling and working on-site with the development team. If this is not well organized, the most cannot be made of the testers' time.

Linguistic testers will need to familiarize themselves with the game before they begin testing. The game's functionality test plan can also help them become familiar with the game and all of its features.

Testers will need a localization test plan to show them where to check all of the translations. One way to do this is to have them check the text in the game against the text translation spreadsheet they already completed. Figure 13.4 is an example where more information has been added to the translation sheet to aid the testers in checking the game.

Location	English	French	Notes
AI(M01)	A police officer is down! Mission failed.	Un officier de police a été abattu. Echec de la mission.	Failure condition that appears as pop-up message in game
M01	1. Disarm the security system.	1. Désactivez le système de sécurité.	Appears in loading screen, set-up screen, and in-game start menu
Install	Would you like a shortcut placed on the desktop that can be used to launch the game?	Souhaitez-vous créer un raccourci pour pouvoir lancer le jeu à partir du bureau?	Appears during installation
Uninstall	Do you wish to clean up the entire game folder? This will delete the folder the game was installed to and everything in it.	Souhaitez-vous effacer complète-ment le dossier du jeu? Cela détruira l'ensemble du dossier dans lequel le jeu a été installé et les éléments qu'il contenait.	Appears during installation
Equip	The primary weapon assigned is the M4, with a 9 mm pistol as a secondary. Flashbangs are pro-vided to suppress enemies, and a heartbeat sensor should help in locating them.	Les armes assignées sont le M4, comme arme principale, et le pistolet 9mm, comme arme secondaire. Les grenades aveuglantes sont fournies pour éliminer les ennemis. Le détecteur cardiaque devrait vous aider à les localiser.	Appears on the help screen for equipment selection
IFF(M03)	a guard	un garde	Appears when you place reticle over a character

❙ FIGURE 13.4   Sample localization test plan.

Bug #	Language	Game Location	Bug Description	Incorrect Text	Correct Text	Bug Status
2	German	UI–Options menu	Please use lower-case letter.	Schritt Nach Rechts	Schritt nach rechts	CLOSED
4	German	UI–Options menu	Text not translated.	Use item	Gegenstand benutzen	FIXED

❙ FIGURE 13.5   Linguistic bug report template.

Determine in advance how linguistic bugs will be reported. If the developer does not require the bugs to be written in a specific format, the linguistic testers may not provide enough information about the bug and how to fix it. This is especially true when fixes are being made by people who don't speak the language. Figure 13.5 is a

PREPRODUCTION	Y/N	NOTES
TECHNICAL CONSIDERATIONS		
Does the game support Unicode?		
Are all language assets in an easily accessible directory in the game?		
Will subtitling functionality be needed?		
Are localized keyboards supported for player input?		
Will several languages ship on a single CD-ROM?		
Will localized versions be multiplayer compatible?		
Do boxes in UI scale accommodate to different sizes of text strings?		
Is any additional software needed to aid in localization?		
Are international currency and date/time formats supported?		
Has a version control system been decided on for the localizations?		
Has the localization pipeline been decided on?		
OTHER CONSIDERATIONS		
Will the localized versions ship simultaneously with the English version?		
Has the asset overview form been filled in and sent to the translator?		
Have the languages been determined?		
Will external vendors be producing the localizations?		
If so, are the bid packages prepared?		
Has the budget been completed and approved?		
Has the level of localization been determined for each language?		
Has the overall schedule been completed and finalized?		
Are there development resources available for the localizations?		
Has a method for integrating text assets been determined?		
Has a method for integrating VO assets been determined?		
Has a pipeline been determined for fixing bugs?		
Have the appropriate measures been taken to comply with all of the international ratings boards?		
Have the third-party publishers been contacted about the localized versions?		
Will PAL support be necessary for console versions?		
Is there enough hardware for functionality and linguistic testing?		

I FIGURE 13.6 Sample localization checklist.

PRODUCTION	Y/N	NOTES
Has a detailed schedule been completed and communicated to the team?		
Has the localization overview document been sent to the localization coordinator or translators?		
Has all the preproduction game documentation been sent to the localization coordinator or translators?		
Has the latest English build of the game been sent to the translators?		
Have the text assets been organized for translation and sent to the localization coordinator?		
Have the voiceover script and character casting notes been sent to the localization coordinator?		
Have the final English voiceover files been sent to the localization coordinator?		
Have all the art assets to be localized been sent to the localization coordinator?		
Have all the cinematic assets and time codes been organized and sent to the translator?		
Are the translations for the text assets complete?		
Have the localized voiceover files been recorded and processed?		
Have the text and voiceover files been integrated?		
Have the cinematics been localized?		
Have the localized versions been sent to the appropriate ratings board for approval?		
Does the master contain demos from other games that were requested by marketing?		
Is functionality testing complete?		
Are all functionality bugs fixed and has the game been code released?		
Is linguistic testing complete?		
Are all linguistic bugs fixed and has final linguistic approval been given?		
Have the localized versions been sent to the replicator (PC) or submitted to the third-party publisher (consoles and cell phones)?		
POSTPRODUCTION		
Have the manual and box text been sent for translations?		
Does a localized demo need to be produced?		
Have localized screenshots been taken for the manual and box?		
Has a closing kit been created for all the localized versions?		
If necessary, have all patches been localized and made available?		

| FIGURE 13.6   (*Continued*).

sample bug report template for linguistic bugs. It includes information on where to find the bug, a description of the bug (usually an incorrect translation), and the solution for the bug (usually the correct translation).

■ 13.7   Localization Checklist

Figure 13.6 is a localization checklist that lists major tasks to address during the pre-production, production, and wrap-up phases of localizations. This checklist can provide a good starting point for formulating a localization plan from start to finish. For more detailed information on localizations, please refer to *The Game Localization Handbook* (2004) by Heather Chandler.

■ 13.8   Chapter Summary

Quality localizations are becoming an expectation in today's international markets. Gamers want to feel that they are playing a game made for them, not just some hastily translated game that has poor voice acting and typos in the translations. If developers plan ahead for localizations at the beginning of the production process, it is possible to create high-quality localizations that ship at the same time as the primary version of the game. This chapter gave a general overview on how to plan for and execute localizations. Topics discussed included organizing assets for translation, integrating assets, and testing the localized versions.

■ 13.9   Questions and Exercises

1. What is localization-friendly code?
2. What are some things to keep in mind when designing a localization-friendly UI?
3. What are the different levels of localization and what does each one contain?
4. What occurs during linguistic testing? How is it different from functionality testing?
5. Fill out an asset overview form for a fictitious game.

14 Testing and Code Releasing

In this chapter:

- Testing Schedule
- Test Plan
- Testing Pipeline
- Testing Cycle
- External Testing
- Determining Code Release
- Code Release Checklist
- Gold Masters
- Postmortems

■ 14.1 Introduction

To many people outside the game industry, testing seems like a glamorous job. After all, you get to play games all day! However, if you talk to anyone who has tested games for a living, you know that it is anything but glamorous. In reality, testing is an extremely stressful and difficult job. Most testers spend at least five to eight months testing the same game day in and day out, looking for defects, confirming bug fixes, and play-testing missions. This becomes pretty tedious after a few weeks, no matter how fun the game is. Oftentimes, because testers are looking for specific issues with the game, they don't even have a chance to actually just play and enjoy the game.

Another thing that adds to the stress of testing is that many game development schedules rarely allot ample time to test everything thoroughly, which means the testers are often working massive overtime (late nights, weekends, and holidays) to get the game tested and ready for code release. One reason this occurs is because testing is the last thing to happen in the production cycle. So if things are running behind schedule for art, engineering, or design, these delays are amplified by the time testing begins. Testing time is often the first thing cut when extra production time is needed.

The producer must work closely with the lead QA analyst to alleviate as many of the testing problems as possible. The lead QA analyst is responsible for testing the game, closing bugs, and determining whether a game is ready to be code released. Involve the QA analyst in preproduction so he or she can comment on any features that may pose testing challenges. For example, if there are plans to include 200 options in the character creation system, the QA analyst can comment on how much testing time it will take to test each option and the different combinations. The testing time alone is probably reason enough to drastically limit the options for this feature. Things like this will help create a tighter loop between the development team and the testing team, which will hopefully translate into more manageable testing schedules.

■ 14.2   Testing Schedule

Since testing time is often cut short to accommodate other schedule slips, create a solid testing schedule during preproduction. This ensures that everyone on the team has a clear understanding of the testing schedule and what the expectations are. If the team understands how their delays negatively impact testing, they will be more conscientious about meeting their deadlines in a timely fashion. Refer to Chapter 10, "Game Plan," for detailed information on creating a schedule.

Build the testing schedule directly into the production schedule and show the testing dependencies so that delays affecting the test cycle can be immediately seen and mitigated. Also, add in testing time for each major milestone of the game so the testing department can spend a few days with a single build to evaluate the game's progress against the milestone deliverables. Refer to Chapter 9, "Game Requirements," for details on milestone deliverables.

Other things to include in the testing schedule are as follows:

Play-testing: During production, make sure to schedule time for QA to play-test the game and offer feedback to the developers. Ideally, conduct these play tests with people who haven't already spent months playing the game so the feedback is based mainly on the fun factor of the game.

Demo: Marketing will want a demo, and it will need to be tested. If the demo is already in the schedule, everyone will be prepared to fulfill this request when marketing makes it.

Marketing builds: If marketing is sending development builds out during production, schedule time for the testing department to check them before they leave the building. Even though journalists expect to see bugs and unfinished work in these builds, there might be critical errors uncovered in testing that must be added to the build notes.

Code release candidates: After beta, the development team's main goal is to get the bugs fixed as quickly as possible and create a suitable code release candidate. Schedule a few weeks at the end of the testing cycle for the QA department to thoroughly check each code release candidate against the test plan. If things go well, the first code release candidate will pass with flying colors, but more than likely, several code release candidates will need to be submitted and tested.

During preproduction, the testing team is mainly used as a resource for play-testing the prototype and offering feedback on proposed features. At this point in the testing schedule, the QA analyst can be on the project part-time, as long as he or she can provide feedback on all the deliverables being generated at this time. If there are prototypes or playable builds to check, he or she can arrange to have a few testers available for a few days at a time to test these deliverables during preproduction.

Production is where the bulk of testing takes place. The QA analyst will be on the project full-time after production starts—working on the test plan, testing gameplay features, and working with leads on managing the production pipeline. A few testers will be needed for a few weeks here and there before alpha, but a team of full-time testers is not necessarily needed until the game reaches alpha. However, if the game is very large and complex, there might be plenty to test before the game reaches alpha. Remember that the sooner something can be tested, the sooner bugs are uncovered and fixed. In some cases, a difficult bug to fix found later in the development cycle was an easy bug to fix earlier in the cycle.

At alpha, the QA analyst will put together a group of full-time testers who can test the features as they are implemented. At this point, it is likely the testing team will not have reached full capacity, as the full game is not completed. After code freeze happens, about three to four months before the game is scheduled to code release, expect to have a full group of testers looking at the game until it is finished. If the game is especially content heavy, the full group of testers might begin looking at the game before code freeze.

■ 14.3 Test Plan

The QA department follows a test plan in order to thoroughly check all areas of the game. The QA analyst will base an initial test plan on the design documentation and then will work with the team to keep it updated during the production process. As discussed earlier, it is useful to have the QA analyst on the team as soon as possible so they can start flagging potential testing issues and start writing the test plan. Depending on the scope of the game, the test plan could be hundreds of pages. The test plan is usually presented in some type of pass–fail format or a checklist. For example, a checklist may include a list of playable characters, and the tester needs to play the game and check off which playable characters are actually in the game. In a pass–fail format, the tester may need to check each button on the UI screen and note if it passes (meaning it functions as expected) or fails (meaning it does not work at all or does not function as expected).

It is critical for the test plan to be updated to reflect the latest changes to the game and the design documentation. Valuable time is wasted if the QA department is using an outdated version of the test plan to check a build. For example, the lead artist may have approved cutting some of the playable characters in the game but didn't inform the QA department or update the character asset lists. A QA tester starts checking the list of characters against his or her test plan and finds that several characters are missing. This gets logged into the database as a bug and now needs to go through the testing process in order to verify that the game is correct. This scenario can be avoided if the test plan is kept up-to-date.

Figure 14.1 is an example of a pass–fail test plan. In this example, the test plan is written in Microsoft® Excel® in order to best organize the information to be checked. As testers play through level 1, they check the items detailed in the test plan and mark whether items pass or fail. If an item fails, the tester will include some notes as to why. If testers are unable to check a specific item, they will mark an item as "CNT," which

	A	B	C	D
1	**Level 1: BulletPoint's Office**	**Requirements**	**Pass/Fail**	**Notes**
2	**Mission** Intro	Intro cut-scence played correctly		
3		Voiceover audio is correct	PASS	
4		Intro cut-scene can be skipped	FAIL N/A CNT	
5	**Objective 1: Find the blue key**	Objective triggered		
6		Objective is displayed		
7		Objective cannot be bypassed		
8		Objective completed when requirements are met		
9	**Interactive Objects**	Copy machine is functional		
10		Light switches turn off/on		
11	**Enemy Boss: Cleaning Lady**	Cleaning lady scripted sequence plays		
12		Cleaning lady goes after player with mop		
13		Cleaning lady AI		
14		Cleaning lady pathing		
15	**Objective 2: Make copies of blueprints**	Objective triggered		
16		Objective is displayed		
17		Objective cannot be bypassed		
18		Objective completed when requirements are met		
19	**Map Integrity**	Map has no holes, soft geometry, or invisible boundaries		
20	**General Enemy Interaction**	All enemies behave as designed		
21	**Audio**	Music is present and does not cut out		
22		Sound effects are audible and correct		
23				
24				
25				
26				

Level 1 / Level 2 / Level 3 / Level 4 / Level 5 / Weapons /

FIGURE 14.1   Sample pass–fail test plan.

	A	B	C	D	E	F
1	**Weapons**	Level	Ice Queen	Caribou	BulletPoint	**Notes**
2		1				
3	9mm Handgun	2				
4		3				
5		1				
6	Shotgun	2				
7		3				
8		1				
9	Knife	2				
10		3				
11		1				
12	Grenade	2				
13		3				

❙ FIGURE 14.2 Sample checklist test plan.

stands for "Cannot Test," and add notes as to why. Note that each level is listed on a separate worksheet, and each level will have unique objectives and enemies listed in the test plan. Figure 14.2 is an example of a checklist test plan. In this example, there are three playable characters and they can use any of the weapons listed in the sheet. Each weapon has up to three levels, with a level 1 weapon being less powerful than a level 2 weapon, and so on. The tester selects one of the playable characters and a weapon, and then cycles through the weapons levels while playing the game. He or she checks off each combination as it is completed. If there are any problems, the tester will enter a note about it, and the item will remain unchecked.

The test will be comprehensive, but the QA department will not test every build they get against the test plan. Instead, they will focus on rotating through certain sections of the test plan on each build they get. If they receive specific instructions to test through a portion of the game, they will consult the test plan for information on how to best fulfill this testing request. Milestone builds are also fully checked against the test plan, as this is a good way to benchmark the progress of the game.

As the game gets closer to shipping, it becomes more important to check the test plan thoroughly. Once there is a gold master candidate for the game, it is critical to schedule enough testing time so that the QA department can run through the entire test plan from start to finish on the gold master candidate. The testers may discover some minor errors that need to be addressed before the game ships.

■ 14.4 Testing Pipeline

Before testing begins, the testers and the development team need to determine the pipeline for tracking and reporting bugs. If this is not established, there will be confusion about how the testers are reporting bugs and which bugs are most critical for the development team to address first. In addition, everyone needs to understand how to access and use the bug-tracking database.

14.4.1   Bug-Tracking Database

In order to efficiently track bugs, a centralized bug-tracking database is critical. Don't rely on emails as a reliable form of bug tracking. Instead, set up a bug-tracking database, such as Seapine's TestTrack™ or Bugzilla™. Both of these programs offer robust bug-tracking functionality for writing and closing bugs.

After the database is set up, the QA analyst can conduct a tutorial to train the team on using it. The team must understand how to use the database correctly so they can enter bugs, comment on bugs, change the status on bugs, and basically understand what they must do to address the bugs in the database. During the tutorial, the QA analyst can also discuss bug definitions so that everyone has a common understanding of the differences between crash bugs, critical bugs, minor bugs, and feature requests.

14.4.2   Bug Definitions

When bugs are added to the database, make sure the correct bug definitions are used so that the bugs can be fixed in the most efficient order. For instance, crash bugs should be addressed well before any minor bugs or feature requests. If the bug is not properly defined in the database, crash bugs might not be addressed for a while and will ultimately become more difficult to fix as production continues. Additionally, if feature requests are defined incorrectly as bugs, feature creep will sneak up on you before you know it. Common bug definitions are as follows:

> **Crash bug:** A crash bug is extremely serious as it prevents the player from progressing in the game. Crash bugs can freeze the game or, in the worst cases, kick the player out of the game and display an error message. The "blue screen of death" sometimes seen in Microsoft Windows® is a crash bug.

> **Critical bug:** A critical bug is a major functionality problem with the game, but it does not prevent the player from progressing in the game. A critical bug is a level missing all of its textures or a major gameplay feature not functioning as designed.

> **Minor bug:** A minor bug is one that is noticeable to the player but does not detract greatly from the overall game experience. Stretched textures and typos can be considered minor bugs.

> **Feature request:** A feature request is not a bug, so be sure everyone entering bugs in the database clearly understands the difference. A feature request is additional functionality that would be nice to add but that is not part of the defined feature set. For example, someone might request an option to turn the in-game heads-up display (HUD) on and off, but if this feature was not an original part of the design

scope, it is considered a feature request and not a bug. If the user is supposed to have the ability to toggle the HUD on and off and this is not working in the game, then this is a bug.

When writing up the bug, there is usually a section for including information on the type of bug it is. Please refer to the "Writing Up Bugs" section later in this chapter for detailed information on writing bugs.

■ 14.5 Testing Cycle

The testing cycle for a build begins when the development team officially submits a build for testing. Even though builds will be available on a daily basis around alpha, it is not useful for QA to test each and every build, as they would never make it through the entire game before a new build was ready. Instead, if the build is stable, the QA department can spend a few days or a week with a single build and test as much as possible.

As development progresses and the game becomes more robust, the QA analyst will test different sections of the game on different builds. For example, when a level artist checks in a new level, the testers will do a pass-through on the geometry and textures and submit any bugs to the database. This level will not be tested again until the artist has fixed all the bugs and resubmitted the level for testing, which could be several weeks. Meanwhile, the testers will concentrate on testing other levels and features in subsequent builds as they wait for things to be fixed. Work with the QA analyst to schedule certain sections of the game for testing. If it is indicated in the schedule when certain parts of the game are supposed to be ready for testing, the development team is better able to plan their work so they can accommodate the testing schedule.

After the build is in testing, the testing cycle is fairly straightforward. The testers will run through the test plan, find bugs, and enter them in the database. When the bugs are in the database, they are assigned to the appropriate person for fixing. This person fixes the bug and resubmits his or her work for verification in a future build. The tester will then check the fix in the build and indicate that it is ready to be closed out of the database.

14.5.1 Writing Up Bugs

Once production and testing are in full swing, the central bug-tracking database is the most valuable resource for tracking the progress of the game. Members of the development team should be required to input any bugs they encounter into the database, along with any feature requests or feedback that requires a change in the game. While a feature request and feedback are not bugs, it is good to include them in the database so they can be tracked, addressed, and verified in the game. If a feature request is not approved for inclusion in the game, it can be tagged as a feature request and addressed for any future patches or sequels to the game. During a code freeze, engineers usually don't make any changes to the code unless it is specifically recorded in the bug database and assigned to someone to be fixed.

Because the team will have so many people writing up and entering bugs in the database, it is imperative to establish a standardized process for writing up bugs and training everyone to use it. The bugs need to contain pertinent information so that the development team can easily figure out what the bug is, find it in the game, and fix it. Most bug-tracking databases have a standard set of information fields to be filled in when writing a bug. These fields include:

Version: This is the version of the build where the bug was found. The version number is useful for tracking the progress of the bug from the time it is found to when it is fixed and verified. If the bug pops up again later on in the cycle, the version history will be useful information for tracking down the cause of the bug.

Category: This indicates whether it is an art, design, or engineering bug. Usually this is fairly easy to figure out, but if in doubt, the tester will make a best guess as to the category. When the appropriate lead takes a look at the bug, he or she may recategorize it.

Component: A subcategory of "category." This offers more details on what behaviors the bug is exhibiting. For example, subcategories in "engineering" might be networking, AI, UI, physics, load/save, and so on.

Summary: A quick one-sentence summary of the bug. The team may establish specific guidelines on how to write the summary so that the bugs can be easily sorted. For example, all art bugs found in mission one need to begin with "M01—Art."

Description of bug: The person writing up the bug needs to describe what happened. In some cases, he or she may want to include information on what he or she expected to happen and what actually happened. This allows the team to easily identify any bugs that are not working as designed or, in some cases, features that *are* working as designed but for some reason are perceived as bugs.

Severity: This indicates whether a bug is a crash, critical, or minor bug, or a feature request. Severity 1 bugs are addressed first, as they are usually crash bugs that prevent the player from progressing in or playing the game. Critical bugs are classified as Severity 2 and usually indicate bugs that block gameplay. Minor bugs are usually considered to be Severity 3, while a feature request is Severity 4.

Priority: This category is another way to classify bugs and indicates which ones are highest priority. For example, you may have three crash bugs all designated as Severity 1. However, one of the crash bugs happens at the beginning of the game, while the other two happen at the end. The producer or lead may designate the crash bug that happens at the beginning of the game as Priority 1 and the others as Priority 2. This helps the team make decisions about which bugs need to be addressed first.

Steps to reproduce: This provides a step-by-step description of how to reproduce the bug (if it is reproducible). If the bug is not reproducible, the tester should note in a chronological order what he or she was doing when the bug occurred. People should make it a practice to reproduce the bug whenever possible.

Screenshots: Including a screenshot of what was happening on-screen at the time the bug occurred is very helpful in pinpointing the location and cause of the bug.

Crash log files: The engineer can create a debug executable that will generate a log file each time the game crashes. The log file will note which line of code the crash occurred in, so the engineer has a good starting point for tracking down a bug.

14.5.2 Assigning and Closing Bugs

Assigning bugs is a large part of the testing cycle because the bug has to get to the right person in order to be fixed and verified. The process for assigning bugs should be clearly defined and presented to the team during the testing tutorial conducted by the QA analyst. The goal of assigning bugs is to get bugs addressed as quickly as possible.

A simple process for assigning bugs involves the tester, the QA analyst, and the lead:

- The tester finds a bug in the game, writes it up, and submits it to the database.

- The bug is automatically assigned to the QA analyst, who will check the bug to ensure that it is indeed a bug and not a duplicate. He or she will also check the information in the bug report to make sure the problem is clearly written.

- The QA analyst will assign the bug to the appropriate lead. The art lead receives all the art bugs and so on.

- The lead will review the bug, verify that it is assigned to the appropriate discipline, and assign it to the appropriate person on the team. In some cases, a bug appears to be one type (such as art) and is really another type (such as engineering), which is why it is helpful for the lead to review the bugs. If the bug is a crash bug, the lead might request that it be addressed right away so it can be fixed for the next build.

- The team member assigned to fix the bug will implement a fix and assign it back to the QA analyst for verification. If the bug can't be fixed for one reason or another, the person should add a comment to the bug explaining why and assign it back to his or her lead for verification.

- After the analyst is assigned a bug for verification, he or she will assign it to a tester to check in the next build to make sure that it is fixed. If the bug is not fixed, the tester will add a comment to the bug, and the process will begin again. If the bug is fixed, it is closed by the analyst.

Fixing every single bug in the game is not possible, especially as you get closer to code release. Most developers have a list of "will not fix" bugs that will remain in the game when it ships. Some of these bugs may be addressed later with an update or patch, but most will not. Bugs categorized as "will not fix" are minor bugs that will not demonstrably impact the player's game experience. The bugs may be cosmetic, such as a stretched texture or a visible seam in a 3D model. Other bugs may be related to gameplay but are prioritized as low risk and are not worth jeopardizing the ship date to fix. Each developer has different standards for designating a bug as "will not fix," and will likely need to get approval from senior management for anything on this list.

14.5.3   Checking TCRs

As discussed in Chapter 2, "The Game Industry," each console manufacturer has a predefined set of technical certification requirements (TCRs) to which each game must adhere. The console manufacturer will provide a complete checklist of each requirement the game must follow, and in some instances will provide tools to assist in checking the title for compliance with the appropriate requirements. Noncompliance with these requirements puts your game at risk of not being approved by the console publisher. If this happens and the error is not fixed, your game will not be approved for release. Therefore, testing for compliance to the requirements is extremely important.

Designate a single person on the QA team to be responsible for knowing the technical requirements and how to test them in the game. If this process is centralized under one person, there are less likely to be mistakes when the game is checked against the requirements. It is very frustrating when a game fails submission because incorrect terminology was used or a required error message is not present. This tester should have extensive knowledge of the technical requirements and an understanding of how to interpret them and should be the main point of contact with the console manufacturer if there are any questions about the requirements. Finally, this person should be familiar with how to use the proprietary development tools provided by the console manufacturer that automate the checks for many of the requirements. Any time a noncompliance bug is entered into the database, it should be rated a high priority and addressed as quickly as possible. While it may not be a crash bug, a noncompliance bug is as serious as a crash bug, as it is possible for the game to fail submission if the bug is found during the approval process.

■ 14.6   External Testing

At some point in the project there may be a need to outsource the testing to an external vendor. This usually occurs when the developer has a very small testing team and wants a second pair of eyes to thoroughly test all areas of the game. External testing also occurs when the localized versions of the game need to be tested by native speakers of each language. Finally, money might be better spent on external testing if there is a specific area to test that requires specialized resources. For example, checking PC compatibility on a variety of computers, video cards, and sound cards might be best handled by an external vendor that has a compatibility lab already set up for testing. It may be worthwhile to hire a testing vendor that has extensive experience checking technical requirements in order to ensure your game has the best chance of passing the console submission process in a timely fashion.

If you are planning to use external testing vendors, be sure to do your research on the vendors and secure recommendations from other satisfied (or unsatisfied) clients when you are able. Questions to ask the vendor about include:

What is the best way to get them a build of the game? Will they set up an FTP site for you to use, or do you need to mail them discs?

How are the testing rates determined? Do they charge by the hour or by the day?

How far in advance do they need to be notified if you want to cancel testing? Do they require 24 hours' notice?

Will they write a test plan? Will they create their own version of the test plan, or will you need to provide one for them? If they write the test plan, find out how much this costs. Also, keep in mind that they will need design documentation and playable builds of the game in advance so that the test plan is ready when they begin testing the game in earnest.

What additional costs are adding to the testing rate? Do they charge a project management fee or tack on an additional percentage of the total testing cost for overhead? You don't want to be surprised when you get the bill.

Can they provide an estimate of how long it will take to test the game? Will they do a free gameplay evaluation in order to determine how much testing time they need in order to fulfill your request?

Who will be the main point of contact? Will they provide a project manager who you can contact on a daily basis and who will send daily progress reports?

What bug-tracking software do they use? Do you have to use their software, or can they accommodate other types of bug-tracking software?

Once a vendor is selected, you will need to do your part to get the most out of the testing as well. For example:

Check builds before sending them to the vendor to ensure they install and load correctly. If the vendor has to spend a few hours troubleshooting a broken build, the costs can add up quickly.

Provide clear direction about what needs to be tested. Are they only focusing on the console technical requirements, or do they need to test other areas of the game as well? Are they supposed to only check 16-player multiplayer functionality, or are they supposed to also check the single-player campaign? Are they focusing only on regressing bug fixes from the previous build? If so, be sure the bug database clearly indicates which bugs are ready for regression.

Establish a schedule for sending new builds. Are they supposed to test a build from start to finish and then wait until you are ready to do another round of testing? Are they supposed to continually test for the next two months; if so, how often do they need a new build (every day, every week)?

Answer questions as quickly as possible. If the vendor has a question, get them the necessary information as soon as possible, as testing may be put on hold until the question is answered. The longer the wait, the more testing time is lost, and the more money is wasted.

■ 14.7 Determining Code Release

When a game is code released, it means the content is final, the bugs are addressed, and the master disc is ready to be replicated and packaged. A code release process should be in place to ensure that everything that needs to be done on the game has been completed correctly. This process will involve daily meetings to discuss bugs, a code release checklist, procedures for submitting to a third party for approval, and information on where to send the code for replication. A game doesn't get code released overnight; the process can take anywhere from five days to two months, depending on the complexity of the game and who needs to approve it before it is code released.

Define a code release process so that the development team and QA department are in agreement about when a game is ready for code release or final submission if it needs to be submitted to a third party for approval. Treat this as a separate phase in the testing process, and be sure to check the code release candidate against the entire test plan and, if necessary, the technical requirements checklists for Sony, Microsoft, or Nintendo. In addition, this is an ideal time to double check that the copyright and other legal information is correct, that all the appropriate age ratings have been secured, and that the localized versions of the game have been approved by the appropriate people.

The main purpose of the code release process is to fully verify that the actual master disc of the game that is sent for replication and manufacturing contains all the correct code and assets. The process should be able to uncover any major issues that need to be addressed before the game ships. The process should include enough time to run through the entire testing plan and technical requirements list at least three times, plus any additional time needed for Sony, Microsoft, and Nintendo approvals (usually four to eight weeks). Additional time in the code release schedule allows time to address any issues with potential gold master candidates and prepare a new master that can then be verified.

A code release candidate (CRC) is a version of the game that has addressed all the bugs, has all the final assets, and is deemed ready to ship by the development team. A game may have several CRCs during the code release process in order to address any major issues that are uncovered. When QA receives a CRC, they will check the game against the test plan and other code release requirements. Depending on how extensive the test plan is, this could take anywhere from five to seven days. You may want to staff up the QA department in order to get through the process more quickly, as saving a day or two at the end of the testing phase can make the difference between making or missing a ship date.

Note that any game appearing on proprietary hardware such as a console or cell phone must be submitted to a third party for approval. Each hardware manufacturer has different requirements to fulfill before the game is approved for replication. More information on the third-party approval process is discussed later in this chapter.

■ 14.8   Code Release Checklist

Create a code release checklist to ensure that code release requirements are clearly defined and understood by everyone. Figure 14.3 is an example of a code release checklist. This provides a general overview of the types of things to include; add or modify anything that relates specifically to your game.

In addition, you may want to include information about the following on the checklist, as all of these items should be double-checked on the CRC as well:

Copyright information: Usually listed in the game and on the packaging. This includes checking the placement of all logos from third parties, such as middleware providers, developers, and third-party manufacturers.

End-user license agreements: Usually included in the manual. PC games may also have a version that displays during the installation process.

Licensor approval: If the game is based on a specific license (such as Harry Potter™), be sure to secure appropriate approvals from all licensors.

Customer support information: This includes phone numbers and websites. International versions will have different customer support information.

Localized assets: Double check that localized assets display correctly in the game.

Demos: If including demos from other games, be sure they have the appropriate age ratings for any territories in which the game is released.

General Information	P / F	Additional Notes
Have all bugs been addressed?		
Have all "will not fix" bugs been approved?		
Can game be played from beginning to end?		
Has cheat code been removed?		
Is debug software removed?		
Has game passed all areas of the test plan?		
Are PC compatibility checks completed?		
Is correct customer support information listed?		
Is this version approved for submission to third parties?		
Are the correct age ratings and disclaimers being displayed?		
Third-Party Approvals		
Has this version passed the technical requirements checks for Microsoft?		
Has this version passed the technical requirements checks for Sony?		
Has this version passed the technical requirements checks for Nintendo?		
Localizations		
Is correct customer support information listed?		
Is game text displaying in the correct language?		
Are voiceovers playing in the correct language?		
Are packaging manuals translated correctly?		
Has game received linguistic approval?		
Does correct legal text and copyright information display?		
Does game have all necessary age ratings?		
Legal		
Have appropriate licensors signed off on the game?		
Are clearances secured for all licensed content (such as music)?		
Does game contain correct version of the End User License Agreement (EULA)?		
Is warranty and customer support information correct?		
Packaging		
Does package contain legal and copyright information?		
Are logos and other icons on package correct?		
Is the manual finalized and approved?		
Gold Master Checks		
Have gold masters been virus scanned and determined to be virus free?		
Is gold master identical to the approved gold release candidate?		
Has gold master been installed and verified on appropriate hardware?		

I FIGURE 14.3   Code release checklist.

Software ratings: Ensure the game has the appropriate rating for each territory in which the game will ship, and that the game and packaging include the required icons and logos.

Console submission requirements: Check the game against the technical requirements checklist for Sony, Microsoft, and Nintendo.

■ 14.9   Gold Masters

The replication and packaging of gold masters for PC games will be handled directly by the publisher. The publisher selects a replication vendor and sends the vendor the final code when it has been approved. Many vendors have an electronic submission process set up to receive code, while other vendors require you to give them actual gold master discs. In either case, be sure you know who is supposed to get the final code and what format is required.

Console gold masters require one more step before they can be sent to the replication house. Sony, Microsoft, and Nintendo need to approve the game before it can be released for any of their systems. An account manager is assigned to work with the developer and publisher and is responsible for guiding the game through the approval process. Each company has a different process, so the account manager is an invaluable resource in understanding the technical requirements, approval phases, and packaging requirements. The account manager will work closely with the team to determine when the game needs to be submitted in order to hit the target ship date. Keep in close contact with your account manager throughout the process in order to navigate the approval process as smoothly as possible.

Build time into the schedule for the approval process. Not only does the final submission need to be scheduled (which on average takes about 10 to 20 days), but other submissions are also required during the course of development. Most console manufacturers require a beta version of the game to be submitted several weeks or several months before the final submission. This gives them an opportunity to check the game's progress and offer any feedback on things that may get written up during final approval. Think of it as a sneak preview and an opportunity to address any areas in the game that may impact final approval.

Once the game enters the final submission phase, it may take the console manufacturer 10 to 15 days to come back with a decision. Hopefully, everything goes smoothly and the game passes on the first try. While games do pass on the first try, it doesn't happen very frequently, so it is better to assume the game needs to be submitted at least twice before it gets final approval.

If the game fails the initial submission, the console manufacturer will generate a report detailing what caused the game to fail. The failures are all related to things in the technical requirements checklist, so the report will reference the specific requirement that was not fulfilled. Depending on how severe the issues are, the development team can expect to implement the bug fixes and feedback in a few days or weeks and submit the game for a second time. Hopefully, the issues have been addressed and the game passes.

Console packaging also needs to be submitted for approval. In most cases, the packaging has a submission process that is separate from the gold master; this is usually handled by someone from marketing or creative services. However, add this task to the production schedule to be sure it's not forgotten; if the packaging is not submitted in a timely fashion, the game's ship date can be jeopardized, even if the code has already been approved. Packaging approval takes about 9 to 10 days, and can be submitted whenever it is finalized by the publisher.

Once the PC and console gold masters are approved and ready for manufacturing, they will be sent to the replication vendor. The vendor generally needs about 10 days to copy discs and get them packaged. This assumes that they receive all the printed parts on time and don't run into any issues with copying the discs. Before mass copies of the discs are created, the vendor will make a few test masters (sometimes called "glass masters") and have someone from the publisher verify that the discs are working correctly.

As the project comes to a close, keep people informed of any changes to the code release schedule because this will also affect the ship date. Figure 14.4 provides a general overview of a production and release schedule for a console game. The schedule begins with submitting the beta version of the game to the console manufacturer for feedback on June 2, 2008. The team has about six more weeks to polish the code, implement feedback, and prepare a CRC. The CRC process starts on July 28, 2008, and is ready for console submission 10 days later. After scheduling two rounds of submissions, manufacturing, and shipping dates, the game is estimated to hit store shelves on October 7, 2008. Note that it took about two months after internal code release for this console game to ship. Of course, every project is different, but it is good to be aware of each of these phases so you can more accurately plan for the ship date.

	Task Name	Duration	Start	Finish	Predecessors
1	Beta console submission	10 days	Mon 6/2/08	Fri 6/13/08	
2	Additional development	30 days	Mon 6/16/08	Fri 7/25/08	1
3	CRC testing	10 days	Mon 7/28/08	Fri 8/8/08	2
4	Console certification	10 days	Mon 8/11/08	Fri 8/22/08	3
5	Fix certification bugs	5 days	Mon 8/25/08	Fri 8/29/08	4
6	Console certification - 2nd pass	10 days	Mon 9/1/08	Fri 9/12/08	5
7	Replication and manufacturing	10 days	Mon 9/15/08	Fri 9/26/08	6
8	Ship to retail	7 days	Mon 9/29/08	Tue 10/7/08	7

❘ FIGURE 14.4   Production and release schedule for a console game.

■ 14.10 Postmortems

Usually, postmortems are conducted at the end of the game development cycle because they provide closure to the entire development cycle. They are an opportunity for you and your team to discuss the ups and downs of the project and how this knowledge can be applied to improving future projects. It's also an opportunity to celebrate the game's completion with each other. The postmortem must involve feedback from the entire team in order to be useful. After the actual postmortem meetings are completed, the information from these discussions is distilled into a Lessons Learned document that outlines a plan for implementing some changes in the process for the next game. The following sections provide information on why a postmortem is important and how to successfully conduct one, write up an action plan, and implement changes.

14.10.1 Purpose of a Postmortem

The main purpose of a postmortem is to learn which methods worked and didn't work during game development. These items are usually focused more on the production process—scheduling, planning, implementing features, and so on—rather than the actual design features of the game. Although successes and failures in the game are discussed in postmortems, they are usually tied to something that was done correctly or incorrectly in the production process. For example, if the game is not play-balanced correctly, it could be that time was not scheduled to do this, or if the character models are getting rave reviews, it could be that the production process included some validation steps that allowed the character artists to get the most out of the tools and technology when creating assets.

Postmortems tend to be overlooked in the development process for a variety of reasons, such as there is not enough time, it's not a high priority, or people are not interested in improving the process (after all, the game got done, didn't it?). However, postmortems are a vital way to learn from mistakes and validate new ideas that improve the process. By not doing one, developers are overlooking the greatest source of concrete information they have on making things more efficient, less costly, and better on future projects.

In order to extract this knowledge from the team, postmortems should focus on answering these questions:

Did we achieve the goals of the game? In order to document the answers to this question, you will need to prepare a project overview of the original goals and the goals the game actually fulfilled. For example, the original goals might have included four character classes for the player to choose from, and the game actually has only three. The purpose of this question is not to highlight where the team fell short of the goal but rather to evaluate why the goal wasn't achieved, such as changing scope, shifting priorities, or limited time. Solutions to these impediments can be examined and implemented to prevent this on the next game.

Were the project's schedule, resources, feature set, and quality expectations realistic for achieving the set goals? When discussing this question, you will want to bring up concrete examples of where these areas were properly planned for and areas where they weren't. This is not an opportunity for the team to personally attack others about their shortcomings. Instead, this question should focus on the facts of what happened to impede goals of the project. For example, people could say something like the schedule did not account for bug fixing the levels and therefore three levels were cut from the game in order to get the rest of the levels finished, or the approval process took too long and impacted the amount of time available to implement a feature.

What went right? What went wrong? This is an opportunity for the team to relay personal experiences of what worked and didn't work on the project. By discussing both the positive and the negative, the team can carry over expertise to other projects about which procedures to implement and which ones to avoid. Additionally, if a procedure did not work, solutions can be discussed for ways to make something different work on the next project with the same desired results.

What are the lessons we learned? The team examines all the information gathered from the previous questions asked and determines the core lessons learned during development. These lessons should focus on big-picture items and less on small details. The details can be used as methods for implementing the lesson learned on the next project. For example, "communicate deadlines clearly to the team" might be one lesson learned, whereas the methods for communicating these deadlines (email, status reports, weekly meetings) provide the details on how to accomplish this. The regular postmortems featured in *Game Developer* magazine provide some great examples of lessons learned.

When working on a project that takes more than a year to develop, try to schedule a mini-postmortem after each major phase of the project: preproduction, alpha, beta, and code release. This way, you can continually improve the production process instead of waiting until the next project to make improvements. When you are working on a project that takes a year or less, you can schedule a single postmortem at the end. Additionally, encourage people to take notes during the development process of things to discuss in the postmortem. This will ensure that the details are not forgotten and can be used to formulate solutions for the Lessons Learned document.

14.10.2   Lessons Learned Document

In addition to the postmortem meeting minutes, the Lessons Learned document is a written deliverable of the postmortem process. As discussed earlier, the lessons learned focus on big-picture items that can be applied to future projects. Ultimately, the Lessons

Learned document will be published to the team, the studio, and perhaps even the publisher so that everyone can benefit from your team's experiences.

Writing the Lessons Learned document should not take too much time, especially if the notes from the postmortem are detailed and accurate. The lessons that will be included in the document will have been determined in the postmortem meeting. The author of the document can be a single person, like the producer, or several authors, such as the leads, who can contribute to each section to speed up the writing process.

Limit the number of lessons learned in the document to five. Anything more than that is daunting to implement, thereby reducing the effectiveness of publishing the lessons in the first place. Focus on lessons that have the highest probability of being implemented. For example, one lesson might be "Schedule time for risk assessment after each phase of the project." This is something that can be implemented fairly easily and does not require any up-front monetary investment. Conversely, a lesson that states "Send everyone on team for training in team software process" might not actually have a chance of being implemented due to schedule and budget constraints. However, lessons like these can be implemented if the company is committed to it, so gear each Lessons Learned document toward what the company can willingly commit to implementing.

Provide an example of why the lessons learned are important. This is where the team's personal experience really helps define why change in a certain area is necessary. If scheduling time for risk assessment is a lesson, include the example that makes this important. For example, if a risk assessment had been done after the preproduction phase, the team would have realized that the personnel needed to implement the graphics features would not be available until later in the project, putting the level production at a huge risk for missing the beta deadline.

When the document is written, have it reviewed by the team, make any necessary corrections, and then publish it to the rest of the studio. You can publish it by posting it on the company website, emailing it to everyone, or sharing it in a specified place on the network. If your studio has multiple postmortems, centralize their location so they are readily accessible to everyone.

In order to ensure that lessons are being implemented, follow up with the team on what changes they've made. For example, before beginning production on the next project, sit down with the core team, review the lessons learned from the last project, and formulate an action plan to implement them. This action plan can become one of the preproduction project deliverables.

■ 14.11 Chapter Summary

Testing is a time-consuming and stressful aspect of game development. As you are trying to get the game out the door, the tester might find a crash bug that was not uncovered earlier in development. If this happens, tensions run high as the developers scramble to prepare another code release candidate as quickly as possible. This scenario is bound to happen on some game development teams, but if the producer, leads, and team are constantly keeping the QA needs in mind during production, some of these instances can be avoided.

The code release process is one of the most critical steps in developing a game. This is the point at which the developer and publisher agree that the game has been thoroughly tested and is ready to be sent to the manufacturer for replication. If a game is code released too soon, there is a risk that a crash bug will be discovered after the game ships, which will have a negative impact on the game's sales.

This chapter discussed general information on how to work effectively with the QA department from preproduction to code release. Topics included the testing schedule, the testing cycle, and closing bugs. Additionally, this chapter discussed a process for code releasing builds to make sure that all the details are accounted for and the game is really ready to go.

■ 14.12   Questions and Exercises

1. What types of testing should be included in the testing schedule?

2. What bug definitions are used when categorizing bugs in the bug-tracking database?

3. What elements are included when writing up a bug?

4. What is the process for assigning and closing bugs?

5. What things do you need to know when considering a testing vendor?

6. Research QA vendors and determine which would be the best one to test a fictitions game.

7. Based on the core feature set of the game, write up a brief test plan.

8. Discuss the code release process and its main purpose.

9. Why is a code release checklist useful?

15 | Marketing and Public Relations

In this chapter:

- Software Age Ratings
- Working with Marketing
- Packaging
- Demos
- Marketing Assets
- Game Builds
- Working with Public Relations
- Asset Deliverable Checklist

■ 15.1 Introduction

The marketing team, in conjunction with the game's producers, coordinates the game's marketing campaign with its release date. The marketing team's mission is to generate game sales through advertising, so they need input from the development team in order to ensure that the game's key features are communicated effectively to the audience. However, marketing's last-minute asset or feature requests can create friction with the development team. This chapter discusses ways to keep the relationship between the marketing department and development team harmonious.

■ 15.2 Software Age Ratings

Most countries have an established board that assigns an age rating to entertainment software, similar to assigning a rating to a movie. The producer must be aware of what rating is desired when developing a game. For example, if the game's target market includes children 13 and older, the game content should stay within the appropriate rating guidelines for young teens. If a game depicts graphic violence, drug use, or sexuality, it will run the risk of being banned in certain countries—which is definitely not good for sales.

Publishers will apply for a rating for each country in which the game is released. The normal procedure is for the publisher to submit a beta or near final version of the game, along with documentation, to the appropriate rating board. The board then reviews the materials and assigns a rating. In some countries, the rating is not required by law, but many retailers will not stock unrated games, so it is in the publisher's best interest to submit all of their games for a rating. In other countries, such as Germany, a game is required by law to receive a rating before it can be released for sale. There is usually a fee involved that can run from several hundred to a few thousand dollars.

Any games released internationally must be reviewed by the appropriate ratings board for each country it is released in. A game to be released in the United States, Europe, Asia, and Australia will need to secure ratings from at least six different ratings boards, and each one has a different process and set of guidelines for securing a rating. For example, the Entertainment Software Rating Board (ESRB) rates games that are released in the United States; Pan European Game Information (PEGI) rates games distributed in most of Europe; and the Office of Film and Literature Classification (OFLC) rates games released in Australia.

The guidelines are fairly subjective, so it can be difficult for publishers to determine what rating a specific game will receive. For example, the ESRB does not have specific rules on what constitutes a Teen (T) or Mature (M) rating. They are happy to offer some feedback on what rating the game might get, but nothing is guaranteed until the game is officially submitted and reviewed by the ratings board. Other countries have different guidelines, and so something that is rated as appropriate for teens by the ESRB may be rated as inappropriate for teens by the OFLC. When in preproduction, think about the game's target audience and determine what ratings best suit this audience, and then develop the game within acceptable guidelines.

In general, the ratings boards are concerned with the behavior and actions depicted in the game, not necessarily whether the game is challenging and fun. The boards' main goals are to prevent children and teenagers from being exposed to content that is deemed inappropriate for their age group. As mentioned previously, this is a subjective process, but the boards make a concerted effort to provide ratings within reason. The main areas of concern are:

- Violence
- Language
- Drug use
- Adult themes
- Sex and nudity
- Criminal acts

The ratings boards are not opposed to games containing these elements; they just prefer that the depiction of these themes is age-appropriate to the rating. For example,

PEGI distinguishes between violence against realistic humans and violence against nonrealistic humans. Games that depict strong violence against realistic human characters can receive an automatic 18+ age rating. Games that depict strong violence against nonrealistic humans, such as aliens or fantastical characters, usually receive a 16+ age rating.

In addition to the overall rating, which indicates the general age range the game is appropriate for, there are content descriptors that provide more information about which areas of the game had an impact on the rating. For example, the ESRB has a list of more than 30 descriptors that cover a wide range of levels concerning violence, sexuality, and drugs. Some of these descriptors include "Blood," "Blood and Gore," "Language," "Tobacco Reference," "Tobacco," and "Comic Mischief." In contrast, PEGI has fewer than 10 descriptors, including "Violence," "Fear," and "Discrimination." Icons for each of these categories are presented next to the age ratings logo.

Other game components may also need to be submitted to the ratings board, such as:

- Demos
- Game trailers
- Expansion packs
- Downloadable content
- Bonus content

If the game does not have a final rating, and the publisher wants to release a demo or game trailer, the publisher will need to submit the content to the board for review; in this case, it is likely to be classified as "rating pending" or some other equivalent. The boards will not use a demo or trailer to determine the final rating for a game; only a full version of the game can be used to determine the rating.

If the game is released on multiple platforms, the board may require each version to be submitted separately for a rating. If the content is exactly the same across all platforms, the rating will be the same as well. However, if one platform has some additional content that may be considered mature, that version of the game may receive a different rating than the other versions.

Build time in the production schedule for submitting the game to the ratings boards. Once a game is submitted, it can take anywhere from 10 to 45 days (depending on the board) to receive a final rating. If you wish to contest the rating and resubmit, it will take another 10 to 45 days to get another rating. Most boards want to review a game that is at beta, meaning all the content is in and the game can be played all the way through. Some boards will also require the game to be fully localized before they review it. Finally, console manufacturers require the rating certificates as part of the final submission process and will not allow any game to begin the process without having the appropriate age ratings confirmed.

SOFTWARE RATING RESOURCES

Software Ratings Boards
- Entertainment Software Rating Board (ESRB): www.esrb.org
- Pan European Game Information (PEGI): www.pegi.info
- PEGI Online: www.pegionline.eu
- Unterhaltungssoftware Selbstkontrolle (USK): www.usk.de
- Office of Film and Literature Classification (OFLC): www.oflc.gov.au
- Computer Entertainment Rating Organization (CERO): www.cero.gr.jp
- Korean Media Rating Board (KMRB): www.kmrb.or.kr

Classification Boards
- Video Standards Council (VSC): www.videostandards.org.uk
- British Board of Film Classification (BBFC): www.bbfc.co.uk
- Netherlands Institute for the Classification of Audio-visual Media (NICAM): www.nicam.cc

Software Publishing Associations
- Entertainment Software Association (ESA): www.theesa.com
- Interactive Software Federation of Europe (ISFE): www.isfe-eu.org
- Entertainment and Leisure Software Publishers Association (ELSPA): www.elspa.com
- Syndicat des Editeurs de Logiciels de Loisirs (SELL): www.sell.fr
- Asociación Española de Distribuidores y Editores de Software de Entretenimiento (ADESE): www.adese.es

---

■ 15.3 Working with Marketing

It's important to involve the marketing department early in the development process, as they have access to a great deal of information about competing games, focus testing, sales, and industry trends. During the concept stage, the game's core hook is usually decided on, and marketing often has useful feedback on this hook.

To facilitate communication with marketing, establish a single point of contact on the development team whose job is to work with the marketing team. If marketing requests demo code from one developer, game code status reports from another, and manual assets from a third, the situation can become confusing and frustrating for the development team. Misunderstandings about product features can create ill will among the fans if misinformation is disseminated through interviews or the game's site. A solid communication pipeline will minimize the risk of such problems.

The development team will need to furnish the marketing department with screenshots, demos, game builds, and the manual text. The marketing team's requests can seem overwhelming, particularly if the team doesn't know in advance what to expect. However, if the development team's contact is working closely with the marketing team and can schedule requests for deliverables, this can streamline the process, reducing the pressure on the developers.

15.3.1   Development Milestone Schedule

Prior to making requests, the marketing team needs to be aware of the development schedule in order to avoid requests for assets during critical development dates. The marketing contact will be aware of major milestones and can help the marketing team establish a schedule, which should include the following:

- Alpha
- Beta
- Submission
- Code release
- Release date

Figure 15.1 is a schedule with the key development milestones and general timeline information.

15.3.2   Game Documentation

Marketing will need information about the game's story, main characters, and features in order to create an effective ad campaign. They'll also need to know what the game's target audience is, and they'll need to be apprised of any assets or features that are available in different versions of the game. The marketing team may request that dif-

Milestone	General Timeline	Deadline
Alpha	~6–8 months before ship date	March 15, 2009
Beta	~1–2 months before ship date	August 15, 2009
Console submission	~4–6 weeks before ship date	September 15, 2009
Code release	~2–4 weeks before ship date	October 1, 2009
Ship	Ship date	October 15, 2009

❙ FIGURE 15.1   Key development milestones.

ferent versions of the game feature platform-exclusive content, such as characters or levels. The development team should present the following information to marketing:

Feature list: This list includes the game's major features, levels, characters, and gameplay mechanics. It also details any platform-exclusive elements.

Story: The plot is summarized, along with any story elements that impact gameplay.

Control scheme: This gives the marketing team an idea of how to navigate in the game world, which can be communicated to the audience through marketing materials.

Core gameplay rules: These documents delineate the way that the game works. The marketing team must understand the game's mechanics, or they won't be able to communicate these to the audience. A brief summary may be more effective than core design documents, particularly if the latter are complicated or lengthy.

Character descriptions: These detail each character's appearance, voice, and personality. Characters are often used as part of a game's marketing campaign, so these documents can be quite useful. If celebrity voice actors are used, be sure to note that here.

Cheats and walk-throughs: In order to demo the game to journalists and buyers, the marketing team will need cheats and walk-throughs. This will allow marketing to complete the game in a competent manner and thus show off its key features.

15.3.3   Focus Groups

During the preproduction phase, marketing will probably arrange for focus testing of the game. This will result in feedback on the game's concepts, features, story, and characters. The marketing team usually works with an external vendor to set up the focus testing.

Often, developers find it useful to receive direct feedback from the target audience, particularly if the game in development represents a major change to the direction of a franchise. In this case, the game's producer may communicate specific questions that the development team wants to ask the focus group. Any developers attending the focus testing can gain firsthand knowledge about the group's reaction to a feature or aspect of the game.

When formal focus testing isn't possible, the developers might choose to arrange informal focus testing on their own. In this case, it's important that the participants sign nondisclosure agreements (NDAs). See Chapter 2, "The Game Industry," for more information on NDAs.

When conducting informal focus testing, establish the exact objectives beforehand. If the developers are hoping for some feedback about the control configuration, ensure that the build is stable, make sure that there's enough hardware for all participants, and establish some method for gathering information about the testing, such as a questionnaire that the participants need to fill in.

■ 15.4 Packaging

The marketing team will need all necessary assets for the creation of the box, manual, and inserts, and it's the developer's job to furnish all of these. Deadlines for these deliverables should be factored into the development schedule in order to avoid unnecessary delays (such as being forced to wait for the completion of the user manual). Smaller developers will need to create the packaging and deliver it to the printer, but larger studios typically rely on a creative services department that produces all packaging. Still, the developer will need to furnish the necessary assets to this team on time, such as manual text, screenshots, and controller configuration.

15.4.1 Manuals

The producer will need to work closely with the marketing team in order to ensure the successful creation of the user manual. The development team is responsible for creating the final draft of the manual text. Early on, the producer will need to establish a deadline for the final draft's completion to allow the marketing team enough time to edit, lay out, proofread, and print the manual before the game's ship date. In order to reach that deadline on time, the marketing department may ask for the final manual draft before the game's features have been implemented. You will need to furnish the most accurate information possible and make sure the marketing team and manual writer are kept up to date on any changes to gameplay.

Because of the localization process, it's likely that the international marketing department will need a copy of the English manual before their American counterparts. For PC games, marketing typically needs the final manual about six to eight weeks prior to ship date. This will give them enough time to get the printing and delivery taken care of.

For consoles, the timetable is different because the packaging needs to be approved by the console manufacturer prior to replication. Therefore, it's important to work closely with marketing to be certain that all of the packaging assets are received in time. Games have missed their initial ship dates because the packaging didn't receive approval in time. To avoid this, be sure to verify the packaging submission dates with the appropriate third-party account managers.

Early in the process, you need to establish a process for updating and correcting the manual text. After the final version has been sent to the marketing team, critical issues will be discovered, such as feature cuts or additions.

An easy way to furnish these updates is to provide a 95 to 99 percent complete draft of the manual to the marketing department on the requested due date, but allow time in the schedule for another round of revisions and updates. These changes should be scheduled as late as possible to make sure that the developers have sufficient time to adjust the text to accompany any gameplay changes. Be sure to communicate all these changes to the team members responsible for the localized version of the manual.

When discussing the manual with your marketing team, find out if there are any word limits and communicate this information to the manual writer. In some cases, localized manuals will have a maximum word count that is less than their English counterparts, so it may be necessary to create a shorter version of the manual for them. Otherwise, the international marketing department may need to edit the manual themselves, which could result in the inadvertent omission of important information.

Screenshots often appear in the manual in order to present UI elements to the user. Localized manuals will require localized screenshots. You don't need screenshots of the final build for the localized version; the important thing is that the shots are legible and clean.

The marketing team may request an electronic version of the manual for the gold master of the PC version. On budget-priced games, for example, this can help save on manual printing costs. Electronic manuals are also effective if a game ships with several languages on a single disc or if the game is released as part of a bundle.

If an electronic manual is needed for the gold master, be certain that everyone is aware of the deadline for getting the final electronic manual to marketing. The development team can use a placeholder manual file until the final version is ready.

15.4.2 Box Art

The final layout and packaging for the box are typically created by the marketing team. Providing assets for the box is usually easier than furnishing assets for the manual because the marketing department usually writes the box text. The developer just needs to double-check the box text, providing corrections or suggestions as necessary. Typically, the developer just provides screenshots for the back of the box. As always, it's important to be aware of packaging deadlines for console versions, as these require third-party approval prior to printing.

■ 15.5 Demos

Demos are marketing tools that build enthusiasm for a game by allowing consumers to play a game prior to purchasing it. You can provide demos to players via the Internet or as a stand-alone disc. Demos can be created after the game's code release, but it is sometimes necessary to create a demo during the game's production. Though this is far from the ideal situation for the development team, releasing a demo near the game's ship date can create a buzz and boost sales.

15.5.1   Planning for a Demo

A demo should be planned for months in advance. Even if the marketing team decides during the preproduction phase that a demo isn't necessary, it's good to plan for one just in case. A demo will be required at some point, whether it's for a trade show, as an incentive to preorder the game, or as a way to build consumer interest in the game. Planning for a demo costs nothing, and it ensures that you're ready to deal with a last-minute request to create a demo. The demo plan doesn't need to be detailed; it can be formulated during preproduction and updated throughout the development process. It should outline:

Content: Talk to the marketing team to determine the specific content for the demo. Which levels are featured? Which characters are playable? Which features will be showcased? The content should provide players with a good feel for the game but should leave them wanting more.

Preliminary production schedule: After the scope of the demo has been determined, the team can begin work on specific assets and features. If a specific level will be showcased in the demo, that level should be built and polished first. All of these details need to be worked into the production schedule so that the demo features can be planned for in advance. If a feature is cut, you can update the demo schedule as you're updating the production schedule.

Testing schedule: The QA department can schedule time for testing the demo if they know far enough in advance when the demo will be ready. It may be necessary to pull some testers off of game testing in order to test the demo, particularly if the demo is being produced while the game is still in development. QA can also hire more personnel during that time period to ensure that there are enough testers to cover both projects.

Key magazine deadlines: Ideally, the marketing team prefers to receive a demo prior to the game's release. If the demo is going to be featured on a magazine disc, note that there are specific deadlines for each issue. The lead times for print magazines can be long, and a completed demo may be required months in advance. For instance, if the demo will be featured in a magazine's October issue, the developers need to submit the final version of their demo in July.

Technical guidelines: If the demo is included on a magazine's disc, it may need to adhere to certain technical guidelines, such as file size limits. If the demo is for a console game, it will need to function with the magazine's demo launcher. It's important to check with the magazine to gather the necessary information prior to submitting the demo.

In the unlikely event that the marketing team decides that the game doesn't require a demo, this plan can be used to create a strong, polished version of the game, which can then be featured at press events, conferences, and trade shows.

■ 15.6 Marketing Assets

The marketing department also needs other assets from the development team, such as high-resolution art and footage. To prepare for the delivery of these assets, work with the marketing team to establish a schedule during the preproduction phase. Some of these additional assets include:

- Screenshots: High-resolution screenshots of in-game action
- Gameplay footage: Used for creating game trailers and commercials
- High-resolution artwork: Artwork that is suitable for use as a magazine cover or posters

■ 15.7 Game Builds

During the development cycle, the marketing team will want builds of the game that they can show to journalists, retail buyers, and potential customers in order to build buzz for the game. The press and retail buyers are aware that they're looking at a game in development, so they don't expect to see a polished version of the game until it ships. Whenever builds are made available, be sure to include a document that details features, bugs, installation instructions, and any other pertinent information. Since members of the development team can't demo the game to all potential buyers and journalists, it's good to include any instructions or caveats pertaining to the demo. The document should be easy to read and should provide contact information in case assistance is required. The demo should also include information that details how to demo the game in order to show it off in the best possible light.

You should consider "fingerprinting" builds that are sent outside of the development team. This entails attaching a unique marker to every build that is delivered outside the team. A master list is then maintained of all fingerprinted builds and the recipients of said builds. If a build leaks on the Internet, the unique marker can be used to determine which build was leaked. Commercial software programs and proprietary solutions are available for software fingerprinting.

Other builds that the marketing team may request include trade show builds, preview builds, review builds, and builds on request, such as builds that allow for the capture of gameplay footage.

■ 15.8 Working with Public Relations

The public relations department is responsible for interfacing with members of the media in order to create publicity for the game. Members of the PR team set up interviews and press tours, and they advise the development team on what core elements of the game should be communicated.

15.8.1   Press Tours

Press tours are one method of promotion for high-profile titles. Confirm dates for press tours as early as possible in the development process, particularly if you're working on a high-profile title. Make sure that the schedule is built around the development team's timetable; it's not advisable to have developers traveling during critical milestones.

Prior to the press tour, be sure that developers who are slated for international press tours are carrying valid passports to avoid delays. Also, plan in advance for any builds that will be shown during the press tour. As is the case with trade show builds, some parts of the game may be shown while access to other parts of the game is restricted.

If the developers are too busy for a press tour, the marketing team might bring in a small group of journalists to visit the development studio. The hands-on presentation and gameplay can be accompanied by PR representatives from the game's publisher who assist the development team in presenting the game.

15.8.2   Interviews

During the game development process, journalists will conduct interviews with various members of the development team. Most of these can be handled via email and require no advance planning. However, it's important to note the deadline for emailed interviews. For interviews with international journalists, time needs to be allotted for translation prior to publication.

15.8.3   Developer Diaries

Developer diaries are created by the development team to help with PR and marketing. These are written by the developers and describe the work that's being done on the game. Typically, there's dedicated space on the game's website where developer diaries are posted and updated.

15.8.4   Trade Shows

Trade shows are a powerful tool for generating publicity for a game. For larger trade shows, like E3, developers may need to attend and demo the game. This is a big draw for journalists, who enjoy speaking directly to members of the development team about the game and its core features.

If developers are going to demo the game at a trade show, it's a good idea to practice playing the game in front of a crowd so that they don't appear flustered or confused if interrupted or questioned. They should be familiar with the game's core

Product Title	Estimated Date	Notes
Localizations: French, German, Spanish, Italian		
Production		
First playable	See production schedule	
Alpha	See production schedule	
Code freeze	See production schedule	
Beta	See production schedule	
Pre-cert submission to Microsoft®	See production schedule	
Code release candidate	See production schedule	
Certification submission to Microsoft	See production schedule	
Target ship date (all platforms, all languages)	See production schedule	
Box and Docs		
First draft of manual	~10 weeks before U.S. submission or ship date	
Final draft of manual with screenshots	~6–8 weeks before U.S. submission or ship date	
Box and manual layout for developer approval	~4–6 weeks before U.S. submission or ship date	
Marketing Assets		
Demo Build	Varies; marketing may want demo to ship a few months before main game or at the same time as the main game	
Preview code for journalists	~3–4 months before ship date	
Review code for journalists	As soon as U.S. version is code released or submitted	
Production milestone schedule	~8–10 months before ship date	
Design summary	~8–10 months before ship date	
Feature list	~8–10 months before ship date	
Game assets for website (sound, art)	~6–8 months before ship date	
Game concept sketches	~6-8 months before ship date	
High-resolution images (for magazine covers)	~6-8 months before ship date; varies depending on need	
Gameplay footage for trailers	~4-6 months before ship date	
Cheat codes and walk-through	~4-6 months before ship date	
Screenshots	Weeky deliveries; determine number in advance	
Developer interviews	Varies, depending on need	
U.S. press tour	Varies, but may happen around beta	
International press tour	Varies, but may happen around beta	

❙ FIGURE 15.2 *Sample asset deliverable checklist.*

features, both those present in the demo and those that will be available in the final version.

■ 15.9 Asset Deliverable Checklist

Figure 15.2 shows a sample asset deliverable checklist. The first column lists the asset, the second column gives a general time frame for when the asset will be needed, and the third column provides space for notes. Some projects have an accelerated development schedule, which means that the deliverables are also on an accelerated schedule. Depending on the scope of the PR and marketing campaign, a project might have a much longer asset deliverable schedule. This schedule provides an overview of the kinds of assets that are usually requested and time estimates for planning purposes.

■ 15.10 Chapter Summary

As the game's producer, it's crucial that you manage the relationship between the marketing department and the development team in order to ensure that they're working together harmoniously. While the developers are working on the game, the schedule needs to include key marketing deliverables. The game's publicity will suffer if useful assets aren't provided to the marketing team in a timely fashion. In this chapter, we examined the types of assets needed by marketing, as well as the general deadlines for when these assets are required.

■ 15.11 Questions and Exercises

1. What is marketing's role on the game development team?
2. What things need to be considered when creating packaging for the game?
3. What types of things need to be planned for when working on a demo?
4. What is the role of the public relations department in game development?
5. Refer to Figure 15.2 and create an asset deliverable checklist for a fictitious game.
6. What is the purpose of the software age ratings boards?
7. What types of things need to be considered when creating game content for a specific target audience?

Case Study—Justice Unit

This appendix is a case study of the production cycle for a fictitious game called Justice Unit that is being developed by Supergame Studios and published by Digital Fun, Inc.

■ A.1 Introduction

Digital Fun recently acquired the intellectual property (IP) rights to create games based on a popular film franchise called Justice Unit. They are willing to approve a generous budget for the game but want to keep costs in line where they can. Their main goal is to get the game completed in 24 months so that it can ship when the next movie is released. They put out a request for proposal (RFP) to several independent game developers and got several interesting pitches in return. The one they are most interested in comes from Supergame Studios.

Supergame Studios is a small but established studio that specializes in developing games for the console and PC platforms. They have an industry reputation of creating quality games on time and on budget. They are a midsize studio, about 60 to 80 people, depending on development needs, and they usually have two projects in production at a time. They are licensed developers for Sony and Microsoft.

Supergame Studios is very excited to work on Justice Unit and created a pitch that addressed Digital Fun's main goals for the game. The pitch indicated that Supergame Studios can create a multiplatform game in 24 months for around $15–20 million. They will develop the game in iterative cycles so that they have something ready to ship in 18 months, in case the movie release date is pushed earlier. They will continue adding features to the core functionality as time allows. They sign a contract with Digital Fun to create a game for Justice Unit, with the understanding that there are a lot of unknowns about the game, such as:

- Genre
- Platform
- Localization plans
- Setting
- Story

These items and many others will be defined during the preproduction phase and presented to Digital Fun for final approval before production begins.

■ A.2 Preproduction Phase

The main preproduction phase will take about six months, beginning in October 2007 and ending in March 2008. During this time, the team will define the concept and requirements and create a game plan for developing the game so that it is ready to ship in October 2009.

There will be additional preproduction phases during the 24-month development cycle for additional features, localizations, voiceover recordings, and other subprojects that occur within the game development cycle. The team also knows that the main preproduction phase will not have a hard stop date and that production will start on some parts of the game before preproduction is completed on other parts of the game. Preproduction is covered in more detail in Chapters 7–10.

During the preproduction phase, the team consists of five people: a full-time producer, full-time lead artist, full-time lead engineer, full-time lead designer, and full-time QA lead. They will work closely together during preproduction and will solicit feedback on the game ideas from outside resources as necessary.

Concept

The initial concept phase is scheduled to start on October 1, 2007, and end on October 31, 2007. During this month, the team will review the original pitch they made for the Justice Unit game and make a decision on the genre, platform, and key features. In addition, they will do some research on the competition and put together both a SWOT analysis and a competitive analysis. Once this information has been organized and presented to management for approval, the team will continue refining the concept.

The team's goal is to refine the concept and create some prototypes before the holidays, as the office will be closed the last week of December 2007. When they return to the office in January 2008, the prototypes and initial design documents will be presented to management for approval. At this point, the concept phase of the game is close to completion. Figure A.1 is an estimated schedule for the Justice Unit concept phase. Refer to Chapter 7 for more information about the concept phase.

Initial Concept

The initial concept for the game is based on the initial concept for the movie: *Can a group of misfits come together as the Justice Unit and save the world from super villains?* As the concept phase progresses, the team will build on this initial concept and figure out if the game should recreate the events that happen in the movie or if the game

Initial Concept	Resources	General Timeline	Est. Start	Est. End	Tasks
Brainstorming	Producer runs sessions; team participates	1 week	1-Oct-07	5-Oct-07	Brainstorm initial concepts for game, including genre and platform.
Initial Concept	Lead designer	1 week	8-Oct-07	12-Oct-07	Review brainstorming notes. Define initial concept, genre, and platform. Incorporate feedback from team.
Competitive Analysis	Producer, marketing	2 weeks	15-Oct-07	26-Oct-07	Review current and potential competition, complete SWOT analysis based on initial concept.
Approve Initial Concept	Producer runs meeting, leads attend	2–3 days (2–3 weeks after preproduction begins)	29-Oct-07	31-Oct-07	Present initial concept with genre and platform for approval. Initial competitive analysis completed. Incorporate management feedback.

Define Concept	Resources	General Timeline	Est. Start	Est. End	Tasks
Mission Statement	Producer runs sessions, team participates	1–2 days	1-Nov-07	2-Nov-07	Define mission statement for the game.
Game Setting	Lead designer, lead artist	3–5 days	5-Nov-07	9-Nov-07	Define game setting, including look and feel.
Gameplay Mechanics	Lead designer	2–4 weeks	12-Nov-07	6-Dec-07	Create general overview of how major game elements will function: challenges, rewards, learning curve, control scheme, audio elements, multiplayer.
Story Synopsis	Lead designer, writer	3–5 days	10-Dec-07	14-Dec-07	Create game's backstory, character biographies, and general outline of how the story unfolds in the game.
Concept Art	Lead artist, concept artist	3–5 weeks	12-Nov-07	7-Dec-07	Create concept art for game setting, characters, and objects.
Audio Elements	Lead designer, sound designer	2–4 days	17-Dec-07	21-Dec-07	Create general overview of how voiceover, sound effects, and music will be presented in the game.
Prototyping	Lead designer, producer	4–6 weeks	12-Nov-07	21-Dec-07	Prototype major game elements.
Risk Analysis	Producer runs sessions; team participates	2–3 days	19-Dec-07	21-Dec-07	Assess risks on project, determine resolution strategy, and publish to the team.
Pitch Idea	Producer, leads	2–3 days (2–3 months after approval of initial concept)	2-Jan-08	4-Jan-08	Present all major gameplay elements to management for approval and incorporate their feedback.
Project Kickoff	Producer	1 day (after management approves pitch)	7-Jan-08	7-Jan-08	Meet with team to celebrate the concept approval. If working on console title, submit game concept to console manfacturer for approval.

FIGURE A.1 Concept phase schedule estimate for Justice Unit.

should present a different story experience and maybe a new character (either a villain or an ally).

Supergame Studios will have a contact at the movie studio who will provide them with the updated script, the casting information, and other things related to the movie that will be needed by the development team in preproduction.

Genre

There is a lot of material to work with in Justice Unit, which makes it easier to create different genres for the game. For example, Justice Unit could be any of the following genres:

Fighting game: If Justice Unit were a two-player fighting game, it might feature a roster of superheroes and villains from which to choose. Selling points could include unlockable characters, combination moves, and possibly a crossover with another licensed property, such as an existing comic book hero.

Real-time strategy: As an RTS, the game would feature an army of superheroes fighting against waves of alien invaders.

Role-playing game: As a first-person RPG, the player takes on the role of a single character, fighting evil in a superhero universe of masked villains and crime fighters.

The team will take some time to brainstorm the various genres and do some paper prototypes if possible. The type of genre will be influenced by the movie storyline and also by the game platform.

Platform

The publisher wants the game to release on multiple platforms—console, PC, and handheld. The game will essentially be the same on these platforms in order to reduce development time and cost, but each platform will need to feature some unique characteristic or asset that is not available in the other platforms. For example:

PC: A PC-based version of Justice Unit would feature customizability as a primary feature because the keyboard controls allow for a high degree of customization and interaction with the game world.

Handheld: As a handheld game, Justice Unit would have a simple UI and the gameplay will focus on one easy-to-learn feature, such as jumping on platforms or collecting items. This version will be the most different from the PC and console versions, as the art assets will be lower resolution and the engineering and design will be less complex.

Console: A console game would contain similar gameplay and assets as the PC version but will contain more enemies and obstacles for the player to interact with in order to keep the action fast-paced and exciting. The UI will not be as complex as the PC version. The console version of Justice Unit will also include a unique character that does not appear in the PC version.

SWOT Analysis

Figure A.2 is a sample SWOT analysis for Justice Unit that analyzes ways to deal with a rival game named PostMortal that will release at the same time.

In addition, the team creates a SWOT analysis that examines the genre and platform they are using for the game. They want to identify any potential problems in creating Justice Unit as a multiplatform game and figure out some good opportunities to market the game.

The producer schedules a series of brainstorming meetings to discuss the various SWOT analyses. It is important to get input from everyone on the team in order to make the analyses as useful as possible.

SWOT ANALYSIS			
The primary competition for Justice Unit is PostMortal, a first-person shooter set in a superhero universe.			
INTERNAL FACTORS		**EXTERNAL FACTORS**	
Our Strengths	**How to Exploit**	**Our Opportunities**	**How to Exploit**
Compared to rival PostMortal, Justice Unit features a strong multi-player experience, including a customizable multiplayer avatar, dozens of gameplay types, and several maps.	Emphasize these features in the marketing plan.	Justice Unit will launch at the same time as the movie sequel, which will garner additional attention for the game.	Cross-promote game and movie. Create a separate story for the game that intersects with some plot points in the movie.
Our Weaknesses	**How to Neutralize**	**Our Threats**	**How to Neutralize**
Justice Unit features a free-roaming, nonlinear single-player experience, which will not deliver the same thrills as the linear, heavily scripted PostMortal.	Downplay this feature in the marketing plan and focus on the multiplayer features.	PostMortal is scheduled to release two months before Justice Unit and this may have a negative impact on sales; people may buy the PostMortal superhero game instead of Justice Unit.	Build early buzz about the player's ability to play as his or her favorite character from the Justice Unit. Sponsor an enemy contest, where the winner gets to meet the cast of the movie and get an advance copy of the game.

❙ FIGURE A.2 SWOT analysis for Justice Unit.

Competitive Analysis

The team will also work on a competitive analysis of games that have already been released and games that will be released in the future. This information will help Supergame Studios determine how to set Justice Unit apart from the competition. Several games will be researched for the competitive analysis. Figure A.3 is a sample competitive analysis that discusses PostMortal, a competing game about superheroes that will be released at the same time as Justice Unit. Other games will be added to the competitive analysis as the team continues to research the competition.

Define Concept

Once the initial concept is approved, Supergame Studios will further define the concept and start working on documentation and a playable prototype. Refer to Chapters 7, 8, and 9 for more information about defining the concept.

Mission Statement

The mission statement details what is being made and for whom it is being made. The goal of the mission statement is to succinctly define the essence of the game. The mission statement becomes a yardstick that the features and game setting are measured against—anything that does not support the mission statement won't be included in the game. The initial mission statement for Justice Unit is:

Justice Unit is a mass-market superhero game with streamlined controls. It is intended for fans of comic books and superheroes who want to experience the larger-than-life adventure of being a hero.

The initial mission statement is revised slightly in preproduction after the team receives feedback on the first draft of the core design document. The publisher wants the connection between the game and movie to be stronger in the mission statement. The new mission statement for Justice Unit is:

Justice Unit is a mass-market superhero game with streamlined controls. It is intended for existing fans of the Justice Unit movies and also for fans of comic books and other superhero movies who want to experience the larger-than-life adventures of their favorite heroes.

Game Setting

The game setting is closely related to the movie setting. For now, the team defines the game setting in general terms, but will flesh out the setting and storyline in the design documents over the next few months. The setting for Justice Unit is:

The game is set in a classic world of fiendish villains and gun-toting thugs. The player's team consists of oddball heroes with superpowers. In a universe full of

Game	Developer	Publisher	Platforms	Est. Release Date	Game Summary	Features	Avg. Review	Sales Figures
PostMortal	Funtime Studios	A-1 Publishing	Xbox 360, PS3	Oct-09	PostMortal is a new IP about super-heroes. It is a third-person action adventure game and the player assumes the role of Avenger Boy. Other superheroes will be in the game, but the player controls only a single hero throughout the game. The game features traditional costumed super-heroes in a 1950s world setting. Avenger Boy will band together with the other heroes to battle Dr. No Good.	• Avenger Boy is the main player character. • New IP that has no cross-over appeal. • Limited multiplayer modes, although it will have a small online co-op campaign. • Traditional third-person action adventure; uniqueness is based on settings and characters. • Each character has one unique super-power they can use against the enemy. They will help in the game if their assistance is requested by the player.	n/a	n/a

FIGURE A.3 Competitive analysis for Justice Unit.

straight-faced heroes and villains, the Justice Unit is a group of bizarre misfits with strange powers and wacky personalities. Justice Unit is part parody of and part tribute to the classic superteams of the sixties, complete with improbable origin stories and larger-than-life villains.

Gameplay Mechanics

The gameplay mechanics describe how the player will interact with the game. This includes how the control scheme works, the types of multiplayer modes that are available, and the types of challenges the player will encounter, along with the strategies used to overcome these challenges. While the designer is responsible for documenting the gameplay mechanics, he or she will work closely with the other leads to prototype some basic gameplay in order to figure out what will work best in the game.

The key gameplay mechanic for Justice Unit is based on the powers the superheroes have. The powers available in the game will match the powers that are depicted in the movie. For example, BulletPoint has the ability to fly, and this ability will be present in the game. The lead designer is working with the lead engineer to create a flying prototype to determine how the player will control BulletPoint when he is flying.

The designers will spend some time in preproduction figuring out the rest of the main gameplay mechanics. The gameplay features will be prioritized so that the most important gameplay mechanics will get defined and prototyped first.

Story Synopsis

Supergame Studios decides to create a unique storyline for the game that has some tie-ins to the movie. They don't want to be too dependent on the movie content, as the final version of the movie will have some differences from the original script. The game will focus on the origination of these superheroes and how they became the Justice Unit.

The story synopsis for Justice Unit is:

When marketing executive Mark Ferrier was struck by lightning during a presentation, he developed astonishing powers. At first, he kept these to himself, but after witnessing the Justice Unit in a pitched battle with the villainous Wire Hanger, he joined in their defense. The Unit recruited Ferrier, who chose the name BulletPoint. Along with Montezuma, Ice Queen, Major Malfunction, and The Caribou, he fights crime and those who commit it.

Audio Elements

The sound design for Justice Unit will be very high quality and will support Dolby Digital® 5.1 surround sound. The superheroes in the game will be voiced by the same actors who play them in the movie. The voiceover design will be fairly complex, as voice cues are used to convey a lot of information to the player about the story, characters, missions, and gameplay mechanics. Fifty thousand lines of dialogue is a ballpark estimate for the game. Each platform may feature some additional voice cues that will be unique to that platform.

Supergame Studios is planning to license the theme music from the movie and will use this as the main theme music for the game's introductory cinematic. They will also hire a composer to create some variations on this theme to use throughout the game. The music will be adaptive and will change based on what the player is doing in the game. For example, if the player is exploring the world, one type of music will play; if the player engages in combat, another type of music will play.

Justice Unit will use a unique sound effect for each superhero power. This will allow the player to easily identify which superhero is helping him or her, even when the superhero is off-screen. Stock sound effects will be used for things like footsteps, environmental sounds, and selecting items in the UI screen. Supergame Studios is planning to use the same sound effects for the superheroes' powers that are used in the movie. The sound designer from Supergame Studios will have a direct contact with someone on the sound design team for the movie.

Prototyping

The superhero powers are one of the key gameplay mechanics featured in the game. Design is working with engineering to prototype at least one superhero power for each of the playable characters in the game. For example, Ice Queen has the ability to freeze anything, and work is being done on a prototype to figure out how to change the state of an object from normal to frozen. Water is going to be challenging, especially running water that is frozen in midair. BulletPoint's flying ability will also be prototyped.

The team will also use some paper prototypes to test out the statistics for the game mechanics. Each superhero power has to be equal to the others so that one superhero is not going to become dominant during the course of the game. The designers are working on a system that balances the superpowers. The system is based on a series of dice rolls, so the designers are able to use dice to prototype the system. Once they have worked it out on paper, they will work with engineering to create a working digital prototype.

Risk Analysis

At this point in the project, before the concept documents are submitted to senior management for approval, the producer conducts a risk analysis. The producer will continue tracking the risks throughout the project in order to be prepared for any unforeseen circumstances. Figure A.4 is a sample risk analysis for Justice Unit.

At this time, the number of actual risks may be quite low. These risks will increase as the team continues to develop the gameplay mechanics and storyline. The technology used to make the game will have a big impact on the risks, especially if it is a new technology that no one on the team has worked with before.

Risk	Probability of Occurring	Impact on Project	Risk Classification	Mitigation Strategies
Licensor who owns Justice Unit IP may not deliver feedback and approvals in a timely fashion. If they don't approve content of gold master, console sub-mission process will be delayed, which may impact the ship date.	HIGH	HIGH	1	• Schedule kickoff meeting with licensor early in preproduction to review the project goals and schedule constraints. • Work out defined approval process that both parties agree to. • Deliver game assets on a regular basis in preproduction to get feedback and approval before production begins. • Once playable builds are available, deliver builds on a regular basis for licensor to review. • If possible, include caveat in contract that if they don't respond with written feedback in 10 days, the item will be considered approved. • Establish good working relationship with licensor contact and try to include them in the development process whenever possible; make them feel like they are part of the team and have ownership in the game.
Design might be able to create a workable gameplay system where the superhero powers are balanced equally against each other.	LOW	HIGH	2	• Focus on prototyping the core superhero powers for each character to limit the number of variables that must be balanced. • Work with engineering to get a digital prototype up and running as quickly as possible. • Create a system that allows variables to be easily changed and tested in gameplay. • Continue brainstorming ideas for superpowers until the core features are prototyped and approved.
During the two-year development cycle, some employees may leave the company.	HIGH	LOW	3	• Train at least two people to handle specific tasks on the project. • Schedule time for hiring and training new people midproject. • Focus on creating a positive working environment to increase employee retention. • Be aware of any sudden changes in employees' work habits so you can identify at-risk people and improve their job satisfaction before they start looking elsewhere. • Require everyone to document the work they are doing and to check all assets into source control system at the end of each day.
Initial game concept art may not accurately depict what the Justice Unit characters will look like in the game.	LOW	LOW	4	• Concept art will be based on character design bible provided by the licensor. • Feedback from licensor can be quickly implemented until they are satisfied with the concept drawings. • Make sure the artists get all available character concept art from the movie.

FIGURE A.4 Risk analysis for Justice Unit.

Define Requirements

The requirements phase for Justice Unit roughly begins after senior management approves the concept documentation and any prototypes. They had some feedback on the characters and setting and also some good suggestions on how to balance the superhero powers. The team will integrate this feedback into the game during the requirements phase. At this time, the team will start to define specifics about the game, including the core feature set, a list of the necessary art assets, and a rough milestone delivery schedule. The producer is working on a detailed game plan as well and works closely with the leads to determine how much time, money, and people are needed to complete the game. Refer to Chapter 9 for more information on defining requirements.

Figure A.5 is an example of the requirements phase overview for Justice Unit.

The requirements phase will start in early January 2008 and will continue until mid-March 2008. The designers will be busy defining the core features of the game and spending a lot of time creating and refining prototypes.

Engineering is evaluating several possible game engines. They have an in-house engine they can use, but this engine may not be the best choice for the type of game being made. They are also looking at some other engines and will spend some time evaluating the features and tools for each. The licensing fees are also something that will impact the decision, but the game has a big budget, so this will not be the primary deciding factor.

Art will continue working on concept art and will start creating the art bible and figuring out how many art assets will be needed. This includes the number of levels, objects, characters, and so on. The list will not be definitive by mid-March, but will provide a core set of assets that will be needed to get a prototype working with near final art.

Define Game Features

The team conducts a few brainstorming sessions to talk about all the features that can be included in Justice Unit. Not only do they discuss the in-game features, they also discuss features that will improve the tool sets and production processes for the game. The producer organizes these features in a spreadsheet and assigns them categories. The team brainstorms about 100 features they want to include in the game. Figure A.6 is a partial list of some of the initial features for Justice Unit.

The goal of the feature brainstorm is to think of everything that could possibly be included in the game and then scale down the list and prioritize the features. The team starts the process of prioritizing the features by having each project lead rank the features on a scale from 1 to 3, with 3 being most important and 1 being least important. These rankings are then averaged and the features are sorted from most important to least important. Figure A.7 is an example of a ranked and sorted feature list for Justice Unit.

The production team takes time to review this list together and will further refine the rankings. For example, the lead designer is able to make a case that the lowest

Step	Resources	General Timeline	Est. Start	Est. End	Tasks
Define game features	Lead designer	1–2 weeks	7-Jan-08	18-Jan-08	Core features are defined. Secondary and tertiary features also defined.
Define milestone deliverables	Producer	Ongoing; each milestone deliverable list completed about four weeks before the official milestone delivery.			Define the main project milestones and the deliverables for each milestone. Rough milestone estimates based on desired ship date.
Evaluate technology	Lead engineer	4–6 weeks	7-Jan-08	1-Feb-08	Evaluate the technology needs for the game and make a recommendation.
Define tools and pipeline	Lead engineer works with other leads	2–3 weeks	4-Feb-08	15-Feb-08	Define the production pipeline that will produce a playable build with updated assets.
Create concept art	Lead artist	2–3 weeks	1-Jan-08	18-Jan-08	Generate concept for key characters and settings in the game.
Design documentation	Lead designer	6–8 weeks	21-Jan-08	14-Mar-08	Document the key features in the game, including prototypes where possible.
Art documentation	Lead artist	6–8 weeks	21-Jan-08	14-Mar-08	Document the artistic look and feel of the game, generate asset lists, and write up instructions on how to use the art tools.
Technical documentation	Lead engineer	4–6 weeks	18-Feb-08	14-Mar-08	Document the coding standards, technical design, and tools instructions for the game.
Risk analysis	Producer	Ongoing during requirements phase	7-Jan-08	14-Mar-08	Assess risks on project, determine resolution strategy, publish to the team.
Approval	Studio management, publisher	2–3 months after requirements phase begins	17-Mar-08	21-Mar-08	Present all major gameplay elements to management for approval and incorporate their feedback.

FIGURE A.5 Requirements phase overview for Justice Unit.

Category	Feature
Gameplay	Dynamic missions objectives.
Process	Mission review process should also include multiplayer levels.
Process	Establish a system for circulating design documents and updates to documents to the team.
Gameplay	Easy-to-understand user interface.
Gameplay	Replayable missions.
Production	Improve physics so explosions look more realistic.
Gameplay	Ability for player to customize character appearance.
Production	Support cut-and-paste functionality in scripting tool.

FIGURE A.6 Initial feature list for Justice Unit.

ranked feature (support cut-and-paste functionality in scripting tool) should actually be moved higher up the list, because this feature will save the designers a lot of time on the overall design schedule. This time can be better spent play-testing and polishing the game. Engineering agrees that this feature can be ranked higher, as it will take only two days for one engineer to implement this functionality.

Each of the features is reviewed in a similar manner until all the features have been categorized as "must have," "like to have," or "nice to have." The producer tries to limit the number of features included in the "must have" list to 25 percent of the total feature list. For example, if there are a hundred features on the list, the number of "must haves" is limited to around 25. The goal for "like to have" features is around 35 percent of the list, and all the other features will be prioritized as "nice to have." By limiting the number of features that can be listed in each category, the team is forced to really consider the importance of a feature and generate a core feature set that is well-defined and manageable within the schedule.

Define Milestones and Deliverables

Now that the core features have been generally determined, the producer puts together an initial milestone overview for these major milestones:

- First playable
- Alpha
- Code freeze
- Beta
- Code release
- Third-party submission (console platform only)

Category	Feature	Prod.	Art	Design	Eng.	QA	Average
Gameplay	Dynamic mission objectives.	3	3	3	3	3	3
Process	Establish a system for circulating design documents and updates to documents to the team.	3	3	3	3	3	3
Gameplay	Easy-to-understand user interface.	3	3	3	3	3	3
Process	Mission review process should also include multiplayer levels.	3	3	3	2	3	2.8
Production	Improve physics so explosions look more realistic.	2	3	1	3	1	2
Gameplay	Replayable missions.	2	2	2	1	2	1.8
Gameplay	Ability for player to customize character appearance.	1	2	3	1	1	1.6
Production	Support cut-and-paste functionality in scripting tool.	1	1	3	1	1	1.4

3 = MUST HAVE
2 = LIKE TO HAVE
1 = NICE TO HAVE

FIGURE A.7 Rated features for Justice Unit.

Because the team knows that the game has a hard ship date of October 13, 2009, the producer estimates some general deadlines for completing each of these major milestones. The producer also loosely defines the content of each milestone and later on will create more detailed milestone deliverable lists. The milestone deadlines may change a bit during preproduction and production as the team gets a better idea of the progress they are making on Justice Unit, but this initial milestone overview provides a good idea of when each milestone should be completed. Figure A.8 is a milestone overview for Justice Unit.

Milestone Deliverable Checklist

Once the overall milestones are determined, the producer can start working on the specific deliverables for each milestone. The deliverables will include more specific details, such as which features are completed, which assets are playable in the game, and how many missions are scripted. Figure A.9 is a partial milestone deliverable checklist for the alpha milestone for Justice Unit.

These milestone deliverable lists will not be fully complete during preproduction, as there will still be a lot of unknowns about the project. During preproduction, the producer begins working on these lists and will add to them as development progresses. More detailed information can be added as the producer completes the schedule and staffing plan. Eventually these lists will be used by the QA department and the publisher when they test the milestone build. The list is the yardstick they will use to measure the progress of the game. If the milestone list is not defined and sent with the milestone build for approval, it will be difficult to track the work that's been done.

The goal is to have a fully defined milestone deliverable list about four to six weeks before the actual milestone deliverable. This provides enough time for the team to understand all the expectations of the milestone build, and they can adjust the deliverable list based on the remaining time in the schedule. This also gives the producer time to identify any risks to the milestone or any areas where the milestone might slip. Digital Fun. wants the defined lists a few weeks ahead of time as well so they are prepared to check the content of each milestone when it is delivered by Supergame Studios.

Pipeline

The lead engineer is evaluating which engines will work best for the game and figuring out the best way to structure the production pipeline. He is leaning toward using a licensed engine, mainly because they have money in the budget and it will save them some time in the long run, especially if they use an engine that is stable and established and has a good customer support program. There are a few modifications that will be made to any licensed engine. The lead engineer wants to make sure the engine licensor will provide suitable technical support so that any issues with the engine

	First Playable	Alpha	Code Freeze	Beta	Code Release	Third-Party Submission—CONSOLE ONLY
General Time Frame	12–18 months before code release	8–10 months before code release	3–4 months before code release	2–3 months before code release	First code release candidate available to QA 3 weeks before final code release deadline.	Submit code release candidate at least 8–12 weeks before desired ship date.
Engineering	Basic functionality for a few key features are in to demonstrate very basic gameplay.	Key gameplay functionality is in for all game features. Features work as designed, but may be adjusted and changed based on feedback. Game runs on target hardware platform. Tools completed. Production pipeline completed.	Code complete for all features. Only bug fixing from this point forward. No new features are added, unless approved by senior management.	Code complete. Only bug fixing from this point forward.	Full code freeze. During this phase; only crash bugs can be fixed. Critical bugs can be fixed with approval.	Code final. If submission is rejected, only specific bugs as requested by the third party will be fixed for resubmission.
Art	Two to three key art assets are created and viewable in the build. The assets demonstrate the look and feel of the final version of the game.	Assets are 40–50% final, with placeholder assets for the rest of the game.	Assets are 80–90% final, with placeholder assets for the rest of the game.	All art assets are final and working in game. Only major bug fixes from this point forward.	Full art freeze. No art fixes, unless it is to fix a crash bug.	Art final. If submission is rejected, only specific bugs as requested by the third party will be fixed for resubmission.
Design	Basic features are defined, key gameplay mechanics have basic documentation, and playable prototype if possible.	All design documentation is completed. Feature implementation is in progress. 40–50% of design production tasks are completed. Major areas of game are playable as designed.	Game is 80–90% playable. Play-testing feedback is being incorporated.	All design assets are final and working in the game. Only major bug fixes from this point forward. Minor gameplay tweaks can be done, based on play-test feedback.	Full design freeze. No design fixes, unless it is to fix a crash bug.	Design final. If submission is rejected, only specific bugs as requested by the third party will be fixed for resubmission.

FIGURE A.8 Milestone overview for Justice Unit.

	First Playable	Alpha	Code Freeze	Beta	Code Release	Third-Party Submission— CONSOLE ONLY
Sound	The sound of the game is determined, including voiceover, music, and sound effects. Samples are available to communicate the sound vision of the game.	40–50% of sound effects are working. Voiceover design is in progress, placeholder VO files are recorded. Music in process of being composed.	Final voiceover is recorded and in game. Final music is in game. Sound effects are 80–90% implemented.	All final sound assets are in and working in the game.	Full sound freeze.	Sound final. If submission is rejected, only specific bugs as requested by the third party will be fixed for resubmission.
Localization	Work with publisher to determine which languages are needed. Select localization vendor and send them design documents and first playable. Define localization pipeline.	Work with vendor to determine asset delivery schedule. Send glossaries, cheat codes, and walk-throughs to vendor. Test localization pipeline to ensure translations are displayed correctly.	Final text and VO assets are sent for translation. Translations are completed and returned to developer for integration.	Final language assets are integrated into the game. Linguistic testing is completed. Send builds to appropriate age ratings boards to secure final rating.	Full localization freeze.	Localization final. If submission is rejected, only specific bugs as requested by the third party will be fixed for resubmission.
Production	Basic game requirements and game plan are completed.	Full production has begun. The game requirements and game plan are fully completed and approved. If working with licenses, all licenses are secured and an approval process is in place.	Manual is in process of being written. Marketing assets are being generated.	Manual is complete. External vendors are finished with work. All approvals for licenses are secured. Development team can start rolling off project.	All production tasks are completed. If submitting game to console manufacturer, the submission forms are filled in and ready to go.	Production final. Only managing submission process.
QA	Can test game against the first playable milestone deliverables defined in the game requirements phase.	Game is now playable as a full game, although there are some rough edges and holes in some of the functionality. Play-testing can begin. Can test against the alpha deliverables expected for this milestone.	Test plan is 100% complete. Full game functionality can be tested and debugged. Play-testing continues. Can test against the code freeze milestone deliverable list.	All aspects of game can be fully tested and debugged. Some play-testing continues in order for design to put the final polish on the game.	Test code release candidates for any crash bugs that will prevent the game from shipping.	Testing continues on submission candidate(s) until game receives final approval.

FIGURE A.8 (*Continued*).

JUSTICE UNIT
Alpha Deliverable for Sept 28, 2008
Last Updated Aug 29, 2008
Levels
<ul><li>The following levels are asset complete, with gameplay scripting:<ul><li>Justice Hall</li><li>Villain's Lair</li></ul></li><li>The following levels have basic geometry and are viewable in-game, but have no gameplay scripted:<ul><li>City Hall</li><li>Office Complex</li></ul></li></ul>
Characters
<ul><li>The following characters are asset complete:<ul><li>BulletPoint</li><li>Montezuma</li></ul></li><li>The following characters are viewable in-game, but don't have final textures:<ul><li>Caribou</li></ul></li></ul>
UI
<ul><li>UI color scheme and font are final and approved</li><li>UI flow is prototyped in Flash®</li><li>Basic UI screens are implemented and functioning:<ul><li>Start screen</li><li>Profile screen</li><li>Options screen</li></ul></li><li>In-game UI has placeholder art with basic functionality for:<ul><li>Health bar</li><li>Inventory</li></ul></li></ul>
Sound
<ul><li>Placeholder VO cues and sound designs are implemented for the following levels:<ul><li>Justice Hall</li><li>Villain's Lair</li></ul></li><li>Sound designs completed for remaining levels in the game</li></ul>
Engineering
<ul><li>Scripting tools completed and functioning</li><li>Art tools completed and functioning</li><li>Networking APIs are implemented</li><li>Build process finalized and in place</li></ul>

FIGURE A.9 Milestone deliverable checklist for Justice Unit.

modifications can be quickly resolved. He has received SDKs for each engine he is evaluating. He also seeks input from the artist and designer on the level design and scripting tools for each engine (if these tools are available as part of the license).

Special consideration is given to creating a pipeline that will allow the team to easily generate multiplatform builds. The ideal situation is to create a pipeline where the artists need to check in only one set of assets that can be used on each platform, instead of having to check in three sets of assets—one for the PC version, one for the console version, and one for the handheld version. The lead engineer is investigating the best way to handle asset conversion for each platform and is hoping to generate a way for the pipeline to automatically incorporate the appropriate assets from the source control system in order to build each version of the game.

The lead engineer also wants to have a process that is easy to work with. People should be able to check assets in and out with a problem. He also wants to add in some checks that are run each time something new is checked into the build, so that any simple errors can be remedied right away. The engineer plans to make a recommendation on how to structure the pipeline sometime in preproduction. The sooner he makes a decision, the sooner he can get an engineering team working on the pipeline.

Documentation

During preproduction, Supergame Studios will generate some design, art, and technical documentation. The QA lead also works on some play-testing plans and will begin putting the main test plan together. These documents will be living documents and will change throughout the development process, so the producer creates an area on the team wiki to publish the documents. This solution provides an easy way to update the documents, track the changes, and communicate these changes to the team. Everyone is directed to go to the team wiki for the current version of all documents. When more people are added to the team, one person in each discipline will be assigned the task of checking the documentation on a daily basis and ensuring that all changes have been added to the wiki.

The lead designer has the most documentation to write, and at some point during preproduction an additional designer will join the project to assist with prototyping, play-testing, and writing documentation. The list of design documents needed for Justice Unit includes:

- UI
- Multiplayer
- Character backgrounds and dialogue
- Scoring
- Mission designs

- Control scheme
- Player actions
- Storyline
- AI
- Weapons, special objects, power-ups
- Voice recognition

The lead artist begins working on the style guide early in preproduction. The asset lists will be generated and included in the milestone deliverable lists. Another artist will join the team in preproduction to help with prototyping and defining the asset deliverables. The asset lists and tools instructions will not be fully final at the end of preproduction. Art will continue adding details to these documents throughout production. The art documentation needed for Justice Unit includes:

- Style guide
- Asset list
- Tools instructions

The lead engineer also has a set of documents to write during preproduction. As engineers are added to the team, they will need to understand the coding standards and how the technology works. The list of technical documents needed for Justice Unit includes:

- Coding standards
- Technical design
- Tools instructions

Create Game Plan

While the leads work on their preproduction tasks, the producer is busy creating the game plan. As with the other documents generated in preproduction, the game plan will continue to be updated during production. The goal of creating a game plan in pre-production is to put together an initial plan that serves as the starting point for the project. It is much easier to determine how much progress is actually being made if there is a plan to compare the progress against. The plan also helps identify which variables (schedule, resources, or features) need to be adjusted in order to fulfill the project goals.

Refer to Chapter 10 for more information on creating a game plan.

Figure A.10 is an estimated schedule for the game plan phase of Justice Unit. This plan will detail the budget, schedule, and staffing that is needed to complete the game in time for an October 13, 2009 ship date. The game plan phase will begin in early January 2008 and will wrap up in mid-March 2008.

Step	Resources	General Timeline	Est. Start	Est. End	Tasks
Create master schedule	Producer	Happens in parallel with requirements phase	7-Jan-08	14-Mar-08	Create project schedule with main milestones and break down each milestone into major art, design, engineering, and QA tasks. Add in sections for any localization, voiceover, or other outsource work. Include sections for third-party approvals.
Create detailed schedules for core features	Producer	Happens in parallel with requirements phase	7-Jan-08	14-Mar-08	As design, art, and engineering determine requirements, create schedules for major features to determine scope, cost, and resources for desired features.
Determine budget	Producer	Happens in parallel with requirements phase	7-Jan-08	14-Mar-08	Make educated assumptions about estimated costs and create an initial budget.
Determine staffing needs	Producer	Happens in parallel with requirements phase	7-Jan-08	14-Mar-08	Make educated assumptions about estimated staffing needs and create an initial staffing plan.
Determine outsourcing needs	Producer	Happens in parallel with requirements phase	7-Jan-08	14-Mar-08	Based on staffing needs, team expertise, and budget, make an educated guess about which areas of the game will need to be outsourced.
Research and select vendors	Producer	Happens in parallel with requirements phase	7-Jan-08	14-Mar-08	Research potential vendors to get an idea of cost, quality, and dependability.
Approval	Studio management, publisher	Happens in parallel with requirements phase	17-Mar-08	21-Mar-08	Present budget, schedule, and staffing plan to management for approval.

FIGURE A.10 Game plan phase overview for Justice Unit.

Initial Schedule Estimate

Because Justice Unit has to ship on October 13, 2009, the producer knows that the schedule is the fixed variable for the game plan. This means that the schedule dictates how many people are needed on the team and what the game's budget will be. Luckily, Justice Unit has a 24-month development cycle, so the producer should be able to create a game plan that has a reasonable schedule and budget.

When creating the game plan, the producer notes that some of the secondary features ("like to have" features) might be moved to the "nice to have" feature list. If the game did not have a hard ship date, the producer could create a schedule that is dictated by when the desired features are actually completed, which would mean the game likely would not be ready to ship in October 2009.

The producer begins work on the game plan by creating an initial schedule estimate. Because the producer is familiar with about how long each milestone phase should be, he starts figuring out the development schedule based on the target ship date and works backward to come up with estimates of when each milestone phase should be completed. For example, it normally takes a console project eight weeks to receive final approval from the console manufacturer, so the game's gold master must be ready for submission at least eight weeks before the ship date. The producer wants to schedule three weeks of testing on potential code release candidates so that the gold master will be ready for submission on time. He schedules rough deadlines for the remaining milestones by continuing to work backward from the previous milestones deadline. Figure A.11 is an initial schedule estimate for Justice Unit.

Once the producer determines the milestone deadlines, he estimates dates for submitting the milestones for approval. He also works with the project leads to estimate completion deadlines for key areas of the game. The actual dates will be slightly different once the producer puts a detailed schedule together, but the initial schedule estimate provides a good blueprint for when things need to be done.

In Figure A.11, the producer has not listed specific deadlines for the cinematics. He wants to first put together a more defined schedule in order to determine whether the cinematics should be outsourced. He plans to hold off on making this decision until early in production. There is enough time in the development schedule to wait on this decision. The producer does list the cinematics as a risk on the project, mainly to keep reminding people that a decision needs to made on whether to outsource the cinematics.

For the design, art, engineering, audio, and localization sections, the producer works with the appropriate lead to estimate some ballpark deadlines. The leads determine some key tasks that can provide useful data points for measuring the progress of the project. After they determine these initial tasks and see the breakdown in the initial schedule, they can better plan the content of each major milestone delivery.

Game Name	Estimated Date	Notes
Languages: English, German, French, Italian, Spanish		
Production		
Concept Phase Completed	21-Dec-07	Completed before holiday break (Dec 24, 2008–Jan 2, 2009).
Requirements Phase Completed	14-Mar-08	Phase begins in early Jan 2009.
Initial Game Plan Completed	14-Mar-08	Producer works on this in parallel with requirements phase.
First Playable	27-Jun-08	Once initial plan approved, will schedule three months to prototype main gameplay mechanics and create a first playable with some assets that will represent final art quality and gameplay experience.
Alpha	27-Sep-08	Planning to develop console and PC platforms in parallel, with priority going to console since it must be code released first in order to be submitted to third party for approval.
Code Freeze	27-Apr-09	
Beta	27-May-09	
Pre-Cert Submission to Microsoft	27-May-09	
Code Release Candidate	27-Jul-09	All platforms, all languages ready.
Certification Submission to Microsoft	17-Aug-09	
Target Ship Date (all platforms, all languages)	13-Oct-09	Sim-ship with Europe.
Approvals		
Concept Approval	7-Jan-08	
Requirements Approval	21-Mar-08	
Game Plan Approval	21-Mar-08	
License Approval	Ongoing	Will need to approve initial design documents and each major milestone delivery. They have 10 days to approve any assets presented to them.
Console Manufacturer Approval	28-Sep-09	Need to get approval by this date in order to have three weeks for manufacturing and shipping.

FIGURE A.11 Initial schedule estimate for Justice Unit.

Design		
Deliverables Completed for Concept Phase	21-Dec-07	
Deliverables Completed for Requirements Phase	14-Mar-08	
Detailed Documentation Completed for Game Features	27-Jun-08	Will continue writing core feature documentation until first playable is ready at end of June 2008. At this time, will determine which secondary features to document and implement.
Character and Story Documents Complete	27-Sep-08	Completed by alpha so there is ample time to implement any feedback.
Voiceover Scripts Completed	27-Mar-09	Will record placeholder VO in Jan 2009 to test out voice cues and determine how much content needs to be written.
Mission and Scenarios Designed	27-Sep-08	Plan to complete all mission designs by alpha. Mission designs will have staggered deliveries between April 2008 and Sept 2008 so that prototype scripting can be completed for each mission by Dec 2008.
Mission Prototypes Scripted	21-Dec-08	Planning to have all art and design prototypes completed by end of year. This allows for playtesting and feedback in Jan and Feb 2009. Once a level is play-tested, final scripting can begin.
Play-testing	27-Feb-09	All play-testing completed by this deadline. Play-testing begins in Jan 2009.
Final Missions Scripted	27-May-09	Final mission scripting completed by beta. After this date, minor scripting feedback can be implemented. Other changes evaluated on a case-by-case basis.
Art		
Deliverables Completed for Concept Phase	21-Dec-07	
Deliverables Completed for Requirements Phase	14-Mar-08	
Prototypes Completed	5-Dec-08	Art prototypes completed in early December so that design has all necessary art assets to complete scripting by Dec 21, 2008. Art prototyping will begin in April 2008 after design completes first mission scenario.
First Playable Level Completed	1-Jun-08	Design needs to deliver level scenario by May 1, 2008 in order for art to have prototype completed by this date. This dates allows four weeks for design to script the level, and for art to continue polishing the level and implementing feedback so that the first playable deadline is met on Jun. 27, 2008.

FIGURE A.11 (Continued).

Special Effects Completed	27-Apr-09	Placeholder special effects to be completed by alpha. All special effects must be completed by code freeze (Apr 27, 2009) so that artists can begin final UI polish.
UI Completed	27-Apr-09	Placeholder UI to be completed by alpha. All UI art assets must be completed by code freeze (Apr 27, 2009) so that artists can begin final UI polish.
Cinematics Completed	15-Jul-09	Placeholder cinematics completed before beta (Apr 27, 2009); final cinematics completed by Jul 15, 2009.
Engineering		
Deliverables Completed for Concept Phase	21-Dec-07	
Deliverables Completed for Requirements Phase	14-Mar-08	
Engineering Prototypes Completed	27-Jun-08	Prototyping of new technology completed by first playable. Ideally first playable is built on technology prototypes.
Art and Design Tools Completed	27-Sep-08	Tools must be completed by alpha at the latest so that design can test tools, provide feedback, and have everything working so they can begin scripting in Jan 2009.
Production Pipeline Completed	27-Sep-08	Build process must be running smoothly by alpha. Once team hits alpha, daily builds will be automatically generated.
All Major Gameplay Features Implemented	27-Mar-09	Would like all features to be implemented one month before code freeze, so there is time to provide feedback or fix any major issues before full code freeze.
Code Freeze	27-Apr-09	Ideally, code can freeze at this time. Will consult with lead engineer about any feature requests that occur after this deadline.
Audio		
Sound Designs Completed	19-Dec-08	Sound design will use mission design documents as basis for sound design. Casting notes and VO samples will also be ready at this time. Will begin recording placeholder VO.
Sound Prototypes Completed	27-Feb-09	Sound can continue work on prototypes while scripting is being play-tested. This allows them ample time to finish final sound designs by beta (May 27, 2009).

FIGURE A.11 (*Continued*).

Task	Date	Description
Placeholder VO Recorded	30-Jan-09	Will work with design to record some placeholder VO so it can be implemented in the level prototypes for feedback. Will also use placeholder as a way to test different types of voices and accents for various characters.
Final VO Recorded	27-Apr-09	Final VO must be recorded by code freeze so that localized VO can be recorded. May schedule a pick-up session in late June 2009 if necessary.
Final Music Implemented in Game	27-May-09	May outsource music to an external vendor. If so, will want vendor to deliver before this deadline to ensure there are no delays.
Localization		
Determine Localization Needs	27-Jun-08	Ideally publisher will let us know by first playable which languages they want. External vendors will be researched and one will be selected by this deadline.
Organize Assets for Translation	27-Mar-09	Design will have VO scripts and in-game text completed at this point. May send assets in batches for translation if some areas of text are not fully final.
Integrate Assets	27-May-09	Planning for translations to be ready at beginning of May 2009. The localized VO for cinematics will need some additional time for integration.
Functionality Testing	27-Jun-09	Will begin functional testing at end of May.
Linguistic Testing	27-Jun-09	Will begin linguistic testing at end of May. This will allow time to submit localized builds to ratings boards for certification. Linguistic testing to be completed by beta.
QA		
Test Plan Completed	27-Jun-08	Initial plan completed by first playable. Plan will continue to be updated as new design documents and prototypes are completed.
First Playable Testing Completed	7-Jul-08	QA will begin checking first playable against milestone deliverables on Jun 30 (next working day after first playable is completed).
Alpha Testing Completed	3-Oct-08	QA will spend five days checking alpha against milestone deliverables.
Play-testing Completed	27-Feb-09	
First Code Release Candidate to QA	27-Jul-09	
Code Release	17-Aug-09	

FIGURE A.11 (*Continued*).

Cinematics (External Vendor)		
Deliver Initial Specs to Vendor	???	Need to determine whether cinematics should be outsourced.
Storyboard from Vendor	???	
Animatic from Vendor	???	
Rough Cut from Vendor	???	
Final Movie from Vendor (no sound)	???	
Movie to Sound Designer	???	
Final Movie Ready for Game	???	
Marketing		
Demo Build	6-Jul-09	Marketing wants fully approved demo by Aug 7, 2009, so it can be included on cover disc for *Official Xbox* magazine. Demo needs to be submitted at least four weeks before this deadline to make this date.
Preview Code for Journalists	27-May-09	Planning to send the beta build as preview code.
Review Code for Journalists	17-Aug-09	The build submitted to Microsoft for final approval will be used as review code.

FIGURE A.11 (*Continued*).

Budget

As the producer is putting together the schedule, he also needs to define the budget and staffing plan. As discussed in Chapter 10, all of these elements must be considered together when creating the game plan. The budget must account for how many people are needed, but the number of people needed can't be accurately determined until the producer has an idea of what the schedule is going to be.

Digitial Fun is already willing to make a substantial investment in getting the game made and has given a budget range of $15–20 million. This budget must include the costs for all licensed music, internal personnel, hardware, external vendors, testing, and anything else directly related to the production of the game. With this in mind, the producer creates a budget with a fairly large team so that he can easily meet the milestone deadlines he estimated earlier in preproduction.

Figure A.12 is an estimated budget for the personnel needed to create Justice Unit. The producer estimates that up to 80 people will be needed to get the game completed on time. He will need to figure out a plan for adding more people to the team as production begins and also create a plan for rolling people off the project as production winds down.

This estimates how long someone will be needed on the project. The staffing may change on the project depending on the feedback the producer gets on the budget. If he is told to reduce the budget, he may decide to also reduce the number of new staff he adds to the game production team.

Figure A.13 is an estimated budget for the other production costs. This includes external vendors to do voiceover, music, cinematics, and localization. There is also a significant royalty for the Justice Unit IP that must be included in the production budget. Note the large amount of software licensing fees. This section of the budget may be reduced if the team decides to use a different engine with a lower-cost licensing fee.

Staffing

As discussed earlier, the producer plans for a large staff on this project in order to realistically meet the desired ship date. If the budget is not approved as it currently stands, the producer may look for cheaper staffing alternatives by outsourcing the work to India or other parts of Asia. For now, he keeps as much internal staff as possible, since he will have better control over the game and will have more flexibility in adding or changing features.

Team Organization Flowchart

Figure A.14 is the team organization chart for Justice Unit. The team includes around 60 people and the producer works with the leads to determine how to organize the team. They decide that a traditional team structure will work best, with each lead heading up his or her discipline. This means that the art director will manage all the artists,

Production Personnel	Number	Monthly Rate	# of Months	Cost
Producer	1	$8,000	24	$192,000
Associate Producer	3	$6,000	18	$324,000
Art Personnel				
Lead Artist	1	$10,000	24	$240,000
Technical Artist	1	$8,000	24	$192,000
Concept Artist	2	$6,000	10	$120,000
World Builder	10	$6,000	12	$720,000
Object Artist	3	$6,000	8	$144,000
Texture Artist	4	$6,000	12	$288,000
Marketing Artist	1	$6,000	12	$72,000
Animator	3	$8,000	8	$192,000
Engineering Personnel				
Lead Engineer	1	$10,000	24	$240,000
Networking Engineer	2	$8,000	16	$256,000
Graphics Engineer	4	$8,000	18	$576,000
UI Engineer	1	$8,000	12	$96,000
AI Engineer	4	$8,000	18	$576,000
Sound Engineer	1	$8,000	12	$96,000
Tools Engineer	3	$8,000	18	$432,000
General Engineer	5	$8,000	18	$720,000
Engineer	2	$8,000	12	$192,000
Design Personnel				
Lead Designer	1	$8,000	24	$192,000
Designer	4	$6,000	18	$432,000
Sound Designer	1	$6,000	12	$72,000
Writer	1	$6,000	6	$36,000
QA Personnel				
Lead QA Analyst	1	$8,000	24	$192,000
Tester	20	$6,000	10	$1,200,000
GRAND TOTAL	**80**			**$7,792,000**

Based on a 24-month development cycle.
Monthly rates are for example only; they do not reflect actual rates.

FIGURE A.12 Estimated budget for personnel costs for Justice Unit.

the engineers will manage the engineers, and so on. All the leads will report directly to the producer, and the producer will have an associate producer who will assist in the day-to-day management of the production cycle.

The leads also select some people on the team to head up subgroups within each discipline in order to improve communication flow and to reduce the number of direct

Hardware	Number	Rate	Cost
Computers	80	$3,000	$240,000
Console Development Kits	40	$10,000	$400,000
Controllers	60	$100	$6,000
Graphics Cards	80	$300	$24,000
Software			
Perforce®	76	$750	$57,000
3ds Max	19	$4,000	$76,000
Photoshop®	4	$600	$2,400
Microsoft Project	5	$1,000	$5,000
Unreal Engine™ 3	1	$1,000,000	$1,000,000
Visual C++®	23	$3,000	$69,000
Licensing Fees			
Justice Unit Royalty	1	$500,000	$500,000
External Vendors			
Voiceover	1	$250,000	$250,000
Music	1	$50,000	$50,000
Cinematics	1	$300,000	$300,000
Localization	4	$50,000	$200,000
Other			
Travel	24	$1,000	$24,000
Food	24	$500	$12,000
Shipping/Postage	24	$200	$4,800
GRAND TOTAL			**$3,220,200**

Based on a 24-month development cycle.

Rates are for example only; they do not reflect actual rates.

| FIGURE A.13   Estimated budget for other production costs for Justice Unit.

reports the leads have to manage. For example, the engineering lead creates subgroups for networking, tools, AI, sound, and graphics, and each of these is headed up by an experienced engineer.

Completing Preproduction

Supergame Studios has completed preproduction and consults their checklist to confirm that they have completed all the major preproduction tasks. Figure A.15 is the preproduction checklist.

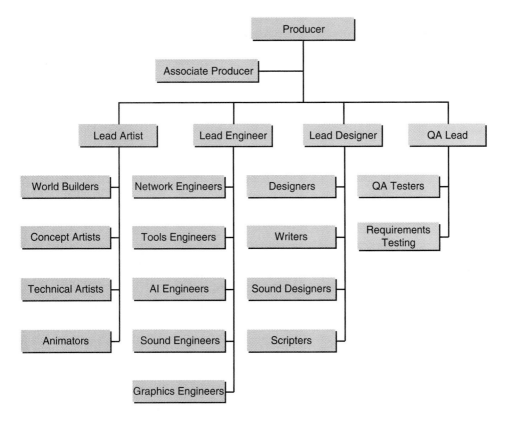

FIGURE A.14 Team organization chart for Justice Unit.

■ A.3 Technical Production

During the preproduction phase, the producer makes some decisions on how to handle the voiceover and music during production. He is going to outsource these parts of the project but still needs to organize and schedule them within the production cycle. The voiceover will need to be carefully managed because there is a lot of dialogue to record and because the actors from the movie will also be voicing the characters for the game.

The theme music from the movie will be used in the game, so Digital Fun will work with the movie studio on a licensing deal. Supergame Studios is hiring a composer to create original music based on the theme, so the producer needs to schedule this so that all the music is completed by beta. Chapter 12 contains more details about audio.

Voiceover

The voiceover needs for Justice Unit are quite large. There are five main characters and 30 minor characters who will have recorded dialogue. The designer and sound

PREPRODUCTION CHECKLIST	Y / N	NOTES
CONCEPT		
Is initial game concept defined?		
Are platform and genre specified?		
Is mission statement completed?		
Are basic gameplay elements defined?		
Is prototype completed?		
Is risk analysis completed?		
Is the concept pitch ready for approval?		
Have all stakeholders approved the concept?		
Is project kickoff scheduled?		
GAME REQUIREMENTS		
Are "must have," "want to have," and "nice to have" features defined?		
Are constraints defined and accounted for in feature sets?		
Are milestones and deliverables defined?		
Has technology been evaluated against the desired feature set?		
Are tools and pipeline defined?		
Is basic design documentation completed?		
Is basic technical documentation completed?		
Is risk analysis completed?		
Have all stakeholders approved the game requirements?		
GAME PLAN		
Is budget completed?		
Is initial schedule completed?		
Is initial staffing plan completed?		
Have core team members approved the schedule and staffing plan?		
Have all stakeholders approved the game plan?		

❙ FIGURE A.15 Preproduction checklist.

Task	Resource	Deadline
Initial dialogue written	Writer	30-Jan-09
Placeholder VO recorded	Sound designer	30-Jan-09
Send bid packages to sound studios	Producer	27-Feb-09
Book time for VO recording session	Producer	13-Mar-09
Updated dialogue written	Writer	27-Feb-09
Additional placeholder VO recorded	Sound designer	27-Feb-09
Audition actors	Sound studio	10-Apr-09
Cast actors	Writer/producer/ sound designer	10-Apr-09
Final dialogue written	Writer	27-Mar-09
Dialogue recorded	Writer/producer/ sound designer	27-Apr-09
Dialogue processed and ready for development team	Sound designer	20-May-09

FIGURE A.16 Estimated VO schedule for Justice Unit.

designer estimate there will be about 100,000 lines of dialogue. The initial recording session will take several weeks, and additional time will be needed for pick-up sessions.

The producer starts planning for the voiceover needs in preproduction. He puts together a schedule estimate of when the major voiceover tasks need to be completed during development. Figure A.16 is an estimated schedule for completing the VO for Justice Unit.

The actual voiceover shoot is scheduled for April 2009. The shoot is scheduled as late in the development cycle as possible in order to give design and sound ample time to polish the voiceover script and make an exact determination of the voiceover needs. The sound designer has already implemented a lot of placeholder VO, so the producer is confident that the VO cues will work as expected in the game. Also, since placeholder voiceover cues with the correct filenames are already implemented, the sound designer will be able to drop the final voiceover files into the game without too many problems. If placeholder VO was not already integrated into the game, the recording session would need to happen much sooner in production so that there is ample time to review the VO files in the game and make any necessary changes.

The producer researches several VO vendors and provides them with information to make a bid. Figure A.17 is a sample of a partially completed bid that will be sent to external vendors the producer is considering for Justice Unit. The producer works with the designer and sound designer to get an exact character and line count for the bid.

Voiceover Assets

Any celebrity talent used? Include celebrity names in "Notes" column in table below.	Yes. The actors who play the main characters in the movie will also voice them in the game.
Union or nonunion (English version)	Union
Bit depth (ex: 8 bit, 16 bit, etc.)	16 bit
Sample rate (ex: 22 KHz, 44 KHz)	44 Khz
Channels (mono/stereo/5.1)	Dolby 5.1
File delivery formats	Uncompressed .wav files
Required processing (list any special effects needed)	Basic edits for pops and clicks, name files according to filenaming system provided by developer.

Character	Est. # of Lines	Male/Female	Age	Notes
BulletPoint	5,000	M	25	Need to get actor who is playing this character in the movie.
Melanie Cole	5,000	F	26	Need to get actor who is playing this character in the movie.
Caribou	3,000	M	24	Need to get actor who is playing this character in the movie.
Teacher	1,000	F	65	Actor needs to speak Chinese and English. The actor can also voice other characters in the game.
Sam	1,000	M	21	Actor can voice other characters in the game.
Woman #1	50	F	mid-40s	This actress will voice three characters.
Woman #2	75	F	early-40s	Voiced by same actress who does Woman #1.
Man #1	50	M	mid-40s	This actor will voice three characters.
Man #2	75	M	mid-30s	Voiced by same actor who does Man #1.

FIGURE A.17 Voiceover bid for Justice Unit.

The producer selects the voiceover recording studio that will be used for Justice Unit. He purposely picks a vendor based in Los Angeles who has experience working with celebrity voices because this makes it much easier to schedule time with the actors from the movie who will also be voicing characters in the game.

The studio requests a set of casting notes for all the major and minor characters in the movie. While the major characters have already been selected, it is useful to have casting notes for the actors to review when they come to the recording session. Casting notes are written up for the minor characters and include an image of the character, the character's history and background, notes on what the character's voice sounds like, and some sample dialogue that actors can record during the audition process.

The recording studio starts the casting process in March 2009 so that final selections can be made by mid-April 2009. Supergame Studios gets a set of audio files to review for each character that needs to be voiced in the game. Because they are trying to reduce the cost for voiceover actors, Supergame Studios chooses actors who can distinctly voice three different characters. Figure A.18 is an example of the casting notes used in Justice Unit.

The vendor books the recording session for late April 2009. The session will take a few weeks because there is a great deal of dialogue to be recorded. The voiceover vendor handles booking and scheduling the actors in the most efficient way in order to complete recording as quickly as possible. The celebrity actors are booked first, since their availability takes priority over any other actors.

While the vendor is organizing the actual recording session, Supergame Studios is working on the final voiceover script. The writer organizes all the VO dialogue into a spreadsheet and reviews it with the designer and producer. Because the recording session is happening so close to the end of the production cycle, there is only time for a single recording session. A three-day pick-up session is scheduled for a few weeks later, but the producer wants to avoid having this session if possible in order to save on costs and time. Figure A.19 is the voiceover spreadsheet that will be used in Justice Unit.

The writer and sound designer attend the recording sessions. A professional VO director was hired to direct the voiceover actors, but it is useful for the writer and sound designer to be on-site in case there are any rewrites or new dialogue needs to be written. They can also advise the director and actors of the context of lines in the VO script and ensure that the performances will work well when they are implemented into the game. They are also on hand to select which takes they want for each line reading, which will save the vendor some time in the editing process. Instead of editing all the VO files, the vendor can concentrate on editing only the high-quality VO files that will be used in the game. The vendor is only responsible for basic editing of the files, such as removing sound artifacts and naming all the files per the established naming convention. The sound designer will do any additional special edits on the VO files.

Name	Ice Queen (real name Melanie Cole)
Background	Born in 1979, Melanie grew up in Virginia Beach, VA. Her father was an architect and her mother worked as a receptionist. An average student, Melanie studied at Tidewater Community College for two years before transferring to Old Dominion University, where she graduated with a degree in history in 2002. Melanie's parents died in 2004, when her sentience manifested itself. The freezing blast leveled three homes, killing a total of seven people. Horrified, Melanie fled, but was later apprehended by police. Later that day, her sentience erupted again, destroying the police station and killing several officers. BulletPoint and The Sensei were called in and were able to incapacitate Melanie. She was taken to Masada, where the Justice Division was able to train her in the use of her powers. Since then, Melanie has learned to control her sentience, and has proven herself a capable member of the Justice Division.
Personality	Melanie is extremely distant and has difficulty forming lasting relationships with people. Though she has fought beside the other members of the Justice Division for two years, she still refers to them by their code names and refuses to socialize outside of work. Members of the Division have joked that her most powerful offensive weapon is the Cold Shoulder. She still grieves for her family and feels a profound sense of remorse for the lives that she ended, even though she's aware that the deaths were accidental. Despite hundreds of hours of training, Melanie fears that she may lose control of her sentience, resulting in more innocent deaths.
Voice	Melanie's voice is low and firm. She only raises her voice when chastising or disagreeing with someone. She often sounds arch or condescending, particularly when explaining things to others, and can come across as callous when delivering bad news. She speaks unaccented English.
References	Gillian Anderson (*The X-Files*)
Sample Dialogue	"That's really too bad, but that's not our problem. We're here to apprehend Zomborg, and that's all I'm really interested in talking about." "What part of 'immediately' did you not understand? You were expected a while ago. Get in there and do your job." "I don't really have time to deal with this. The Division doesn't have time for this either. Suck it up, or quit."

FIGURE A.18　Casting notes for Justice Unit.

Line #	Character	English	Level	Type	SfX	Context	Voice Direction	Filename
1	Bad Guy #13	We're in the van, commander. We're going to lose the police on the interstate.	1	Mission open	Radio futz	The bad guys are trying to outrun the police after they stole a museum artifact.	Serious	01_bg13_01.wav
2	BulletPoint	Sam, they're getting away!	1	Objective		BulletPoint has been monitoring radio chatter and knows what the bad guys are planning.	Serious, raised voice	01_bp_01.wav
3	Sam	I'll cut them off.	1	Objective		Sam received the update from BulletPoint and will cut off the bad guys on the highway.	Serious, calm	01_sam_01.wav
4	Civilian #3	Help me!	1	Nonplayer Character		This civilian got hit by the bad guys as they were trying to escape.	Scared, yelling	01_c3_01.wav
5	Sam	You'll be OK. I've called the ambulance.	1	Cinematic		Sam stops pursuit of the bad guys and aids the injured civilian.	Soothing	01_sam_02.wav

FIGURE A.19 Voiceover spreadsheet for Justice Unit.

The sound designer was able to implement about 90 percent of the placeholder VO recordings to test out the placement of the VO cues and how well they worked in the game. Because he was able to implement most of the placeholder VO files, it will be easy to copy over the final VO files into the build.

As the voiceover tasks are completed, the producer reviews the checklist in Figure A.20 to confirm that he has everything necessary for the game's voiceover. Refer to Chapter 12 for more information on voiceover production.

Music

Supergame Studios plans to license the main music theme that is being used in the movie so it can be used in the game's opening sequence. They think this will be a good way to tie together the movie and game. This is the only track that will be licensed for the game and will play in the opening sequence. Supergame Studios is hiring a composer to create original music for the rest of the game. The composer will be allowed to compose variants on the main theme if this is part of the music design.

The sound designer puts together a plan for the music in late June 2008 when the first playable milestone is completed. Figure A.21 is an estimated schedule for the music tasks to be completed. The sound designer wants to send out bid packages in late September 2008 and receive final music files in late April 2009. The composer will deliver initial versions of all music a few months before the April 2009 deadline so there is ample time to review the music in the game and provide any feedback to the composer on what changes must be made.

The sound designer is able to integrate some existing music tracks into the playable build to get an idea of what type of music will work best in the game. He sends these test music tracks along with the bid information so that the composers can get a good idea of what the music should sound like. Figure A.22 is an example of a music bid for Justice Unit.

Once the composer is selected, he receives a playable build of the game and documentation that describes the characters, setting, and story. This will help him get a better idea of the game and will improve the quality of the music he is composing for the game. The composer and sound designer set up a process for the sound designer to review each track when the composer has an initial version ready. Once the composer receives feedback, he creates another version for review. The sound designer and composer find that two rounds of feedback usually provide the desired results with the music.

As with the voiceover files, the sound designer integrated placeholder music files into the game so that they can easily be replaced with the final music files when they are ready. Because the game supports adaptive music, the sound designer also uses these placeholder music files to test how well the adaptive music is working.

After the composer delivers the final music files in April 2009, the sound designer discovers he needs one more minute of music to loop behind some of the UI screens.

Voiceover Checklist	Y/N	Notes
PREPRODUCTION		
Is initial voiceover design completed?		
Are initial character descriptions written?		
Is initial voiceover schedule completed?		
Is initial voiceover budget completed?		
Is file naming convention established?		
Is file management system established?		
Are file delivery formats defined?		
Are casting notes written with sample dialogue?		
Have bid packages been sent to sound studios?		
PRODUCTION		
Is sound studio selected?		
Has final decision been made on using union or nonunion actors?		
Have recording dates been tentatively booked with the sound studio?		
Is initial voiceover script written?		
Is placeholder dialogue recorded and implemented in the game?		
Are auditions scheduled?		
Are celebrity voices being used? Are they available for the tentative dates?		
Are final actor selections completed? Are they available for the tentative dates?		
RECORDING SESSION		
Are dates finalized and booked with the actors?		
Is the voiceover script final?		
Are audition files available for the actors to listen to?		
Is pronunciation guide final?		
Is game footage available to show the actors?		
Is voice director booked for the session?		
Are all final takes selected?		
POSTPRODUCTION		
Has sound studio edited the final takes of audio files?		
Are files delivered in the correct format? Are uncompressed versions available?		
Has the raw data from the recording session been delivered?		
Has voiceover script been updated with any dialogue changes and alternate lines?		

FIGURE A.20 Voiceover checklist.

Task	Resource	Deadline	General Timeline
Music design determined	Sound designer/ sound engineer	27-Jun-08	Before production starts
Initial music deliverables defined	Sound designer	27-Sep-08	By alpha
Send bid packages to composers (if working with external composer)	Producer	27-Sep-08	By alpha
Start negotiating for music rights (if licensing music)	Producer	27-Sep-08	By alpha
Add placeholder music in the game	Sound designer	21-Dec-08	Before alpha
First set of compositions delivered by the composer	Composer	27-Mar-09	~2–3 months before beta
Composer delivers final music mixes	Composer	27-Apr-09	~1 month before beta
Secure all final music rights	Producer	27-Apr-09	~1 month before beta
Implement all final music in the game	Sound designer	27-May-09	By beta

FIGURE A.21   Estimated music schedule for Justice Unit.

He decides to reedit one of the tracks the composer sent over instead of asking the composer to create an additional minute of music. Because the composer had a work-for-hire contract with Supergame Studios, it is fine for the sound designer to reedit or sample any music files the composer delivers. In fact, when the composer delivers the music files, he also delivers all the source files in case Supergame Studios needs or wants to make any changes. Refer to Chapter 12 for more information on music.

Marketing and PR

Digital Fun assigns a product manager to work with the studio's development team on the marketing plan for Justice Unit. The product manager makes plans to visit Supergame Studios after the alpha milestone is completed in September 2008. By the time the game is at alpha, Digital Fun has some idea of what the gameplay is like and some ideas for a marketing hook from the game. The good thing about this game is that it will benefit from comarketing from the movie. However, Digital Fun also wants to build a unique marketing campaign around the game to emphasize that this is a quality game and not just something that was quickly created to benefit from the release of the movie.

During the visit to Supergame Studios, the product manager spends some time brainstorming marketing ideas with the team. The product manager has some feedback on the game, along with a good idea for handling how the player controls a flying superhero. He also works closely with the producer to create a deliverable schedule for marketing assets. This schedule details the types of assets marketing will need directly from the production team and when they are expecting to get the assets. Figure A.23 is a sample marketing asset deliverable list.

Music Cue	Length	Mixing Details	Location	Format	Notes	Deadline
Main theme	120 secs	Full Dolby 5.1 mix	UI	.wav	Main theme for the game; will be heard whenever players are in the UI shell screens. Must match the look and feel outlined in enclosed music vision document.	27-Mar-09
Loop 1	30 secs	Stereo	In-game	.wav	Heard in game as a looping piece of background music. Must match the look and feel outlined in enclosed music vision document.	27-Mar-09
Loop 2	30 secs	Stereo	In-game	.wav	Heard in game as a looping piece of background music. Must match the look and feel outlined in enclosed music vision document.	27-Mar-09
Intro cinematic	180 secs	Stereo; music + voiceover + sound effects; music must be timed to picture.	Cinematic	.wav	Deliver final music, vo, and sound effect mixes on separate tracks.	27-Apr-09
Midtro cinematic	60 secs	Stereo; music only, back-ground music. No timing.	Cinematic	.wav	Deliver final music, vo, and sound effect mixes on separate tracks.	27-Apr-09
Outro cinematic	90 secs	Stereo; music + voiceover + sound effects; music must be timed to picture.	Cinematic	.wav	Deliver final music, vo, and sound effect mixes on separate tracks.	27-Apr-09

FIGURE A.22 Sample music bid for Justice Unit.

Product Title	Estimated Date	Notes
Localizations: French, German, Spanish, Italian		
Production		
First playable	27-Jun-08	Once initial plan approved, will schedule three months to prototype main gameplay mechanics and create a first playable with some assets that will represent final art quality and gameplay experience.
Alpha	27-Sep-08	Planning to develop console and PC platforms in parallel, with priority going to console since it must first be code released in order to be submitted to third party for approval.
Code freeze	27-Apr-09	
Beta	27-May-09	
Pre-cert submission to Microsoft	27-May-09	
Code release candidate	27-Jul-09	All platforms, all languages ready.
Certification submission to Microsoft	17-Aug-09	
Target ship date (all platforms, all languages)	13-Oct-09	Sim-ship with Europe.
Box and Docs		
First draft of manual	22-Jun-09	
Final draft of manual with screenshots	10-Jul-09	Need to make sure there is enough time to get manual translated.
Box and manual layout for developer approval	20-Jul-09	Marketing needs developer to confirm that correct features, logos, and icons are on the packaging.
Marketing Assets		
Demo build	6-Jul-09	Marketing wants fully approved demo by Aug 7, 2009 so it can be included on cover disc for *Official Xbox* magazine. Demo needs to be submitted at least four weeks before this deadline to make this date.
Preview code for journalists	27-May-09	Planning to send the beta build as preview code.

I FIGURE A.23   Marketing assets needed for Justice Unit.

Review code for journalists	17-Aug-09	The build submitted to Microsoft for final approval will be used as review code.
Production milestone schedule	21-Dec-07	Marketing will have feedback on initial concept documents.
Design summary	21-Dec-07	Marketing will have feedback on initial concept documents.
Feature list	21-Dec-07	Will need to get updated feature lists throughout the project to ensure the features are marketed correctly.
Game assets for website (sound, art)	1-Feb-09	Website will launch in mid-Mar 2009.
Game concept sketches	1-Feb-09	Needed for website.
High-resolution images (for magazine covers)	1-Mar-09	Planning to pitch game articles at beginning of Mar 2009.
Gameplay footage for trailers	1-Mar-09	Initial footage needed in Mar 2009. Will need additional footage in Aug 2009 for TV commercials. Marketing can record this footage if they get a recent build of the game with cheats activated.
Cheat codes and walk-through	Varies	Will need this whenever game is sent out for previews and reviews, and whenever a PR event is scheduled.
Screenshots	Screenshots delivered with each milestone	As game gets closer to ship date, will request screen-shots on a weekly basis.
Developer interviews	As needed	Will mainly be email interviews.
U.S. press tour	Press tour scheduled for Sept 2009	
International press tour	Press tour scheduled for Sept 2009	

I FIGURE A.23 (*Continued*).

The product manager also discusses the plans for a demo, focus group testing, and the PR tour. The real marketing push will begin in early 2009 when the game is officially announced at the D.I.C.E. summit. The producer and product manager are in regular contact with each other throughout production. Refer to Chapter 15 for more information on marketing.

A.4 Production

At this point in development, Supergame Studios is in full production on Justice Unit. The leads put together a detailed plan in preproduction, and everyone on the team has a good idea of the tasks they should do and how long they have to do them. The producer ensures that everyone has the things they need to complete their work. The producer also deals with any issues that come up that need to be resolved. The internal production team is making progress on the game, and the external vendors have begun preproduction on their work for the game. Chapters 11 and 13 contain more detailed information about the production phase.

Production Cycle

The producer is in close communication with the publisher throughout the production cycle and provides weekly status reports. Every two months, the producer participates in an internal project review to gauge the status of the game. Digital Fun is also working with the licensor to secure any approvals that are needed for the Justice Unit game. Refer to Chapter 11 for more information about the production cycle.

Each month, Supergame Studios delivers a milestone to Digital Fun, as per the contract. The publisher takes about five days to review each milestone and will either approve it as is or write up some feedback and a list of required changes. Once Supergame Studios implements this feedback, they will resubmit the milestone build to Digital Fun for approval. Usually Digital Fun approves the milestones on the first submission but may still have some feedback on things they want implemented for the next milestone submission.

Build Process

During preproduction the lead engineer set up an automated build process. He assigned a data manager to be in charge of the build process and to create any additional scripts and processes that are needed to make the automation efficient. For example, the data manager created scripts that check file extensions, filenames, and file sizes. These checks will prevent someone from breaking the build if they check in a file that does not follow the established standards.

Once there is a first playable build, the data manager starts making a new build each day. He sets the build process to begin compiling and making the build at midnight so that a new build is ready first thing in the morning. At the beginning of the day, before the new build is reviewed by anyone else, the data manager checks the build logs to see whether there are any errors that need to be fixed in the build. If there are not any errors to address, the data manager runs the build to make sure that it loads and archives it on the network. The lead engineer will then decide whether this build should be sent to the QA department for testing.

Once the game hits beta, the QA department requests that new builds be available twice a week—Mondays and Thursdays. This gives them enough time in between builds to verify bug fixes and look for new bugs. If they need builds more frequently than that, they will make a request to the lead engineer a day in advance.

As people check assets and code into the build, they will send an email to the "build notes" mailing list. This email details what they checked into the build—either new code and assets or bug fixes that will need to be verified by the QA department. The build notes are useful to the QA department because the notes detail what changes were made in the current version of the build.

When the major milestones are delivered to the publisher for approval, the producer writes up a complete set of build notes that details all the major changes and improvements since the last milestone build. Digital Fun will use these build notes to compare what was delivered in the milestone with what was defined in the contract (see Figure A.9 for an example of how a milestone deliverable is defined in the contract).

Localization

Initially, Justice Unit will be localized into French, German, Italian, and Spanish. The localized versions will ship at the same time as the English version. A single multilingual master will be created with all the languages. The producer starts planning for the localizations in preproduction in order to ensure they will not hold up the final release of the game.

He prepares an asset overview form that is sent to potential vendors so that they can create a bid. He wants to find a vendor who can handle the localization work for all the languages rather than having to find a separate vendor to localize each language. If he is able to find a high-quality multilingual vendor, the localization process will be more streamlined and efficient since his associate producer will have to deal with only one vendor. One of the potential vendors translated the movie script for the first Justice Unit movie, so they are very familiar with the property and already have a good start on how some of the specific terms in the Justice Unit world need to be translated.

Figure A.24 is the asset overview form for Justice Unit. During preproduction, the producer has to make educated guesses about how many assets need to be localized, so he overestimates in each area. This overview form is sent to the vendors so they can start putting together a bid. The producer reviews all the bids and selects the vendor who is familiar with the Justice Unit property. There were cheaper bids, but those vendors

	#	Delivery Format	Comments
In-Game Text Assets			
Number of words to be translated	100,000	.xls file	Will need to use the same localized glossaries for Justice Unit that have already been used for previous movie translations to make sure the character names and special terms are correctly translated.
Number of text files to be modified	0	n/a	Developer will handle all text integration.
Art Assets			
Number of words in art assets	0		
Number of art assets to be modified	0		
Voiceover Assets			
Number of words in VO script	10,000	.xls file	
Number of VO files to be modified	600	.wav files (DVD quality)	
Number of characters to record	25		Will send full character details shortly. Estimate 15 male, 10 female.
Total time of VO (min:sec)	60 min		
Cinematics Assets			
Number of words in cinematic script	500		Only intro and outro sections contain VO that needs to be localized.
Number of cinematics to modify	2		
Number of characters to record	3		2 male, 1 female; will need to use the approved celebrity sound-alikes for the U.S. actors.
Total time of lip-synced dialogue	30 secs		Developer will provide the exact time codes.
Total time of cut-scenes (min:sec)	5 min		
Printed Materials			
Number of words in manual	5,000		
Number of manual graphics to be modified	10		Will need to provide localized screenshots to replace the English screenshots in the manual.
Number of words in box text	500		
Number of box graphics to modify	0		Marketing will provide the appropriate localized logos. Box screenshots will not display UI elements; they will be full screen.
Other printed materials	n/a		

FIGURE A.24 Asset overview form for Justice Unit.

were not as experienced. Also, he checked references for the vendors before making the final decision and found that many people highly recommended the vendor that was his first choice.

The producer assigns an associate producer (AP) to manage the localization process. The AP starts putting together an initial localization kit in March 2009. The AP develops a system for sending batches of text to be translated and integrated into the game. The first batch is sent at the end of March 2009, and the last batch is sent a few days after beta.

The text is organized into a spreadsheet for the translators. Figure A.25 is a translation spreadsheet for Justice Unit. This is the easiest format for the translators to work with. Since the production team planned ahead of time for localizations, they were able to create a localization pipeline that could easily pull out all the game text that needed to be translated and organize it into a spreadsheet. The translations are added

Location	English	French	Notes
AI(M01)	A police officer is down! Mission failed.	Un officier de police a été abattu. Echec de la mission.	Failure condition that appears as pop-up message in game
M01	1. Disarm the security system	1. Désactivez le système de sécurité	Appears in loading screen, set-up screen, and in-game start menu
Install	Would you like a shortcut placed on the desktop that can be used to launch the game?	Souhaitez-vous créer un raccourci pour pouvoir lancer le jeu à partir du bureau?	Appears during installation
Uninstall	Do you wish to clean up the entire game folder? This will delete the folder the game was installed to and everything in it.	Souhaitez-vous effacer complète-ment le dossier du jeu? Cela détruira l'ensemble du dossier dans lequel le jeu a été installé et les éléments qu'il contenait.	Appears during installation
Equip	The primary weapon assigned is the M4, with a 9 mm pistol as a secondary. Flashbangs are pro-vided to suppress enemies, and a heartbeat sensor should help in locating them.	Les armes assignées sont le M4, comme arme principale, et le pistolet 9 mm, comme arme secondaire. Les grenades aveuglantes sont fournies pour éliminer les ennemis. Le détecteur cardiaque devrait vous aider à les localiser.	Appears on the help screen for equipment selection
IFF(M03)	a guard	un garde	Appears when you place reticle over a character

FIGURE A.25 Translation spreadsheet for Justice Unit.

Bug #	Language	Game Location	Bug Description	Incorrect Text	Correct Text	Bug Status
2	German	UI–Options menu	Please use lower-case letter.	Schritt **N**ach **R**echts	Schritt **n**ach rechts	CLOSED
4	German	UI–Options menu	Text not translated.	Use item	Gegenstand benutzen	FIXED

FIGURE A.26   Sample linguistic bug report for Justice Unit.

to the spreadsheet, and the team has a tool that allows them to easily pull out the translations and integrate them into the game.

The integration process for all languages takes about a week, and the first fully localized builds are ready around the end of June 2009. This provides enough time to conduct a few weeks of functionality and linguistic testing. The linguistic testing is also handled by the localization vendor. The linguistic testers will fill in a bug report form and Supergame Studios will be responsible for implementing the bug fixes. Figure A.26 is a sample linguistic bug report for Justice Unit. Testing takes about five weeks and involves three rounds of testing. Once testing is completed, the localization work is reviewed and approved by the publisher, Digital Fun.

Completing Localization

Supergame Studios has completed localization and consults their checklist to confirm that they have completed all the major localization tasks. Figure A.27 is the localization checklist.

Refer to Chapter 13 for more information on localization.

Production Scenarios

Following are two production issues that occur during the development cycle on Justice Unit. Think about how you would deal with these situations.

Scenario #1

The design team is ready to start scripting the levels but just found out that the copy-and-paste functionality has not been added to the tool yet. This is a feature that engineering agreed to add to the scripting tool because it would save the designers a lot of time. The lead designer based the design schedule on the assumption that this functionality would be in the tool. Because it's not implemented, it is going to take the designers 25 percent more time to script the levels in the game. This is going to have a negative impact on the overall schedule and will definitely jeopardize the ship date. The lead designer goes to the producer right away with this issue so they can work out a solution.

PREPRODUCTION	Y/N	NOTES
TECHNICAL CONSIDERATIONS		
Does the game support Unicode?		
Are all language assets in an easily accessible directory in the game?		
Will subtitling functionality be needed?		
Are localized keyboards supported for player input?		
Will several languages ship on a single CD-ROM?		
Will localized versions be multiplayer compatible?		
Do boxes in UI scale accommodate to different sizes of text strings?		
Is any additional software needed to aid in localization?		
Are international currency and date/time formats supported?		
Has a version control system been decided on for the localizations?		
Has the localization pipeline been decided on?		
OTHER CONSIDERATIONS		
Will the localized versions ship simultaneously with the English version?		
Has the asset overview form been filled in and sent to the translator?		
Have the languages been determined?		
Will external vendors be producing the localizations?		
If so, are the bid packages prepared?		
Has the budget been completed and approved?		
Has the level of localization been determined for each language?		
Has the overall schedule been completed and finalized?		
Are there development resources available for the localizations?		
Has a method for integrating text assets been determined?		
Has a method for integrating VO assets been determined?		
Has a pipeline been determined for fixing bugs?		
Have the appropriate measures been taken to comply with all of the international ratings boards?		
Have the third-party publishers been contacted about the localized versions?		
Will PAL support be necessary for console versions?		
Is there enough hardware for functionality and linguistic testing?		

FIGURE A.27 Localization checklist for Justice Unit.

PRODUCTION	Y/N	NOTES
Has a detailed schedule been completed and communicated to the team?		
Has the localization overview document been sent to the localization coordinator or translators?		
Has all the preproduction game documentation been sent to the localization coordinator or translators?		
Has the latest English build of the game been sent to the translators?		
Have the text assets been organized for translation and sent to the localization coordinator?		
Have the voiceover script and character casting notes been sent to the localization coordinator?		
Have the final English voiceover files been sent to the localization coordinator?		
Have all the art assets to be localized been sent to the localization coordinator?		
Have all the cinematic assets and time codes been organized and sent to the translator?		
Are the translations for the text assets complete?		
Have the localized voiceover files been recorded and processed?		
Have the text and voiceover files been integrated?		
Have the cinematics been localized?		
Have the localized versions been sent to the appropriate ratings board for approval?		
Does the master contain demos from other games that were requested by marketing?		
Is functionality testing complete?		
Are all functionality bugs fixed and has the game been code released?		
Is linguistic testing complete?		
Are all linguistic bugs fixed and has final linguistic approval been given?		
Have the localized versions been sent to the replicator (PC) or submitted to the third-party publisher (consoles and cell phones)?		
POSTPRODUCTION		
Have the manual and box text been sent for translations?		
Does a localized demo need to be produced?		
Have localized screenshots been taken for the manual and box?		
Has a closing kit been created for all the localized versions?		
If necessary, have all patches been localized and made available?		

❙ FIGURE A.27 (*Continued*).

The producer first talks to the lead engineer to figure out when this functionality can be added and who is available to do the work. The lead engineer wants the engineering team to finish up some work on the graphics engine first, and then he says he will have one programmer available who can complete the feature in two days. The lead engineer estimates that the tool will have the feature working in about two weeks.

The producer relays this information to the lead designer, and they look at the design schedule to see whether there are some other tasks the designers can work on in the meantime. The lead designer decides to keep half of the design team on the original task of scripting levels and assigns other designers to work on the next set of mission walk-throughs. This allows them to stay on schedule because when the scripting tool is finally ready to use, more than half of the missions will be designed on paper and ready for prototype scripting. The lead designer also puts in a request for an additional designer on the project. If he can get someone on the project during the last six months of production, the lost time can easily be made up.

Scenario #2

Justice Unit is at beta and is asset complete. The game is right on schedule for the final submission to Microsoft. Digital Fun informs Supergame Studios that they are close to finalizing a deal with Coca-Cola® for in-game advertising. They want to add Coke signs to all the levels in the game and possibly build a drink stand where the player's character can purchase Coke as part of a health boost. This deal is worth $1 million in ad fees to Digital Fun, so they are really pushing for it, but on the other hand, they also need the game to ship on time.

The producer discusses this feature request with the team leads to get an idea of how much work is required to implement the feature as requested by marketing. Adding Coke signs throughout the levels doesn't take too much time, as long as the team is able to get prerendered art assets in the correct size and resolution for the signs. If the team has to create the signs, it will take one artist five days to complete. In addition, the team needs specific instructions on where the signs are to be placed in the levels and information on how many signs need to be added to each level. The schedule is pretty tight, so even the few days it would take to implement a few 2D signs in the level will impact the level of polish on the game.

The request for building a drink machine for a health boost is more complex and would impact the engineering, art, and design schedules. Since the game doesn't already include a health boost drink, the team has to spend some time prototyping this functionality to figure out how to make it work in the game. Art needs to prototype some drink machines and drinks, and engineering needs to figure out how to implement this functionality in the game. In addition, the animator may need to create a new drinking animation and an animation of a character getting a drink out of the machine.

After reviewing the production schedule, the producer writes up a proposal that details the feature request and the impact that implementing it would have on the game. He concludes that adding three 2D signs in 10 levels, while not ideal timing, could be done without putting the schedule in jeopardy. This is contingent upon:

- Receiving the final art assets for the signs from the publisher or licensor by June 27, 2009. The art team does not have time in the schedule to create these assets.
- Getting final approval on the in-game logo placement in five business days. Supergame Studios will have a build ready for review around July 15, 2009, and needs to get the approvals quickly so the game is ready for the code release process.

If the team does not get the appropriate art assets from the licensor, it is highly unlikely this feature request can be accommodated. In this case, the production team might be able to create a splash screen with the Coca-Cola logo that can be displayed while missions are loading.

The request for a drink machine cannot be accommodated at this time without having a huge impact on the gameplay and schedule. This is a feature that can be considered for the next version of the game. If this feature is absolutely required, the team will have to cut a mission out of the game to free up a designer and will have to pull one engineer and one artist from bug fixing. This means the final game will not be as polished as it could be, and there is still no guarantee that the drink machine feature will work correctly in the game and be done on time. Given all of these factors, the producer strongly recommends not pursuing this feature at this time.

Completing Production

Supergame Studios has completed production and consults their checklist to confirm that they have completed all the major production tasks. Figure A.28 is the production checklist.

■ A.5   Testing Phase

Supergame Studios begins testing with a small QA team around alpha. The QA lead has been on the project since preproduction, so she is very familiar with the game and has written up the test plan and other testing documentation. A few more testers are added to the team with each major milestone, and by the time the game hits code freeze, there is a full QA team checking the game. The code release process is scheduled to begin July 27, 2009, and the game is scheduled to be code released on August 17, 2009. Testing is covered in more detail in Chapter 14.

Testing

The QA lead writes up a detailed test plan for the game based on the design documents. As development continues, the test plan is updated. The QA lead also works

PRODUCTION CHECKLIST	Y/N	NOTES
PLAN IMPLEMENTATION		
Is game plan clearly communicated to team?		
Is game plan in publicly accessible place?		
Can plan be easily updated with changes by producer?		
Does everyone on team have the necessary resources to do their work?		
Is process in place for controlling feature creep?		
Is risk assessment happening on a regular basis throughout production?		
Is process in place for managing task dependencies?		
PROGRESS TRACKING		
Is there a game plan to track progress against?		
Is process in place for producer to track all task progress?		
Is progress posted in visible areas in the team rooms?		
TASK COMPLETION		
Does each task have clearly defined exit criteria?		
Are these exit criteria publicly available to the team?		
Are all stakeholders in agreement on what the exit criteria are?		

I FIGURE A.28 Production phase checklist for Justice Unit.

with the other leads to clarify any questions about the game so they can be accounted for in the test plan.

The QA lead writes documentation on how to correctly write up bugs for the game. She will use this to train new QA testers. She also works with the leads to establish a well-defined process for fixing and regressing the bugs. The bug-fixing process will go more smoothly if everyone understands how a bug is entered into the database, fixed by the team, and then assigned back to QA so the fix can be verified. Finally, she works with the producer on milestone checklists. These are the QA checklists used to compare the milestones against the producer's milestone deliverable list. The QA team needs to know her expectations for each milestone and then confirm whether the game actually fulfilled all the milestone requirements.

The testing plan is written in two parts. Part one is a test plan that is written in a pass–fail format. This is useful for checking whether the levels are loading correctly,

	A	B	C	D
1	**Level 1: BulletPoint's Office**	**Requirements**	**Pass/Fail**	**Notes**
2	**Mission** Intro	Intro cut-scence played correctly		
3		Voiceover audio is correct	PASS	
4		Intro cut-scence can be skipped	FAIL N/A CNT	
5	**Objective 1: Find the blue key**	Objective triggered		
6		Objective is displayed		
7		Objective cannot be bypassed		
8		Objective completed when requirements are met		
9	**Interactive Objects**	Copy machine is functional		
10		Light switches turn off/on		
11	**Enemy Boss: Cleaning Lady**	Cleaning lady scripted sequence plays		
12		Cleaning lady goes after player with mop		
13		Cleaning lady AI		
14		Cleaning lady pathing		
15	**Objective 2: Make copies of blueprints**	Objective triggered		
16		Objective is displayed		
17		Objective cannot be bypassed		
18		Objective completed when requirements are met		
19	**Map Integrity**	Map has no holes, soft geometry, or invisible boundaries		
20	**General Enemy Interaction**	All enemies behave as designed		
21	**Audio**	Music is present and does not cut out		
22		Sound effects are audible and correct		
23				
24				
25				
26				

◄ ◄ ► ►I \ **Level 1** / Level 2 / Level 3 / Level 4 / Level 5 / Weapons /

FIGURE A.29   Pass–fail test plan for Justice Unit.

whether the music and sound are playing correctly, and so on. Figure A.29 is an example of a pass–fail test plan for Justice Unit. Part two is written in a checklist format and is useful for checking the various combinations of characters, weapons, and difficulty levels in the game. Figure A.30 is an example of a checklist test plan for Justice Unit.

Code Release Candidate

The code release process is covered in more detail in Chapter 14. July 27, 2009, is the date the producer plans to have the first code release candidate (CRC) ready for review. Only the CRC for the console version needs to be ready on this date because it still has to go through the console submission process. The PC CRC doesn't technically need to be ready for final checks until September 25, 2009. However, the producer is trying to keep all the platforms on a similar schedule if possible, so that people can take some time off and then start working on another project as soon as possible.

The QA department has a complete testing plan and process in place for the code release candidates. This process checks the code, assets, and gameplay on the potential gold master. The process also checks that the correct languages display for the

	A	B	C	D	E	F
	Weapons	Level	Ice Queen	Caribou	BulletPoint	Notes
1						
2		1				
3	9mm Handgun	2				
4		3				
5		1				
6	Shotgun	2				
7		3				
8		1				
9	Knife	2				
10		3				
11		1				
12	Grenade	2				
13		3				

❙ FIGURE A.30 Checklist test plan for Justice Unit.

localizations, that the correct customer support information is listed for all versions, and that all the legal text and other information is correct. Figure A.31 is a code release checklist that details the main areas the QA department will double check in this process.

The team submits the first CRC on July 27, 2009. The QA department starts by checking that all major areas of the game load and that the localizations are correct. The QA team then starts going through the test plan. While the QA testers check the game against the test plan, the associate QA analyst begins checking the documentation, legal text, logo, and customer support information to ensure that everything is correct and ready to go. All of these items are in order and so the QA team continues to work through the test plan.

While the QA department checks the CRC, the production team also continues checking the build as well. The producer has locked everyone out of source control to prevent anyone from checking in any changes or bug fixes to the game. The production team is not planning to make any additional bug fixes unless the QA department finds an issue with the code release candidate. One of the designers finds some minor typos in some of the in-game text and would like to implement the correct text if a second code release candidate is needed. The producer approves this fix since it is a low-risk change to a text file.

The artists find some issues with the way one of the special effects is working and also ask whether they can implement a fix in a second CRC. After discussing the issue with the artists and engineers, the producer decides against making this fix. The fix is a bit risky since some of the code would need to be changed and some art assets would need updating. This issue is a cosmetic one and doesn't have a large impact on gameplay, so the producer decides that it is too risky to make this change for a second code

General Information	P/F	Additional Notes
Have all bugs been addressed?		
Have all "will not fix" bugs been approved?		
Can game be played from beginning to end?		
Has cheat code been removed?		
Is debug software removed?		
Has game passed all areas of the test plan?		
Are PC compatibility checks completed?		
Is correct customer support information listed?		
Is this version approved for submission to third parties?		
Are the correct age ratings and disclaimers being displayed?		
Third-Party Approvals		
Has this version passed the technical requirements checks for Microsoft?		
Has this version passed the technical requirements checks for Sony?		
Has this version passed the technical requirements checks for Nintendo?		
Localizations		
Is correct customer support information listed?		
Is game text displaying in the correct language?		
Are voiceovers playing in the correct language?		
Are packaging manuals translated correctly?		
Has game received linguistic approval?		
Does correct legal text and copyright information display?		
Does game have all necessary age ratings?		
Legal		
Have appropriate licensors signed off on the game?		
Are clearances secured for all licensed content (such as music)?		
Does game contain correct version of the End User License Agreement (EULA)?		
Is warranty and customer support information correct?		
Packaging		
Does package contain legal and copyright information?		
Are logos and other icons on package correct?		
Is the manual finalized and approved?		
Gold Master Checks		
Have gold masters been virus scanned and determined to be virus free?		
Is gold master identical to the approved gold release candidate?		
Has gold master been installed and verified on appropriate hardware?		

FIGURE A.31 Code release checklist.

release candidate. However, if the QA department finds a major crash bug with the game that would entail a code change, the producer will consider the request to fix the special effect again. If the code needs to be changed anyway to fix a bug, it might not be as risky to implement a code change to fix the special effect.

On the third day of testing (July 29), the QA department does find a major bug in the game that they feel should be addressed. While it is not a crash bug, it does prevent the player from progressing in the game. The bug is reproducible and QA is able to isolate the exact steps to reproduce it. While they are investigating the bug, they determine that at least 25 percent of the players will encounter this issue and decide that it needs to be fixed for the final game. The QA lead also recommends that three other bugs be addressed at this time—they are not major issues, but the changes are low risk and will improve the final gameplay experience.

The production team starts working on a second code release candidate and the QA department continues testing the first CRC to see if any more issues are uncovered. Fortunately, they don't find any other issues during the code release checks. It takes the team three days to generate another CRC, which they give to the QA lab on August 3. The producer presents a detailed list of each bug change to the QA lead. The QA lead tests these changes to confirm that the fixes are made and working correctly. Once these changes are confirmed, the QA department starts running through the test plan and code release checklist again.

The second CRC is in testing for four days, and another major issue is uncovered. At the end of the day on August 6, the QA lead asks the team to make a third CRC. The team works over the weekend so they can have the third CRC ready for testing first thing Monday morning on August 10. For the third CRC, the production team addresses only the specific fixes that were requested by QA.

The third CRC goes into testing first thing Monday morning. The QA team works extended shifts to check the third CRC as quickly as possible. The console submission deadline is quickly approaching, and the QA team feels confident that the third CRC can be ready to go. By working extended shifts, the QA department is able to complete all the code release checks by the end of the day on August 13, 2009. They approve the third CRC for submission.

Code Release Schedule

In order to meet the October 13, 2009, ship date for the console version, the producer works with Microsoft or Sony to make sure the game gets approved in a timely fashion. The final approval process generally takes six to eight weeks if the code is relatively bug free, the game has no major issues, and all of the technical requirements are fulfilled. Supergame Studios has a lot of experience working on console titles, so they are confident of their ability to fulfill the technical requirements and get the game approved in no more than two submissions.

	Task Name	Duration	Start	Finish	Predecessors
1	Microsoft Pre-Cert Submission	10 days	Wed 5/27/09	Tue 6/9/09	
2	Additional Development	38 days	Wed 6/10/09	Fri 7/31/09	1
3	CRC Testing	10 days	Mon 8/3/09	Fri 8/14/09	2
4	Console Certification	10 days	Mon 8/17/09	Fri 8/28/09	3
5	Fix Certification Bugs	5 days	Mon 8/31/09	Fri 9/4/09	4
6	Console Certification - 2nd Pass	10 days	Mon 9/7/09	Fri 9/18/09	5
7	Replication and Manufacturing	10 days	Mon 9/21/09	Fri 10/2/09	6
8	Ship to retail	7 days	Mon 10/5/09	Tue 10/13/09	7

❙ FIGURE A.32   Code release schedule for Justice Unit.

Figure A.32 is a general code release schedule for Justice Unit. This schedule allows the game to have a pre-certification submission go through two approval cycles in the final certification process, and meet the desired ship date. The pre-certification submission is scheduled for May 27, 2009. This is when the game is basically at beta and all the technical requirements are implemented. The console manufacturers check the technical requirements in the game and write up a detailed report about any requirements that need to be fixed before the final certification process. The team gets the report back in early June, which offers them plenty of time to implement any necessary feedback and changes.

Final console certification is scheduled for August 17, 2009. The team is actually able to submit the game several days earlier on August 9. This turns out to be a good thing because they forgot to submit the PEGI software ratings certificate and Microsoft puts a hold on the submission until the PEGI certification is sent on August 17. There was some chance the ship date could slip if it had taken a few days to get the certificate to Microsoft. The producer has built some padding into the submission schedule to account for any unexpected minor delays.

Microsoft starts reviewing the final submission August 17, 2009, and after reviewing it for 10 days, fails the submission because there were a few areas in which the game was not following the technical requirements correctly. They also encountered one reproducible crash bug.

The team reviews the report and investigates the crash bug. It takes them about five days to fix and test the crash bug and to make some adjustments to how the technical requirements are implemented in the game. They submit the game for a second time on September 7, 2009. This time the submission is approved on September 18. The game is sent immediately for replication and manufacture.

Because there is ample time for the replicator to press the discs and package the game, the game is able to easily make the October 13, 2009, ship date. If the approval process had taken more time, the publisher would have worked with the replicator to reduce the amount of time in the schedule to package and ship the game. For extra money, the publisher could have the replicator put a rush on the order and work over the weekend, which could save 7 to 10 days in the schedule. The publisher could also pay extra shipping costs to get the product to stores in two days instead of the normal five to seven days. Luckily, Supergame Studios came through and completed the game on time, so the publisher did not have to negotiate with the distributor or pay any extra to get the game on the store shelves in time.

Completing Testing

Supergame Studios has completed the testing phase and consults their checklist to confirm that they have completed all of the major testing tasks. Figure A.33 is the testing checklist.

TESTING CHECKLIST	Y / N	NOTES
VALIDATE PLAN		
Is test plan written?		
Is game plan updated for QA?		
Has test plan been updated with any changes to the game plan?		
Are testing milestones accounted for in the schedule?		
Is bug-tracking software available for the testers and development team?		
Are all areas of the game tested?		
Are all bugs regressed and closed?		
CODE RELEASE		
Has development team submitted a final code release candidate?		
Is there sufficient time in the schedule for QA to complete the test plan on the code release candidate?		
Has QA approved the product for code release?		
CONSOLE ONLY: Has code-released game been submitted to console manufacturer for approval?		
CONSOLE ONLY: Has console manufacturer approved game for final replication?		

FIGURE A.33 Testing phase checklist.

■ A.6 Postproduction Phase

The team worked very hard on Justice Unit and is looking forward to taking some time off before the next project gets under way. However, before they can go on vacation, the producer wants to conduct a postmortem and create a closing kit. These tasks will not take more than a week or so to complete.

Postmortem

The producer asks the team to prepare for the postmortem by listing five things that worked and five things that didn't work on the project. Some people have been anticipating a postmortem at the end of the project and have been jotting notes throughout the project. Other people start thinking about these items at the end of the project.

While everyone will have a slightly different list of good and bad—for example, the artists may be more focused on things that directly impact the art production cycle, while the engineers are focused on the engineering aspects—these items will have some common elements. The producer and associate producer organize everyone's items into broad categories and then schedule a meeting to discuss the information. Each category is discussed for about 10 to 15 minutes. At the end of the meeting, the team selects three categories that can be improved upon for the next project. The producer writes up a brief Lessons Learned document for these three categories and publishes it to the team. The team's goal is to focus on improving these three items on the next project.

The other items on the list aren't considered any less important, but the producer has found that it is more effective to concentrate on three areas of improvement at a given time rather than a whole list. Once the team has successfully implemented the first three lessons learned on the project, the producer will then work with the team on the next three items on the list. Every few months, the team will work on integrating improvements in the development process.

B | Glossary

AI: Abbreviation for artificial intelligence.

API: Abbreviation for application programming interface. APIs are sets of protocols and tools for programming software. Software that uses a common API will have a similar user interface.

cinematics: Prerendered or in-game movies that are part of the gameplay experience. They are used to further the game's story during gameplay.

code release: A term describing a product that has been fully tested, bug fixed, and deemed ready to ship by the publisher.

developer producer (DP): A producer who heads up an internal development team comprised of artists, engineers, and designers.

ESRB: An acronym for Entertainment Software Rating Board, the entity in the United States that assigns age ratings to games.

EULA: Abbreviation for end user license agreement, a legal agreement between the game publisher and the game purchaser.

FIGS: An acronym commonly referring to localizing a game into French, Italian, German, and Spanish.

gold master: The final version of the game code that is code released and sent to manufacturing.

HUD: An acronym for heads-up display. This is a common user-interface element in an interactive game that usually indicates the player character's statistics, such as health, time elapsed, weapon status, and so on.

intellectual property (IP): Ideas that are protected under federal law, including copyrightable works, ideas, discoveries, and inventions.

NDA: acronym for nondisclosure agreement. A legal document used to protect proprietary information.

NTSC: An acronym for National Television System Committee. U.S. televisions adhere to NTSC video display standards, which means that the video image delivers 525 lines of resolution at 60 half-frames per second. U.S. console games are developed according to these standards so that they will display on NTSC televisions and other NTSC-compatible video monitors.

OEM: Acronym for original equipment manufacturer. They manufacture hardware add-ons for computers, such as video cards, headsets, and joysticks.

operating system (OS): The operating system performs basic tasks for the computer such as recognizing input from the mouse, displaying output to the monitor, and providing a base for running applications. It also manages peripheral devices, such as printers and scanners. The OS is language specific and can detect which languages to display when running applications. The application needs to have this capability programmed into the code before the OS will detect the correct language setting.

PAL: An acronym for phase alternating line. European televisions adhere to PAL video display standards, which means that the video image delivers 625 lines of resolution at 50 half-frames per second. European console games are developed according to these standards so that they will display on PAL televisions and other PAL-compatible video monitors.

patch: A piece of game code created to deal with existing bugs in an already shipped product. The patch will modify game files on the user's hard drive to fix any critical bugs that inadvertently shipped with the game. The patch is usually offered for download on the Internet.

PEGI: Abbreviation for Pan European Game Information, the entity in Europe that assigns age ratings to interactive games.

P&L: A profit-and-loss statement generated by the publisher to determine whether a product will be profitable. Production, marketing, and distribution costs are compared against the money made from a projected sale of the game.

platform: The type of hardware that is required to run a game. Some examples are PC, Nintendo DS™, Sony PSP®, and Xbox®.

proprietary software: Software that is created and owned by the developer. The software is not authorized for public use, and the source code is not available publicly. For example, the developer can write proprietary software to convert .bmp files to a graphic file format that is recognized by the game.

publisher producer (PP): A producer who works for the publisher and interfaces with external development teams.

SAG: Abbreviation for Screen Actors Guild. This is a union representing actors working in the entertainment media.

SDK: Abbreviation for software development kit. An SDK is a programming package that can be used to develop software. An SDK usually includes APIs, tools, and documentation. If you are working with middleware, the vendor will provide you with an SDK with all the pertinent information.

user interface (UI): Areas of the game where the user can input or receive information. For example, the user can select a character from a list of choices or get information about his or her character's health from a health bar indicator.

C Resources

■ C.1 Books

Bethke, Erik. 2003. *Game Development and Production*. Plano TX: Wordware.

Chandler, Heather Maxwell. 2004. *The Game Localization Handbook*. Hingham, MA: Charles River Media.

Drucker, Peter. 2008. *The Essential Drucker*. New York: Harper Paperbacks.

Entertainment Software Association. Essential Facts About the Computer and Video Game Industry 2009. http://www.theesa.com.

Koster, Raph. 2005. *A Theory of Fun for Game Design*. Scottsdale, AZ: Paraglyph Press.

Laramée, François Dominic, ed. 2005. *Secrets of the Game Business*. 2nd ed. Hingham, MA: Charles River Media.

Lewis, James P. 1998. *Team-based Project Management*. New York: American Management Association.

Lewis, James P. 2003. *Project Leadership*. New York: McGraw-Hill.

Lewis, James P. 2005. *Project Planning, Scheduling, and Control*. 4th ed. New York: McGraw-Hill.

Lewis, James P. 2008. *Mastering Project Management*. 2nd ed. New York: McGraw-Hill.

Liverman, Matt. 2004. *The Animator's Motion Capture Guide: Organizing, Managing, and Editing*. Hingham, MA: Charles River Media.

McConnell, Steve. 1996. *Rapid Development: Taming Wild Software Schedules*. Redmond, WA: Microsoft Press.

Mencher, Marc. 2003. *Get in the Game! Careers in the Game Industry*. Indianapolis: New Riders.

Williams, Dimitri, Nicole Martins, Mia Consalvo, and James D. Ivory. 2009. *The Virtual Census: Representations of Gender, Race and Age in Video Games*. New Media & Society, vol. 11, no. 5, 815–834.

■ C.2 Websites

Organizations

Academy of Interactive Arts + Sciences (AIAS)—www.interactive.org: This academy promotes common interests in an interactive entertainment. They also host the annual D.I.C.E. Summit.

ACM SIGGRAPH—www.siggraph.org: This association focuses on graphics in interactive entertainment. They host an annual conference every year for digital content creators.

International Game Developers Association (IGDA)—www.igda.org: This is an association dedicated to the game development community. They are also one of the sponsors of the annual Game Developers Conference.

Conferences and Trade Shows

Consumer Electronics Show (CES)—www.cesweb.org: This annual trade show showcases the latest consumer technologies.

D.I.C.E. Summit—www.dicesummit.org: D.I.C.E. is an annual summit focused on the creative challenges of game development. It is hosted by the AIAS.

Game Developers Conference (GDC)—www.gdconf.com: This week-long conference held each March features lectures, tutorials, and roundtables presented by working members of the game development community. GDC also features a job fair and vendor expo.

Game Developers Conference online—www.gdc.online.com: Formerly the Game Developers Conference system, this annual conference is held each fall and features lectures, roundtables, and tutorials presented by members of the game development community.

IGDA Leadership Forum—www.igda.org/leadership: This annual conference focuses mainly on production and leadership in the game industry.

Montreal International Game Summit (MIGS)—www.sijm.ca: This annual conference held each fall in Montreal focuses on game development.

Penny Arcade Expo (PAX)—www.pennyarcadeexpo.com: This annual conference was started by the writers of the comic strip "Penny Arcade." The conference is geared toward game development professionals, students, and anyone interested in video games.

General Game Industry Information

Blue's News—www.bluesnews.com: Website that presents the latest industry news, game reviews, and other information about games.

Develop—www.developmag.com: Game development magazine published in Europe.

Edge—www.next-gen.biz: Website with daily news and articles pertaining to the game industry.

The Escapist—www.escapistmagazine.com: Online magazine that covers gamers and gaming culture.

Gamasutra—www.gamasutra.com: Website with all kinds of game development resources such as job postings, industry news, and articles about game development.

Game Developer magazine—www.gdmag.com: Magazine published in the United States that features articles on game development. It also includes job postings.

Game Development Search Engine—www.game_developer.com: A great resource for game development job postings and potential candidates.

GameDev.net—www.gamedev.net: Website containing technical articles about game development, book reviews, forums, job postings, and other useful information.

Game Rankings—www.gamerankings.com: Website that posts all the reviews of a given game and determines an overall average based on these reviews.

Metacritic—www.metacritic.com: Website that posts and averages all the reviews of a game.

MobyGames—www.mobygames.com: Website that collects and posts information on game credits and other news about the game industry.

D | Star Trek Online

1. **Tell us about your background and how you became an executive producer on STO.**

   Sure! I've been at Cryptic Studios for quite some time now. I worked as a producer for both *City of Heroes* and *City of Villains*. For a while, I was the director of production of all projects at Cryptic, but was looking to get back to a more hands-on approach. So, with my experience, passion for *Star Trek*, and a little pleading on my part, I was chosen to be the executive producer for *Star Trek Online*. It's been a privilege to work on an IP as rich as *Star Trek* and I'm extremely grateful for the opportunity that was given to me.

2. **What was it like to work with such a well-established IP? Does the game have anything new to the ST universe? Is there anything that you wanted to do but couldn't because of IP restrictions?**

   It was great to work with such a well-established IP. It gets you excited because you know the fan base is really excited for the game, and of course, it's *Star Trek* so that right there is exciting in itself because we're all really big fans.

   We were able to do most of the things we wanted to. We had a great working relationship with CBS, who holds the license. Every now and then they would say we can't do that or ask us to switch something on a ship design, but overall they were great to work with. I think they recognized pretty quickly that we were all fans, so we weren't trying to do anything way out there. Some of the new things we added were the uniforms, new ship designs, and then of course the year in which the game takes place.

3. **What was the biggest production challenge that you faced during development? How did you overcome it?**

   Probably the biggest challenge was adding in both space and ground missions. A lot of games just choose one or the other. This being *Star Trek*, we felt we had to have both because both the TV series and the movies the characters were constantly switching back and forth between environments. The reason this was tricky is because on the ground you have your away team, so you have to not only control yourself but them as well. In space it's different because you want to make space feel big and vast, but not so big and vast that the player gets disorientated. Also, there is another plane to take into consideration. So all in all, getting both styles of gameplay to flow and complement each other was one of the harder challenges we faced.

4. Tell us about the creation of the game's episodic model. How did it come about?

We didn't want the game to follow the same mission/quest model of other games. This being *Star Trek*, we thought, Why not make it like the TV series? So that's what we did. We wrote out mission chains in five-act structures to emphasize that you're a star in this universe, even though it's still an MMO. Players have been responding positively to it, and it's something we're going to support as the game grows and evolves.

5. The "Genesis System" allows your team to algorithmically make new star systems for STO. What was the development of this system like?

It was a great combination from both some folks on the design team and folks from the development and core team to make things happen. What's so difficult about something like the Genesis System is its dependance on a machine to create some things that only humans can really do well. So not only did we have to teach the system to design maps and spawn points and such in a way that a designer would, we also had to make sure the tools we built were powerful and elegant enough for designers to make tweaks to the maps that the system produced. It was very much a combination of technology and art.

6. STO features two combat systems (away-team missions and space combat). What was the design process like for these?

As I mentioned in one of the earlier questions, it was tricky to get both to complement each other. We really felt strongly about having both styles of gameplay available. When designing the combat systems we wanted to have space feel very tactical in that you had to position yourself, knock down your enemy's shields with your phasers, then fire your torpedos to the exposed hull. Also, you have to pay attention to your own shields, speed, and your crew's special abilities, so space combat is very tactical with a lot going on. On the ground, we wanted it to have more of an action feel. It's more fast paced and visceral, demanding quicker decisions and reaction times from the player.

7. Were any Star Trek cast members involved in the game's voice acting?

Yes! We had Leonard Nimoy do the opening narrative and narration as you move from sector to sector. We also had Zachary Quinto as the EMH character that guides you through the tutorial.

Interview Biographies

The following people were interviewed for this book. Their knowledge and insight of the game industry provided useful information that is featured throughout the book.

■ E.1 Tom Buscaglia

Tom Buscaglia, The Game Attorney, practices law around the world from his offices in Miami, Florida (www.gameattorney.com). Tom is dedicated to the computer and video game industry, assisting developers in all aspects of their legal and business needs, and has been representing game developers since 1991. Tom is a member of the board of directors of the International Game Developers Association (www.igda.org), as well as the coordinator of the South Florida Chapter. He has published numerous articles to help those wishing to start their own game development studios and recently launched www.GameDevKit.com to further assist start-up game developers. Tom is a perennial presenter at the annual Game Developers Conference, the Indie Games Com, and numerous other game-related conferences. He is also the executive director of the Interactive Entertainment Institute, the presenters of the G.A.M.E.S. Synergy Summit (www.SynergySummit.com) and of Games Florida (www.Games-Florida.org). As *FaTe[F8S]*, Tom plays online on a regular basis with FaTe's Minions (www.f8s.com) and has a gamer's appreciation and understanding of the game industry.

■ E.2 Carey Chico

Carey Chico has been working in the game industry since 1996, after graduating from the University of California, Los Angeles with a bachelor's degree in design. His foray into the game industry began when he started at Activision Studios as an animator on Planetfall™. From there, he rose through the ranks as lead artist on Battlezone™ and then as a founding member of Pandemic Studios where he completed Battlezone II™ as art director. After working again as art director on Star Wars™: The Clone Wars™, he stepped up as studio art director to oversee more global and long-term art interests. Some of the most recent titles under his supervision are Full Spectrum Warrior™, Star Wars: Battlefront™, Mercenaries™, and Destroy All Humans!®

■ E.3 Don Daglow

Don Daglow has served as president and CEO of Stormfront Studios since founding the company in 1988. At the 2008 Technology & Engineering, Emmy® Awards he accepted the award for creating Neverwinter Nights™, the first massively multiplayer online role-playing game (MMORPG), and in 2003 he received the CGE Award for "groundbreaking achievements that shaped the video game industry." Electronic Games has called him "one of the best-known and respected producers in the history of the field." Stormfront's major hits include The Lord of the Rings™: The Two Towers™ (based on the film by Peter Jackson), EA Sports' NASCAR Racing and Madden NFL and the original Neverwinter Nights on AOL.

Prior to founding Stormfront, Don served as director of Intellivision game development for Mattel, as a producer at Electronic Arts, and as head of the Entertainment and Education division at Broderbund. He designed and programmed the first-ever computer baseball game in 1971 (now recorded in the Baseball Hall of Fame in Cooperstown, NY), the first mainframe computer role-playing game (Dungeon for PDP-10 mainframes, 1975), the first sim game (Intellivision Utopia, 1981), and the first game to use multiple camera angles (Intellivision World Series Major League Baseball, 1983). Don codesigned Computer Game Hall of Fame title Earl Weaver Baseball (1987), as well as the original Neverwinter Nights for AOL (1991–1997). He was elected to the board of directors of the Academy of Interactive Arts & Sciences in 2003 and again in 2007. He is also a past winner of the National Endowment for the Humanities New Voices playwriting competition. He speaks extensively on the topics of game design, interactive media, and the video games industry, and has delivered keynote addresses in Canada, Germany, the United Kingdom, and the United States. Don holds a BA in writing from Pomona College (Claremont, California) and an EdM from Claremont Graduate University (Claremont, California).

■ E.4 Stephanie O'Malley Deming

Stephanie O'Malley Deming is a software development producer with over 10 years of experience in worldwide award-winning educational and entertainment products for companies including Activision, Electronic Arts, and 2K Games. She specializes in localizations and has successful sim-shipped multiplatform, multilanguage versions of high-profile titles including the Call to Power® series, the Guitar Hero® series, Rock Band™, NBA 2K8™, and numerous Tony Hawk® titles. With her partner, Stephanie founded XLOC, Inc. (www.xloc.com), a company that offers web-based applications for easy localization management, and works as a consultant for interactive game companies.

◼ E.5 Jamie Fristrom

Jamie Fristrom's history with the industry dates back to 1991. Though he has never held the title "producer," he has worked on projects large and small in various roles including programming, technical direction, project management, design, and creative direction. Currently he's a partner, technical director, and designer at Torpex Games where he helped create the game Schizoid® for Xbox Live® Arcade. Prior to Schizoid, Jamie was most recently a technical director and designer on Spider-Man™ 2, his biggest claim to fame being that he invented its dynamic, physical swinging system. Other games he's worked on include Spider-Man 1 for PS2™, XBox®, and GameCube™, Tony Hawk for the Dreamcast, Die by the Sword™ for the PC, and the Magic Candle™ series of RPGs. Jamie wrote the "Manager in a Strange Land" column for Gamasutra and holds the world record for writing game development postmortems in Gamasutra and *Game Developer* magazine.

◼ E.6 Tracy Fullerton

Tracy Fullerton is a game designer, educator, and writer with more than a decade of professional experience. She is currently an assistant professor in the Interactive Media Division of the University of Southern Calfornia School of Cinema-Television where she serves as codirector of the new Electronic Arts Game Innovation Lab. Tracy is also a coauthor of *Game Design Workshop: Designing, Prototyping, and Playtesting Games*, a design textbook in use at game programs worldwide.

Prior to joining the USC faculty, she was president of the interactive television game developer Spiderdance, Inc., which produced games based on NBC's *Weakest Link*™, MTV's *webRIOT*™, The WB's *No Boundaries*™, History Channel's *History IQ*™, and Sony Game Show Network's *Inquizition*™, along with Cyber Bond™ for TBS's "15 Days of Bond." Before starting Spiderdance, Tracy was a founding member of the New York design firm R/GA Interactive. As a producer and creative director, she created games and interactive products for clients including Sony, Intel, Microsoft, Ad Age, Ticketmaster, Compaq, and Warner Bros. Notable projects include Sony's multiplayer Jeopardy!® and multiplayer Wheel of Fortune® and MSN's NetWits™, the first multiplayer online game show.

Tracy's work has received numerous industry honors including Best Family/Board Game from the Academy of Interactive Arts & Sciences, *I.D.* magazine's Interactive Design Review, Communication Arts Interactive Design Annual, several New Media Invision awards, iMix Best of Show, the Digital Coast Innovation Award, IBC's Nombre D'Or, and *Time* magazine's Best of the Web. In December 2001, she was featured in the Hollywood Reporter's "Women in Entertainment Power 100" issue.

■ E.7   Raymond Herrera

Los Angeles-based drummer and producer Raymond Herrera has spent the last nine years writing, recording, and touring with his bands Fear Factory, Brujeria, and Kush. Raymond is a cofounder of 3volution Productions and Koolarrow Records. He has produced and acted as a music supervisor on many video game and movie sound tracks. He has earned three gold records, one platinum record, and the California Music Award for Best Hard Rock Act.

■ E.8   Clint Hocking

Clint Hocking has an MFA in creative writing from the University of British Columbia, where he completed his thesis at the same time he was working on Splinter Cell™ and Splinter Cell: Chaos Theory™. Along with writer J. T. Petty, Clint was honored for his work on the first Splinter Cell with the first-ever Game Developers' Choice Award for Excellence in Scriptwriting at GDC 2003. Clint is on Montreal's IGDA advisory board and also sits on the advisory board for the Electronic Game and Interactive Development degree program at Champlain College in Vermont. He is currently working as a creative director at Ubisoft in Montreal, where he lives happily with his fiancée Anne-Marie and their dog.

■ E.9   Lee Jacobson

Lee Jacobson never quite grew up as a kid, programming his first video game at the age of 16 on his Atari 400 computer (he couldn't afford the 800 model) between all-night sessions hacking away at Ultima® and Wizardry™. In 1988, he cofounded one of the first interactive media-based advertising companies in Dallas, Texas, which was acquired in 1990.

He then headed west to manage business development at Virgin Interactive Entertainment/Viacom in Irvine, California, and joined Midway Games, Inc. in 1998 where he serves as vice president of business development and acquisitions. Lee's career spans more than 15 years in the entertainment industry and includes managing product and business development, acquisitions, domestic and international licensing, and strategic planning for Midway.

■ E.10   Jeff Matsushita

Jeff Matsushita is a 10-year veteran of the video game business. After gaining production experience through careers in film, video, IT, and the then-emerging Internet, he joined Activision in Tokyo where he helped localize U.S. titles for the Japanese market. He moved back to the United States where he continued working for Activision as an associate producer in development. As the industry transitioned to separate publishing and development, he decided to bring his experience to bear on the publishing side of the business where he oversaw several externally developed titles as both a producer and a senior producer before transitioning to a role at Activision as greenlight czar where he helped ensure the health of all titles in development. Jeff currently serves as the executive producer overseeing development for Red Octane's Guitar Hero franchise.

■ E.11   Jay Powell

Jay Powell comes to Digi Ronin Games with 10 years of industry experience and a degree from the University of North Carolina. Jay began work in the game industry with Octagon Entertainment as an agent who represented developers around the world. During his time as an agent, he negotiated countless contracts for his clients. From European distribution deals to multiplatform development agreements, he has just about seen it all. In the last several years he has overseen the development of more than a dozen titles based on a variety of licenses, such as Garfield, Holly Hobby, Strawberry Shortcake, and a wide selection of Disney characters. These titles spanned the Nintendo Game Boy® Advance and DS, Microsoft Xbox 360®, and the PC. Jay has developed and continues to maintain relationships with companies such as Disney, Cartoon Network, MTV, Nickelodeon, and Microsoft.

■ E.12   Stuart Roch

Stuart Roch has been a member of the interactive industry for over a decade working in quality assurance, design, production, and strategic capacities. While at Shiny Entertainment, Stuart had design and production roles on Wild 9™, R/C Stunt Copter™, Messiah™, and the critically acclaimed Sacrifice™. Stuart led the Shiny team in production of Enter the Matrix™, which shipped in 2003 and eventually sold more than six million units worldwide. Later, as an executive producer at Treyarch, Stuart joined the development team late to help complete Ultimate Spider-Man™. During his tenure at Treyarch, Stuart worked on Quantum of Solace™ before moving to parent company Activision. During his ongoing career at Activision, Stuart worked as an executive producer on various titles before being promoted to senior director of franchise strategy in 2008.

■ E.13   Amanda Rubright

Amanda Rubright joined the production team at Aspyr in the spring of 2006. Since then she has led the production of Supreme Commander® (Xbox 360), Turok® (PC), The Shield™ (PC), Top Spin 2™ (PC); and Save the Dinos™ (PC); lent a hand to the game designs for the Sims™ Pet Stories and the Sims Castaway Stories; and supported Aspyr's internal IP department in developing pitches. While currently working toward obtaining her PMP certification through PMI, Amanda is also busy leading the production of Guitar Hero: Aerosmith® (PC/Mac) and Guitar Hero III: Legends of Rock (PC/Mac). Prior to working with Aspyr, Amanda spent the previous eight years as a game and level designer with Ubisoft Entertainment (Tarzan™: Untamed), Retro Studios (Metroid Prime®), Amaze Entertainment (Shrek 2™ for the PC), and Edge of Reality (Shark Tale™, Fear & Respect) developing AAA titles for both console and the PC. Aside from providing team leadership, she also spearheaded the design work flow process at many of these companies, providing efficient and communicative design procedures. Her solid understanding of game development fundamentals, coupled with her leadership and experience in game and level design, has made for a natural transition into production.

■ E.14   Tobi Saulnier

Tobi Saulnier is CEO of 1st Playable Productions, an independent game studio located in Troy, New York, that specializes in creating fun games for entertainment and learning. Previously, in her five years as vice president of product development for Vicarious Visions, Tobi was responsible for the delivery of more than 60 game titles ranging from Blue's Clues for the Game Boy Color to Doom III for the Xbox, with teams ranging from four people to more than 60 and project schedules from two months to two years. She also served as producer and contributed to the design on a number of these titles, with a particular interest in games for nontraditional demographics. Before joining the game industry, Tobi managed R&D in embedded and distributed systems at GE R&D. Tobi holds a PhD, MS, and BS in electrical engineering from Rensselaer Polytechnic Institute (Troy, New York).

■ E.15   Coray Seifert

Coray Seifert is an associate producer at THQ's Kaos Studios, working on his 24th title, Frontlines™: Fuel of War™. A coordinator of the International Game Developers Association's New Jersey chapter since 2002, he also cofounded the IGDA game writers Special Interest Group Quarterly Report and continues to work with the SIG as a committee member and contributing author for their Game Writing book series. Coray has developed games as a writer, designer, and producer for companies like Large Animal Games, Creo Ludus Entertainment, and the U.S. Department of Defense, and has appeared on Gamasutra.com, Forbes.com, NY1, in *Game Developer* magazine, and at numerous game industry events as an editor, panelist, lecturer, or host. An advocate for the aspiring game developer, Coray also teaches game design as a visiting lecturer at Bloomfield College and the New Jersey Institute of Technology. When not distributing gratuitous high-fives and D&D jokes, Coray lives in Summit, New Jersey, with his amazing wife Katie and their two highly eccentric cats.

■ E.16   Wade Tinney

Wade Tinney cofounded Large Animal Games (www.largeanimal.com) with partner Josh Welber in 2001. Since then, Large Animal has developed more than 45 games for a variety of platforms, including the Web, mobile devices, and PCs. They've created Web-based promotional games for clients such as LEGO, MTV, Cartoon Network, and Mattel, and their original downloadable game titles are distributed through the leading casual game portals. Large Animal's puzzle game AlphaQUEUE was a finalist in the 2004 Independent Games Festival (IGF), and RocketBowl was a 2005 IGF Award winner. Wade is an active member of the International Game Developers Association, a regular contributor to their annual Web and Downloadable Games Whitepaper, and the founding editor of the IGDA *Online Games Quarterly*. He also teaches game design at Parsons School of Design and New York University.

Index